THE NAZI GENOCIDE OF THE ROMA

War and Genocide

General Editors: Omer Bartov, Brown University; A. Dirk Moses, European University Institute, Florence, Italy/University of Sydney

There has been a growing interest in the study of war and genocide, not from a traditional military history perspective, but within the framework of social and cultural history. This series offers a forum for scholarly works that reflect these new approaches.

"The Berghahn series Studies on War and Genocide *has immeasurably enriched the English-language scholarship available to scholars and students of genocide and, in particular, the Holocaust."*—**Totalitarian Movements and Political Religions**

For a full volume listing, please see back matter

THE NAZI GENOCIDE OF THE ROMA

Reassessment and Commemoration

Edited by

Anton Weiss-Wendt

berghahn
NEW YORK · OXFORD
www.berghahnbooks.com

First published in 2013 by
Berghahn Books
www.berghahnbooks.com

©2013, 2015 Anton Weiss-Wendt
First paperback edition published in 2015.

All rights reserved.
Except for the quotation of short passages for the purposes
of criticism and review, no part of this book may be reproduced in any form
or by any means, electronic or mechanical, including photocopying, recording,
or any information storage and retrieval system now known or to be invented,
without written permission of the publisher.

Library of Congress Cataloging-in-Publication Data

The Nazi genocide of the Roma : reassessment and commemoration ; edited by Anton Weiss-Wendt.
    pages cm. — (Studies on war and genocide ; volume 17)
  Includes bibliographical references and index.
  ISBN 978-0-85745-842-1 (hardback : alk. paper) — ISBN 978-1-78238-923-1 (paperback : alk. paper) — ISBN 978-0-85745-843-8 (ebook)
 1. Romanies—Nazi persecution—Congresses. 2. World War, 1939–1945—Atrocities—Congresses. 3. Romanies—Germany—History—20th century—Congresses. 4. Germany—Ethnic relations—Congresses. I. Weiss-Wendt, Anton, 1973– editor of compilation.
  D804.5.G85N39 2013
  940.53'1808991497—dc23

                                                                    2012037868

British Library Cataloguing in Publication Data

A catalogue record for this book is available from the British Library.

Printed on acid-free paper.

ISBN: 978–0-85745–842–1 hardback
ISBN: 978-1-78238-923-1 paperback
ISBN: 978–0-85745–843–8 ebook

*To Michael Zimmerman (1951–2007),
historian and humanitarian*

Contents

Acknowledgments	ix
Introduction *Anton Weiss-Wendt*	1
Chapter 1 Assimilation and Persecution: An Overview of Attitudes toward Gypsies in France *Shannon L. Fogg*	27
Chapter 2 Genocidal Trajectory: Persecution of Gypsies in Austria, 1938–1945 *Florian Freund*	44
Chapter 3 Ustaša Mass Violence Against Gypsies in Croatia, 1941–1942 *Alexander Korb*	72
Chapter 4 Ethnic Cleansing or "Crime Prevention"? Deportation of Romanian Roma *Vladimir Solonari*	96
Chapter 5 Nazi Occupation Policies and the Mass Murder of the Roma in Ukraine *Mikhail Tyaglyy*	120
Chapter 6 The Nazi Persecution of Roma in Northwestern Russia: The Operational Area of the Army Group North, 1941–1944 *Martin Holler*	153

Chapter 7
The Justice System of the Federal Republic of Germany and
the Nazi Persecution of the Gypsies   181
Gilad Margalit

Chapter 8
Disentangling the Hierarchy of Victimhood: Commemorating Sinti
and Roma and Jews in Germany's National Narrative   205
Nadine Blumer

Chapter 9
The Aftermath of the Roma Genocide: From Implicit Memories
to Commemoration   229
Sławomir Kapralski

Selected Bibliography   252

Notes on Contributors   260

Index   263

Acknowledgments

I want to acknowledge several individuals who have been very helpful at the earlier stage of this book project: Charles Westin and Mats Deland of Stockholm University, and Joackim Scheele and Oscar Österberg of Living History Forum. A special thank you goes to Winfried Etzel, who has translated from German Florian Freund's chapter, and Samantha Fox, who has copyedited several chapters in this volume. I also thank my colleagues at the Center for the Study of the Holocaust and Religious Minorities in Oslo who have lent their full support to this book project. Finally, I want to express my gratitude to the editorial staff of Berghahn Books and the two anonymous readers whose pointed comments have helped to improve the overall quality of the manuscript.

More than anyone else, however, this volume owes to the late Michael Zimmermann, the scholar who has perhaps contributed most to the study of the Nazi genocide of the Roma. Published in 1996, his magisterial work *Rassenutopie und Genozid. Die nationalsozialistische "Lösung der Zigeunerfrage"* remains the most comprehensive account to date. Based on the broadest possible reading of sources, Zimmermann's analysis struck an effective balance between the Intentionalist and Functionalist interpretations. Zimmermann was also the first to make a comparison between Nazi and Soviet policies toward the Roma in the 1930s. Zimmermann advanced research in his capacity as a founding member of the Sinti and Roma working group at the Fritz Bauer Institute in Frankfurt am Main and the co-editor of *Romani Studies*. Beside his mastery of sources and ability to contextualize, Zimmermann has projected a certain sense of humanity. Unlike many other scholars,

Zimmermann exhibited compassion toward the victims in whose name he has carried out research, without either succumbing to social activism or lowering the standards of historical inquiry. He was articulate in his writings and soft-spoken in real life. His premature death in early 2007 not only impoverished the academic community but also left the Roma people without one of its champions. This collection of essays is dedicated to his memory and the cause of humanity that he has pursued throughout his career as a historian.

INTRODUCTION

Anton Weiss-Wendt

This volume uses the framework of genocide to analyze the patterns of persecution of the Roma in Nazi-dominated Europe. The new archival evidence presented in this anthology confirms the earlier findings that placed the victimization of the Roma within the definition of genocide. Without departing from the actual wording of the UN Genocide Convention, the contemporary legal practice in establishing criminal intent suggests a common design that rendered the comprehensive destruction of the Roma communities unequivocally genocidal. Naturally, the extent and means of persecution varied from country to country and the differences sometimes overruled commonalities. The context in which the process of destruction evolved, however, invites certain generalizations.

Due to the lack of reliable statistics on the size of prewar Romani population for each country and Europe as a whole, the estimates of the death toll vary greatly, from 96,000 to 500,000, with the likely figure in excess of 200,000. Following the years of conventional and legal discrimination instituted in Nazi Germany, but also in other European countries, the invasion of the Soviet Union in 1941 provided for a radical solution of the "Gypsy Question." The *Einsatzgruppen* (mobile killing units) of the German SS executed en masse tens of thousands of itinerant and sedentary Roma in the occupied Soviet territories. Some 5,000 Austrian Roma, who had been deported to the Jewish ghetto at Litzmannstadt (Łódź) in Poland in late 1941, died of typhus, and the remainder was shortly murdered by gas at the nearby Kulmhof (Chełmno) death camp. Mass deportations and executions of Roma continued in satellite countries while in Germany proper so-called pureblood Sinti became subject to forced sterilization. Eventually, in December 1942 the head of the German SS and Police Heinrich Himmler ordered a European-wide deportation of Roma to a newly created "Gypsy family camp" at Auschwitz-Birkenau, where all but a few perished.

The volume focuses mainly on the countries and regions outside Germany proper. Written by experts in the field using a variety of sources in half a dozen languages, the detailed case studies of France, Austria, Romania, Croatia, Ukraine, and Russia generate a critical mass of evidence that indicates criminal intent on the part of the Nazi regime to destroy the Roma as a distinct group. However inconsistent or geographically limited, the mass murder acquired a systematic character over time and came to include ever larger segments of the Romani population, regardless of the social status of individual members of the community. From the long-term Nazi perspective, anything that contradicted this pattern was only a temporal deviation. The occupied Soviet territories, which until now have received only scarce attention from historians, serve as a compelling illustration of the widening circle of genocide that engulfed the European Roma.

The chapters in this collection suggest two patterns that came to play a complimentary role in the destruction of the Romani minority during World War II. With the bewildering number of contradictory decrees and regulations issued by various agencies, the ultimate faith of the Roma usually rested with local authorities. As a rule, the civil, police, or military authorities interpreted their mandate upward. Consequently, criminality became a collective label and police surveillance often led to incarceration, children were forcibly separated from their families, many sedentary Roma were included into the category of *itinerants*, mass deportations degenerated into indiscriminate shootings, and mass murder escalated to genocide. While some Roma survived due to loopholes in legislation and the chain of command, many more perished for that very reason. In short, the lack of centralized decision making with regard to the Roma rarely ameliorated their situation, but rather aggravated it. An apolitical, stateless minority, the Roma were rarely a priority on the list of potential enemies anywhere in Nazi-dominated Europe. The arbitrary interpretation of a potential security threat, then, constitutes the second aspect that made genocide possible. The Nazis variably defined the Roma in racial and social terms. This duality enabled a malicious interpretation, according to which the sum total of the Roma's purportedly inherent social traits amounted to a certain negative racial type. This false reasoning made some military commanders and civil administrators in the dismembered Yugoslavia and the occupied Soviet territories collectively label Roma as spies and saboteurs.

Obviously, this survey is not exhaustive. Research have been done in recent years on certain aspects of Nazi genocide, such as Robert Ritter and his notorious institute, the relationship between the social and racial categorization of the Roma, the mass deportation to Auschwitz-Birkenau, restitution and indemnification, or even postwar cultural representation.[1] At the same time, comprehensive studies of a number of countries with a substantial Romani minority (e.g., Italy, Greece, Bulgaria, Hungary, Poland, and Slovakia) are yet to come.[2] A specific aspect of the genocide that has not yet found its historian is the Nazi treatment of Soviet prisoners of war who happened to be Roma.[3] The present anthology may, therefore, be regarded as a call for further research and discussion.

The Issue of Genocide

As far as the Roma are concerned, the discussion of genocide began in earnest only a decade or so ago. Beside several articles by Philip Friedman in 1950 and 1951 and a few general studies published in the intervening two decades, over a dozen case studies dealing with Nazi persecution of Roma in various parts of Germany or specific concentration camps (e.g., Buchenwald, Dachau, Flossenbürg, Mauthausen, Natzweiler, Ravensbrück, Sachsenhausen) appeared in the 1980s and 1990s.[4] The significance of Auschwitz in the "Final Solution of the Gypsy Question" has been captured in a multivolume memorial book compiled by the State Museum of Auschwitz-Birkenau.[5] In the United States, Sybil Milton and the late Henry Friedlander sustained academic interest in the Nazi persecution of the Roma.[6] As early as 1987, the US Government Printing Office published a pamphlet called *In Memory of the Gypsy Victims of Nazi Genocide*.

In his groundbreaking book, *Rassenutopie und Genozid. Die nationalsozialistische "Lösung der Zigeunerfrage,"* Michael Zimmermann made perhaps the strongest case for racism, alongside traditional stereotypes, as a defining factor in the Nazi treatment of the Roma. He concluded that, despite the contradictions in the Nazi anti-Roma policy, the effective synthesis was mass murder.[7] *Rassenutopie und Genozid* was succeeded by two important monographs in English: Gilad Margalit's *Germany and Its Gypsies: A Post-Auschwitz Ordeal* and Guenter Lewy's *The Nazi Persecution of the Gypsies*. In his book, Margalit examined the postwar legal and political debates surrounding the Nazi persecution of the Roma. Lewy settled for a lower estimate of Roma victims and, in contrast to Zimmermann, doubted whether genocide applies.[8] Although he offered new insight into the dynamics of persecution at the local level, his argumentation displayed certain tendentiousness.

Most recently, Tomislav Dulić and Martin Holler made significant contributions to the analysis of genocide with regard to the Roma. With his book, *Utopias of Nation: Local Killing in Bosnia and Herzegovina, 1941–42,* Dulić has successfully bridged empirical research and genocide theory. Using the three-dimensional model accounting for intent, level of organization, and magnitude of destruction, he concluded that the consistency and ideological determination with which the Ustaša regime had targeted Jews and Roma for destruction qualifies it as genocide.[9] Although Holler does not engage in theoretical discourse in his book, *Der nationalsozialistische Völkermord an den Roma in der besetzten Sowjetunion (1941–1944)*, his overall conclusion matches that of Dulić. Based on extensive archival research in Russia, Ukraine, and Germany, Holler demonstrated the totality of destruction of the Roma in the occupied Soviet territories under military control. The Roma were murdered as Roma, he observed.[10]

Where it should have ended assertively with the statement of genocide, historians such as Yehuda Bauer, Gilad Margalit, Guenter Lewy, and others continued emphasizing the nonontological difference between genocide and the Holocaust, genocide and the Final Solution, and genocide and mass murder, respectively. The question of intent (or the lack thereof) is the main point of contention. Bauer, for example, has observed "no clear policy, not intention" to annihilate the Roma.[11] Indeed, genocidal intent is notoriously difficult to prove, whether historically or in a court of law. Whether we deal with the Nazi attack against the Jews, the Young Turks' campaign against Ottoman Armenians, or the Rwanda Hutu onslaught against the Tutsi, what we have is usually circumstantial evidence of intent. I would invite scholars to apply the same method of inquiry to the case of Romani minority in World War II.

Beside the prerequisite of intent, as Martin Shaw has stressed, the crime of genocide has an element of knowledge to it. Within the context of genocide, awareness that a circumstance exists, or a consequence will occur in the ordinary course of events, can be interpreted as awareness that the acts committed will lead to the destruction of the targeted group.[12] Despite the narrow interpretation of "intent" in law, in practice, proof of intent is rarely a formal part of the prosecution's case, as William Schabas has explained. Rather, the intent is a logical deduction that flows from evidence of the physical act itself. In other words, the intent could be inferred from presumptions of fact, the general context in which criminal acts have been systematically directed against the same group.[13]

The scholars who have advanced the genocide argument are not immune to methodological pitfalls either. Quite often, they failed to differentiate between different phases of destruction process, or to clearly state the principles and objectives of a comparison. For example, the single fact that the Nazis deported the Roma from eleven European countries to Auschwitz-Birkenau does not automatically imply genocide, contrary to what Romani Rose, the chairperson of the Central Council of German Sinti and Roma, has argued.[14] The symbolism of Auschwitz alone is not enough to ascertain the plan to murder the European Roma entirely or in part. Furthermore, we can now say with certainty that Himmler's decree did not affect Polish, Soviet, or French Roma. Indeed, over 80 percent of the Roma registered in the camp's records came from Germany, Austria, and the Protectorate of Bohemia and Moravia. Of those who had perished at Auschwitz-Birkenau, two-thirds died of malnutrition and diseases.[15]

In the context of genocide, the fact of forced sterilization is at least as important as racial categorization, indiscriminate executions by *Einsatzgruppen*, or mass deportation to Auschwitz. Those few among the Roma exempted from deportation (i.e., "racially pure" itinerant Sinti and Lalleri, as well as "good Mischlinge" and a small number of "socially adjusted" individuals) were coerced to consent to sterilization. As Gilad Margalit argues, the act of sterilization had a racial underpinning. The label "Mischling" (a person of mixed origin) implied criminal traits and carried with it a sentence of sterilization. For the Roma, as a people, it meant biological death. Fortunately, the British and American air raids and general social disintegration during the final war years put an end to the sterilization program. The actual number of victims who were subject to sterilization (approximately 2,500[16]) does not change the conclusion, namely, that the Nazis intended to destroy the Roma as a group.

The fact that the comprehensive picture of the Nazi mass crimes began emerging only recently complicated the previous attempts to engage with the issue of genocide. For example, emphasizing the similarity of the discriminatory policies, Christopher Browning viewed the Nazi persecution of the Roma and Jews in the period between 1939 and 1941 developing in parallel. The emergence of the "Final Solution" following the invasion of the Soviet Union, however, had different consequences for the two peoples. Browning qualified as "amorphous consensus" the likely intent on the part of the Nazi leadership to destroy the German and Austrian Roma and Sinti as a group, yet he denied the existence of a similar intent for the German-occupied Soviet territories.[17] Dieter Pohl, on the other hand, regarded Operation Barbarossa as a breaking point while arguing for a less systematic Nazi drive against the Roma than that against the Jews during the preceding period.[18] A great many local variations within the broader pattern of Nazi persecution has no doubt influenced these and similar conclusions by historians.

Whenever mass deportation preceded mass murder, or when the Nazis faced obstacles in implementing their immediate plans, the Reich Security Main Office (RSHA) invariably prescribed a "final solution" at a later point. Spelled out and/or interpreted differently, the "near future" referred either to a window of opportunity dictated by the situation on the ground or the period immediately after the (successful) end of World War II. In either case, the existence of the Roma as a cohesive group was in danger. The variations in form and degree became irrelevant within the overall design that Hitler's regime held for postwar Europe. As Florian Freund eloquently sums up with regard to Austria: the surviving Roma were doomed. When surveying the case of France, Shannon L. Fogg finds it difficult to qualify the treatment of itinerant Roma by the Vichy regime as genocide. At the same time, she speculates that—among other reasons that spared the French Roma—the Germans had different priorities at that particular moment, and the Roma would have been likely deported en masse had the outcome of the war been different. The dynamics of mass violence in the former Yugoslavia may indicate what lay in store for the Roma. In August 1942, Dr. Harald Turner, the head of civil administration in Serbia, announced, "In the interests of pacification, the Gypsy question has been fully liquidated. Serbia is the only country in which the Jewish question and the Gypsy question have been solved!"[19] Indeed, with clear indications of the murderous intent emanating from the occupied Soviet territories, the shadow of genocide hovered over the entire people whom the Nazis defined as "Gypsies."

The new evidence emerging from East-European archives consistently pushes the arrow of the barometer toward genocide. As Martin Holler convincingly argues in his chapter, "the Soviet case study plays a key role in establishing genocidal intent in the Nazi persecution of Roma insofar the German attack on the Soviet Union on 22 June 1941 marked the transition toward systematic mass murder." By closely examining mass atrocities committed in the occupied Soviet territories, Holler and Mikhail Tyaglyy concur that the Nazis had murdered *all* Roma irrespectively of their social status. Romani and non-Romani survivors alike frequently observed a particular animus on the part of the German police and the military coated in the allegations of treachery and penchant for spying. Within the same geographic location, German combat operations against Soviet partisans typically prompted reprisals against the civilian population. However, as Holler pinpoints, while in the case of ethnic Russians only certain adults became a target, in the case of Roma, entire families were murdered, including members of the Communist Youth Organization, railway officials, collective farm workers, teachers, musicians, and others. Whenever German agencies exploited Roma as a source of free labor, inevitably the economic rationale had been abandoned in favor of a policy of mass murder.

Tyaglyy eloquently sums up the factors that accelerated the destruction of the European Roma, dividing them roughly into chronological, geographical, administrative, and circumstantial. In the case of the former Soviet Union, the deteriorating situation on the ground made Nazi policy toward the Roma more radical. The priorities accentuated by respective authorities in any given area determined the extent and nature of the "Final Solution of the Gypsy Question" at a local level. Aspects such as the scale of combat operations or (the lack of) economic considerations proved equally important in the ultimate demise of the Romani communities. The great variation in anti-Roma practices gives a whole new, sinister meaning to the Latin expression *e pluribus unum*: out of many emerged the contours of genocide.

This conclusion is grounded in primary sources. Contrary to what scholars have believed until recently, the documentary evidence of the genocide was quick to come, already during World War II. For one, the *Einsatzgruppen* reports provide some statistics on the Nazi mass murder of the Roma in the occupied Soviet territories, though they only document a part of atrocities. The Soviet partisans and the Red Army had both reported on Nazi atrocities against the civilian population, including the Roma, according to Holler. War crimes investigations in the Soviet Union and West Germany included detailed information about specific cases of mass murder. Most extensively, however, the Nazi crimes against Roma found coverage in the records of the Soviet Extraordinary State Commission for the Investigation of the Crimes Committed by German Fascists and their Collaborators on the Territory of the USSR (ChGK), which came into existence in late 1942 with the purpose of collecting incriminating evidence in the run-on to the International Military Tribunal at Nuremberg. Both Holler and Tyaglyy make extensive use of this particular source in their respective chapters. Simultaneously, Tyaglyy pinpoints the methodological problem of generalizing from the divergent, yet numerous, instances of mass murder documented by the Soviet Extraordinary Commission. He warns that the image of a monolithic Nazi war machine in pursuit of a uniform policy toward the Roma may not be entirely correct. In this sense, Holler may be overstating the significance of the Commission's reports in asserting genocidal intent of the Nazis, while misconstruing the uncoordinated efforts to erase the Romani presence in the Baltic States as the lack of criminal intent. As a general proposition, Tyaglyy urges scholars using a wide range of primary sources, including the documents produced by the German civil administration, the Security Police, and the Wehrmacht, as well as the ChGK records and survivor testimonies. Oral history in particular remains an untapped source. The University of Southern California Shoah Foundation Institute Archives (formerly the Steven Spielberg Shoah Foundation) currently contains 397 audio interviews with Romani survivors. Even though this number pales in comparison with 48,361 testimonies of Jewish survivors stored in the same archives, it nevertheless constitutes a significant collection.[20] The United States Holocaust Memorial Museum in Washington, DC, and several Romani nongovernmental organizations hold further survivor testimonies. In Russia, Nikolai Bessonov has been collecting an oral history of the Nazi genocide against the Roma.

The Victimization of Roma and Jews Compared

The first scholar to raise the issue of genocide with regard to the Roma was, unsurprisingly, Raphael Lemkin, who coined the very word *genocide*. In one of his speeches, in January 1951, Lemkin mentioned Roma, alongside Jews and Slavs, as victims of the Nazi genocide. In a radio broadcast in October 1955, he further emphasized that, "almost all the Gypsies in Europe were destroyed by the Nazis."[21]

Until very recently, the issue of genocide has often been treated as a matter of comparison between Jewish and Romani victimization. Guenter Lewy, for example, argued that the Nazi attitude toward the Roma was a mixture of traditional prejudice and racist thinking and therefore did not constitute a consistent policy of extermination based on heredity. He further noted that the Nazi attack against the Roma lacked the kind of fanaticism that fueled their anti-Jewish campaign.[22] In his study of Ustaša Croatia, Alexander Korb picks upon this particular difference between the treatment of the Jewish and Romani minority during World War II, namely, negative emotional investment on the part of the perpetrators. The collective representation of the Jews involved a great deal of anti-Semitic imagination, proactive hostility, while the comparable image of the Roma rarely stirred passions beyond the matter-of-fact resoluteness to "do away with the Gypsy nuisance." Otherwise, the deportation of Croatian Roma to Jasenovac camp (where all of them perished) in May 1942 came on the heels of the mass arrest of the Jews prior to their deportation to Auschwitz-Birkenau.

As a student of Jewish history, Michael Zimmermann was fully aware of dissimilarities between the Nazi treatment of Jews and Roma, especially the fact that the former were defined strictly in racial terms while the latter in both racial and social terms. Since the legal definition of the main target group "Gypsy Mischlinge" was missing, however, local authorities could interpret it as they pleased. And so they did, having swept off an increasing number of sedentary, socially adjusted Roma. While the German population largely proved indifferent toward the fate of the Jews, resentment against the Roma kept rising throughout the war. However infrequent were protests against the deportation of Jews, even fewer individuals objected to the deportation of Roma.[23] As Henry Friedlander has pointedly noted, "Any system that categorizes all members of a group as anti-social is obviously establishing a racial definition based on heredity."[24] The rationale behind selection of itinerant Roma for execution by the *Einsatzgruppen* exposes the salience of the racial categorization. The Roma were sentenced to death as "spies" and "saboteurs," because they moved around uncontrollably, because they were "Gypsies." Then and again, circular logic merged the social and racial criteria into one threatening image of the enemy. The interaction between central and local agencies was crucial to the development of a policy that culminated in forced sterilization and murder. Racial ideology accelerated the traditional "fight against the Gypsies." The tension between local initiatives to expel the Roma and initial government attempts to settle them affected the decision-making process. Whether expulsion or settlement—death was the outcome, concluded Zimmermann.[25] Most recently, Donald Bloxham has reinforced Zimmermann's conclusions by arguing that "to suggest, as some have, that Nazi Romani policy was fundamentally different to Jewish policy because Romanies were seen as a social rather than a racial problem is to fail to appreciate the extent to which biological and social concepts coalesced in the period."[26]

In the context of a global military conflict aptly described by Nazi ideologists as "the war of extermination," the fluctuating definition of the "Gypsy" disadvantaged potential victims. Typically, the ambiguous criteria reflected the desire of the local authorities to get rid of the Romani population from a territory under their control. As Vladimir Solonari observes in the case of the mass deportation from Romania, the broad categorization of sedentary versus itinerant Roma effectively enabled the police to exercise unlimited discretionary powers. The percentage of Roma deported from any given county in 1942 reflected the outlook and the extent of the prejudice harbored by individual police officers. In rare cases, they regarded the lack of criminal record a sufficient reason to erase somebody's name off the list of deportees. Otherwise, they routinely snatched off as "itinerants" the Romani men who were used to traveling long distances in search for work. Perhaps most dishearteningly, the deportee lists had also to include spouses and children. When unable to establish the identity of a suspect, policemen based their judgments on sweeping criteria such as place of residency, purported "Gypsy lifestyle," and sometimes skin color. Collectively labeled a threat to public health and security, Roma appeared to match the image of "criminal Gypsies." Solonari thus concludes: "Although not all Gypsies were subject to deportation, no individuals other than Gypsies (and Jews) were deported."

The farther East, the more ambiguous became the criteria for identification of Roma. Extending his conclusions to the entire occupied Soviet territories, Tyaglyy argues that German authorities lacked a uniform policy vis-à-vis the Roma, effectively delegating decision-making power to local agencies. In November 1941, the supreme German military commander in Northwest Russia ordered "roaming Gypsies" to be segregated from sedentary Roma. However, the latter category did not apply to those deemed "politically or criminally suspicious," which invited a broad, malevolent interpretation by the Security Police and the military. Fleeing from combat areas, if apprehended, war refugees risked entering the former category. In the administrative entity that encompassed the Baltic States and parts of Belorussia, the German civil authorities in December 1941 issued an order that listed the following means of discovery: self-identification, lifestyle, social conditions, and testimonials of other group members. By continuously shifting in policy documents between associating and disassociating itinerant and sedentary Roma on the one hand, and Jews and Roma on the other, by late 1943 the Nazis had decimated the Romani communities.[27] Throughout the former Soviet Union, the flimsy distinction between sedentary and itinerant Roma existed only on paper, insists Tyaglyy. Hence, as far as the persecution of the Roma is concerned, he finds no qualitative difference between the regions of Ukraine under civil and military administration. Holler's research confirms that none of the sedentary Roma ever apprehended by the German military authorities had avoided a firing squad.

The extent to which the history of the Nazi persecution of the Jews and Roma was intertwined is reflected in the Holocaust scholarship of the past decade or so. Many scholars, including several represented in this anthology, have begun their historical quest with the study of the

Nazi mass murder of the Jews. Working with primary sources, inevitably they came across the evidence of the Nazi brutalities committed against the Roma. The archival records project an integrated picture of parallel rather than separate developments leading to Jewish and Romani victimization. The locally and centrally devised schemes for the solution of the "Jewish Question" and "Gypsy Question" were often strikingly similar. An idea originally explored by the Polish government, the Nazis for some time seriously considered deporting European Jews en masse to Madagascar. Before any of these plans ever emerged, in 1933 a representative political gathering in Austrian Burgenland toyed with the idea of deporting the local Roma to unsettled islands in the Pacific Ocean. In 1941, some Ustaša officials weighed the option of creating a similar reservation for Croatian Jews and Roma, probably on an island in the Adriatic Sea.

All too often, the Nazi decision making incorporated the Roma into the initial schemes designed for the Jews, from the earlier plans for mass deportations to Poland to mass executions in the Soviet Union during the opening months of Operation Barbarossa. The two best known examples include the deportation of Austrian Roma from Burgenland to the Litzmannstadt ghetto in late 1941 and the establishment of the so-called Gypsy family camp at Auschwitz-Birkenau in spring 1943. Florian Freund discusses in detail the decision to deport Burgenland Roma to the Litzmannstadt ghetto and its consequences; much less information is available about the Roma who had been dispatched to Jewish ghettos other than Litzmannstadt. Warsaw, for example, had served as a brief stop for several hundred Polish, but also a few Hungarian, Romanian, and Bulgarian Roma. The head of Warsaw *Judenrat* Adam Czerniaków registered in his diary the arrival of Roma inmates for the period April–July 1942. From that month onward, and through January 1943, the Nazis gradually dispatched the Roma, along with thousands of Jews, to their death to Treblinka. One eyewitness recalled that, unlike their fellow Jewish inmates, the Roma did not seem to realize it was their last journey.[28] Tyaglyy narrates that, during the liquidation of ghettos in District Galicia (then part of the General Government of Poland) in 1943, the Roma were murdered along with the Jews across towns and villages, for example, in Sambor.

The fact that the Jews and Roma in the Litzmannstadt ghetto were murdered in experimental gas vans at the Kulmhof death camp in January 1942 has often been mentioned in the literature. Tyaglyy relates at least two instances from March 1942 when the Germans used gas vans to dispose of over one hundred Roma at Dzhankoi railway junction in Crimea. In the long list of crimes committed by the Nazis against the civilian population, it reads as a mere footnote that a single largest concentration of Roma in the Soviet Union was probably in Leningrad, and that a great many of them died of starvation during the 872-day siege of the city. Tyaglyy describes several cases from Ukraine when Jews and Roma died side by side. In one such instance in Volyn province in August 1942, the German Security Police murdered seventy-six Roma. Prior to the mass execution, Romani and Jewish victims spent their last hours in the same concentration camp. Entire Romani caravans perished at Babi Yar near Kiev—the site of one of the first and largest massacres of Jews during World War II. The local Ukrainian population, anxious about their own survival, had composed a rhyme that identified both Jews and Roma as a target group for the Nazis. The Soviet records confirm that, as a rule, the *Einsatzgruppen* first murdered all the Jews in any given locality and only then the Roma. In some cases mass executions of Jews and Roma were carried out simultaneously, and only infrequently the killing of Roma preceded that of Jews.[29]

In Ustaša Croatia, as Korb argues in his chapter, the animosity reserved for the Serbs had exponentially increased to include the Jews and the Roma. However, since the German-Croatian agreement dealt exclusively with the expulsion of Serbs, the Ustaša started exploring other options vis-à-vis non-Slavic minorities. Korb observes that, as far as the Roma were concerned, the Ustaša racial laws proved more radical than the notorious Nuremberg Laws, defying them as a non-Aryan minority. As elsewhere in Nazi-dominated Europe, the mass violence in Croatia was directed in the first place against so-called nomadic Gypsies. Aptly analyzed in the case of the Nazi "Final Solution of the Jewish Question," the phenomenon of cumulative radicalization had translated various resettlement schemes into a full-fledged deportation to concentration camps and the exploitation of forced labor into mass murder.

It is not just the comparable scope, means, and brutality of persecution that the Nazis applied to Jews and Roma, but also its explicit dehumanizing aspect. Among other instances, Holler describes how members of a Security Police unit forced a group of Roma to dance half-naked in freezing temperatures prior to killing them. This deliberate act of degradation and public humiliation was not dissimilar from that of the Nazi policemen cutting off beards of the observant Jewish men slated for execution. In a detailed study of a massacre at Novorzhev, Holler relates horrendous torture to which a German Field Police unit subjected a group of three hundred-odd Roma, including women and children. As I have argued elsewhere, the comparison between the Nazi persecution of Jews and Roma is an important first step toward a comprehensive study of minority policies, both interethnic relations and the purposeful assault on minorities under Nazi rule. The issue at stake has never been comparative victimization, but contextualization.[30]

The Continuity and Break in the Persecution of the Roma

No doubt, the World War II period saw the most methodical and ruthless implementation of anti-Roma policies resulting in internment, deportations, mass murder, and eventually genocide. Like in the case with the Jews, it is inconceivable that without the connivance of the Nazi authorities, the Pavelić regime in Croatia or Antonescu in Romania would have implemented anti-Roma measures amounting to genocide. At the same time, having clearly allocated the destruction of the European Roma only a secondary priority, the Nazis did not pressure the satellite governments to solve the "Gypsy Question" once and for all. Indeed, the client states such as Croatia, Romania, or Vichy France could operate with a significant degree of autonomy, in accordance with the perceptions and laws that harked back to the interwar period and beyond. From the persecutory assimilation, as argued in the case of Vichy France by Shannon L. Fogg, to ethnic purification, as analyzed in the case of Romania by Solonari—the persecution of the Roma reflected the present status of any given dependent territory and the preexisting minority-majority relations.

Traditionally, the Romani minority has been very heterogeneous. Factors such as geography, religion, language, and lifestyle came to define both the self-identity and the prescribed identity of the Roma. The distinction between urban and rural, sedentary and itinerant, Orthodox and Muslim made it difficult to speak of a single people. These divisions, sometimes real, but sometimes superimposed, usually worked against the Roma, who had been arbitrarily put in one category or another depending on the whim and agenda of local authorities. However disadvantageous their situation was across interwar Europe, the Roma, as a loosely defined group, were at the mercy of the Nazi racial ideology. The doctrine of biological purity sat well with the Nazi satellites, which were all too eager to ascertain their racial worth by, among other means, purging the body national of "undesired elements." Occasionally, within the context of a war of extermination, the persistent image of Roma as social deviants merged with the label of racial inferiority. With some exceptions, the Roma followed Jews on the list of the imaginary enemies to be purged from society. One such exception was Ustaša Croatia, which regarded the Serbs as its archenemy. Remarkably, the fascist regime in Zagreb had intensified the persecution of both Jews and Roma while having been forced by the German Big Brother to scale back its onslaught against ethnic Serbs. In a peculiar twist, as Korb observes, the Ustaša purposefully dispatched the Roma to Jasenovac concentration camp as Serbs' spies. Symbolically, the Roma came to define the ethnic boundary with Serbia that the Ustaša was eager to draw. This kind of rhetoric did not prevent the Croatian police and military from expelling Roma under conventional pretexts. Despite the multitude of justifications, the result was all the same: 75 percent of local Roma had been wiped out. The Nazis had provided the framework for destruction, but the actual murder was committed by Pavelić's regime.

In Romania, the Roma had historically been treated as second-rank citizens. As Solonari pinpoints, the Romanian intellectual elites were keen to elevate the status of Romania internationally by drawing a line between the ethnic Romanians and the Roma. Perpetually marginalized in interwar Romania, the Roma fell victim to violent nationalist rhetoric and, increasingly, homegrown eugenic discourse that taunted assimilation of "biologically inferior" minorities. The growing calls for segregation, internment in concentration camps, and forced sterilization had assumed an ominous meaning following the German invasion of the Soviet Union in 1941. In May 1942 Romanian dictator Ion Antonescu sanctioned the deportation of Roma to Transnistria, a formerly Soviet territory occupied by Romanian troops. Antonescu was reactive in his decision, even though he had personally determined the selection criteria and the framework for deportation, argues Solonari. Among the factors that framed Antonescu's loathing of Jews and Roma, Solonari singles out prejudice, geopolitics, and copycat. Bound by a special relationship with Nazi Germany, still optimistic about the prospective of Axis victory, and certainly aware of the implementation of the Nazi "Final Solution," Antonescu ordered an assault on the two most vulnerable minorities. By October 1942, however, Antonescu reassessed the possible outcome of the war and, in order to curry favor with the Western Allies, stopped the deportation of Jews to Transnistria. Inadvertently, this policy change extended to the Roma as well. Tyaglyy complements Solonari's account by providing harrowing details of the plight of the Romani deportees in Transnistria: in some districts, due to the typhus epidemics, anywhere between one-fourth and one-third of the Roma had died. While some Roma were occasionally killed by Romanian policemen, SS men, or ethnic Germans, the local non-Romani population viewed the former with suspicion, unwilling to share their limited resources.

In Vichy France, on the other hand, the persecution of Roma continued largely in accordance with the earlier, discriminatory legislation targeting so-called nomads. The policy of forced assimilation pursued by Philippe Pétain's government, contends Fogg, did not incorporate an element of race. The typical discourse that linked vagrancy to nomadic lifestyle and nomadism to criminality made it into the 1912 law, which had clear implications for France's Roma. The assignment of all those deemed "nomadic" to certain areas continued through the June 1940 armistice, except that the Vichy regime regarded internment as the best means of assimilation. The German order of October 1940 prescribing the confinement of all Roma—based on a broader definition of "Gypsy"—to camps ran into a problem since no comprehensive census of the itinerant and sedentary populations alike ever been conducted on the territory of France. In March 1942, however, the Vichy government established, on its own initiative, a special camp for itinerant Roma. The camp at Saliers in Southeast France, which for the following two years accommodated close to seven hundred Roma, served as a propaganda showcase for the regime's efforts to assimilate the "nomads." Needless to say, these efforts failed miserably. The policy of reeducation through work (remotely resembling the early Soviet model) aimed specifically at children and youth, who had been forcefully separated from their families. Ultimately, writes Fogg, the victims only remembered persecution and privation, scoffing at the "benevolent intentions" proclaimed by the Vichy regime.

The case of Austria, and specifically Burgenland, presents a striking example of continuity of the persecution. Tracing the discriminatory legislation in Austrian lands back to the mid-eighteenth century, Freund follows what he calls a "genocidal trajectory" all the way to the November 1941 deportation of Burgenland Roma to Litzmannstadt ghetto. Incorporated into Austria in 1921, the formerly Hungarian province of Burgenland contained a sizable, overwhelmingly sedentary Romani minority. Differently from other federal states, local authorities in Burgenland from early on defined the Roma in ethnic terms. The world economic crisis pushed the Roma out of jobs and onto welfare, which fueled resentment on the part of the relatively poor rural population of Burgenland. Despite the tendency toward social marginalization of the Roma, until 1938 the existing legal safeguards had prevented a further application of pressure. Freund makes a bold statement that, in the period following the annexation, Austrian officials in general and regional authorities in Burgenland directly contributed to the radicalization of the Nazi anti-Roma policy. Not coincidentally, the Austrian Roma became the first victim of that policy in Western Europe.

Freund argues that the collaboration between Burgenland politicians, welfare officials, the Reich Criminal Police, and the Nazi leadership in Berlin had engendered the calls for a more drastic solution. Local district heads (*Gauleiter*) referred to recurrent complaints from the municipalities when they proposed to dispatch all the Roma to a purpose-built camp. The German invasion of Poland offered Burgenland authorities an opportunity to get rid of the Roma in their respective districts. The decision to deport about thirty thousand German and Austrian Roma dates from early 1940. The adopted criterion for deportation was social, even though nearly all work-fit Roma who ended up in forced labor camps prior to the deportation had previously held steady jobs. Due to the complex power relations in German-occupied Poland, the initial plans for deportation had to be postponed. The attack on the Soviet Union in the summer of 1941, however, pushed further the demands for a wholesale deportation of Jews and Roma. The 5,007 Roma deported to Litzmannstadt ghetto never came to perform labor, as had been originally envisaged, but died in the hundreds of a typhus epidemic. Subsequently, the survivors were murdered at the nearby Kulmhof death camp.

The issue of continuity and break in the persecution of the Roma can also be considered from the perspective of popular opinion—a crucial, yet largely understudied subject. Generally, the expression of public sympathy toward the Roma increased from West to East as the plight of the victims deteriorated from random incarceration to systematic mass murder. It is partially explicable, since the very same people who may otherwise cheer the removal of the "Gypsy nuisance," would hardly fathom the physical destruction of individuals or entire communities. The other side of the coin is that bringing about the desired outcome (i.e., expunging the Roma from any given area) blanked the imagination of the officials involved as to the ultimate faith of the affected population. For instance, Freund cites a summary of the reports that came from the districts following the mass deportation of the Austrian Roma to Auschwitz-Birkenau in April 1943: "All in all, the removal of Gypsies, which is seen as the long-awaited liberation from a menace, has generated the greatest satisfaction."

In places like Ukraine or Russia—aptly described in this volume by Tyaglyy and Holler respectively—where the scope of designated enemies expanded exponentially to include the Slavic peoples, the issue of survival strengthened the bonds of human solidarity; hence the more numerous cases of rescue that have been documented until now for Eastern vs. Western Europe. A common faith sometimes served as a key to survival, too. Although it rarely, if at all, played a role in the case of the Orthodox religion, for example in Romania, the Islamic creed, or at least a declaration thereof, at times saved person's life. Tyaglyy documents several such cases for Crimea in the Ukraine, while Korb does so for

Bosnia. In Crimea, a substantial number of Roma had adopted the religion and culture of the indigenous Tatar population. When the systematic destruction of the Roma and Jews commenced, simultaneously, in Crimea in late 1941–early 1942, some of the former managed to survive by posing as Tatars. The Muslim Committees installed by the Germans sometimes directly intervened on behalf of the Muslim Roma before occupation authorities, for example, in Bakhchisarai and the regional capital Simferopol. In an attempt to win over the Crimean Tatars, the Nazis relented their pressure, especially since a majority of the Roma were already dead by the time of the intervention. In Bosnia, too, Muslim officials sometimes intervened on behalf of the Roma who practiced Islam. An act of pure humanitarianism it probably was not. More likely, Korb suggests, the Bosnian Muslim leadership sought to stave off a potential large-scale attack against the multiethnic society as a whole. Keen on merging Bosnia's Muslims into the Croatian nation, the Ustaša backtracked, further differentiating between different categories of Roma. Subsequently, the Croatian foreign minister even intervened with the German authorities in Serbia on behalf of Muslim Roma. Sometimes, officials in position of power rendered individual assistance by merely ignoring or deliberately misinterpreting the anti-Roma ordinances that they had received. In the essence, however, these and similar random initiatives rarely provided a lasting relief for the Roma: whenever some of them were reclassified as "Aryans," the remainder were cast even deeper into prejudice, just to balance the policy.

Solonari finds no evidence that the Romanian society as a whole was opposed to the deportation of Roma. In spite of a number of individual petitions presented to Romanian authorities to exempt a certain Roma from deportation—often on utilitarian grounds—public protests against the deportation of persons deemed "itinerant and/or dangerous sedentary Gypsies" were conspicuous by their absence. Similarly, in the case of Vichy France, Fogg detects little public sympathy toward the Roma, or the regime's assimilation project for that matter. Local residents and officials alike expressed their strong desire to see the "nomads" go and therefore approved of the internment of the Roma.

Tyaglyy spends much time in his chapter discussing the attitudes of the local population toward the persecution of the Roma. As with other aspects of the genocide, the patterns of individual and collective behavior varied greatly under different circumstances. Tyaglyy qualifies the earlier findings, according to which the ethnic Russian population universally extended support to the Roma (but not necessarily the Jews). He argues that this generalization applies exclusively to itinerant Roma and that it ignores the persistence of traditional stereotypes. Besides, this overtly positive assessment does not take into account the segment of the local population who collaborated with the Germans. Thus, the Organization of Ukrainian Nationalists (OUN) initially lashed against the Roma with the same vehemence they did against the Jews. The Romani survivors reserved no other words but "bandits" for the members of the organization, as opposed to describing Soviet partisans as "brothers" or even recalling some "good Germans." Tyaglyy evokes the cases in which village elders drew up lists of Roma that served as a basis for their subsequent arrest and execution, auxiliary policemen participated in atrocities, and local officials misappropriated the meager possessions of the dead. Remarkably, when confronted with the truth that they did not intervene on behalf of the persecuted minority, local Russian eyewitnesses after the war conventionally described the victims as "nomads"—no differently from the German perpetrators, remarks Holler. As all-out civil war flared up in the dismembered Yugoslavia, even Tito's communist partisans occasionally killed Roma suspected of espionage for the Germans; some of their fellow inmates at Jasenovac camp accused the Roma of working for the Ustaša. In effect, the deep-seated resentment against the Roma did not subside even under the most precarious circumstances for the latter.

The Aftermath: Persecution Continues

The persecution of the Roma across Western and Central Europe had been a continuous process engrained in collective prejudice. It did not begin with the Nazis, nor did it end with the collapse of the Third Reich. It is ironic as it is tragic that the new, democratic governments in countries as different as France and Austria decided to uphold the discriminatory ordinances against the Roma that had been applied most systematically under the Nazi domination. The Soviet NKVD picked up Romani survivors as part of a wholesome deportation of the Crimean Tatars in May 1944 following the withdrawal of the German troops. In West Germany, unsympathetic lawyers came to effectively subscribe to the findings of Nazi racial pseudoscience in their argument against financial compensation to the Roma victims.

Since the Nazi policy of persecution exceeded in brutality any anti-Roma legislation that had ever been passed anywhere in Europe, the governments in countries like Austria and France had no misgivings in reenacting the discriminatory laws that had regulated the Roma's life since the late nineteenth century. Thus, shortly after the end of World War II, the notorious Gypsy Edict of 1888 was again in effect in Austria. Even more grotesque, writes Freund, was the official statement as to the Roma undeservingly claiming the victim status. The traditional stereotypes had persisted well beyond 1945. Even the suspicion of liaison with the enemy—this time around the Soviet occupation authorities and communists in general—did not let go. The Austrian police stopped the routine surveillance of Roma only by the early 1960s, and even then rather unofficially. The 1912 French law that had introduced the category of *nomadism* remained in force until 1969. The itinerant Roma who fell under this category still languished in camps by the end of 1945; unlike in the case of other prisoners, French authorities denied them a blanket release. The new government effectively continued with the policy of assimilation codified in prewar France, except for the provision for internment, concludes Fogg.

Margalit pinpoints the persistence of racial bias in the West-German legal investigation of the crimes committed by Hitler's regime against the Roma. When dealing with the issue of compensation, the judicial authorities refused to recognize the Roma as victims of the Nazis. Instead, all the way through the mid-1980s, the West-German judiciary consistently ruled in favor of the perpetrators, including the notorious Dr. Robert Ritter and his aide Dr. Eva Justin. The defendants convinced the judges that racial biology was a legitimate science, that their acts actually benefitted the Roma, and that they altogether opposed Nazism. The sympathetic justice officials readily accepted the arguments that any discriminatory act committed prior to Himmler's December 1942 decree, which provided for a wholesome deportation of Roma to Auschwitz-Birkenau death camp, did not qualify as racial persecution. With the major Nazi criminals dead or missing, individuals like Ritter and Justin walked out free while the Romani plaintiffs were denied a fair hearing in court. Remarkably, German-Jewish officials routinely supported claims for compensation by the Roma. In so doing, argues Margalit, they acted out of a genuine sympathy for the victims. Simultaneously, they were worried that the negative verdict might serve as a precedent to deny Jews compensation for the persecution as well.

On a side note, Margalit contradicts himself by situating anti-Roma prejudice within German culture while maintaining that the West German justice system proved dysfunctional in investigating the Nazi crimes committed against minorities in general. The chapters in this volume attest to what has since long been known, namely, the strength of anti-Roma sentiments across Europe. When looking from a comparative and longitudinal perspective, the German Sinti and Roma have fought for and received perhaps more justice than any other Romani community outside Germany.

Nadine Blumer takes further the issues of comparison, victimhood, and representation in her chapter on commemoration of the Nazi genocide against the Roma people. She builds her narrative around the debates surrounding the creation of a central memorial to the Romani victims of the Nazi regime in Berlin. When analyzing public and political debates in Germany, she pays particular attention to the position taken by the Central Council of the German Sinti and Roma and its leader Romani Rose. Since the idea was first broached in 1988, the memorial and a politics of commemoration generally is still a work in progress. From the outset, the discussion centered on incorporating the suffering of non-Jewish minorities, and specifically the Roma, under Nazi rule into the narrative of the Holocaust. As the debate evolved over time, it eventually converged on a broader issue of the memorialization of Nazi victims in the new Germany. After years of heated polemics, a narrow consensus has emerged among all the parties involved that the prospective Roma memorial should stand apart from the Central Memorial to the Murdered Jews of Europe, which was unveiled near the German parliament in 2005. At the same time, it was decided that the new monument would be situated in direct proximity to the Jewish memorial whose historical exhibit covers the suffering inflicted by the Nazis on numerous victim groups, including the Roma. Notwithstanding the occasional acrimony of the debate examined by Blumer, it is obvious that the Nazi persecution of the Jews and Roma belong together when it comes to historical context and commemoration.

The level of organization made the German Sinti and Roma a coherent group often speaking in one voice, which is rarely the case elsewhere in Europe today. The judicial proceedings of the earlier decades and the more recent politicized debate over the Berlin memorial tell a great deal about Germans coming to terms with their past. No less important is how the Romani people as a whole embrace the memory of persecution, the question that Sławomir Kapralski examines in the final chapter of this book. Kapralski explicates the forms and means of commemoration as an essential element in constructing Romani identities. In his critique of the notion that the Roma are a "people without history," he stresses the structural factors that discouraged retelling and sharing the stories of violence. The Roma are not "mute," but have been "muted" by mainstream society, argues Kapralski. Until recently, the Roma had to fit their narrative within the traumatic discourse developed by non-Roma for the lack of own cultural codes of transmission. Moreover, the sheer plurality of Romani communities makes it difficult to generalize for the entire Romani people.

Not unlike the cumulative diversification of Holocaust research, however, the initial Holocaust discourse provided a context from which Roma could derive concepts and ideas to essentialize their suffering at the hands of Nazis and their collaborators. The growing interaction with non-Roma has over time introduced shared cultural practices. Using the annual Romani commemorative event in Polish Tarnów as an example, Kapralski insists that the synthesis of tradition and modernity is indeed possible. Kapralski concludes that, as far as the Nazi genocide is concerned, the lack of expression does not mean the absence of historical memory among the Roma. The evolution of the Romani civil rights movement aptly supports his conclusion.

Social Activism and Terminology

The renewed academic interest in the Roma victimization during World War II has in part to do with history and the development of the international Romani civil rights movement. The starting point was probably the creation of the International Romani Union in London in 1971. Donald Kenrick and Grattan Puxon's book, *The Destiny of Europe's Gypsies,* which has brought the issue into the open, owes much to the International Romani Union and its regular gatherings. (Kenrick was a linguist, whereas Puxon then served as the secretary of the British Gypsy Council.) Among other issues, the First World Romani Congress (held in 1971) raised the issue of compensation from West Germany. The participation of the Central Council of German Sinti in the Third Congress in Göttingen in 1981 pushed this issue to the fore.[31]

The Central Council of German Sinti and Roma (the word *Roma* has been added to make the organization sound more representative) was born out of a public campaign by the Society for Endangered Peoples. The Society for Endangered Peoples is a left-leaning organization, established in Hamburg in 1970. A few months after the screening of the TV miniseries "Holocaust" in early 1979, the society put together a conference with the title, "The Holocaust Means Also the Extermination of 500,000 Gypsies in the Third Reich." The same year, the Society for Endangered Peoples published a collection of essays, *In Auschwitz vergast, bis heute verfolgt. Zur Situation der Roma (Zigeuner) in Deutschland und Europa* (Gassed at Auschwitz—Persecuted Until Today), which became its rallying point. Since 1981 the Central Council has emerged as a leading Romani organization in Germany, with financial support from the federal government.[32]

The Central Council of German Sinti and Roma is certainly the most important Romani organization with a research agenda. The Central Council has successfully lobbied for the erection of monuments to Gypsy victims on the former sites of Nazi concentration camps, including Buchenwald and Ravensbrück. Through the efforts of its longstanding chairperson, Romani Rose, the Central Council has established a Documentation and Cultural Center of German Sinti and Roma. Founded in 1990, the center moved into a purpose-built building in Heidelberg seven years later. From the inception, the center took on a proactive approach to the study of Nazi persecution of Roma. In 1993 it joined forces with the Auschwitz-Birkenau State Museum to publish the *Memorial Book: The Gypsies at Auschwitz-Birkenau*. The Center's own publication, *Der nationalsozialistische Völkermord an den Sinti und Roma* (1995), was essentially the catalog for an exhibition that went on display in 1997. The book that followed, *"Den Rauch hatten wir täglich vor Augen." Der nationalsozialistische Völkermord an den Sinti und Roma* (1999), reflected back on the exhibition.[33] The educational mission of the center came the farthest in the permanent exhibition at the Auschwitz-Birkenau State Museum that opened in 2001. The concept and the contents of the exhibition were closely coordinated with the Heidelberg Center, which for that matter engaged the Association of Roma in Poland. It has received the most international attention, however, through an English-language traveling exhibition modeled on the German prototype. The exhibition focused on the Nazi mass murder but linked it to the continuing discrimination against Roma in Europe. It also traced the genesis of the Romani civil rights movement and the debates on financial compensation. Since its launch at the European Parliament in Strasbourg in January 2006, the exhibition has been to a dozen countries, with a stop at the UN Headquarters in New York City.

The study of the Nazi persecution of the Roma has generated heated debates but minimum consensus, starting with the name of the victim group. The word most often used in contemporary discourse is *Roma*. *Roma* is a politically correct term that comes from within the community rather than being enforced from outside. The word *Gypsy* (corrupted form of *Egyptian*), or *Zigeuner/цыган* (derived from a Greek root meaning untouchable), on the other hand, reflects prejudice and ignorance of the surrounding society. The fact that the Nazis and their collaborators purposely defined the persecuted group as "Gypsies" makes it in the eyes of many, particularly human rights activists, a word of abuse. Yet for the purpose of analysis, I contend, the context of World War II provides for the use of both words. One can argue, for example, that the collective term *Gypsies* refers to an entire minority rather than distinctive tribes that compose it. Beside, not all groups identify themselves as Roma. The construct *Sinti and Roma,* which since 1980 has become normative in German-speaking countries, may be more precise yet semantically deficient. The Nazis committed a mass murder predominantly against the Roma people. As far as the notion of genocide is concerned, however, both Roma and Sinti were the victims. Unsurprisingly, the difference of opinions as to use of the word *Roma* versus *Gypsies* is reflected in his volume. The contributors who explore the application of genocidal policies in various parts of Europe predominantly use the former word, whereas the authors who deal with the legacy of the genocide use the latter. In either case, the underlining motive that runs through all the chapters is identification with the victims.

Scholars use specific terms to mark crucial events or historical periods (e.g., the Reformation, the Great Depression, the Thaw). Other terms denote particular instances of mass violence or massive loss of life (e.g., Black Death, the Great Terror, the Great Leap Forward). The collective memory of the ethnic groups who were subject to mass terror or genocide generates specific terms in the native languages to define that tragic experience. Thus, we have the Hebrew word *Shoah,* Armenian word *Aghet,* Ukrainian word *Holodomor,* and Arabic word *Anfal* (used by the Kurds to describe Saddam Hussein's attack against their people in 1986–89).[34] Terminology has a consolidating function as it can help to shape ethnic or national identity. Otherwise, common terminology is useful for identifying sets of related problems, doing research, and teaching. It is not surprising, therefore, that Roma and non-Roma, professional historians, and social activists alike have been searching for the right word to describe the experience of the Romani people under Nazi rule.

The most commonly used word at the moment is *Porrajmos,* coined by Ian Hancock, a professor of English and linguistics at the University of Texas. Hancock made use of the Vlax dialect of Romanes to argue that *Baro Porrajmos* means "great devouring" and thus is an appropriate term to denote the suffering of the Roma at the hands of the Nazis. The term took off thanks to the international Romani congresses. Historians started using it as a politically correct term; it has made an appearance in some of the contributions to the now-classic volume, *The Gypsies in Eastern Europe,* published in 1991. Unfortunately, the word *Porrajmos* is misleading from both a linguistic and ethic point of view. The verb *porrav-* literally means "open wide," and has a sexual connotation. The root of the noun *poravipe* means in Romanes simply "rape." Essentially, the word *Porrajmos* denotes sexual violence. Outside this context it is only used by a small but growing group of Roma activists with an international flair, but not by the Roma at large. As Michael Stewart and Nikolai Bessonov wrote, the term *Porrajmos* is not carved in the historical memory of the Roma people.[35]

Another less frequently used Romani word is *mudaripen* (sometimes also rendered as *samudaripen*), which means total killing or murder. The German language, due to its peculiarity, has added to the academic vocabulary a one-word construct, *Zigeunermord* (by analogy with *Judenmord*), which can be rendered as mass murder of Gypsies. When it comes to verbal constructs, however, by far the most popular is *Roma Holocaust* or *Romani Holocaust*. In my view, most sensible is to neither devise new, ethnocentric terms nor try to adapt the existing ones, but to use emotionally neutral scholarly terminology. The legal term *genocide* in fact carries as much moral weight as the word *Holocaust,* thus rendering the issue of comparison between Jewish and Romani victimization into an intellectual exercise in pursuit of a deeper understanding of the nature of mass violence and of the extent of human suffering. The bulk of historical evidence and the growing legal consensus pinpoints the accurate definition of the wartime persecution of the Roma, namely, genocide.

Notes

1. M. Zimmermann, ed., *Zwischen Erziehung und Vernichtung. Zigeunerpolitik und Zigeunerforschung im Europa des 20. Jahrhunderts* (Stuttgart, 2007), esp. pt. 3; F. Fischer von Weikerstahl et al., ed., *Der nationalsozialistische Genozid an den Roma Osteuropas. Geschichte und künstlerische Verarbeitung* (Cologne, 2008); Julia von dem Knesebeck, *The Roma Struggle for Compensation in Post-War Germany* (Hatfield, 2011).
2. The three-volume anthology edited by Donald Kenrick and published by University of Hertfordshire Press between 1997 and 2006 provides rather sketchy, uneven accounts of the Romani plight in individual European countries.
3. In his study of Jewish POWs, Pavel Polian stated that "there is no information on the selection and murder of Gypsy POWs." See Pavel Polian, "First Victims of the Holocaust: Soviet-Jewish Prisoners of War in German Captivity," *Kritika: Explorations in Russian and Eurasian History* 6, no. 4 (Fall 2005): 764.
4. Philip Friedman, *Roads to Extinction: Essays on the Holocaust* (New York, 1980); Joachim Hohmann, *Zigeuner und Zigeunerwissenschaft. Ein Beitrag zur Grundlagenforschung und Dokumentation des Völkermords im "Dritten Reich"* (Marburg, 1980); Joachim Hohmann, *Geschichte der Zigeunerverfolgung in Deutschland* (Frankfurt, 1988); Joachim Hohmann, *Robert Ritter und die Erben der Kriminologie. "Zigeunerforschung" im Nationalsozialismus und in Westdeutschland im Zeichen des Rassismus* (Frankfurt, 1991); Donald Kenrick and Grattan Puxon, *The Destiny of Europe's Gypsies* (New York, 1972); Donald Kenrick and Grattan Puxon, *Gypsies Under Swastika* (Hatfield, 1995); Grattan Puxon, "The Forgotten Victims," *Patterns of Prejudice* 11, no. 2 (1977): 23–28; Deutlev Peukert, *Volksgenossen und*

Gemeinschaftsfremde. Anpassung, Ausmerze und Aufbegehren unter dem Nationalsozialismus (Cologne, 1982). For a comprehensive overview of literature see Michael Zimmermann, *Rassenutopie und Genozid. Die nationalsozialistische "Lösung der Zigeunerfrage"* (Hamburg, 1996), 30–1, 389–90; Michael Zimmermann, "Zigeunerbilder und Zigeunerpolitik in Deutschland. Eine Übersicht über neuere historische Studien," *Werkstatt Geschichte* 9, no. 25 (May 2000): 35–58.

5. State Museum of Auschwitz-Birkenau, *Memorial Book: The Gypsies of Auschwitz-Birkenau*, 4 vols. (Munich, 1993).
6. Henry Friedlander, *Origins of Nazi Genocide: From Euthanasia to the Final Solution* (Chapel Hill, NC, 1995); Sybil Milton, "The Context of the Holocaust," *German Studies Review* 13, no. 2 (1990): 269–83; Sybil Milton, "Nazi Policies Toward Roma and Sinti," *Journal of the Gypsy Lore Society* 2, no. 1 (1992): 1–18.
7. Zimmermann, *Rassenutopie und Genozid*, 369–81. See also his chapter, "Der nationalsozialistische Genozid an den Zigeunern und der Streit zwischen 'Intentionalisten' und 'Funktionalisten,'" in *Von der Aufgabe der Freiheit. Festschrift für Hans Mommsen zum 5. November 1995*, ed. C. Jansen et al. (Berlin, 1995).
8. Gilad Margalit, *Germany and Its Gypsies: A Post-Auschwitz Ordeal* (Madison, WI, 2002); Guenter Lewy, *The Nazi Persecution of the Gypsies* (Oxford, 2000). For example, with regard to mass executions in the summer and fall of 1941, Lewy wrote (220): "Yet since the main reason for subjecting the Soviet Gypsies to the murderous actions of the roving *Einsatzgruppen* (special task forces) was their alleged tendency to spy, in practice most of the victims were itinerating Gypsies." In reference to the mass murder at Auschwitz-Birkenau in 1944, he had this to say (221): "It is possible that had it not been for the overcrowding of the gas chambers and the need to find temporary housing for the doomed Hungarian Jews, the killing of Gypsies who were deemed not suitable for work would never have taken place."
9. Tomislav Dulić, *Utopias of Nation: Local Killing in Bosnia and Herzegovina, 1941–42* (Uppsala, 2005); Tomislav Dulić, "Mass Killing in the Independent State of Croatia, 1941–1945: A Case for Comparative Research," *Journal of Genocide Research* 8, no. 3 (September 2006): 255–81.
10. Martin Holler, *Der nationalsozialistische Völkermord an den Roma in der besetzten Sowjetunion (1941–1944)* (Heidelberg, 2009).
11. Quoted in David Young, "The Trial of Remembrance: Monuments and Memories of the *Porrajmos*," in *Genocide Perspectives I: Essays in Comparative Genocide*, ed. C. Tatz (Sydney, 1997), 121.
12. Martin Shaw, *What Is Genocide?* (London, 2007), 82–5.
13. William Schabas, *Genocide in International Law* (Cambridge, 2000), 214, 218, 222.
14. Thus, Rose wrote in the Preface to the *Memorial Book* regarding the deportation of Roma to the Auschwitz death camp: "These names—each name speaks for itself—attest to the genocide committed under the National Socialist regime" (*Memorial Book*, vol. 1, xiii).
15. Zimmermann, *Rassenutopie und Genozid*, 374–75.
16. Michael Zimmermann, "The National Socialist 'Solution of the Gypsy Question': Central Decisions, Local Initiatives, and Their Interrelation." *Holocaust and Genocide Studies* 15, no. 3 (Winter 2001): 20–21.
17. Christopher Browning, *The Origins of the Final Solution: The Evolution of Nazi Jewish Policy, September 1939-March 1942* (Lincoln, NE, 2004), 178–84, 473.
18. Dieter Pohl, *Die Herrschaft der Wehrmacht. Deutsche Militärbesatzung und einheimische Bevölkerung in der Sowjetunion 1941–1944* (Munich, 2008), 271–73.
19. Quoted in Dennis Reinhartz, "The Genocide of the Yugoslav Gypsies," in *The Gypsies During the Second World War: The Final Chapter*, ed. D. Kenrick (Hertfordshire, 2007), 90.

20. The testimony catalog is accessible online at: http://tc.usc.edu/vhitc.
21. Lemkin's statement at a luncheon in his honor organized by the American Jewish Congress, New York City, 18 January 1951 [?], American Jewish Archives (Cincinnati, OH), Ms 60, Box 4, Series 4; "Genocide" by Lemkin, broadcast, October 1955, American Jewish Archives, Ms 60, Box 4, Series 2.
22. Guenter Lewy, "Gypsies and Jews Under the Nazis," *Holocaust and Genocide Studies* 13, no. 3 (Winter 1999): 398.
23. Zimmermann, *Rassenutopie und Genozid,* 373–75.
24. Henry Friedlander, "Euthanasia and the Final Solution," in *The Final Solution: Origins and Implementation,* ed. D. Cesarani (London, 1996), 51.
25. Zimmermann, "The National Socialist 'Solution of the Gypsy Question'," 423–24.
26. Donald Bloxham, *The Final Solution: A Genocide* (Oxford, 2009), 142.
27. For Estonia see Anton Weiss-Wendt, "Extermination of the Gypsies in Estonia During World War II: Popular Images and Official Policies," *Holocaust and Genocide Studies* 17, no. 1 (Spring 2003): 31–61; for Latvia and Lithuania see Christoph Dieckmann, *Deutsche Besatzungspolitik in Litauen 1941–1944,* vol. 2 (Göttingen, 2011), 1392–97.
28. Adam Czerniaków, *Im Warschauer Ghetto. Das Tagebuch des Adam Czerniaków 1939–1942* (Munich, 1986), 247, 264, 265, 268, 275; Zimmermann, *Rassenutopie und Genozid,* 278–81.
29. Nikolai Bessonov, "Ob ispol'zovanii terminov 'Porajmos' and 'Holocaust' v znachenii 'genotsid tsygan,'" *Golokost i suchasnist: studii v Ukraini i sviti* 2, no.1 (2007): 79 (also available online at http://www.holocaust.kiev.ua/news/Research_note.pdf).
30. For further analysis see introduction in Anton Weiss-Wendt, *Eradicating Differences: The Treatment of Minorities in Nazi-Dominated Europe* (Newcastle, 2010), 1–22.
31. Elena Marushiakova and Veselin Popov, "Kholokost i tsygane. Konstruirovanie novoi natsional'noi mifologii," *Golokost i suchstnist: studii v Ukraini i sviti* 4, no. 2 (2008): 29–30 (also available online at http://www.holocaust.kiev.ua/news/chasopis_2008(4).html).
32. Margalit, *Germany and Its Gypsies,* 180–82, 187, 199–202.
33. R. Rose, ed., *Der nationalsozialistische Völkermord an den Sinti und Roma* (Heidelberg, 1995); R. Rose, ed., *"Den Rauch hatten wir täglich vor Augen." Der nationalsozialistische Völkermord an den Sinti und Roma* (Heidelberg, 1999). Chancellor Helmut Schmidt was probably the first high-ranking German official who has evoked the issue of genocide, when he stated in 1982 that Gypsies were persecuted on racial grounds in Nazi Germany.
34. The word *al-Anfal* (also used as a term—*the Anfal Campaign*) was introduced by the perpetrators themselves. Originally, it referred to a chapter in Koran, *Surat Al Anfal.* I am indebted to Chalak Kaveh for pointing it out to me.
35. Bessonov, "Ob ispol'zovanii terminov," 73–76; Michael Stewart, "Remembering Without Commemoration: The Mnemonics and Politics of Holocaust Memories Among European Roma," *Journal of the Royal Anthropological Institute* 10, no. 3 (2004): 578.

CHAPTER 1

ASSIMILATION AND PERSECUTION
AN OVERVIEW OF ATTITUDES TOWARD GYPSIES IN FRANCE

Shannon L. Fogg

During World War II, Gypsies in France faced identification, restrictions, arrests, internment, and death. Repressive laws and anti-Gypsy measures were nothing new for those who circulated within the country's borders when the war broke out in 1939, however. Gypsies in France had faced discrimination and marginalization since medieval times, with the first French law aimed specifically at the mobile population appearing in 1539.[1] A wave of anti-Gypsy legislation sparked by republican values, war, and French assimilationist tendencies had affected Gypsies throughout the late nineteenth and early twentieth centuries. World War II brought yet another set of circumstances and restrictive measures. The French army's surrender in June 1940 led to Nazi occupation of three-fifths of the country and the establishment of the Vichy regime in its southern, unoccupied zone. Itinerant Gypsies thus found themselves the potential targets of two different authoritarian governments between 1940 and 1944. Known for its conservative, exclusionary politics, it seems only natural that the Vichy regime would target Gypsies as part of the National Revolution that sought to create a renovated nation purged of "undesirable" elements. Yet the reality was much more complicated and somewhat unexpected. Unlike Jews, Gypsies in France were never officially persecuted on racial grounds during the war, and the Vichy regime continually argued for the assimilation of this minority group into the mainstream. In many ways the treatment of Gypsies under the Vichy regime was a clear extension of policies initiated during the French Third Republic (1871–1940). This chapter traces the evolution of modern French attitudes towards Gypsies and demonstrates the importance of persecutory assimilation as a guiding factor in their treatment during World War II.

A History of Persecution

A policy of forced assimilation was not unique to Marshal Philippe Pétain's wartime government. From the sixteenth century onward, assimilation attempts throughout Europe became more violent, but the Gypsies have proven to be remarkably resistant to such attempts at social integration. European marginalization in combination with Romani culture has limited the amount of interaction between the Roma and *Gadje* (the Rom word for non-Gypsies) resulting in the preservation of Romani language, social structures, and culture in spite of centuries of persecution.[2] Despite earlier exclusionary acts against the peripatetic population, it was not until the 1860s that France first considered a national surveillance program for "Bohemians." As a result, French and foreign travelers (*ambulants*) were required to carry identification papers beginning in 1863. By 1895, the government ordered a census of all "nomads, bohemians, and vagabonds" in a further surveillance attempt. Following the French loss in the Franco-Prussian war, many citizens supported such a measure that promised to help locate and identify potential "foreign" enemies.[3] These actions coincided with increasing concerns about vagrancy in the Third Republic, which ultimately facilitated surveillance of Gypsies and helped further associate nomadism with criminality. Xenophobia and safety thus became the major themes of anti-Gypsy propaganda and stereotypes in the late nineteenth and early twentieth centuries.

On 16 July 1912, the government of the French Third Republic channeled these sentiments into a law with clear implications for Gypsies. The 1912 law regulated travelling professions in France, identified three different categories of itinerant merchants, and introduced a new, anthropometric identity card for "nomads."[4] The first three articles of the law differentiated between travelling salesmen (*marchands ambulants*), stallholders at fairs and markets (*forains*), and nomads (*nomades*). Each category was delineated by nationality, required some form of registration and/or identification, and outlined penalties for failure to conform. A travelling salesman was anyone (French or foreign) with a fixed domicile, living in France and practicing a mobile trade. These salesmen were required to make a declaration at the prefecture or subprefecture in their place of residence and would receive a receipt in exchange for the declaration. Failure to register could result in a fine of five to fifteen francs and imprisonment for one to five days. *Forains* were defined as French nationals who practiced a recognized profession yet were without a fixed residence. They (and their family members) were required to carry an identification card with a photograph. Public authorities could demand that an individual produce this identity card at any time. Punishment for infractions included a fine of sixteen to one hundred francs and prison time ranging from five days to one month. Finally, the law defined nomads as anyone without a fixed residence, regardless of nationality, falling into neither of the two previous categories. Nomads were required to carry anthropometric identity cards, which were to be presented upon arrival and departure in any commune as a kind of travel visa. The cards thus allowed authorities to track nomads' movements. The law did not provide that everyone subject to Article III would be granted a card. Furthermore, all people falling into this administrative category were also required to carry a separate, collective identity card for the entire family and to display a special plate on their vehicles. The laws governing vagabondage would determine punishment in all cases of infractions related to the requirements for nomads outlined in Article III.

The 1912 law thus created a new administrative category and introduced a new type of identity card without explicitly defining who could be considered a "nomad." The document contained neither racial references nor any ethnic identifiers (e.g., *Tsigane, Gitan, Bohémien, Romanichel,* or *Manouche*) in keeping with republican principles. Despite these omissions, it was "exactly Gypsies (*Tsiganes*) that the legislator meant to designate by the term 'nomad.'"[5] The vagueness of the definitions of *marchands ambulants, forains,* and *nomades* in the law also meant that mobile families of Gypsy (Roma or Sinti) heritage could be classified as *forains* while sedentary Gypsies would be considered travelling salesmen. The key to understanding future actions against Gypsies is recognizing that these were not absolute categories; not all Gypsies were classified as nomads though most scholars agree that all nomads were Gypsies.[6] The actual categorization was determined on an individual basis by local officials and depended upon certain characteristics and perceptions that can best be labeled as racial.[7] In daily practice, most ordinary people did not distinguish between ethnically Gypsy *fo-*

rains and nomads, but the law did.⁸ For these reasons, I will use the term *Gypsy* throughout the rest of this chapter to describe the perceived racial heritage of this group or as a general term to describe a varied population. I will employ the word *nomad* to reflect the official administrative terminology embodied in the French word *nomade,* as defined in the 1912 law.⁹

Nomads were viewed as "foreign" to French society regardless of their nationality; they were legally linked to criminal vagabondage by the 1912 law; the creation of anthropometric cards further underscored the government's association of Gypsies with criminality. Recording physical characteristics previously only collected for the identification of criminals, the cards exhibited the holder's name, date and place of birth, height, chest measurement, size of head, length of right ear, length of left middle and little fingers, length of left arm from elbow to middle fingertip, eye color, all ten fingerprints, and full-face and profile photographs.¹⁰ One goal of the 1912 law was to force nomads off the road and encourage them to acquire a permanent residence, thereby placing them within the "travelling salesman" category. In lawmakers' eyes, conforming to the French norm of having a fixed domicile would encourage regular work and the Gypsies' assimilation. Nomadism was not a racial but rather a social and cultural problem that could be solved.¹¹ The Great War and the immigration concerns of the 1920s and 1930s further increased the surveillance of itinerant groups and helped crystallize the distinctions between French citizens and all types of "outsiders."¹²

The Persecution of French Gypsies During World War II

The 1912 law, which remained in effect until 1969, would form the basis for Vichy's attitudes and laws concerning Gypsies. In fact, Third Republic laws laid the foundation for the legal treatment of Gypsies during World War II, underlining the continuities between the republican and authoritarian regimes. This is not to say that the Gypsies in France did not experience additional discrimination, persecution, and extreme maltreatment during the war. Indeed, they faced surveillance, regular checks, forced immobilization, arrest, and internment in camps. However, official persecution was never explicitly racial (laws applied only to nomads and not all Gypsies) and offered the opportunity for rehabilitation—a combination that can best be described as a policy of persecutory assimilation. On 6 April 1940, after the outbreak of war in Europe but before the German invasion of France in May, President Paul Lebrun issued a law forbidding the circulation of nomads (as defined by the

1912 law) within French borders during wartime. The law, upheld by the Vichy regime after its establishment in July 1940, forced nomads to reside in a designated area under police surveillance. Nomads could move about freely only within these circumscribed areas, and they had to present themselves to the local gendarmerie within fifteen days of the law's publication. Failure to do so would result in a one- to five-year imprisonment. The preface to the law made it clear that such measures were necessary for "national defense" since the incessant movement of nomads with no national ties presented them with ample opportunities to pass military information to the enemy.[13] Xenophobia and long-standing stereotypes that associated Gypsies with spying certainly contributed to the lawmakers' push to immobilize the peripatetic population.[14]

The assignment of nomads to certain areas or even to fixed residences continued after the armistice of 22 June 1940 officially ended the hostilities between France and Germany. Although the Vichy regime touted itself as fundamentally different from the decadent Third Republic and promised to renovate French society through a National Revolution that would purge the nation of undesirable elements such as Jews, Communists, and foreigners, the regime continued to support the idea of nomad assimilability throughout the war years. Ethnic Gypsies who had a fixed residence (*marchands ambulants*) and *forains* of Roma extraction were exempt from the laws related to nomads and were shielded from harsher measures as the war progressed. In other words, Vichy maintained the distinction between *forains* and nomads throughout the war and did not use race as a determinant for internment. In fact, government officials sometimes worked to free travelling salesmen and *forains* who had been wrongly interned regardless of whether they were of Roma origin.[15] Nomads were offered a path to social reintegration, that is, by accepting French cultural norms regarding work and family. For the Vichy regime, the best way to encourage nomads' assimilation was through internment.

Internment Camps: A German Order

French authorities originally discouraged incarcerating nomads in concentration camps due to the additional policing, provisioning, economic, and cultural problems it would create. This attitude would change, however, after the defeat and the establishment of the Vichy regime in the summer of 1940. By early September, Nazi officials had received reports on the Gypsy situation in France. This was followed by the German ordinance of 4 October 1940, which explicitly ordered the confinement of all Gypsies in the occupied zone in French-run camps. This order posed problems, however. The Germans operated with a broader, racial definition of "Gypsy," but were unable to apply it because a comprehensive census of both itinerant and sedentary Gypsies did not exist in France. Since the French were responsible for the application of the ordinance, they arrested and interned only nomads as defined by the July 1912 law.[16] Over thirty camps would be used to intern nomads during the war, with the majority of them (twenty-five) in the northern, occupied zone. Somewhere between 6,000 and 6,500 men, women, and children (out of an estimated population of 40,000 nomads in France) would experience internment at some point after 1940.[17] The French were in no position to challenge the German ordinance despite the financial burden it would create and the challenge to Vichy's sovereignty it implied; Pétain's regime thus began the census and round-up of Gypsies later in October. By the beginning of 1941, approximately 1,700 people were interned in ten camps in the northern zone.[18]

Fears about the financial and material burden that concentration camps would place on local communities proved to be well founded. After legislators voted full powers to Marshal Pétain, the Vichy regime quickly discovered that the cost of running camps was substantial. At the Linas-Montlhéry camp (Seine-et-Oise) the cost of caring for internees was 1.3 million francs per year, not including the cost of salaries for police surveillance, which could reach 2.4 million francs.[19] These high costs often meant that the authorities cut back on surveillance, which helped to contribute to the ease with which some detainees were able to escape from the camps.[20] The costs associated with internment also created tension between the Vichy regime and the German occupation authorities. Initially the costs fell on the French Ministry of the Interior despite the fact that German orders created the camps. The French government believed the Germans should pay the costs since they had ordered the internment in the first place. The Germans, harboring the belief that Gypsies' internment served French interests, refused financial responsibility until the fall of 1942. Negotiations finally led to an agreement, according to which the expenses incurred by the internment of all "undesirables" based on German orders (i.e., Jews and nomads) would be included in French occupation costs and paid out of these accounts.[21]

Internment Camps: The French Experiment at Saliers

The French did take the initiative in one specific case, which is indicative of the regime's ideas about nomads and its ultimate failure to achieve its goal of assimilation. After March 1942, all nomads that had been assigned residence in the southern, unoccupied zone were to be dispatched to a new camp created in the town of Saliers (Bouches-du-Rhône) in the Camargue region of southeastern France. Established by the Vichy government, the camp was the only one instituted uniquely for the internment of Gypsies.[22] The regime created the camp on its own initiative and endowed it with an explicit political agenda: "Above all, the Saliers camp must be a governmental propaganda argument. This argument consists of giving a concentration camp the look of a village and of allowing family life there and respecting the customs and beliefs of the internees."[23] In other words, the camp would re-create a typical French village in the attempt to help nomads become accustomed to "normal" life while upholding some Gypsy traditions. The Vichy regime intended to use the concentration camp system in general, and the Saliers camp in particular, as a means to introduce nomads to the French notions of family, community, and productive labor, and thereby enforce assimilation.[24]

Close to seven hundred Gypsies were transferred to the Saliers camp between 1942 and 1944 in the attempt to convince them of the "inutility of nomadism" while creating "a sort of living document to refute the foreign propaganda campaign against French internment camps." Specific instructions from the Ministry of the Interior required the good maintenance of the camp's exterior: "It must have a beautiful décor."[25] In the attempt to achieve these ends, the Vichy regime chose the location carefully. The camp's architect claimed that "the Roma consider ... this region [the Camargue] as the cradle of their race." Therefore, it was assumed that itinerant Gypsies would happily settle there. Furthermore, by choosing a suitable site with access to materials traditionally used by the Gypsies in their work (unlike the other camps that were often located in unfavorable areas where inmates struggled with wind, floods, mud, and sand in addition to incarceration), it appears that the government hoped to encourage permanent settlement in this area.[26] Rather than building traditional-style wooden barracks to hold the internees, the camp featured huts built of local materials in the style of a Camargue village. Yet the area around Saliers was also relatively isolated and the land was "absolutely unsuitable" for agriculture due to its aridness and the soil's high salt content.[27] Thus the camp would resemble a real French village with access to primary materials in a region that authorities believed held a traditional place in Romani culture. At the same time, the poor agricultural land used for the camp would not interfere with the needs of the local French population. It seemed to be the perfect location to prevent complaints from both internees and the region's natives and to achieve the ultimate goal of assimilation.

Despite the government's intentions and the propaganda, the actual conditions in the camp did little to encourage assimilation. Originally under the control of the Commissariat for the Fight against Unemployment (*Commissariat à la lutte contre le chômage*), the living situation was so bad in the model camp by 1943 that the Ministry of the Interior took over direct administration of the camp. The architect's Camargue-style reed huts were overcrowded and had dirt floors, little light, and no ceilings beneath the thatched roofs. They did little to protect their inhabitants from rats; the thatching, which could not be disinfected and posed a fire risk, quickly became the home for disease-carrying insects. The camp's physical site posed additional problems: its proximity to marshlands meant poor drainage and mosquitoes; the region's famous *mistral* winds often reached over 60 miles per hour; and temperatures could be extreme.[28] Therefore by 1943, anyone wrongfully interned (i.e., someone without an anthropometric card and therefore not a "nomad") was released, while some children were separated from their families and placed with people outside the camp due to the "bad sanitary conditions."[29] Adults who had escaped from the camp often cited the physical conditions as the reason for their flight. Berthe Renard, for example, was dispatched to Saliers on 15 September 1943. She illegally left the camp with her brother and sister-in-law's help on the night of 6 December, "only because the food there is very bad and because of this I couldn't send any packages to my husband who is a prisoner [of war]."[30] Rather than creating a livable atmosphere and incorporating itinerant Gypsies into the national community envisioned by Vichy, the camp ordeal pushed them into illicit activities.

One young girl recollected the difficult living conditions in the camp, which effectively undermined assimilation efforts, as follows:

> I must have been around three or four years old when I was interned with my whole family at the Saliers camp, but I remember plenty of things. We were assigned residence in a small village next to Limoges. It was the Germans who came looking for us. They burned our caravans and put us in trucks to drive us to the Saliers camp. On the road they threw out the sheets that my mother had taken so that we wouldn't be cold during the trip. My parents knew a lot of people interned in the camp. We were eleven people in the same barracks with my parents, my uncles and aunts as well as my five brothers and sisters. They were small, low houses. There was nothing inside if it wasn't for a few small stoves to heat ourselves. There wasn't any food either. We were as unhappy as rocks. Me, I was sick because of the bad living conditions inside the camp. So I went to the infirmary and I had to stay there for about a week.... And then one day my mother passed by the infirmary and said to me: "Come, my little one, come!" So I left the infirmary running and it was bombed just after.[31]

This young girl, like many others, did not recognize the "benevolent intentions" proclaimed by the government; she felt and remembered only persecution and privation.

Internment and Assimilation

The existence of the Saliers concentration camp, as well as the experiences of those interned there, raises several issues regarding persecutory assimilation. First, the camp was intended to introduce itinerant Gypsies to a life of regular, socially acceptable work. The minister of the interior under the Third Republic had identified establishing "the habits of regular work" as one of the goals of the 6 April 1940 law that immobilized nomads during wartime.[32] Work was also a cornerstone of Vichy's National Revolution, ingrained in its slogan of "Work, Family, Homeland" (*Travail, Famille, Patrie*). The itinerants' customary occupations of bringing in seasonal crops or selling items at markets and fairs required freedom of movement, something that was now legally prohibited. The government hoped that regular employment would be encouraged by the new, sedentary lifestyle forced upon nomads. Confinement at Saliers would serve the same purpose. The first thirty inhabitants of Saliers were nomads transferred from the internment camp at Rivesaltes to aid in the new camp's construction.[33] The location was chosen, in part, due to the availability of materials such as reeds and willow for basket weaving traditionally used by Gypsy artisans.[34] The work proceeded under the supervision of the Commissariat for the Fight against Unemployment, which regarded Gypsies' occupations as irregular and unproductive. The theme of reeducation through work was consistent throughout the internment system, though the type of work varied: some were forced to work as lumberjacks and agricultural laborers while others provided labor in construction or sawmills. Grueling manual labor was meant to make Gypsies abandon their so-called laziness.[35]

Second, while adults were working, assimilation efforts focused on the youngest and most vulnerable internees, the children. Social reformers who believed that the nation's strength rested on the health and morals of its youth had often targeted children in attempts to rejuvenate French society. Secular and religious summer camps abounded in France during the interwar years with the intent of improving children's hygiene and education.[36] Jewish organizations, for example, believed that poor, foreign children could be "emancipated" (i.e., assimilated) by improving their hygienic habits and diets, changing their clothing, and introducing them to sports.[37] At the same time that Third Republic legislators became increasingly concerned about crime, vagrancy, and monitoring nomads, they were also implementing mandatory secular education for children under thirteen. Education was seen as the means of generating political support for the republic and inculcating its values into younger generations.[38] The Vichy regime also emphasized the importance of youth and education in regenerating France.[39] Thus, unsurprisingly, the regime concentrated on the socialization of children in its attempts to assimilate Gypsies during the war. The need to aid these children was visibly reinforced by their perceived dirtiness. In Romani culture, unkempt children in torn clothing were viewed as a natural consequence of healthy, outdoor playing. For French society, however, one's outward appearance was seen as an indication of one's internal moral worth.[40] Unwashed and disheveled Gypsy children thus only reinforced societal beliefs about criminality and difference. Inadequate hygiene, like at Saliers, could also be used as an excuse to remove children from "dangerous" surroundings and place them in a more "appropriate" environment. Rather than working to improve living conditions for all internees in the camp, the government used the sanitation problems as a means to more rapidly assimilate young people by integrating them into sedentary, non-Roma families and French institutions.[41] Proportionally, children represented the majority of nomads in internment camps[42] and thus the government could have access to a large pool of potential converts.

Before resorting to separation, however, authorities turned to education in their attempts to socialize and integrate Gypsies. Children under the age of fifteen were viewed as more malleable, and education thus presented an opportunity to shape these young minds. Camp rules required children, many of whom had never had any formal education, to attend school. Classes were established within concentration camps, provided there was a sufficient number of students between the ages of six and fourteen. If there were not enough children to justify a school inside the barbed wire, the Gypsy inmates were to attend classes alongside local schoolchildren, though this scenario rarely occurred. Finding people willing to teach in the camps proved altogether difficult. Whenever a class was established, children were taught only the basics: French language, reading, writing, and arithmetic. Large class sizes, differences in children's ages, the students' poor command of French, and the fact that they had no previous experience in school further complicated matters. Yet some educators noted great improvement and even success in their assimilation efforts: Children became polite and disciplined rather than wild and unruly; they learned songs that glorified Marshal Pétain; and they could now read and write.[43] In other words, they were on their way to becoming ordinary French children!

In theory, education would allow children to escape their parents' "negative" influence, and would lead them to renounce the older generation's irrational customs and traditions. The family bond, however, was so strong that some officials felt the only way to save children was to cut family ties altogether. Despite official rhetoric and attempts undertaken in other camps, the greatest number of children who were eventually removed from their parents' care occurred at the Saliers model camp. The camp's director placed abandoned or orphaned children with public assistance organizations in Marseille, while others were placed—supposedly with their parents' consent—in religious institutions. Some were placed with families in the countryside, and still others were adopted.[44] Altogether, some two hundred Gypsy children from Saliers were placed in secular and religious institutions outside the camp.[45] Emmanuel Filhol and Marie-Christine Hubert have asserted that authorities supported such separations out of "humanity ... but also with the secret hope that they would succeed in making them into beings different from their parents, members entirely part of society. Not so that they would take an active role in the community, but so that they would no longer represent a 'moral and social danger' to the French population."[46] Internment and persecution would thus benefit both the Gypsy minority and society as a whole.

A Genocidal Process?

There is no question that itinerant Gypsies in France faced repression and persecution in the name of assimilation, but was this persecution part of a larger genocidal process? The case of France seems to complicate the picture. First and foremost, the French Gypsies were never deported to death camps in Poland on a large scale. Of the 20,943 Gypsies listed in the Auschwitz-Birkenau records, there were 145 French Gypsies (74 women and 71 men).[47] However, none of these victims had been deported from France, but rather from a camp in Malines, Belgium, on 15 January 1944. Although nomads were the first victim group to face internment and the deplorable conditions of French concentration camps, these camps were never intended as instruments of death.[48] Some scholars attribute the survival of the majority of French Gypsies to fundamental differences in national attitudes toward the itinerant population. Thus, Marie-Christine Hubert has argued, "If the Gypsies of France were not deported, it is in part because the Germans could not apply their racial criteria to French Gypsies. France had the sole objective of eradicating Gypsies' nomadism."[49] Since the Germans left Gypsy matters largely up to the French during the war, it was the French government's attitudes and actions that had the greatest impact. There are few German documents regarding the Gypsies in French archives; available evidence demonstrates that most German orders were given verbally. The French thus turned to their own laws regarding nomads, all promulgated before the German occupation.[50] The persecution model advanced in France had deep roots in sociocultural attitudes toward assimilation while the Germans focused on racial attributes, which meant the Gypsies could never be assimilated.[51] Others have contended that the Vichy regime never acted with the "intent to destroy" the Gypsies as a whole or in part (a key aspect in the definition of genocide), and therefore their persecution cannot be considered genocide.[52] This is a sustainable argument in the French context since no Gypsies were deported from French soil to extermination camps, internment did not lead to systematic mass murder, and Gypsies were never defined as a racial group.[53] Guy Hantarrède, who has studied Gypsies incarcerated in the Alliers camp, reached a similar conclusion: "We have no indication of this intention [to exterminate Gypsies], but instead a vague and paternalist desire to help [nomads] and transform them through regular employment."[54] Whether or not we label the marginalization of Gypsies in France as part of the genocidal process, it is clear that racist stereotypes did exist and that a majority of French citizens did support the exclusion of Gypsies from mainstream society.

Despite Heinrich Himmler's decree of 16 December 1942 authorizing the deportation of all European Roma to Auschwitz-Birkenau, none were deported from French soil. The concentration of nomads in camps certainly provided a large, captive population that the Vichy government could have used to meet the total deportation quotas imposed by Nazi officials over the course of the war. Unlike the sympathy displayed toward persecuted Jews in France (especially after 1942), there was little public support for Gypsies or for Vichy's project to assimilate them into mainstream society. Local officials and residents called for Gypsies' internment in petitions and statements such as "I wish with all my heart that the administrative authorities rid us of [the nomads] as soon as possible" or "I would be especially happy to be rid of their presence."[55] Even the promise of a model camp did not arouse enthusiasm from neighboring communities. Thus, the mayor of Arles noted: "It is indisputable that the hamlet of Saliers, one of the Camargue's most prosperous, would become practically uninhabitable if the proposed camp was permanently realized; that the crops, the livestock, and the harvests of neighboring properties will be subjected to a permanent threat from the undesirable Bohemians, that no surveillance could prevent them from engaging in the thefts and destruction to which they are accustomed."[56] The archival material leaves little trace of the reasons why most French Gypsies were protected from extermination, and, therefore, one is forced to speculate. Possible explanations include the following: (1) French, rather than German, implementation of the internment decree and the government's belief in assimilation; (2) a shortage of German personnel to carry out the deportations or the lack of French desire to do so; (3) a higher priority given to other issues; (4) a question of timing, which suggests that had the war continued the Gypsies would have been deported; (5) that it was part of the Vichy regime's attempts to assert and maintain its sovereignty in the face of the German occupiers; and/or (6) that the French government truly believed its own paternalist rhetoric.

Conclusion

Paris was liberated in August 1944 and the war in Europe ended in May 1945, but neither event meant the end of internment for many nomads. At the time of the Allied landing in Normandy on 6 June 1944, there were still 1,600 nomads interned in seven camps throughout France. Four hundred of them still languished in camps by the end of 1945. The last internees were finally released at the end of May 1946.[57] The provisional French government issued the following proclamation in August 1944: "All persons detained by order of the German occupation authorities for any motive whether in a prison, a concentration camp, an administrative internment center, a work group or any similar establishment or organization will be immediately released."[58] Given this definition, the declaration should have applied to nomads as well. In November of the same year, however, the Ministry of the Interior informed regional representatives that nomads would not be liberated until each case had been examined individually. The new government implicitly accepted the laws regarding nomads originally instituted under the Third Republic, viewing them as legal and necessary.[59] A circular issued by the Ministry of the Interior clarified the government's position on 27 March 1945: internment was viewed as a "preventive" measure against individuals considered "dangerous for national defense and public security."[60] Thus, the same justifications used by the Third Republic in 1939–40, and reconfirmed by the Vichy regime, continued into the postwar period. The law of 6 April 1940, assigning nomads residences and justifying the continued internment of a certain proportion thereof, was finally abrogated on 10 May 1946; the earlier law of 16 July 1912, however, remained in effect. The new government effectively committed to continuing the policy of persecutory assimilation codified under the Third Republic, yet without the provision for internment introduced by the Germans under the Vichy regime. The minister of the interior declared his intention to keep a close eye on nomads in a telegram dated 20 July 1946, which lauded the "fortunate results" of the 1912 law including the "stabilization" of some of them. In order to continue this trend, he recommended strictly enforcing the articles related to nomads in the 1912 law. Four days later he reemphasized the law's achievements (gained primarily under Vichy), especially pinpointing nomads' acquisition of a fixed domicile and "exercising an occupation or trade under normal conditions."[61] Thus assimilation through forced settlement would continue despite government change, leading one to conclude that the experience of Gypsies in France throughout the twentieth century can be summarized as a story of continuous persecution pursued in the name of assimilation.

Notes

1. Donald Kenrick and Grattan Puxon trace the origins of European discrimination against the Gypsies in their book, *The Destiny of Europe's Gypsies* (New York, 1972). On the French case specifically see Emmanuel Filhol and Marie-Christine Hubert's first chapter "Une histoire chaotique (XIXe–XXe siècle)," in *Les Tsiganes en France: un sort à part (1939–1946)*, (Paris, 2009), 15–70. For a brief overview of the "Gypsy Problem" in France on the eve of the Second World War see Shannon L. Fogg, *The Politics of Everyday Life in Vichy France: Foreigners, Undesirables, and Strangers* (Cambridge, 2009), 87–93.
2. Ian Hancock, "Romani Americans ('Gypsies')" in *Roma and Sinti: Under-Studied Victims of Nazism*, ed. Center for Advanced Holocaust Studies (Washington, DC, 2002), 3–4.
3. Filhol and Hubert, *Les Tsiganes en France*, 27–31.
4. The law originally appeared in the *Journal Officiel* on 19 July 1912, 6410–11. The full text of the law is reproduced in Denis Peschanski, *Les Tsiganes en France 1939–1946* (Paris, 1994), 125–30.
5. See Marie-Christine Hubert, "Les réglementations anti-tsiganes en France et en Allemagne, avant et pendant l'occupation," *Revue d'histoire de la Shoah: le monde juif* 167 (1999): 20–52, quotation at 25; Christophe Delclitte, "La catégorie juridique 'nomade' dans la loi de 1912," *Hommes & Migrations* 1188–89 (June–July 1995): 26.
6. See, for example, Filhol and Hubert, *Les Tsiganes en France*, 57.
7. In making their determination, officials looked for things such as travelling in caravans, certain physical characteristics, certain professions, large numbers of children, and appearance of poverty (Filhol and Hubert, *Les Tsiganes en France*, 58).
8. See Fogg, *Politics of Everyday Life in Vichy France*, 95.
9. On terminology, see especially Filhol and Hubert, *Les Tsiganes en France*, 12. The authors explain that the French Gypsies prefer to be called "travelers" (*gens de voyage*) but that *Gypsy* is the most commonly used term to describe the heterogeneous population. Although some people may see the French words *romani, romanichel,* and

nomade as pejorative, Filhol and Hubert view them as interchangeable with *tsigane* since none of the terms have any significance for the population they represent.
10. Biological determinism of criminality was widely accepted by the time the anthropometric cards appeared in 1913. See, for example, Robert A. Nye, *Crime, Madness, and Politics in Modern France: The Medical Concept of National Decline* (Princeton, NJ, 1984).
11. On France and assimilation see Gérard Noiriel, *The French Melting Pot: Immigration, Citizenship, and National Identity* (Minneapolis, MN, 1996). The literature related to France's civilizing mission in Africa is also instructive, as is the discussion of Jewish assimilation. For examples see Alice L. Conklin, *A Mission to Civilize: The Republican Idea of Empire in France and West Africa, 1895–1930* (Stanford, CA, 1997) and Michael R. Marrus, *The Politics of Assimilation: A Study of the French Jewish Community at the Time of the Dreyfus Affair* (Oxford, 1971).
12. On the policing of immigrants in the interwar period, see especially Clifford Rosenberg, *Policing Paris: The Origins of Modern Immigration Control Between the Wars* (Ithaca, NY, 2006).
13. *Journal Officiel*, 9 April 1940, 2600, quoted in full in Emmanuel Filhol, "Le sort des Tsiganes dans le Limousin pendant la Second Guerre mondiale," *Revue des sciences, des lettres et des arts de la Corrèze* 108 (2006): 67–90. A circular sent to prefects on 29 April 1940 provided more details on the specifics of enforcing this law. See letter from the Interior Minister to Prefects, Archives Nationales (hereafter: AN), F7/16044.
14. Gypsies had been accused of spying in the Franco-Prussian war of 1870 and were interned during the Great War for the same reasons. On 1870 see Jacques Sigot, "La longue marche vers l'internment des Tsiganes en France pendant la seconde guerre mondiale," *Etudes tsiganes* 13, no. 1 (1999): 20. On the First World War see Hubert, "Les réglementations anti-tsiganes," 29–30, and Filhol, *Un camp de concentration français: Les Tsiganes alsaciens-lorrains à Crest 1915–1919* (Grenoble, 2004).
15. See Marie-Christine Hubert, "L'internement des Tsiganes en France 1940–1946," *Etudes tsiganes* 13, no. 1 (1999): 17.
16. Filhol and Hubert, *Les Tsiganes en France*, 89–91.
17. For a list of the camps see Emmanuel Filhol, *La mémoire et l'oubli: l'internement des Tsiganes en France, 1940–1946* (Paris, 2001), 12. The anthropometric cards reveal that in 1924 there were approximately 40,000 nomads in France, a number that appears again in wartime and postwar estimates (Filhol and Hubert, *Les Tsiganes en France*, 61). The cards reveal 17,544 French nomads and 12,524 foreigners. The additional 9,900, reaching the total of 40,000, represent an estimate of the number of children under the age of thirteen not required to carry an anthropometric card. No official census statistics exist since the French did not collect information based on race or ethnicity.
18. The number had increased to 3,100 nomads in fifteen camps by October 1941 (Filhol and Hubert, *Les Tsiganes en France*, 102–4).
19. Ibid., 123.
20. Ibid., 119. The Saliers camp provides a good example of the number of nomads' evasions. In the summer of 1943, 21 out of the 78 nomads dispatched to Saliers escaped. In August 1944, 137 nomads fled the camp after it was bombed by the Allies; altogether, 214 individuals (70 percent of the internees) escaped during that month. On evasions more broadly, see Filhol and Hubert, *Les Tsiganes en France*, 199–207.
21. Ibid., 123–24. The Armistice required the French to pay 400 million francs per day for the costs of German occupation.
22. Other camps were often referred to as "nomad camps" but housed other "undesirables" such as black marketeers, political opponents, Jews, prostitutes, work draft dodgers, and others. Filhol and Hubert note, however, that the different groups were

separated by barbed wire and the nomads lived entirely separated from the other prisoners (Filhol and Hubert, *Les Tsiganes en France,* 108–9).
23. Quoted in Mathieu Pernot, ed., *Un Camp pour les Bohémiens: Mémoires du camp d'internement pour nomades de Saliers* (Arles, 2001), 5.
24. For an extended discussion of these attitudes and a comparison with the treatment of Jews in France see Shannon L. Fogg, "'They Are Undesirables': Local and National Responses to Gypsies during World War II," *French Historical Studies* 31, no. 2 (Spring 2008): 327–58.
25. Pernot, *Un Camp pour les Bohémiens,* 20.
26. Chris Pearson, *Scarred Landscapes: War and Nature in Vichy France* (Houndsmill, 2008), 78.
27. Ibid., 79.
28. Ibid., 79–80.
29. Pernot, *Un Camp pour les Bohémiens,* 22–24.
30. Extract from a gendarme's report after Renard's arrest in Limoges reproduced in Pernot, *Un Camp pour les Bohémiens,* 75. There are several examples of nomads who fled the camp after a similar amount of time (approximately three months) citing the food situation as the reason for their evasion. See the arrest reports for Irène Blanvin and François Reinhardt (Pernot, *Un Camp pour les Bohémiens,* 76–77).
31. Ibid., 110. The Saliers camp became the target of Anglo-American bombing on 17 August 1944. The Allies mistook the concentration camp for a German military camp since it was located in the middle of German troop activity (Filhol and Hubert, *Les Tsiganes en France,* 119).
32. Letter from the Interior Minister to Prefects, 29 April 1940, AN, F7/16044.
33. Filhol and Hubert, *Les Tsiganes en France,* 118.
34. Pearson, *Scarred Landscapes,* 78.
35. Filhol, *La mémoire et l'oubli,* 61–62. See also Filhol and Hubert, *Les Tsiganes en France,* 224–52.
36. Laura Lee Downs, *Childhood in the Promised Land: Working-Class Movements and the Colonies de Vacances in France, 1880–1960* (Durham, NC, 2002).
37. Ph. E. Landau, "L'Oeuvre de secours aux enfants ou les péripéties d'une organisation juive," in *Au secours des enfants du siècle: Regards croisés sur l'OSE,* ed. M. Lemalet (Paris, 1993), 48–52.
38. On attitudes towards children and crime see especially Sarah Fishman, *The Battle for Children: World War II, Youth Crime, and Juvenile Justice in Twentieth-Century France* (Cambridge, MA, 2002). On the importance of education for assimilation during the Third Republic see Eugen Weber, *Peasants into Frenchmen: The Modernization of Rural France 1870–1914* (Stanford, CA, 1976).
39. See, for example, W. D. Halls, *The Youth of Vichy France* (Oxford, 1981).
40. On Gypsies and attitudes toward children see Isabel Fonseca, *Bury Me Standing: The Gypsies and Their Journey* (New York, 1996). Julian Jackson has noted that "moral hygiene was inseparable from social hygiene" during the war years (Jackson, *France: The Dark Years 1940–1945* [Oxford, 2001], 329). Fishman notes this connection as well (Fishman, *The Battle for Children,* 97). For rural attitudes toward Gypsy families see Fogg, *The Politics of Everyday Life in Vichy France,* 103–8.
41. Pernot, *Un Camp pour les Bohémiens,* 24.
42. Filhol and Hubert, *Les Tsiganes en France,* 150–51; Filhol, *La mémoire et l'oubli,* 28–31.
43. Filhol and Hubert, *Les Tsiganes en France,* 252–59.
44. Ibid., 262.
45. Ibid., 263.
46. Ibid., 264.

47. Peschanski, *Les Tsiganes en France*, 147.
48. On mortality rates see ibid., 68–72.
49. Hubert, "L'internement des Tsiganes en France," 16.
50. Filhol and Hubert, *Les Tsiganes en France*, 94–95.
51. Guenter Lewy has argued that Nazi policies toward Gypsies were not entirely racial and that "social adjustment could override racial origin" (Lewy, *The Nazi Persecution of the Gypsies* [Oxford, 2000]). Lewy has also discussed the complex evolution of German Gypsy policy from cultural to racial exclusion. See his article, "Gypsies and Jews Under the Nazis," *Holocaust and Genocide Studies* 13, no. 3 (Winter 1999): 383–404.
52. Cf. "Convention on the Prevention and Punishment of the Crime of Genocide," *United Nations Treaty Series* 78 (1951), 280.
53. Hubert, "Les réglementations anti-tsiganes," 51.
54. Guy Hantarrède, "Les Tsiganes au camp des Alliers (novembre 1940–mars 1946)," *Etudes Tsiganes* 13, no. 1 (1999): 126.
55. National Gendarmerie Historical Service, 24 March 1942, Service Historique de la Gendarmerie Nationale (hereafter: SHGN), 12754/115; ibid., 24 March 1942, SHGN, 12754/125.
56. Quoted in Pernot, *Un Camp pour les Bohémiens*, 21.
57. Filhol and Hubert trace the decline in the camp numbers in *Les Tsiganes en France*, 318.
58. Quoted in ibid., 319.
59. Ibid., 320.
60. Ibid., 321.
61. Ibid., 330–32.

CHAPTER 2

GENOCIDAL TRAJECTORY
PERSECUTION OF GYPSIES IN AUSTRIA, 1938–1945

Florian Freund

During the first decades of the nineteenth century Gypsies were scarcely a priority for the authorities in the Austrian Lands.[1] The emergence of the modern nation-state and the parallel development of the legal system and the modern police force had created a legal groundwork conducive to the persecution of Gypsies in the years 1850 to 1938. This groundwork included passport matters and social rights and, needless to say, did not take Gypsies into account. Furthermore, state and local authorities almost never made distinctions between beggars, vagabonds, and Gypsies. The Vagabond Law (*Landstreichereigesetz*) enacted on 10 May 1873—coincidentally, just one day before the Vienna stock market crash—remained in force in Austria until the 1970s. Instrumental in the proclaimed "fight against the Gypsy nuisance" (*Bekämpfung des Zigeunerunwesens*), this law nonetheless did not define the term *Gypsy*. Otherwise, the negative image of Gypsies—typically portrayed as an imaginary threat provoking fear and hatred—began to emerge around 1850.[2] As Jacques Sémelin has perceptively observed in his general analysis of genocide, the genocide of the Austrian Gypsies further demonstrates "that massacres are mainly born out of a mental process, a way of seeing some 'Other' being, of stigmatizing him, debasing him, and obliterating him before actually killing him."[3] Thus, it can be described as a dynamic, complex, and decade-long process that had been greatly accelerated in the context of World War II.

Constructing the Negative Image of Gypsies

During the second half of the nineteenth century the negative image of Gypsies had acquired an instrumental function in Austrian politics increasingly preoccupied with the issue of class. In 1848 the imaginary fundamentals of society were shaken to the core. Not just the middle class, but also the working class suddenly became the center of attention. Even though the 1848 Revolution was crushed, the military defeat at the hands of the Germans in 1866 significantly weakened the absolute rule of Franz Joseph, who had been forced to elevate Hungary to the same status as Austria and to cede more power to the bourgeoisie through the 1867 Constitution. The stock market crash of 9 May 1873 prompted the fear of a proletarian uprising. The perceived need to prevent the workers from gaining mobility—even though the number of employed workers fluctuated significantly—fueled the talk of the danger of "vagabondism."

The 1867 constitution, which introduced equality before the law and for the first time ever granted freedom of movement, tied the local authorities' hands. However, the 1873 Vagabond Law, even though it did not mention any specific ethnic groups, proved an effective tool in preventing the mobility of the impoverished underclass. Comparing underclass to Gypsies was by no means the only use of anti-Gypsy stereotypes. In the decades after 1848 the police authorities deliberately evoked the "Gypsy nuisance" in order to modernize the police force. The state and local politicians who had supported this initiative decried the executive powerlessness in the face of the "Gypsy nuisance," the impossibility to establish the personality of offenders, and the high maintenance cost of bureaucracy.

Significant in this context proved a speech by a high-ranking Church official Dr. Josef Lechner, held in the beginning of October 1884 during a debate on the "increased vagabond adversity" (*überhandnehmende Vagabundennoth*) at the Upper Austrian state parliament. The contemporaneous term used in the debate was *Landstreicher* (vagrant), until after Lechner at once substituted it for *Gypsy* in the meaning "vagabond." Those three terms continued to be used interchangeable, with no ethnic or racist connotation. Lechner saw the cause of vagrancy, or the Gypsy Problem, in the 1848 unrest marked by the freedom of movement, the dissolution of the guild organization, and economic reforms: "Now that everyone can travel freely, Gypsies wander around as artists and musicians, saying it's their business."[4] Evidently, Lechner had been using the word *Gypsy* to stress the alleged risk posed by mobile workforce. That is also when the negative profiling of Gypsies began in earnest. According to Lechner, the only effective means in the fight against vagabonds would be penal colonies, to be established overseas.[5] Otherwise, the instrumentalization of Gypsies for the purpose of disciplining the mobile underclass was nothing new, built upon conventional anti-Gypsy stereotypes.[6]

It took fifteen years since the enactment of the Vagabond Law in 1873 to standardize the legal procedures against Gypsies in the Austrian lands. To proceed with the systematic eviction of foreigners, especially those of them who were poor yet retained their mobility, however, became more difficult after the establishment of the German Empire (excluding Austria) in 1871. In addition, Austrian authorities anticipated an influx of Gypsies from Hungary as well as the principalities of Moldova and Wallachia in which slavery and serfdom was abolished as late as 1855–56. The so-called Gypsy Edict (*Zigeunererlass*) issued in 1888 by the Ministry of the Interior (and remained in force until the 1960s, with a brief interruption during the Nazi period) did not provide a definition of "Gypsy" or member of a "Gypsy band."[7] It was effectively left to the whim of the local authorities to determine who was "Gypsy." Otherwise, the only category of Gypsies directly affected by the edict was itinerant Gypsies, in particular those without certificate of residence (*Heimatschein*).[8]

According to the edict, the designation *Gypsy* would apply to those individuals without a certificate of residence who led an itinerant lifestyle. As the most common reason behind the introduction of the edict, at least in the Austrian lands, officials cited "vagrancy of the poor." The Gypsy Edict encouraged the cooperation between state authorities and the municipal councils in deporting "itinerating Gypsies" into their respective countries of origin. All those who could prove a right of residence, or simply could not be deported, were allowed to stay, that is to say, their mobility should be enforced. However, since all neighboring countries had enforced similar regulations, no Gypsies could be deported there. The persons stigmatized as "Gypsies" were thus caught in a vicious circle, since the Gypsy Edict explicitly forbade their integration. The actual number of stateless Gypsies is not known, though it could not possibly be a big group judging by the infrequent mention of foreign or stateless Gypsies in the provincial governors' reports to the Ministry of the Interior.

The 1888 edict effectively introduced a policy of harassment against local and foreign Gypsies through the use of compulsory health checks and, supposedly as a hygienic measure, forced shaving in the case of detected lice infestation. The veterinarian law was to be extensively applied to draft animals belonging to Gypsies. Local Gypsies were entitled to receive identification papers, issued upon the most stringent inspection. Most difficult for Gypsies to obtain were the documents required in order to open a new business; existing business permits and music licenses could be revoked at the slightest suspicion of irregularities.

In order to implement the edict as well as to differentiate between foreign and local Gypsies, on 3 July 1890 the Ministry of Interior requested the local authorities to create lists of resident Gypsies, to be updated annually.[9] According to the statistics thus collected, the actual number of Gypsies legally residing in Lower Austria, Upper Austria, Salzburg, Tyrol, Vorarlberg, Styria, and Carinthia was fairly insignificant. Thus, according to the census conducted at the end of 1887 a mere 486 Gypsies, or rather Gypsy families, resided in the Austrian lands.[10] The consistently evoked "threat" of massive Gypsy immigration from the Hungarian part of the empire proved nothing but rhetoric. The Hungarian "Gypsy Census" of 1893 registered 8,938 itinerant Gypsies, 20,406 semisedentary, and 243,423 sedentary—the relatively low numbers that surprised even the local statistics office.[11] The Hungarian Statistics Bureau used *Gypsy* as an ethnic designation whereas the Austrian authorities used one developed by the police, which was particularly concerned with itinerating.[12]

This crucial difference further underlined that the process of definition of "Gypsies" was still ongoing. In 1916 the Ministry of the Interior attempted to come up with the working definition in the new draft edict, the Fight Against the Gypsy Nuisance (*Bekämpfung des Zigeunerunwesens*). The edict defined "Gypsy" as a "habitually itinerating person, alone or as part of a larger family or band, without fixed abode who makes a living from petty trading or from begging or by any other illicit means."[13] Even though this particular edict was never enacted, it displays the criteria that the authorities used in their definition of "Gypsy." While the Vagabond Law referred exclusively to destitute persons, the new definition expanded the application of law by including traveling traders without fixed residence or itinerant families and bands. From then onward, legal authorities considered itinerating and the lack of fixed abode as exclusive features of the Gypsies. This, strictly sociological, definition—regardless of the actual status of Gypsies—signified the transition at the policymaking level from the fight against the poor to the stamping out of itinerating as a social phenomenon.

The end of World War I had created a new situation in Austria. On 1 October 1920, the Austrian parliament unanimously approved a new constitution that would not only incorporate citizen rights from the previous constitution but also guarantee equal voting rights for men and women.[14] Formerly a part of Hungary, Burgenland was in 1921 incorporated into Austria. The new authorities upheld the ethnic criteria for sedentary Gypsies in Burgenland, as exercised earlier in the Hungarian lands. Consequently, in 1924 the Burgenland police authorities defined "Gypsy" in a different way from the other federal states: "The term *Gypsy* denotes the persons who differ from the settled population due to their strange lifestyle, who speak their own language along with the national language, and who are generally identified as 'Gypsies' in the municipalities. Persons who enter a common law marriage with a Gypsy or a child born from a mixed family should be regarded as 'Gypsies.'"[15] In their definition of "Gypsy" local authorities in Burgenland thus emphasized ethnicity, or race, and poverty endemic to the sedentary rural population, while the other federal states continued using the definition predicated on itinerating as a behavioral trait.

In the absence of a common definition, it was left up to the local authorities to determine who was or was not a Gypsy. In practice, the local authorities were rarely concerned if a group of itinerant Gypsies conducted a legal trade or had money. The debates regarding a prospective "Gypsy law" in 1928–29 did little to change this element of arbitrariness. Such a law, modeled after a Bavarian law of 1926 and a Czechoslovakian law of 1927, was never enacted due to the conflicting clauses in both the Treaty of St. Germain and the constitution. Ascribing ethnicity to Gypsies became an objective criterion since a minority-protection clause in the Treaty of St. Germain (1919) provided for the notions of *race* and *language* to be used as relevant criteria in the definition of "nationality."[16] As the only ostensibly objective criteria, the Austrian Supreme Administrative Court determined in 1921 that "race is to be evaluated objectively as 'affiliation to a tribe,' which can be traced back through ancestry and therefore cannot be part of a subjective decision."[17] However, this pronouncement had no direct impact—after all, race cannot really be objectified—especially on the police procedures, which had had been consistently informed by traditional anti-Gypsy stereotypes. Nevertheless, it provided certain legal basis in Austria that had predated Nazi racial theories. No one in the nineteenth century had questioned the "truth" that Gypsies constituted a separate race. As I will demonstrate below, the identification and registration of the Gypsy population during the interwar period was a crucial step for the subsequent deportation to Litzmannstadt (Łódź) ghetto and eventually to Kulmhof (Chełmno) death camp.

Fear Factor: Gypsies as an Imaginary Threat

Josef Lechner, who I mentioned earlier, challenged in 1884 the recently established freedom for traveling merchants to legally conduct their trade. As the technical progress accelerated the mobility of the rural population and the mass production of goods, however, the kind of business conducted by traveling merchants became obsolete. When lodging complaints against traveling merchants, businessmen increasingly used Gypsies as scapegoats, regardless of whether the latter had a valid trade license. The campaign against Gypsy businessmen remained an essential factor in the anti-Gypsy policymaking for decades. The animosity toward Gypsies was in no small part a result of economic insecurity prompted by modernization. Cheap, industrial production of goods made redundant craftsmen operating within the guild system. The middle class, threatened by social descent, could not or did not want to recognize the changes in the mode of production. The craftsmen and the middle class both projected their problems onto traveling merchants, drawing upon the support of the politicians and the police.

While the local authorities continued talking about a "Gypsy plague" throughout the 1880s, their rhetoric became increasingly more virulent in the 1890s. For example, the delegate Franz Roser ranted in 1891 in the House of Representatives as follows: "The rural population has been molested, damaged by the itinerating vagabonds and Gypsies. I know it is [happening] in my electoral district, especially in localities of the Königinhofer district, which has been plagued by this party [*Gesellschaft*] years on end, especially by Gypsies, who destroy the meadows with their horses, empty the potato fields, and commit not just petty thefts but also burglaries; by fortunetelling and by inducing superstition among the population, [Gypsies] corrupt their morality while emptying their pockets."[18] Although Roser was incapable of pinning any specific crimes on the Gypsies, he nevertheless demanded confining them to forced labor camps or a penal colony in Bosnia-Herzegovina, a demand that was immediately approved by a resolution of the House of Representatives. The House of Representative took up this issue again in 1896, prescribing to "make arrangements for the Gypsies to be placed in a forced labor camp, as demanded by municipal authorities," without specifying the nature of the ostensible threat, though.[19] A majority of the parliamentarians was ready to revoke basic rights from the group of citizens collectively stigmatized as "Gypsies" and to consider a request by a municipality sufficient enough a ground for committing Gypsies to a camp. Meanwhile, the reproaches against Gypsies remained extremely vague. "Gypsies are a threat to property, [and] this is commonly known," claimed Josef Baldinger in the Upper Austrian state parliament in 1902:

> Typically, Gypsies are wandering around the country under the pretext of horse trade or [the false pretense] of being musicians. But their actual business purpose is begging and thievery (cheers from the audience). It is no longer acceptable today to let those Gypsies, a plague and a burden to the country, wander around; it would not be difficult to prove that the Gypsies are just wandering stealthily around and attacking every single farmstead whenever they see nobody around but one or two children, or oftentimes just an elderly woman.[20]

However unsubstantiated these claims were, the Upper Austrian state parliament passed a resolution urging the government in Vienna "to adopt appropriate measures to efficiently counter the ever-growing presence of itinerating cons, begging musicians and singers, imposters and peddlers, who oftentimes endanger the public morals."[21] In spite of the fact that the state governments had reported the consistent decline of "Gypsy plague" from year to year, the calls for action against Gypsies had intensified by 1909. The Bohemian delegate to the House of Representatives, Karl Iro, for example, insisted that all Gypsies should be registered (complete with a mug shot and a tattooed number, "like the cars"), detained, and have their children taken away.[22] Even though the parliamentary inquiry had no immediate effect, it demonstrates a growing radicalization of the parliamentarians, who increasingly perceived Gypsies as the threat that had to be offset by all means. The available sources remain inconclusive whether those statements reflected the prevalent sentiment among the population or if they contributed toward that sentiment.

Upheld by criminology, the notion of Gypsy criminality thus appeared to have been scientifically legitimized. Especially important in cementing this notion, at least in the German-language countries, proved the *Handbuch für Untersuchungsrichter als System der Kriminalistik* (Criminology Handbook for Coroners), which was published in 1893 by the constitutional law professor Hans Gross from Graz and had undergone several reprints within the next fifty-odd years. In effect, Gross added elements of romanticism and racial anthropology to the stereotypical image of Gypsies generated by the police. From the romantic image of Gypsies emerged the idea that "the Gypsy wants to travel free and uninhibited; he does not want to rule over anyone, but neither does he want to take orders from anyone." This notion reoccurred in Gross's discourse, even if the racial imagery remained dominant: "The Gypsy is anything but a person of culture [*Kulturmensch*], not even in its roughest and most debauched form.... However different is the Gypsy from any other crook, they appear strangely similar. Since the Gypsies had moved to Europe they have always stayed the same." Gross ascribed to Gypsies innate physical and psychological characteristics such as "incredible idleness, strong proclivity for revenge and atrocity, and unbelievable cowardliness to no end." He further insinuated:

> [The Gypsy] considers the biggest fortune to indulge in unlimited laziness, wishing to take as much as possible from those who have worked to supply his however humble needs. Honor and fatherland, family and state, the past and future of his own people—the concepts that brought every civilized nation to the absolute height of its accomplishment but remain unknown to the Gypsies; they replace them with unlimited laziness, animal-like appetite, sensuous love, and a bit of vanity.... Gypsies have a distinctive, long-lasting, smell.... It is said to be similar to the typical smell of a Negro.

That smell supposedly reminded of "a smell of grease combined with the stench of mice" and, according to Gross, could even be used as evidence at crime scenes. Gross further intimated that the "itinerating Gypsy" in Transylvania "is a whole lot better than ours."[23] Thus Gross extended the romantic notion that one could meet "the real Gypsies" in the areas unaffected by the Industrial Revolution.

Gross's racial image approximated the eighteenth-century description of Gypsies as a primitive race, originally developed by Heinrich M. G. Grellmann and used for decades by the police and gendarmerie. Subsequently, Nazi "Gypsy scientists" had capitalized on Gross's ideas of inferiority and dangerousness of Gypsies. His books had big print runs and were often used as police manuals. Nonetheless, the alleged threat and (negative) racial features associated with Gypsies did not instantly change the authorities' modus operandi, simply because they were lacking objective identification criteria. The Austrian authorities continued identifying Gypsies by the latter's purported behavior, even if they were aware that the collective portrayal of Gypsies by Gross had become the official doctrine of the newly created discipline of criminology, and that the police and gendarmerie were facing an extremely malicious and dangerous enemy.

The discourse on Gypsies intensified during the interwar period. Even then, one could not come up with any incriminating evidence against Gypsies, neither as a group nor as individuals, beyond evoking the act of itinerating. Regardless of the annual reports of the local authorities that consistently deemphasized the extent of "Gypsy plague," even a few instances proved one too many. Gypsies were advised to avoid Austria altogether: "They have no place [in the country with such] a well-regulated administrative system [*Verhältnisse*]."[24] Thus, Gypsies simultaneously became an administrative problem, apart from the accusation that their draft animals were a cause of diseases, reaffirmed through the 1926 decision of the Upper Austrian state parliament to submit all "Gypsy horses" to a thorough checkup.[25] The campaign of harassment continued as the authorities attempted to deprive Gypsies of even the smallest legal source of income and subsequently condemn them for "antisocial behavior," begging, or vagrancy, which sometimes led to deportation. The authorities used legal charges as an additional proof of "Gypsy menace," which in its turn was used to incite fear and hatred within the population. With no legal basis and/or orders from the center, the federal states of Styria and Burgenland began systematic fingerprinting in 1923 and 1924 respectively. A year later, state authorities ordered every Gypsy to be photographed and issued an identity card as to distinguish them from "foreign, non-sedentary Gypsies."[26] Initially created on an informal basis, the Central Information Office for Gypsies (Zentralevidenzstelle für Zigeuner) in 1937 received an official status.

A discriminatory anti-Gypsy law passed in neighboring Czechoslovakia on 14 July 1927 was preceded by fear mongering in Austria. On 16 May 1927, the newspaper *Der Montag* published a sensational report on a "Gypsy gang" in Czechoslovakia that was accused of having "slain many people in the forest" and subsequently "devoured" them.[27] According to the newspaper, the Czechoslovakian police responded by having carried out a countrywide raid, during which the policemen forcibly shaved Gypsies' heads under the existing law to prevent the spread of infection. (In all likelihood, the police raids served to legitimize the Czechoslovakian anti-Gypsy law.) *Der Montag* evoked the threat of a Gypsy "invasion" of Austria, provoking general hysteria. For example, on 19 May the district authorities in Neusiedl am See alarmed the gendarmerie posts to the existence of "Gypsy gangs" in Upper Austria that supposedly engaged in a gunfight with the intervening gendarmerie.[28] There is no evidence that such an incident ever took place.

The world economic crisis further instrumentalized the notion of a "Gypsy menace" as a means of preventing the uncontrolled movement of the destitute unemployed.[29] The economic crisis also had a negative impact on social welfare sustained through municipal taxes. As many Gypsies had lost their temporary jobs, they came to increasingly rely on social welfare. This fact exacerbated the preexisting resentment against Gypsies among the relatively poor rural population of Burgenland, culminating in the so-called Gypsy conference (*Zigeunerkonferenz*) held on 15 January 1933 in Oberwart.[30] In the presence of a representative of the local government in Burgenland, members of the Christian Socialist Party, the Social Democratic Party, the Rural Federation (Landbund), the local government office, as well as the head of the gendarmerie and the local mayors discussed what should have been done with Gypsies. In view of the failed attempt to forcibly separate Gypsy children from their families, the conference concluded that "the call of blood of that mysterious race is stronger than anything else, so that there is not a chance that they [Gypsies] could ever be influenced to adopt a European way of life. They will effectively remain a foreign body that constitutes a constant threat to the native population and the civilized nations at large. Not even religion was capable of inculcating those people with morals as we understand it. True Christianity appears alien to them." Hence came a suggestion to deport Gypsies to some unsettled islands in the Pacific Ocean, because "every continental state, be it in Europe or on any other continent, would struggle to accommodate Gypsies." When dismissing this proposal as illusory, member of the Burgenland provincial government Hans Wagner indirectly mentioned, for the first time ever, the probability of violence: "proposals to annihilate Gypsies by any means, to sterilize them or to deport them to some overseas country."[31] Due to the unfeasibility of mass deportation, the conference ended with a call to pass an anti-Gypsy law. Hereby Gypsies irrevocably became the "superfluous Other."[32]

By January 1933 a democratic constitution providing for the basic rights of all Austrian citizens was still in place. Yet a great many political parties, mayors, judges, and gendarmes had a consensus that Gypsies were in fact an inferior race and that they eventually had to be removed. The abovementioned conference in Oberwart had no immediate impact on the situation of the Gypsies in Austria. Between 1934 and 1938 the main obstacles to a radical solution of the "Gypsy problem"—as the anti-Gypsy activists often bemoaned—were the constitution, the League of Nations, and the Treaty of St. Germain.

Mass Deportation as a Solution to the "Gypsy Question," 1938–1940

The annexation of Austria by Nazi Germany in March 1938 automatically annulled the constitution and the Treaty of St. Germain. I argue that the Austrian authorities gave impetus to the cumulative radicalization of the anti-Gypsy policy in the Third Reich that followed. This policy was to a larger degree influenced by the radical proposals advanced by the *Gauleiter* (district head) of Burgenland, Tobias Portschy; the *Gauleiter* of Styria, Siegfried Uiberreither; and the head of the Gypsy desk in the Niederdonau district administration, Bernhard Wilhelm Neureiter, who sometimes directly lobbied with the authorities in Berlin. Consequently, the Austrian Gypsies became the first victims of that policy—murdered in an extermination camp as a group. This act of murder signified a qualitative step from the earlier, more conventional, anti-Gypsy policy. The racial ideology effectively laid the theoretical framework for the persecution. Meanwhile, the basic principles that underlined the police fight against the poverty and criminality had changed dramatically in Nazi Germany. Criminality and an antisocial lifestyle were arguably innate features, and a healthy society could thus only be attained through "elimination" of criminal and antisocial elements within the purview of racial hygiene.[33]

The decree of the Federal Chancellery from 16 March 1938 denied Gypsies the right to vote. Performing music in public places, one of the important sources of income for many Gypsies, was prohibited. In Burgenland, Gypsy children were prohibited to attend public schools as early as May 1938. Similar prohibition for the rest of Austria came into effect at the beginning of the school year 1939–40; in the Third Reich at large, school attendance for Gypsies was first prohibited in March 1941. Two months after the Anschluss, head of the SS Heinrich Himmler ordered the census of Gypsies in Austria and prohibited the Austrian Gypsies to cross the border to the *Altreich* (Germany proper), "irrespective of the forthcoming standardized regulation of the Gypsy question for the entire Reich." Without any legal basis, Burgenland authorities in July 1938 introduced forced labor for Gypsies. Although this forced-labor model had certain advantages for the municipalities, it had effectively excluded the Gypsies from routine working life and ultimately drove them into poverty. Simultaneously, Gypsies were prohibited to engage in commercial activity.[34]

In August 1938 the *Gauleiter* of Burgenland Portschy published an exposé, "Die Zigeunerfrage" (The Gypsy Question). In this treatise Portschy compiled the entire repertoire of myths and prejudices against Gypsies. According to Portschy, Burgenland Gypsies were particularly dangerous: "Slackers, the idle, lingerers, and criminals [who pose] the treat to the security of properties and the [overall] economic situation of our communities." Consequently, Portschy demanded that the 1933 German Law for the Prevention of Genetically Diseased Offspring (*Gesetz zur Verhütung erbkranken Nachwuchses*) should be extended to incorporate Gypsies: Men and women should be separately committed to forced labor institutions (*Zwangsarbeitsanstalten*); "optional" emigration to foreign countries should be allowed so as to bring Gypsies into future colonies of Germany. Portschy insisted that Gypsies should have the same legal status as Jews and warned against showing empathy toward them: "The Nordic mindset interprets just any favor extended to those of Oriental descent not as a form of altruism but as criminal carelessness that would victimize the essence of our culture—all things German, Nordic blood, the German man, our friends."[35] A differentiation between *reinrassig* (purebred) and *Mischling* (person of mixed origin), typically drawn by the Nazis, is not to be found in Portschy's exposé; with hindsight, neither did it have any profound impact on the Austrian Gypsies.

Immediately after the Anschluss, around 230 Gypsies from Burgenland were arrested under the Edict for the Preventive Combating of Crime (*Erlass über die vorbeugende Verbrechensbekämpfung*). One year later, on 5 June 1939, the Reich Criminal Police Office (Reichskriminalpolizeiamt, or RKPA) ordered three thousand Gypsies from Burgenland to be committed to concentration camps.[36] This order, for the first time ever, defined Gypsies explicitly as "Gypsies" and not in connection with their alleged antisocial behavior, as had been the case in the past. This radical shift was affirmed in Himmler's circular order, Fighting the Gypsy Plague (*Bekämpfung der Zigeunerplage*) from 8 December 1939, that differentiated between full-bred and half-bred persons.[37] Even if Himmler's order was supposed to impose a uniform Gypsy policy, it did not preclude the local authorities in eastern Austria to interpret the order in a far more radical way.

The 1939 roundup affected at least 1,142 able-bodied men and women who were subsequently dispatched to concentration camps to perform labor. Berlin authorities presupposed that the Gypsies in Burgenland were living on welfare benefits and not regular employment. This assumption could not be further from the truth as Gypsies had easily gained employment due to the growing needs of the armament industry and the resultant labor shortage. With the breadwinners all but arrested, several hundred unsupported children and other family members were left to their own devices. The individuals who stayed behind received no welfare payments from the municipalities to which they were entitled by the law. In the meanwhile, local authorities used those entitlements as a proof of the Gypsies' "antisocial" nature and pushed for their abolition. This kind of method was in line with the general policy of creating consensus for increasingly radical action. The cooperation between the Reich Criminal Police, welfare officials, local politicians, and the Nazi leadership in Berlin had fueled the dynamics that eventually led to the annihilation of the larger segment of the Gypsy population in Austria.[38]

Sometimes, however, policymaking experienced temporary setbacks caused by human factors and/or practical considerations. One of the reports, for example, spoke of the farmers and their wives who had pity on the starving, itinerating Gypsy children. A memorandum on the margins unequivocally stated: "That way the Gypsy question could never be resolved."[39] Because of the steady stream of complaints from the municipalities, the *Gauleiter* of Styria Uiberreither on 1 September 1939 raised the issue of mass arrest with the RKPA. Uiberreither criticized the police round up on the grounds that the arrested Gypsies for a longer time were permanent employees, that it raised operating costs for the municipalities, and that hundreds of children were left unattended following the arrest of their parents. In order to reduce the cost of social welfare, he proposed dispatching all the Gypsies to a special Gypsy camp, "unless one cannot, or will not, just take them all at once to a concentration camp." As an immediate measure, Uiberreither suggested establishing a separate labor camp, because "a Gypsy standing outside of the community of the people [*Volksgemeinschaft*] is always antisocial."[40]

The invasion of Poland offered a new opportunity to the Austrian authorities to get rid of Gypsies in their respective districts. By that time Gypsies were included in the deportation plans for Jews insofar as the authorities sought to join one or two railway carloads of Gypsies to a Jewish transport.[41] In the meanwhile Himmler had gained even more power following his appointment as Reich Commissioner for the Strengthening of Germandom (*Reichskommissar für die Festigung deutschen Volkstums*, or RKF) in October 1939. As far as Gypsies were concerned, the immediate consequence was the mobility freeze. On 17 October 1939, the head of the Reich Security Main Office (Reichssicherheitshauptamt, or RSHA) Reinhard Heydrich issued a decree prohibiting Gypsies and Gypsy *Mischlinge* to leave their current place of residence until further notice.[42] The local police authorities were given three days (25 to 27 October) to recount and register all Gypsies residing in their respective district. The mobility freeze increased the pressure from below, as the municipalities that until then had no Gypsy residents were now obliged to accommodate them and thus to increase welfare spending. Thus the mayor of Schwarzach in Pongau beseeched the *Gauleiter* of Salzburg Friedrich Rainer "to do everything [in his power] to free the municipality from that menace."[43] The mayor of Salzburg Anton Gieger fought as passionately against the presence of Gypsies in that city, citing extra costs for the municipality. Without prior sanction from Berlin, the city of Salzburg drove all Gypsies into the former Gypsy campground

Maxglan. At Maxglan, Gypsies were living behind barbed wire in tents, trailers, and old moving vans.[44]

At the end of January of 1940 Heydrich finalized the plan for deportation of the Poles, Jews, and Gypsies.[45] By deporting some 160,000 Poles and Jews from the annexed Polish territories, the Nazis intended to make room for the incoming ethnic Germans from the Baltic States and Volhynia (Volyn). The General Government of Poland (*Generalgouvernement*) was to become the dumping ground for Jews and up to thirty thousand Gypsies. The initial deportation to the General Government was accompanied by numerous problems. Governor General Hans Frank opposed the arrival of uncoordinated transports, and so on 23 March 1940, Hermann Göring discontinued the deportations until further notice.[46] Gypsies as such played only a minor role in this dispute. The intention to deport around thirty thousand German and Austrian Gypsies—registered in accordance with Heydrich's decree from October 1939—to the *Generalgouvernement* can be dated from early 1940. Upon demand from the Wehrmacht, the "evacuation" to the General Government was temporarily resumed, enabling the deportation of 2,500 Gypsies from the western and northwestern border regions of the German Reich in May 1940.[47] The RSHA covered the costs associated with this particular transport while the municipality in which Gypsies had last resided paid for the meals of the deportees.[48]

Further plans for the deportation of the Austrian Gypsies began to emerge in January 1940. Yet February had passed and, as the head of Styria province Otto Müller-Haccius complained to the RSHA at the end of March, "those measures have not been realized until today."[49] The RSHA assured the local authorities that it was aware of the "difficult situation with regard to the Gypsies in Burgenland" and promised to deal with it as a priority.[50] On 16 July 1940, the RSHA announced that the deportation would now be possible and that by the end of August–beginning of September up to six thousand Gypsies could be deported from Burgenland to the General Government.[51] The preparation for the deportation began instantly. Wehrmacht soldiers, their relatives, the seriously ill, and pregnant women were to be exempted from the deportation while "antisocial Germans who have adopted the Gypsy way of living" were not.[52] Thus the chosen criteria for deportation were clearly social. The municipalities, or local welfare agencies for that matter, had to cover part of the expense in connection with the deportation, calculated at RM 74,000 for the 3,528 Gypsies. However, before the payment issue had been sorted out, on 15 August 1940 the deportation was canceled. The RSHA instantly promised to solve the "Gypsy question" in the near future.[53] As for the reasons why the deportation was cancelled, the evidence is rather scanty. In his letter from 31 October 1940 to the RKPA in Vienna, Heydrich explained cryptically: "The intended relocation of 6,000 Gypsies from the Ostmark to the General Government is being called off until the Gypsy question will have been reconsidered after the war [*weil nach dem Kriege eine andere Regelung der gesamten Zigeunerfrage vorgesehen ist*]."[54]

Simultaneously, the RSHA pointed out a possibility to proceed more radically against Gypsies at the local level by proposing the construction of Gypsy camps to "assure the sustenance of the families and to possibly relieve the municipalities of the current social burden."[55] In Salzburg, the head of the Criminal Police Anton Böhmer took up the initiative to transform the impromptu Gypsy camp into a permanent facility in the case the RKPA would bear the expense for constructing a police barracks and the barbed-wire fence.[56] The RSHA welcomed Böhmer's initiative though declined to finance the project. In a letter to the Reich representative in Styria from 21 August 1940, the head of the German Criminal Police Arthur Nebe emphasized that "[the solution of] the Gypsy problem in Burgenland has for the time being to be considered a local obligation.... Not until this has proven impossible should we try and mobilize Reich funds for Burgenland. I consider this approach to be tactically most appropriate as you would by then come into possession of a substantial amount of statistical data."[57]

The abovementioned Heydrich's letter encouraged local authorities to use newly available data to impose further restrictions with the purpose of disposing of Gypsies.[58] Specifically, Heydrich instructed the Criminal Police in Linz, Innsbruck, Salzburg, and Klagenfurt to lock up *all* Gypsies in one, bigger, camp, whereas in Niederdonau and Styria only workfit Gypsies were dispatched to forced labor camps. The earnings of those Gypsies capable of work should provide an absolute existence minimum, Heydrich argued. Gypsies would receive just 10 percent of their salary while the rest would go to the district welfare offices, which, in their turn, would pay for the food of the Gypsies staying in the "Gypsy settlements." Essentially, Heydrich outlined a model that on one hand should have helped to reduce the cost of welfare and on the other to impose further restrictions on Gypsies. This twofold policy cleared the way for the mass deportation "eastward."

As a result of the failed attempt at deportation in early 1940, the camp sites that meant to be temporary actually became permanent, at least until after the "final evacuation" of the Gypsies could be put into effect. Thus, in fall 1940 the mayor of St. Pölten, the municipality of Vienna, and district councils in Bruck on Leitha, Eisenstadt, Lilienfeld, Oberpullendorf, St. Pölten, and Vienna Neustadt reached an agreement to lease the Esterházy estate in Lackenbach and to share costs for the construction and maintenance of a larger camp—proportionally to the number of Gypsies admitted form each of the participating administrative units. Gypsies who had been imprisoned by 23 November 1940, would live in that guarded camp under most primitive conditions, forced to perform physical labor.[59] The RKPA considered the newly established Lackenbach camp as a model worth emulation.

Authorities in Styria intended to engage seven hundred male Gypsies in railway construction.[60] Those Gypsies had been locked in camps in Upper Styria, forced to mainly build roads. Almost all work-fit Gypsies had held paying jobs before they ended up in forced labor camps purposefully built for Gypsies. As slave laborers, obviously, they could no longer support their families. Whatever they earned had been claimed by the district welfare office, ostensibly to help local municipalities relieve financial burden. However, the intended funds only reached few municipalities, prompting a series of complaints.[61] Even less reached the Gypsies in the so-called Gypsy settlements. Nonetheless, the district welfare office kept defending the established system, requesting even more Gypsies to be dispatched to forced labor camps.[62] Gypsies imprisoned in the Maxglan forced labor camp in Salzburg were used, among other things, for the construction of the Glan canal and as extra workers for Riefenstahl Film. At the beginning of 1941 about three hundred Gypsies from across Upper Austria were deported to the Gypsy camp in St. Pantaleon-Weyer where they were engaged in drainage and land clearing.[63]

The Dynamics of Nazi Mass Murder Following the Invasion of the Soviet Union in 1941

In spring 1941 the authorities in Burgenland were considering how to further proceed with Gypsies. One of the plans, though never realized, was to establish six to seven bigger Gypsy camps in southern Burgenland. Smaller Gypsy settlements, however, continued to be dismantled one by one.[64] In February 1941 the authorities in eastern Austria got a new opportunity to deport Gypsies en masse. It might, or might not, have had something to do with the Nazi invasion of Yugoslavia. Seven weeks after the beginning of the military campaign, on 26 May 1941, Heydrich ordered Gypsies to be deported (to Serbia).[65] However, the deportation was halted in early August 1941 because of the opposition of the German military administration. As the Reich representative in Styria confirmed: "The deportation of Gypsies has currently run into a dead end."[66]

Heydrich prescribed the deportation of 7,000 Gypsies from Burgenland, 3,000 from the Niederdonau district, and another 4,000 from the Styria district by July 1941. The accompanying guidelines established that each "Gypsy and Gypsy of mixed origin [*Zigeunermischlinge*] from the former Burgenland" should be deported on the basis of the census carried out in June 1938.[67] The 1938 census, however, was almost exclusively based on the Gypsy card file created during the interwar period. Thus, the criteria for deportation were essentially those established by Austrian authorities during the 1920s and 1930s. By the same token, individuals excluded from deportation included the sick, those married to a "German-bred" (*Deutschblütigen*), those whose relatives were currently in the military service, and real estate owners.[68] By enumerating the real estate owners, Heydrich unwittingly conceded that some Gypsies did possess property and that there were no legal grounds for its expropriation, in contrast to the "legal" expropriation of Jews. For the time being, however, property owners among Gypsies were exempted from deportation. The deportation would be carried out a few months later, though to a different destination.

On 22 June 1941, Nazi Germany invaded the Soviet Union. The initial military advances of the summer of 1941 pushed the demands for the wholesale deportation of Jews and Gypsies. The war against the Soviet Union caused a further radicalization of the anti-Jewish and anti-Gypsy policies, as *Einsatzgruppen* (mobile killing units) executed tens of thousands of Jews, Gypsies, and other "unwanted elements" behind the frontline. Under the cloak of war, the Nazi and Wehrmacht leadership dropped the last vestiges of civility. It is true that the Final Solution of the Gypsy Question had been postponed, but only "until after the war." Until late summer 1941 the ephemeral solution to the Jewish Question had mainly meant expulsion. However, as the anticipated victory over the Soviet Union did not come true, the Nazis readjusted their plans, unwilling to wait until after the end of the war to do away with Jews and Gypsies.

On 18 September 1941, Himmler informed the *Gauleiter* of the Warthegau Arthur Greiser that Hitler had requested a deportation of Jews from the Reich territory. Specifically, Himmler intended to dispatch before the onset of winter some 60,000 Jews from Germany proper and the Protectorate of Bohemia and Moravia to the Litzmannstadt ghetto.[69] Even though Himmler did not specifically mention Gypsies, one week later the mayor of Litzmannstadt complained to the district president about the forthcoming deportation of 20,000 Jews and 5,000 Gypsies.[70] Already earlier, the capacity of the ghetto came under scrutiny. Since the Warthegau district and the city of Litzmannstadt were officially part of the Third Reich, the local administration had tried hard—for the most part unsuccessfully—to shift the Jews into the General Government. At the same time, an increasing number of Jews from the Warthegau ended up in the Litzmannstadt ghetto. In order to prevent further influx of inmates, the ghetto administration argued for the risk of epidemic and inadequate food provision in the ghetto. The difference of opinions brewed into a conflict over the "resettlement" (the Nazi euphemism for deportation) of 20,000 Jews from Western Europe and 5,000 Gypsies from Austria. The mayor of Litzmannstadt Werner Ventzki insisted that the ghetto administration should renounce any responsibility for the potential impact of the deportation, "particularly in view of the biggest danger posed by the resettlement of the Gypsies." He then speculated that deportation would negatively affect the production in the ghetto, "while Gypsies were the arsonists of the worst kind."[71] Ventzki further spoke of the risk of epidemic, shortages of food, deficient transport, and inadequate supplies of coal and construction materials. Genuine or not, this apprehension was promptly projected onto Gypsies. In any case, the German ghetto administration failed to stop the deportation.

Whose idea it was to include the 5,000 Austrian Gypsies into the discussion of the Jewish deportation to the Litzmannstadt ghetto is unclear. Preliminary negotiations apparently took place in August and September 1941, since Himmler's decree of 1 October concerning the deportation of Gypsies—with reference to the corresponding decree of Heydrich from 26 May—mentioned Litzmannstadt as the final destination.[72] This decree was followed by chaotic and rushed negotiations concerning the number of Gypsies to be deported from Styria and Lower Austria respectively. The decree compelled the district welfare offices in Styria and Niederdonau to pay for deportees' food while all other expenses, including the cost of construction of transit camps, would be covered by the German Security Police.[73]

Although, as a rule, entire families were subject to deportation, the factor of (un)employment proved an important selection criterion. The forced labor camps in Styria and the Gypsy camp in St. Pantaleon were closed down, and their inmates were deported to Litzmannstadt. Altogether, between 4 and 8 November 1941, the five transports originating in Hartberg, Fürstenfeld, Mattersburg, Rotenthurm, and Oberwart carried a total of 5,007 Gypsies—1,130 men, 1,188 women, and 2,689 children. According to the estimate of the German ghetto administration, only 1,925 (or 38 percent) deportees were work fit.[74]

The Gypsy camp at Litzmannstadt consisted of a single housing block, practically without sanitation or any other essentials. The exploitation of forced labor (*Arbeitseinsatz*), as it had been originally envisaged, never came to be. Shortly upon arrival of the Gypsy prisoners, a typhus epidemic broke out in the ghetto. Hundreds of prisoners died of typhus because the German camp administration refused to provide necessary medication and altogether did nothing to improve the hygienic conditions in the ghetto. The risk of typhus epidemic spreading through the city of Litzmannstadt was the likely reason for the mass murder of *all* Gypsies from the ghetto carried out in December 1941 and January 1942 at the recently built death camp at Kulmhof.

Yet a large number of Gypsies still remained in the Ostmark after the November 1941 deportation to the Litzmannstadt ghetto. Thus, at the beginning of 1942 the head of the Oberwart county communicated to the local mayors that "one can count on a further solution of the Gypsy question, even if the timeframe has not yet been established."[75] When it comes to the probable 1942 negotiations that had resulted in the deportation of some 2,900 Austrian Gypsies (out of the total of 22,600 Gypsies deported from all over Europe) to Auschwitz-Birkenau, documentary evidence at the local level is conspicuously missing. Surely, all the crucial decisions were made in Berlin, even if the constant intervention of the local authorities had to a certain degree expedited those decisions. In September 1942 Himmler requested the Ahnenerbe (a research institute dealing with the history of the "Aryan" race) to cooperate with the German Criminal Police for the purpose of establishing scientific grounds for the preferential treatment of a part of Gypsies "due to their valuable traits [*wegen ihres wertvollen Erbes*]," the notion that contradicted the previous police practices. This request made the RKPA, with the assistance of the "Gypsy researcher" Robert Ritter, revise the existing categorization of the Gypsies. Until then the RKPA made a distinction between "Gypsy" and "Gypsy *Mischling*." Now, however, it began distinguishing between Sinti and the Lalleri Gypsies on the one hand and the rest of the Gypsies on the other, upgrading the former into the category of "purebred" (*stammechten Zigeuner*) while relegating every other category of Gypsies. Consequently, Sinti and the Lalleri Gypsies were (supposed to be) exempted from deportation and/or forced sterilization that would affect the rest of the Gypsies.[76] The implementation of the new classification began with the appointment of so-called Gypsy spokesmen, introduced in accordance with a decree from October 1942. The "Gypsy spokesmen" were supposed to prepare lists of those who should be exempted from deportation. In the meantime, the deportation to Auschwitz-Birkenau was already underway, even before those lists had been compiled. The decision to that effect was essentially made by the RKPA, which enjoyed significant executive authority.[77]

On 16 December 1942, Himmler issued the so-called Auschwitz decree that led to the deportation of "Gypsy *Mischlinge,* Roma Gypsies, and Balkan Gypsies" to a special camp in Auschwitz. On 29 January 1943, the RSHA sent out additional instructions (*Schnellbrief*) explaining Himmler's decree in detail. Apparently, Himmler issued a separate decree regarding the deportation of the Austrian Gypsies to Auschwitz. Although the original document has not been found, it is reasonable to assume it had the same provisions as the Auschwitz decree and the accompanying RSHA instructions. The latter two documents specified the categories of Gypsies subject to deportation:

> In accordance with the order of the Reichsführer-SS from 16 December 1942, Gypsy *Mischlinge,* Roma Gypsies, and members of non-German Gypsy tribes of Balkan origin are to be segregated pursuant to the specific guidelines and in a few weeks' time to be committed to a concentration camp in a special operation... The committal to the concentration camp (Gypsy camp) Auschwitz is to be carried out on a family basis, regardless of individual racial composition.[78]

The police effectively ignored the clause in the guidelines that prescribed the deportation of "Gypsy *Mischlinge*" only. Following a meeting on 11 March 1942, regarding the forthcoming deportation to Auschwitz, a high-ranking official in the Waidhofen on Thaya county produced the following memorandum exposing a consensus within the local Nazi leadership to bypass Himmler's order:

> Upon the special request of the *Gauleiter* [of Niederdonau], the Gypsies and Gypsy *Mischlinge* should be dispatched to the concentration camp Auspitz [*sic*] near Kattowitz [Katowice] as soon as possible and as many as possible. ... The main principle, according to the *Gauleiter,* is this: This is probably our last chance to take advantage of the final settlement [*restlose Bereinigung*] of the Gypsy question in order to excise as many Gypsy *Mischlinge* from Niederdonau as possible. To that end, as few exceptions should be made as possible.[79]

Whether racial criteria were used in the selection process it not quite clear. What is certain, however, is that the deportee lists were compiled with help from local authorities. Thus a summary of the reports of the district councils in Feldbach, Fürstenfeld, and Oberwart concerning the deportations to Auschwitz reads as follows:

> From the Feldbach, Fürstenfeld, and Oberwart districts Gypsies were evacuated [*abtransportiert wurden*] on 5 April. 208 Gypsies were removed from Feldbach, and another 1,405 from Oberwart, in addition to 2,000 Gypsies that had been evacuated from Oberwart on 1 November 1942. The entire operation, apart from few attempts at escape, went according to plan. Groups of Gypsies in hiding were discovered the same day or they turned themselves in voluntarily. The question of resettlement is currently under consideration

with regard to the 83 nonpureblood Gypsies remaining in the district Oberwart who in many cases have connections to non-Gypsies. All in all, the removal of Gypsies, which is seen as the long-awaited liberation from a menace, has generated the greatest satisfaction.[80]

The Criminal Police office in Salzburg expressed similar levels of satisfaction. On 5 April 1943, the office informed the district leadership and the Reich representatives in Salzburg that between 1 and 3 April a majority of the Gypsies who had been incarcerated in Salzburg were deported to Auschwitz and the rest to Lackenbach.[81] Gypsy transports from the Styria district arrived in Auschwitz on 3, 5, 9, and 16 April 1943, respectively.[82]

Altogether, over 2,900 Austrian Gypsies were deported to Auschwitz. About 65 percent of the prisoners at the Auschwitz Gypsy camp originally came from Germany and Austria; over 20 percent from Bohemia and Moravia; and slightly more than 6 percent from Poland. The mortality among sick and malnourished prisoners was especially high; the Nazis routinely gassed sick inmates, among them also Austrian Gypsies on 12 May 1943. Until the end of 1943, close to 70 percent of the Gypsy prisoners at Auschwitz had died. Following the deportation of work-fit Gypsy prisoners to other concentration camps at the end of July 1944, on the night of 2 August the SS troops surrounded the Auschwitz Gypsy camp and herded the remaining inmates into the gas chambers.[83]

According to the Criminal Police office in Vienna, there were "still 993 Gypsy-like persons" residing in the Alpine and Donau regions in the aftermath of the mass deportation to Auschwitz. Though in the long term, those Gypsies were doomed too:

> The remaining Gypsies, who fall under one of the exemption categories listed above, have all been registered, have permanent residence and employment. In close cooperation with the respective labor office, they will be subjected to a strict control and continuous supervision. As soon as the labor situation will allow it, they too will be deported to the concentration camp. The rest will be subjected to [forced] sterilization. The preparations to that end are already in progress.[84]

Conclusion: Persecution Uninterrupted

The exact number of Austrian Gypsies murdered by the Nazis is rather difficult to establish. It has something to do with the fluctuating definition of "Gypsy." For example, Gypsies in the concentration camps did not constitute a uniform prisoner category, often having been dispatched to camps as "antisocial," especially outside of the big deportation waves in 1938 and 1939. Thus, the available sources enable only a rough estimate of the number of deportees. It can be established with certainty that out of the 5,007 Gypsies who had been deported to the Litzmannstadt ghetto, no one survived, and that further 237 prisoners died in the Gypsy camp at Lackenbach. Close to 4,700 Gypsies were deported to concentration camps: assuming a 10 percent survival rate, the death toll among the Austrian Gypsies could amount to 9,000–9,500.[85] Among those regarded by the Nazis as "Gypsies" no more than 1,500–2,000 might survive.

The end of Nazi rule did not automatically mean the end of discrimination against Gypsies in Austria. On 28 June 1945, just a few weeks after the liberation, the government of Lower Austria announced that the Gypsy Edict of 1888 was again in effect due to the alleged influx of Gypsies in the province's border regions.[86] Ironically, this piece of the nineteenth-century anti-Gypsy legislation was, among other pre-1933 legal acts, meant to replace the discriminatory laws that had been enacted during the Nazi period. Whether it was a deliberate act on the part of local politicians is difficult to tell now. Otherwise, the Austrian provisional government had many problems on their hands in the weeks after the collapse of Nazi Germany, including the refugee crisis and the division of Austria into several occupation zones. Either way, the Lower Austrian precedent might have influenced the Ministry of Security to officially reintroduce on 20 September 1948 the notion of a "Gypsy nuisance":

> This agency came to know that the Gypsy nuisance again has been on the rise in some parts of federal lands, making an unpleasant appearance. In order to impress the [local, non-Gypsy] population, the Gypsies often pass as [former] concentration camp inmates.... Since the successful implementation of these measures would no doubt run into difficulties, the Gypsies and their movement should be monitored more closely. The individual or group migration from one area to another has to be monitored, passing on the [relevant] information to the authorities in whose jurisdiction they [Gypsies] are supposedly moving in.[87]

Particularly grotesque was the reference to Gypsies' faking the victim status. In Burgenland, for example, the authorities knew full well that, according to the "Gypsy census" (*Zigeunererfassung*) carried out by the gendarmerie in 1948, out of the 870 Gypsies registered in that particular province 636 were survivors.[88] Already due to their small numbers, the Gypsy survivors could not possibly pose "security problem." As during the interwar period, the Austrian authorities were particularly concerned with foreign Roma, which were hard to find due to the closely guarded borders between the Soviet and Western occupation zones. In any case, the prescribed monitoring of Gypsies' movement had its origin in the 1888 edict, and so it was understood by the police authorities. Thus, the police in Burgenland had collected evidence concerning Gypsies until the early 1960s while their counterparts in Linz and Salzburg had filed annual reports on the Gypsy minority in their respective province for the Ministry of Interior.[89]

The police authorities continuously exercised the preconceived notion of Gypsies as criminals, work shy, thieves, smugglers, and innately antisocial. The suspicion of liaison with the enemy—this time around, the Soviet occupation authorities and communists—topped the list of alleged offenses.[90] While the stigmatization of Gypsies continued unabated in the immediate postwar decades, any good will was missing to return the property that had been previously robbed from the victims. As the Directorate of Security for Upper Austria reported to Vienna in early 1956:

> Only few Gypsies have been seen passing through since 1945. By and large, Gypsies can be designated predominantly as work shy and asocial, even though they rarely commit grave offenses (except for bodily injuries incurred during brawls), according to the available data.[91]

Indeed, little had changed in the police practices vis-à-vis Gypsies since the interwar years, notwithstanding the statement by the Directorate of Security in 1956 that saw no need for a separate "Gypsy law":

> During that period [1938–1945] the Gypsy question in Austria (Ostmark) was similarly handled on the basis of decrees issued by the Reich Criminal Police Office, the Reich Security Main Office, and the Reich Ministry of Interior in Berlin. During that time there existed a Gypsy camp in Austria, in Lackenbach in the Oberpullendorf district. As a result of the measures implemented by the Nazi regime, the Gypsy problem in Austria had been resolutely offset [*energisch an den Leib gerückt*]. As for the specific methods applied, there is no need to elaborate on them here, since those measures were the same throughout the German Reich. Since 1945, one can no longer speak of a Gypsy problem in Austria—no doubt a consequence of the Nazi rule of seven years.... Even if the Gypsies should for the most part be regarded as asocial and work shy, their conduct in the recent years does not warrant enacting specific legislation in Austria.[92]

This particular statement marked the beginning of the end of anti-Gypsy policymaking in Austria, even if the police had continued for a few more years to treat the Gypsies in accordance with the 1948 (1888) edict. Otherwise, there was nothing like the official ending to the discriminatory practices. It appears as if the police authorities in the 1960s simply dropped Gypsies from their sight, thus effectively discontinuing the century-old policy of discrimination. This does not necessarily mean that the traditional anti-Gypsy stereotypes disappeared at once from both official and public discourse in Austria, unfortunately.

Notes

1. Florian Freund, *Oberösterreich und die Zigeuner. Politik gegen eine Minderheit im 19. und 20. Jahrhundert* (Linz, 2010), 41. For the term *Gypsy* see Florian Freund, "Der polizeilich—administrative Zigeunerbegriff. Ein Beitrag zur Klärung des Begriffes 'Zigeuner,'" *Zeitgeschichte* 30, no. 2 (March–April 2003): 76–90; Juliane Hanschkow, "Etikettierung, Kriminalisierung und Verfolgung von 'Zigeunern' in der südlichen Rheinprovinz zur Zeit des Kaiserreiches und der Weimarer Republik 1906 bis 1933," in *Zigeuner und Nation. Repräsentation—Inklusion—Exklusion,* ed. Herbert Uerlings and Julia-Karin Patrut (Frankfurt, 2008), 249–71.
2. Freund, *Oberösterreich,* 21. I use the generic word *Gypsy,* which denotes a social construct rather than an ethnic group.
3. Jacques Sémelin, *Purify and Destroy: The Political Uses of Massacre and Genocide* (New York, 2007), 9.
4. "Berichte über die Verhandlungen des oberösterreichischen Landtages nach den stenografischen Aufzeichnungen. VII. Landtags-Periode. Erste Session vom 15. September bis 21. Oktober 1884, 13. Sitzung am 9. Oktober 1884" (Linz, [1884]), 217.
5. Ibid., 218.
6. Leo Lucassen, *Zigeuner. Die Geschichte eines polizeilichen Ordnungsbegriffes in Deutschland 1700–1945* (Cologne, 1996), 40.
7. Edict of 14 September 1888, reproduced in Ernst Hayerhofer, *Handbuch für den politischen Verwaltungsdienst in den im Reichsrathe vertretenen Königreichen und Ländern mit besonderer Berücksichtigung der diesen Ländern gemeinsamen Gesetze und Verordnungen,* vol. 3 (Vienna, 1897), 665.
8. Certificate of residence granted citizen rights, including welfare benefits. Certificate of residence could only be acquired by birth, providing for deportation of all those who did not possess this document.
9. Ministry of the Interior to district authorities, 13 July 1890, Upper Austrian State Archives (hereafter: OÖLA), BH Steyr, 158.
10. Freund, *Oberösterreich,* 57.
11. Königlich Ungarisches Statistisches Buero, ed., "Ergebnisse der in Ungarn am 31. Jänner 1893 durchgeführten Zigeuner-Conscription," in *Ungarische Statistische Mittheilungen* 9 (Budapest, 1895): 19.
12. The head of the police in Munich, Alfred Dillmann, used the same approach as in Austria in his *Zigeunerbuch* (1905), providing personal data on six hundred Gypsies and "Gypsy-like individuals" arrested by the police in Munich. Albrecht Angelika, *Zigeuner in Altbayern 1871–1914. Eine sozial-wirtschafts- und verwaltungsgeschichtliche Untersuchung der bayerischen Zigeunerpolitik* (Munich, 2002), 30, 132.
13. Ministry of the Interior, draft decree, no date [1916], OÖLA, BH, Steyr, 158.
14. Alfred J. Noll, "Entstehung der Volkssouveränität. Zur Entwicklung der österreichischen Verfassung 1918–1920," in *Das Werden der Ersten Republik ... der Rest ist Österreich,* ed. Helmut Konrad and Wolfgang Maderthaner, vol. 1 (Vienna, 2008), 363–80.

15. Burgenland regional gendarmerie office, proposals re. the study of the Gypsy Question, no date, Burgenland Provincial Archives (hereafter: BLA), Zigeunerakt, Mappe Zigeunerunwesen 1930–33.
16. Gerald Stourzh, "Ethnic Attribution in Late Imperial Austria: Good Intentions, Evil Consequences," in *The Habsburg Legacy. National Identity in Historical Perspective, Edinburgh 1994,* ed. Ritchie Robertson and Edward Timms (Edinburgh, 1994), 67–83; Wolfgang Pauser, "Was heisst 'artfremdes Blut'? Identitätsbegriffe in der Geschichte der rechtlichen Verfahren zur 'Feststellung von Volkszugehörigkeit,'" in *Nationalsozialismus und Recht. Rechtssetzung und Rechtswissenschaft in Österreich unter der Herrschaft des Nationalsozialismus,* ed. Ulrike Davy et al. (Vienna, 1990), 97–123.
17. Finding of the Austrian Supreme Administrative Court, 9 June 1921, quoted in Pauser, "Was heisst 'artfremdes Blut'?", 106.
18. "Stenographische Protokolle über die Sitzungen des Hauses der Abgeordneten des österreichischen Reichsrathes im Jahre 1891, 59. Sitzung der XI Session am 27.10.1891," vol. 3 (Vienna, 1892), 2703.
19. "Stenographische Protokolle über die Sitzungen des Hauses der Abgeordneten des österreichischen Reichsrathes im Jahre 1896, 523. Sitzung der XI Session am 26.10.1896," vol 21 (Vienna, 1897), 26743.
20. "Berichte über die Verhandlungen des oberösterreichischen Landtages nach den stenografischen Aufzeichnungen. IX. Landtags-Periode. Sechste Session vom 27. Dezember 1901 bis 3. Jänner 1902 und vom 21. Juni bis 18. Juli 1902," (Linz, [1902]), 12; ibid., Sitzung am 3. Juli 1902, 154.
21. Ibid., 159.
22. Ibid., "Interpellation des Abgeordneten Karl Iro und Genossen, Stenografisches Protokoll, Haus der Abgeordneten, 83. Sitzung der XVIII. Session am 5. Juni 1908," 3012/I, 9388ff.
23. Hans Gross, *Handbuch für Untersuchungsrichter als System der Kriminalistik* (Munich, 1904), 400–06. Cf. Christian Bachhiesl, "Die Grazer Schule der Kriminologie. Eine wissenschaftsgeschichtliche Skizze," *Monatsschrift für Kriminologie und Strafrechtsreform* 91, no. 2 (April 2008): 87–111.
24. "Anfrage des Abgeordneten Johann Gürtler und Genossen an den Herrn Bundesminister für Inneres betreffend Beseitigung der Zigeunerplage, Stenographische Protokolle über die Sitzungen des Nationalrates der Republik Österreich, 91. Sitzung am 24.02.1922," (Vienna, 1923), 277/I.
25. Freund, *Oberösterreich,* 97.
26. Ibid., 105.
27. *Der Montag,* 16 May 1927, BLA, Zigeunerakt, Mappe 1927–1930.
28. District Office Neusiedl am See to local gendarmerie offices, 19 May 1927, BLA, BH Neusiedl, Polizei 1938.
29. Freund, *Oberösterreich,* 134.
30. Minutes of the meeting re. the Gypsy Question in Burgenland, Oberwart, 15 January 1933, Austrian State Archives (hereafter: ÖStA), BKA, Gd 3/37, Kt. 7152, Z. 339.732.
31. Ibid.
32. Sémelin, *Purify and Destroy,* 33.
33. For the German Criminal Police see Patrick Wagner, *Hitlers Kriminalisten. Die Deutsche Kriminalpolizei und der Nationalsozialismus* (Munich, 2002).
34. For the initial Nazi anti-Gypsy polices in Austria see Florian Freund et al., *Vermögensentzug, Restitution und Entschädigung der Roma und Sinti, Veröffentlichungen der Österreichischen Historikerkommission* (Vienna, 2004).

35. Tobias Portschy, *Die Zigeunerfrage. Denkschrift des Landeshauptmannes für das Burgenland PG. Dr. Portschy* (Eisenstadt, 1938), available in Documentation Archives of the Austrian Resistance (hereafter: DÖW), Bibliothek 8085, Nazistica, 23, 33, 35–37.
36. Instructions of the German Security Police for the Criminal Police office Vienna, 5 June 1939, DÖW, 2607. Cf. Michael Zimmermann, *Rassenutopie und Genozid. Die nationalsozialistische 'Lösung der Zigeunerfrage'* (Hamburg, 1996), 116.
37. Himmler's order re. the "fight against the Gypsy nuisance," 8 December 1938, printed in *Ministerialblatt des Reichs- und Preuss. Ministerium des Inneren* 51 (1938): 2106; Martin Luchterhandt, *Der Weg nach Birkenau. Entstehung und Verlauf der nationalsozialistischen Verfolgung der 'Zigeuner'* (Lübeck, 2000), 118.
38. Freund, *Oberösterreich*, 176.
39. Author unknown, memo, late July 1939, Styria Provincial Archives (hereafter: STLA), Landesregierung 384, Zi 1–1940.
40. *Gauleiter* Uiberreither to the German Criminal Police, 11 September 1939, STLA, Landesregierung 384, Zi 1–1940.
41. Hans Safrian, *Die Eichmann-Männer* (Vienna, 1993), 77; Zimmermann, *Rassenutopie*, 168.
42. Zimmermann, *Rassenutopie*, 167.
43. Mayor of Schwarzach im Pongau [?] to *Gauleiter* of Salzburg Friedrich Reiner, 3 February 1940, DÖW, E 18518.
44. Barbara Rieger, "'Zigeunerleben' in Salzburg 1930–1943. Die regionale Zigeunerverfolgung als Vorstufe zur planmäßigen Vernichtung in Auschwitz" (Diploma Thesis, University of Vienna, 1990), 50.
45. Zimmermann, *Rassenutopie*, 171.
46. Safrian, *Eichmann-Männer*, 89–91; Raul Hilberg, *Die Vernichtung der europäischen Juden*, vol. 1 (Frankfurt, 1990), 217.
47. Zimmermann, *Rassenutopie*, 171; Donald Kenrick and Grattan Puxon, *Sinti und Roma. Die Vernichtung eines Volkes im NS-Staat* (Göttingen, 1981), 67; Hans-Joachim Döring, "Die Motive der Zigeuner-Deportation vom Mai 1940," *Vierteljahrshefte für Zeitgeschichte* 7, no. 4 (1959): 419.
48. Zimmermann, *Rassenutopie*, 175.
49. Head of Styria province Otto Müller-Haccius to the RSHA, 30 March 1940, STLA, Landesregierung 384, Zi 1–1940.
50. RSHA to local authorities in Styria, 17 June 1940, STLA, Landesregierung 384, Zi 1–1940.
51. RSHA to the head of Styria province Otto Müller-Haccius, 16 July 1940, STLA, Landesregierung 384, Zi 1–1940.
52. Reich representative in Styria, police department, memo, 22 July 1940, STLA, Landesregierung 384, Zi 1–1940.
53. Criminal Police office Graz, memo, 15 August 1940, STLA, Landesregierung 384, Zi 1–1940.
54. Minister of the Interior (Heydrich) to the Criminal Police office Vienna, 31 October 1940, STLA, Landesregierung 384, Zi 1–1940.
55. Criminal Police office Graz, memo, 15 August 1940, STLA, Landesregierung 384, Zi 1–1940.
56. Head of the Criminal Police in Salzburg Anton Böhmer to the head of the German Criminal Police Arthur Nebe, 6 September 1940, Salzburg Provincial Archives (hereafter: SLA), RSTH I/3, 95/940
57. RSHA to the Reich representative in Styria Sigfried Uiberreither, 21 August 1940, STLA, Landesregierung 384, Zi 1–1940.

58. Minister of the Interior (Heydrich) to the Criminal Police office Vienna, 31 October 1940, STLA, Landesregierung 384, Zi 1–1940.
59. More on the history of the Lackenbach Gypsy camp see Erika Thurner, *Nationalsozialismus und Zigeuner in Österreich* (Vienna, 1983), 60.
60. Criminal Police office Graz, memo, 12 August 1940, STLA, Landesregierung 384, Zi 1–1940. Eventually, Gypsy slave laborers ended up building roads.
61. Freund et al., *Vermögensentzug*, 109.
62. Reich representative in Styria to the city councilors and the mayor of Graz, 5 December 1940, STLA, Landesregierung III b 120, Zi 1/11–1940.
63. Freund, *Oberösterreich*, 191.
64. Reich representative in Styria, police department, memo, 28 February 1941, STLA Landesregierung, 120 Zi 1–1940.
65. Heydrich's order, 26 May 1941, STLA, Landesregierung 384, Zi 1–1940.
66. Reich representative in Styria, police department, memo, 12 August 1941, STLA, Landesregierung 384, Zi 1–1940.
67. RSHA, guidelines re. deportation of Gypsies from Burgenland, 26 May 1941, STLA, Landesregierung 120, Zi 1–1940.
68. Ibid.
69. Himmler to Greiser, 18 September 1941, German Federal Archives (hereafter: BA), NS 19/2655; Cf. Florian Freund et al., "Das Getto in Litzmannstadt (Łódź)," in *"Unser einziger Weg ist Arbeit." Das Getto in Łódź 1940—1945. Eine Ausstellung des Jüdischen Museums Frankfurt am Main* (Vienna, 1990), 17–31.
70. Mayor of Litzmannstadt Werner Ventzki to the district head of Kalisz-Łódź Friedrich Uebelhoer, 24 September 1941, BAK, NS 19/2655; Cf. Safrian, *Eichmann-Männer*, 117.
71. Freund et al., "Das Getto in Litzmannstadt," 25.
72. Himmler's decree concerning the deportation of Gypsies, 1 October 1941, STLA, Landesregierung 384, Zi 1–1940.
73. Reich representative in Styria to Styria district welfare office, 27 October 1941, STLA, Landesregierung, 120, Zi 1–1940.
74. On Gypsy camp in Litzmannstadt ghetto see Jerzy Ficowski et al., *Wieviel Trauer und Wege. Zigeuner in Polen* (Frankfurt, 1992); Julian Baranowski, *Zigeunerlager in Litzmannstadt 1941-1942/The Gypsy Camp in Łódź/Obóz cyganski w Łodzi* (Łódź, 2003).
75. District head of Oberwart county Peter Hinterlechner to local mayors, 6 January 1942, DÖW, 11.293.
76. Luchterhandt, *Der Weg nach Birkenau*, 314–15.
77. Ibid., 246. Zimmermann, *Rassenutopie*, 310.
78. "Auf Befehl des Reichsführers SS vom 16.12.1942 sind Zigeunermischlinge, Rom-Zigeuner und nicht deutschblütige Angehörige zigeunerischer Sippen balkanischer Herkunft nach bestimmten Richtlinien auszuwählen und in einer Aktion von wenigen Wochen in ein Konzentrationslager einzuweisen … Die Einweisung erfolgt ohne Rücksicht auf den Mischlingsgrad familienweise in das Konzentrationslager (Zigeunerlager) Auschwitz" (Zimmermann, *Rassenutopie*, 301); the text of the edict is reproduced in Hans-Joachim Döring, *Die Zigeuner im nationalsozialistischen Staat* (Hamburg, 1964), 215.
79. District head of Waidhofen on Thaya [?] to district head of Zwettl, 12 March 1943, Lower Austrian Provincial Archives (hereafter: NÖLA), BH Zwettl, XI 153/1943.
80. District councils in Styria, report for April 1943, STLA, Landesregierung, 384, La 1–1940.
81. Criminal Police office Salzburg to the *Gauleiter* and the Reich representative in Salzburg Gustav Adolf Scheel, 5 April 1943, SLA, RSTH, I/3 45/1943.

82. Danuta Czech, *Kalendarium der Ereignisse im Konzentrationslager Auschwitz-Birkenau 1939–1945* (Reinbek bei Hamburg, 1989), 429, 432, 436, 443. Cf. Luchterhandt, *Der Weg nach Birkenau*, 248.
83. Czech, *Kalendarium*, 337, 340, 343.
84. Criminal Police office Vienna to the Reich representative Hugo Jury in Niederdonau, 11 May 1943, NÖLA, RSTH XIII 1601/1944 Kt. 1145.
85. Freund et al., *Vermögensentzug*, 51.
86. Government of Lower Austria to district heads and the police department in Neustadt, 28 June 1945, NÖLA, BH Korneuburg, Gr. XI 153/1945, Kt. 450; Cf. Barbara Rieger, "Roma und Sinti in Österreich nach 1945. Die Ausgrenzung einer Minderheit als gesellschaftlicher Prozess" (PhD diss., University of Vienna, 1997), 34.
87. Directorate of Security to all branch offices and police offices, 20 September 1948, ÖStA, AdR, BMI 102.389–13/60. Cf. Rieger, "Roma und Sinti," 53.
88. Burgenland gendarmerie, investigation department, memo, 7 February 1952, ÖSta, AdR, BMI 102.389–13/60; Rieger, "Roma und Sinti," 54.
89. Directorate of Security in Salzburg to the Ministry of the Interior in Vienna, 29 January 1960, ÖStA, AdR, BMI 102.389–13/60; Cf. Erika Thurner, "Ein Zigeunerleben? Als Sinto, Sintiza, Rom und Romni in Salzburg," in *Roma. Das unbekannte Volk. Schicksal und Kultur*, ed. Mozes Heinschink and Ursula Hemetek (Vienna, 1994), 54–96.
90. Baumgarten and Freund, *Die Burgenland Roma 1945-2000. Eine Darstellung der Volksgruppe auf der Basis archivalischer und statistischer Quellen* (Eisenstadt, 2004), 62.
91. Directorate of Security in Upper Austria to the Ministry of the Interior in Vienna, 27 January 1956, ÖStA, AdR, BMI 102.389–13/60; Cf. Rieger, "Roma und Sinti," 41.
92. Directorate of Security, statement [February 1956], ÖStA, AdR, BMI 102.389–13/60; Cf. Rieger, "Roma und Sinti," 44.

CHAPTER 3

Ustaša Mass Violence Against Gypsies in Croatia, 1941–1942

Alexander Korb

Introduction

It has become commonplace among scholars of the Ustaša regime to mention the persecution of the Gypsies. Despite that, the mass killings of Gypsies carried out by the regime during World War II remain largely understudied. This has in part to do with the dominant scholarly focus, especially in the Yugoslav historiography, on the anti-Serb policies of the Ustaša. While the Holocaust has received more attention in Croatia in recent years, this does not apply to the mass murder of the Gypsies. Due to limited availability of documentary sources, only basic facts have been established so far, with the decision-making process of the Ustaša leadership and the actual mass killings at the Jasenovac concentration camp remaining a blind spot.

The perception of the destruction of the Gypsies by the Ustaša has been shaped by two assumptions. First, scholars describe it as a part of single "Ustaša genocide of Serbs, Jews, and Gypsies." By perpetuating a generic narrative of Ustaša genocide, however, historians have blurred the differences between the persecutions of various groups.[1] The link between the persecution of Gypsies and the mass murder of Serbs and

Jews has yet to be established. Second, most scholars assume a strong German influence on the persecution of Gypsies in the Ustaša Croatia. The comparison with neighboring Serbia, where the German Wehrmacht began killing Gypsies as early as summer 1941,[2] suggests the plausibility of German involvement in Croatia. However, the German impact on the Ustaša policies in general and on the persecution of the Gypsies in particular has not yet been analyzed in depth. This chapter provides an overview of the Ustaša mass murder of the Gypsies, challenging the assumptions mentioned above.

The Ustaša was a fascist, terrorist movement that aimed at destroying the multiethnic Yugoslavian state in order to establish an independent, ethnically homogeneous Croatia. Prior to 1941, the movement operated mainly from exile in Italy and Hungary. Following the invasion of Yugoslavia on 6 April 1941, the Germans handed over the newly declared Independent State of Croatia (ISC) to the Ustaša movement. Its leader, Ante Pavelić, became the head of the new state. The Ustaša ideological program put the blame for the alleged subjugation of the Croatian people under the prewar Yugoslav regime onto the Serbs and the Jews, setting out to purge them from Croatia. While the new regime increasingly targeted Jews and Gypsies, its main victims in the spring and summer of 1941 remained Serbs. In the summer months alone, Ustaša units killed over 100,000 Serbs in the countryside and expelled further 200,000 to Serbia. In an act of resistance, Serbs staged a large-scale uprising. Soon, the ISC was ravaged by a bloody civil war that lasted for the next four years.

The Croatian state was subsequently divided into an Italian sphere of interest and a German occupation zone. In the areas under direct control of Italian occupation forces, the Ustaša exercised only limited power. In the German zone of occupation, however, the Ustaša had more room to maneuver. The state's name, Independent State of Croatia, was a misnomer, as it was heavily dependent on Nazi Germany. However, the ISC was more than just a puppet state. Ustaša leaders proved skillful at exploiting German-Italian frictions. Furthermore, it enjoyed substantial independence in its campaign of ethnic cleansing, not least by unleashing an interethnic civil war. Especially on the ground, the Ustaša had significant bargaining power.[3]

However, due to internal and external pressures, the Ustaša was forced to revisit its anti-Serb policies by the end of 1941. Yet this shift did not affect the course of persecution of Jews and Gypsies. In fact, the persecution of these two groups intensified in the course of 1942. The Germans asserted their control over the Final Solution of the Jewish Question, resulting in deportations of Jews from Croatia to Auschwitz in August 1942. Simultaneously, their Croatian counterparts proceeded with deportation of Gypsies to the Jasenovac camp.

Gypsies in Croatia: A Historical Overview

One of the first scholars to address persecution of Gypsies in Croatia was Narcisa Lengel-Krizman, who identified a great many victims and laid the ground for further research.[4] According to Lengel-Krizman, the Ustaša mass murder of the Gypsies—which she qualifies as genocide—had been prepared in advance, prior to the regime's coming to power in Croatia. This interpretation is probably due to the widely held view that regards intent as the main element of genocide. However, there is no evidence of any planning by the Ustaša prior to April 1941. Apart from that, the fact that the Ustaša had committed mass murder of Gypsies is undisputed. In a recent study, Tomislav Dulić has argued that the consistency and ideological determination with which the regime targeted Gypsies for destruction involved disproportionately high death rates of around 75 percent; this line of argumentation made him define mass murder of Gypsies in the ISC as genocide.[5] The more attention paid to local context, however, the more complex becomes the picture. This applies especially to the case of Muslim Gypsies, who were to a certain extent exempted from persecution. (Emily Balić has analyzed the successful attempts of the Muslim elites of Sarajevo to protect their fellow Gypsy citizens.) Obviously, persecution took different forms depending on the regional, social, and religious background of the Gypsies in the ISC.

According to the 1931 Yugoslav census, there were 17,948 Gypsies living on the territory that was later to become the ISC. However accurate the figures of the census might appear, the Yugoslav state authority was weak in many regions, and as a certain proportion of the population was reluctant to register, these numbers are more of a rough estimate. Itinerant Gypsies were more likely to evade registration. Furthermore, in many villages the distinction between Gypsies and non-Gypsies was nonexistent. Indeed, the Gypsy and non-Gypsy populations had blended locally. Nonetheless, the number of individuals identifying themselves as "Gypsies" in 1941 might be anywhere between 20,000 and 30,000. Croatian officials and the propaganda apparatus suggested higher figures.[6]

The Gypsies in the ISC belonged to three different denominations. A majority (55 percent according to the 1931 figures) was Orthodox, around a third (35 percent) Catholic, and the remaining 10 percent Muslim.[7] Likewise, the social status of Gypsies in Croatia and Bosnia varied from one region to another. A small number of Gypsies lived in urban areas, working mainly as craftsmen or blacksmiths. Some cities such as Zemun had Gypsy quarters.[8] The majority of Gypsies, however, lived in the countryside. Itinerant Gypsies tended to be bilingual and traditional in their lifestyle, earning a living mainly from small trade. They rarely itinerated throughout the entire year, usually staying in the same village each winter. Reports from some villages suggest that the Gypsies were an identifiable minority that existed on the margins of the rural society. Yet it was not true for all communities, for the majority of Gypsies were sedentary and therefore did not significantly differ from the rest of the rural population. Apparently, only one-third of the Gypsy population declared themselves "ethnic Gypsies."[9] In some parts of Bosnia it was nearly impossible to make a clear distinction between the local non-Gypsy and Gypsy populations. According to Croatian government officials, intermarriages, assimilation, and lingual and social "Croatization" had resulted in significant intermixing.[10]

The Ustaša Ideology

Anti-Gypsyism played a relatively minor role in Ustaša ideology, at least prior to 1941. Much like anti-Semitism, it was heavily subordinated to, and influenced by, anti-Serb sentiment among the Ustaša. Consequently, Jews and Gypsies were perceived as agents of the Serbs, the fifth column, rather than a biological threat to the racial purity of the Croatian people.[11] Gypsies were said to have embodied an image of the Balkans the Ustaša did not want Croatia to be a part of. The Ustaša propaganda depicted Serbia in general, and the ruling Belgrade elite and the royal dynasty in particular, as representative of a "barbaric culture and Gypsy civilization."[12] Viewed as potential vagrants roaming back and forth between Serbia and Croatia, the Gypsies supposedly undermined the ethnic boundary that the Ustaša was eager to erect.[13] At the same time, Ustaša propaganda failed to draw a clear distinction between Serbs and Gypsies. The term *Vlach,* which originally applied to Latin peoples of southeastern Europe, now became a synonym for Balkan tribes in Croatia and was used altogether arbitrarily.[14] Croatian nationalists claimed that during the Middle Ages an admixture of Balkan tribes, among them Serbs and Gypsies, had poured into the Croatian "living space," destroying its ethnic homogeneity in the process.[15] The Ustaša goal was thus to restore the ethnic purity. While the Ustaša ethnic engineers were mainly concerned how to exclude Serbs, Jews, and Gypsies from the nation-building process, the local police and army officers were guided by more conventional prejudices. They requested the deportation of Gypsies from the areas under their supervision as they believed that the latter spread rumors and carried out intelligence for the Tito Partisans. Itinerant Gypsies in particular were in mortal danger of being accused of subversive activities. This does not imply, however, that sedentary Roma lived in safety. In June 1942 the police in the city of Zemun (a suburb of Belgrade on the Croatian side of the Sava River) proposed deporting the Roma population of four hundred to Jasenovac camp due to the alleged risk of the latter joining the partisans.[16]

Shortly before and during the war, German racial scientists and propagandists dealt intensively with what they called the Gypsy Question in southeastern Europe. Building upon speculations and prejudices, they identified the alleged "eternal wandering" as a constant economic, criminal, and biological threat to the racial order in the Balkans. In their publications they demanded "the removal of these rapidly spreading, alien parasites." Gypsies were branded a minority alien to the races among which they lived. Measures to be undertaken included registration of Gypsies, prevention of interracial marriages, implementation of a large-scale sterilization of the Gypsies in the Balkans, and mass deportation to labor camps.[17]

The Ustaša engaged in the racial discourse combining issues of public health and public security, as it was typical for fascist movements. Regime newspapers depicted the deportation of the Roma as a social-hygienic act.[18] At the same time, there is no strong evidence to suggest that the articles in German journals such as *Volkstum im Südosten, Leipziger Vierteljahrsschrift für Südosteuropa*, or *Volk und Rasse* had shaped the guiding principles of the Ustaša. Even though Nazi racial discourse on sterilization and eugenics had adherents in southeastern Europe, as Rory Yeomans has demonstrated, it did not become dominant—as I will demonstrate later in connection with the Ustaša flexibility when it came to defining who was a "Gypsy."[19] Race was an important, yet not determinant factor within the Ustaša ideology. Moreover, paradigms of social and racial hygiene were not easily applicable in a predominantly rural society such as Croatia. The Ustaša was short of both time and the personnel to convince the population to help advance its racist goals.

Although the Germans persecuted Gypsies in a number of European countries, there is no evidence that the Germans ever tried to directly influence the Ustaša as far as anti-Gypsy policymaking was concerned. The Germans exercised their will indirectly though. In Serbia, the German police and army carried out mass executions of Gypsies. The Croatian government observed closely what was happening in neighboring Serbia, and therefore must have been aware that it became the first country in Europe where "the Jewish and the Gypsy Questions have been solved," as the head of the military administrator of Serbia, Harald Turner, had reported to Berlin.[20] Nevertheless, the claims that the Germans were responsible for the mass murder of Gypsies in the ISC, and that they even deported Gypsies from Croatia to Auschwitz, cannot be substantiated.[21] Unlike German racial scientists, the German men on the ground—the army and the police stationed in the ISC—were not overly concerned with the so-called Gypsy Question. The German ambassador Siegfried Kasche was surprised to learn about the brutality with which the Croatian government treated its Gypsies.[22] The only evidence of German involvement I have discovered so far was the German police attaché in Zagreb prescribing a police informer to keep an eye on the Gypsy minority.[23] In countries such as Romania, Hungary, and Slovakia where retreating German units fought against the advancing Soviet forces during the last phase of the war, those units sometimes assaulted Gypsies on their own accord.[24] No such data exists for Yugoslavia, even though individual instances of murder of Gypsies might have occurred there as well. In any event, the persecution of Gypsies on the territory of the ISC was not German sponsored. It was a mass crime for which the Ustaša regime bears full responsibility.

Ustaša Anti-Gypsy Policies

Neither Nazi racial policies of destruction nor the more traditional prejudices against Gypsies within Croatian society provide a sufficient explanation as to why mass murder of the Gypsies in Croatia occurred in the year 1942. In order to comprehend how the policies of destruction had emerged, I consider the following two questions: why did the Croatian authorities decide to deport Gypsies to concentration camps, and why did the camp administration decide to murder a majority of the Gypsy deportees? While I am able to offer new insights with regard to the first question, more research has to be done to convincingly answer the second.

I argue that the interethnic civil war in the ISC, especially the brutal Ustaša assault on the Serbs, had a radicalizing effect that accelerated the persecution of the Gypsies as well as of the Jews in Croatia. In June 1941 the Ustaša regime reached an understanding with the German government on a policy of population transfer, which foresaw the expulsion of 200,000 Serbs from Croatia to German-occupied Serbia. This population transfer was perceived as a unique opportunity to transform Croatia into an ethnically homogeneous and socially viable nation-state.

The advocates of this policy presented the expulsion as a necessary measure, and rationalized it by referring to the Greek-Turk population exchange carried out in the early 1920s in accordance with the Lausanne Treaty. Expulsion, expropriation, and ethno-social restructuring were understood as an organic part of the nation-building process.[25] The proposed population transfer triggered a certain euphoria among Croatian bureaucrats and planners, who intensified their efforts at designing a nation-state. At this stage, the Croatian government offered increasingly radicalized visions of the nation-state that now encompassed the territorial "solutions of the Jewish and the Gypsy Questions." As we now know from research on the Nazi policies, such visions mark a transition between fantasies of destruction of the Jews and concrete plans for deportation.[26] Even though the arrest and internment of Jews eventually resulted in their extermination, it was the physical removal rather than actual destruction which motivated the original planning efforts.

Similar processes can be identified in the ISC. The large-scale deportation and expulsion of Serbs from Croatia led to a rush of suggestions to expel smaller minorities as well. The option to deport Jews and Gypsies from the country, however, was unavailable in 1941.[27] The German-Croatian agreement on mutual expulsions referred to Serbs solely. None of the neighboring countries was willing to receive deported Jews or Gypsies.[28] In contrast, German authorities sometimes expelled Gypsies to Croatia.[29] To realize the expulsion of Jews and Gypsies, Croatian authorities increasingly started looking for internal "territorial solutions." One option discussed was a Jewish settlement on some islands in the Adriatic Sea where the Jews would work in salt mines or on land amelioration.[30] As for the Gypsies, a governmental office in charge of population transfers within the ISC suggested the restriction on movement and eventual resettlement of Gypsies, without specifying a destination though. Cities such as Križevci proposed resettling their Gypsies to undisclosed areas. Such suggestions customarily entailed exploitation of Gypsy forced labor.[31] A later, even more radical project proposed the creation of a "Jewish reservation" in the vicinity of the Jasenovac concentration camp.[32] This particular proposal makes evident how quickly the transition from resettlement projects to deportations to concentration camps took place. Resettlement plans, however, were not mere propaganda. These plans were publicly discussed, projecting a future Helot-like existence of Jews in specially designated areas within the ISC, where they would be engaged in productive work for the benefit of the Croatian people by mining salt or draining swamps. Accordingly, racial theorists called for the segregation of Gypsies from the Croatian society in order to be able both to control them and to exploit their labor.

The first anti-Gypsy act of the Croatian government was meant to force "nomadic Gypsies" to become sedentary. The creation of forced labor camps was announced, and a newspaper published a photograph of a tent camp set up for Gypsy forced laborers.[33]

Defining the "Gypsy"

The Croatian government was quick at promulgating anti-Gypsy laws. Following acquisition of power, it took the Ustaša regime just twenty days to enact racial laws, which have been frequently depicted in historical literature as a carbon copy of the Nazi Nuremberg Laws.[34] In fact, the Ustaša laws had exceeded the Nuremberg Laws insofar as they defined both Jews and Gypsies as non-Aryan minorities, in contrast to Germany where only Jews were affected by racial laws. In the ISC, persons with three or more Jewish grandparents were regarded as Jews while persons with "two or more grandparents who were members of the Gypsy race" were considered as Gypsies (*Ciganin*). The laws prohibited sexual contact and marriages between "Aryans" and "Non-Aryans," though unlike the Jews, Serbs and Gypsies were not required to wear special badges on their clothes.

The Ministry of the Interior attempted giving its legislation a racial-scientific tone. Thus, the Ministry issued an order that put Gypsies under the neutral category *Indid,* allegedly in order to avoid the pejorative and unscientific connotation of the term *Gypsy.*[35] Despite such semantic nuances, the racial laws remained extremely vague when it came to the definition of Gypsies. Like in the Nuremberg Laws, the grandparent's religion was decisive in the legal definition of a Jew. Such a criterion was altogether missing in the case of Gypsies. The discourse on Gypsies in the ISC remained ambiguous. Some racial scientists claimed that Gypsies could be assimilated once they became sedentary while others called for the total removal of Gypsies. In the end, whether a person was defined as a Gypsy depended on the whim of local bureaucrats. What constituted a "Gypsy"—despite the fact that Gypsies were subject to racial laws—had never been defined, in contrast to a more specific definition of the "Jew." Precisely this vagueness saved many Gypsies' lives.[36]

On 3 July 1941, the Ministry of the Interior instructed local authorities to register the Gypsies and to collect their personal data, including sex, age, and social status. The minister gave an order to expel Gypsies who had migrated to Croatia since the outbreak of World War I. It is unclear, though, to what extent these guidelines had been put into practice.[37] The Croatian government issued a flood of decrees that deprived

Serbs and Jews of basic rights. The extent to which this legal discrimination affected Gypsies, once again, is hard to establish. Otherwise, only in a few cases Gypsies were explicitly mentioned.[38] However, within the following eleven months there had been no further radicalization of the anti-Gypsy campaign. Sometimes, the Ustaša police forced Gypsies to perform labor, mainly grueling physical labor.[39] But unlike in the case of Jews and Serbs, Gypsies were not often assaulted outside the concentration camp territory. The physical destruction of the Gypsies took place almost exclusively within the camp system.[40]

Convinced that the Gypsies were to be excluded from the Croatian nation, the government discussed various options to achieve this goal: forced assimilation, resettlement, or deportation to concentration camps. Plans and initial attempts to "resettle" Jews and Gypsies had failed, however. Islands in the Adriatic Sea could only accommodate a small fraction of deportees, even though the government had continuously advocated for this solution. Gradually, various plans for resettlement and forced labor had escalated into mass murder.[41] The area where Jews and Gypsies would be "settled" had eventually become the Jasenovac concentration camp, and the paradigm of resettlement had transformed into physical destruction. Croatian newspapers were quite clear about that when they called for the "disappearance" or "liquidation" of the Gypsies.[42]

Gypsies and Jews

The Ustaša regarded Jews as a higher priority than Gypsies, who were hardly mentioned in pre-1941 racist pamphlets. At the conceptual level, however, Jews and Gypsies occupied a similar position in the Ustaša ideology—as the fifth column helping the Serbs to weaken Croatia from within. The main difference was that the Jews, according to the Ustaša propaganda, chose consciously to support the Serbs in their attempts to subjugate the Croat people while the Gypsies, wittingly or unwittingly, embodied the Balkan, and thus Serbian order.[43] Consequently, the Ustaša called for the removal of both Jews and Gypsies, yet the process of destruction of the Jews had begun one year before the deportation of the Roma commenced. This fact can be attributed to the home-grown Ustaša anti-Semitism, which became more radical thanks to the German presence. Scholars have not yet been able to establish when exactly the Ustaša leadership began planning a comprehensive deportation of the Gypsies. Apparently, the deportation could not have taken place prior to 1942 due to the limited capacity of the camp system. Mark Biondich has suggested the Ustaša preoccupation with Serbs and Jews, who were perceived as the more dangerous enemy, as a possible reason for the delay of the deportation. The extent of that preoccupation, however, is hard to establish, and therefore I emphasize the Ustaša persecution of the Serbs as a factor that had radicalized their disposition toward other minorities. Lengel-Krizman has contended that the Gypsies had not been deported earlier because of the frozen ground, which would not have permitted the disposal of the corpses in the winter of 1941–42. This, however, is pure speculation, as the author herself has admitted.[44] Such an interpretation suggests an intentionalist presumption that the Ustaša had always wanted to murder the Gypsies of Croatia, just waiting for the opportune moment to do so. This argument cannot be supported by existing evidence of any long-term planning, as well as disregards the probability of Ustaša policies changing and radicalizing over time. If there was indeed a "delay" with the deportation of Gypsies, this had to do with the fact that no consensus on the definition of a "Gypsy" had been reached due to reservations of Bosnian Muslims.

The deportation of the Gypsies in May 1942 overlapped with the preparations to deport Croatian Jews to the Third Reich. A second wave of arrests and deportations targeted Gypsies simultaneously with the mass arrests of Jews prior to their deportation to Auschwitz-Birkenau.[45] Biondich has interpreted this correlation as another probable cause for the timing of the Gypsy deportation. Indeed, the preparation and implementation of the large-scale deportation of Jews might have triggered the deportation of Gypsies in the summer of 1942.[46]

The Case of Muslim Gypsies

In response to the first anti-Gypsy decrees, Muslim officials in Bosnia sometimes intervened on behalf of the Gypsies living within their communities.[47] Emily Balić has suggested that the religious leadership of the Bosnian Muslims "recognized that the racial classification of Roma had broader implications for Muslims in Croatia, [realizing] that if the Ustaša could label some Muslims non-Aryan or non-Croat, nothing would prevent them from reclassifying other Muslims in the future." Thus, by defending the Gypsy members of their community, they aimed at defending the entire community. This remarkable act of solidarity was probably motivated by the growing awareness among Muslims that any assault on Bosnia's fragile multiethnic society would put at risk Muslim Bosnia as a whole.[48]

The policies of the Ustaša aimed at the integration of Bosnia's Muslims into the Croatian nation, and were therefore relatively Muslim friendly. Pavelić's deputy, for example, was one of Bosnia's leading Muslim politicians. The government could not simply ignore the concerns raised by the Muslim elites. Therefore, the Ministry of the Interior established a commission consisting of three Muslim public figures from Bosnia. Their task was to resolve the "questions concerning the racial affiliation of Gypsies with Islamic faith." Ironically, the study of an Austro-Hungarian Jewish anthropologist became the base of the commission's deliberations.[49] The commission attempted to shield Muslim Gypsies from racial persecution. According to the commission's survey, Bosnia's Muslim Gypsies comprised two groups: so-called black Gypsies (*Čergaši*) were regarded as nomadic and traditional in their lifestyle, whereas so-called white Gypsies (*Gurbeti*) were considered sedentary and assimilation prone. The commission stated, "According to scientific evidence, both of the aforementioned branches of Gypsies are considered Aryan belonging to the Indo-European/Indo-Germanic races." The commission concluded by suggesting reemploying all officials who had been previously dismissed as Gypsies, and deleting the names of Muslim Gypsies from the state-run Gypsy lists into which, according to the commission, many Muslims had already been entered, much to the local population's chagrin.[50] A Sarajevo newspaper went even further in its criticism, blaming the government for having forced Muslims to register as non-Aryans. "Although everyone knew that the author was referring to Muslim Roma, the fact that he used the general term 'Muslim' reveals the community's intent to stand together," Emily Balić has interpreted the newspaper's intervention.[51] In conclusion, the commission took up the popular narrative of the division of the Gypsies into "black" and "white" types, claiming that both were of Aryan descent. As the commission consisted solely of Muslim notables, the result of its deliberations was somehow predictable. Not all the recommendations were put into practice. The government tried to avoid a conflict with the Muslim religious communities, while the proposed differentiation between black and white, sedentary and itinerary, Muslim and non-Muslim Gypsies remained unclear. In consequence, such differentiations were not applied consistently. In general, Gypsies who happened to be sedentary as well as Muslim had not been registered.[52] Apparently, this practice was widely accepted among the Ustaša. In 1942, the Croatian Foreign Ministry even intervened on behalf of Muslim Gypsies in Serbia who "were treated like [real] Gypsies" by the German authorities.[53] The German allies tended to accept the distinction between Muslim and non-Muslim Gypsies implemented by the Ustaša. In 1942 German newspapers in Belgrade and Osijek explained somewhat liberally the concept of "white Gypsyness" to its readers, claiming that white Gypsies had proven to be good citizens and brave soldiers within the ranks of the army or the Ustaša.[54] Although neither Muslim nor sedentary Gypsies seem to have been deported from Sarajevo, lists of deportees from other parts of Bosnia contain Muslim names (probably itinerant Gypsies).[55] Having said that, the decrees granting the status of "white Gypsies" imply the precarious status of "black Gypsies," even though the latter group was not explicitly mentioned. Despite that, the Islamic Religious Community continued to intervene on behalf of *all* Muslim Gypsies regardless their social status. Subsequently, the government confirmed that any Gypsy who could prove that he or she was Muslim would be released. Yet as Balić has rightly noted, it is very unlikely that, once deported to a camp, any Gypsy had the possibility of producing such a proof of identity.[56] The vagueness of the regulations posed a constant threat to all Gypsies without exception. Moreover, the government continued persecuting poor Gypsies on nonracial grounds, using decrees against behavior perceived as antisocial by the Ustaša (e.g., begging).[57]

Those concerned with the Gypsy Question were worried that the exclusion of Muslim Gypsies from persecution would be exploited by "real Gypsies." For example, the Ustaša Supervisory Service (UNS) warned that Gypsies might disguise themselves by wearing the traditional Muslim fez.[58] Sometime later, however, Ustaša officials suggested that Muslim Gypsies *should* wear a fez to distinguish themselves from other Gypsies—a meaningless gesture, according to Balić.[59] This anecdote further demonstrates the eagerness with which the Ustaša exposed the minorities who they had perceived as a threat. Those Gypsies who did not wear a fez would become visible, while Muslim Gypsies, by wearing the fez, would fulfill their supposed duty of assimilating into the Muslim society.

Despite the Muslim solidarity with Muslim Gypsies, their overall situation in the ISC was becoming more precarious due to the general increase of ethnic prejudice in times of civil war. This negative sentiment affected in particular smaller minority groups. Not only the Ustaša, but all warring parties committed acts of violence against Gypsies, especially if/when the latter were apprehended wandering about as refugees. Even the procommunist Partisans occasionally executed Gypsies in the belief that they conducted espionage for the Germans.[60] The belligerents leveled mutual accusations of being Gypsy friendly or Gypsy-like. The Serb nationalist Četnici, for instance, accused the Ustaša of being a "Gypsy movement," and identified certain leading Ustaša as "Gypsies" (in other words, Muslim).[61] German soldiers accused Gypsies of bestially torturing and killing captured comrades, thus justifying the persecution of Gypsies.[62]

Mass Deportations

On 16 May 1942, the UNS issued a decree according to which all Gypsies in Croatia were to be transferred to the Jasenovac concentration camp.[63] The Ministry of the Interior instructed the county police chiefs, while the Higher Gendarmerie Command instructed its units to arrest all Gypsies and to hand them over to the district administration. All institutions were asked to cooperate as closely as possible. The Croatian Gendarmerie, sometimes the Army, received orders to escort the deportation transports to Jasenovac.[64]

In connection with the deportations, the debate as to who should be considered a Gypsy had resurfaced. News about the arrests led to repeated interventions on behalf of Gypsy citizens. Many gendarmerie posts were uncertain whom they were supposed to arrest. One gendarme reported that quite a few people in his district were called "Gypsy," but no one knew for sure if they actually were Gypsies. Muslim officials tried to protect local Gypsies by stating that the latter were faithful members of their community who had always voted for Croatian or Muslim nationalist parties, had their own businesses, and owned houses. In short, they tried to counter the most common prejudices about Gypsies.[65] The administration responded by affirming that sedentary Muslim Gypsies "were to be considered Aryan according to a decree of the Poglavnik [the head of state]."[66]

The reports that local gendarmerie and army posts sent back to the Ustaša headquarters reveal an astonishing variety of reactions. Many gendarmes reported that there were no Gypsies on their territory—which sometimes was simply not true.[67] Some authorities effectively ignored the decree. The government apparently did not do much to enforce the laws. This implies that, even though Gypsies were legally stripped of most of their rights by 1941, their everyday life might not be significantly affected by state persecution at least in some localities. Naturally, there are many more examples of Gypsies who had been discriminated against in the local communities. However, the fact that some local authorities displayed no visible interest in the persecution of the Gypsies and therefore ignored governmental decrees raises the question whether the Croatian bureaucracy was at all able to implement its goals.

However, certain latitude in implementation is just one side of the coin. Many police and gendarmerie officers carried out their orders quickly and efficiently, arresting those whom they deemed to be Gypsies and escorting them to the Jasenovac camp. Sometimes army units—or local ethnic German units, for example, in the case of Zemun—assisted in the arrests.⁶⁸ As an army commander succinctly put it: "Finally, it came to a radical solution of the Gypsy question."⁶⁹

A year earlier, in July 1941, the Croatian government had implemented a comprehensive campaign of ethnic cleansing in most districts, in the course of which several tens of thousands of Serbs had been expropriated and subsequently expelled.⁷⁰ This process not only ethnically homogenized many rural communities but also streamlined the mechanisms of expulsion. For example, local police received an order to arrest a group of Serbian villagers. Village councils were put in charge of the houses, crops, and cattle belonging to the arrested Serbs. Their property was then distributed among poor non-Serb villagers or sold at public auctions. This kind of distribution system, which was probably still operational as of spring 1942, might have facilitated the arrest of the Gypsies. Reports from some communities suggest exactly that. In the district of Županja, for example, the belongings of the Gypsies who had been deported to Jasenovac, especially horses and carts, were distributed locally among the needy. The expropriated livestock was sold at public auctions, and the cash went into the communal budget. Houses and gardens of the deportees were to be used by Croatian refugees from other parts of Croatia.⁷¹ This pattern indicates that local officials sometimes used the deportation of Gypsies for the purpose of socially restructuring rural communities.

The deportation of the Gypsies did not significantly differ from the deportation of other groups in the ISC. Locally, gendarmerie, police, or the army herded Gypsies into temporary assembly places such as schools, barns, or public squares. Later, the guards escorted larger groups of Gypsies to the nearest train station. If a train station happened to be farther away, the deportees were habitually brought by busses or army vehicles. From regions close to Jasenovac such as Slavonia, Gypsies had to head toward the camp using their own carts. Thus they arrived in the camp with their horses and their livestock, and sometimes with their show animals such as bears or monkeys.⁷² The insufficient infrastructure might have prevented some of the deportations. Lengel-Krizman has estimated that during the first days of June up to 4,000 Gypsies arrived in the Jasenovac camp, many of them from Zagreb, Zemun, and from western regions such as the Banija. From the Županja district in Slavonia alone some 2,000 Gypsies were deported by three separate trains to the camp.⁷³ The first round of mass arrests was followed by several more in the summer of 1942. Some of these roundups were related to antipartisan operations,⁷⁴ while others to the mass arrests of Jews in the ISC in August 1942.⁷⁵

As a rule, the police did not register Gypsies individually following their arrest. In a few cases, however, the police did issue deportation lists with the names of individuals. Thus, the police in Zagreb sent a list with the names of sixty-nine Gypsies from the Zagreb area to the Jasenovac camp administration.[76] According to the surnames of the deportees, they came mainly from two extended families. The age of the deportees ranged between ten and seventy-eight, which implies that younger children had not been registered. Along with them, the Gypsies brought into the camp twenty-seven carriages, twenty-nine horses, and three cows. Probably, the deportees belonged to an itinerant group that was rounded up by the police and transported to Jasenovac together with all their belongings. If they were sedentary, their livestock would most likely have been distributed within the village community in which they lived.

Upon arrival in Jasenovac, the deportees were registered by Ustaša guards, and their property was confiscated.[77] Without knowing for sure how brutal the actual deportations were, it appears that the Gypsies became the subject of physical violence for the first time following their arrival in the camp. Due to the chaos that ensued following the arrival of groups of deportees from all over Croatia, the guards instantly tried to enforce order by means of violence.

The Dead End: Mass Murder of Gypsies at Jasenovac Camp

By the end of 1942 nearly all of the Gypsies deported to Jasenovac were dead. In order to comprehend the mass murder perpetrated against the Gypsy deportees, it has to be framed within the general, extremely violent history of the Jasenovac camp complex. In the first months of 1942 the situation in the camp aggravated due to a sudden increase in the number of prisoners. At the end of April 1942 Ante Pavelić's headquarters had issued a decree, which proclaimed the Jasenovac camp to be ready to "receive an unlimited number of prisoners."[78] The expanded prisoner capacity of the camp offered new opportunities to the regime. By the time of their deportation in May 1942, Gypsies were by no means the only group locked up in the camp. In July and August, thousands of individuals taken prisoner during a large-scale antipartisan operation conducted by German and Croatian forces in the western part of the ISC ended up at Jasenovac.[79] In September, antipartisan raids in the eastern part of the ISC sent further scores of prisoners into the camp. In August, many of the Jews who had been deported from Croatia to

Auschwitz-Birkenau went through Jasenovac. How the deportations of the summer of 1942 interrelated has yet to be established. One is clear, however: the high levels of violence in Jasenovac facilitated the mass murder of minority groups once they had been deported to the camp.

One reason for the particularly high level of violence against Gypsy inmates was their isolation in a designated section of the camp, which made the Ustaša guards single them out for violent treatment. The first arrivals had to spend some time in a so-called Gypsy camp, which consisted of the village Uštice in the vicinity of the camp whose Serb inhabitants had been previously expelled. Later on, the Gypsy inmates were herded into an unfinished section of the camp designated as IIIC. From the beginning, camp guards subjected the deportees to brutal treatment resulting in cases of manslaughter. As a survivor recollected the situation of Gypsies in the camp, "The Gypsies were in a dead end. The guards perceived them as lowly animals and felt entitled to treat them brutally. No one was ever held responsible."[80] The situation deteriorated dramatically in the course of June, possibly because the number of Gypsy inmates rose to a level that the Ustaša was unable to handle. First mass executions were carried out in the Uštice camp (and this is also where the corpses were buried). At a later point, the victims were transferred to a designated execution site situated in the half-submerged village Gradina on the opposite side of the Sava River. In contrast to the first deportees, the second wave of Gypsy deportees arriving in Jasenovac had to undergo a process of selection upon their arrival. Elderly prisoners were shipped over the Sava to Gradina where they were immediately executed and buried in mass graves prepared beforehand. A small number of Gypsies were deported from Jasenovac to Germany among forced laborers dispatched from the ISC to Nazi Germany.[81] Probably, the fact that they were Gypsies did not play a role, as they were deported alongside Serbian villagers who had been arrested simultaneously. A certain number of prisoners was transferred to the IIIC section of the camp—in fact bare ground behind barbed wire—with the horrendous living conditions that had caused high mortality among the inmates. Only a small proportion of prisoners were used as laborers in brickworks, sawmills, or embankment works at the river. Even though forced labor in Jasenovac was grueling and unsafe, it probably increased the prisoners' chances for survival as compared with slow death in the IIIC section of the camp. Another prisoner group of approximately one hundred was forced to dig mass graves and dispose of bodies in the camp.

Selections and pits prepared beforehand point out that the mass murder of the Gypsy prisoners had been organized from the top. The testimonies of survivors of the Jasenovac camp, most of who were non-Gypsies, lend support to this inference.[82] Otherwise, survivor testimonies are the only available source that provides evidence of mass executions of Gypsies at Jasenovac. Most of the testimonies, however, should be treated with caution. First of all, much of the inmates' information is based on hearsay rather than first-hand accounts. Even though some of the survivors describe the executions as if they were eyewitnesses to a crime, it is rather unlikely that they had been present at the Gradina killing site. Nevertheless, most of them confirm that Gypsy prisoners were beaten to death by guards armed with clubs, sticks, and knives. The painful descriptions of Ustaša cruelty suggest empathy for the victims. Yet, some of the witnesses appear biased against their fellow Gypsy prisoners. Their accounts are filled with exoticisms, depicting the Gypsies as members of a cheerful and naïve tribe that the Ustaša could easily exploit. Anecdotes about Gypsy musicians who played in the camp orchestra further indicate ethnically colored bias.

The divide-and-rule policy introduced by the Ustaša with the purpose of controlling the prisoner population incited prejudice and hatred among the Jasenovac inmates. As a consequence, both Jews and Gypsies were often accused by their fellow prisoners of working on behalf of the Ustaša, heralding the emergence of a particular form of anti-Semitism and anti-Gypsyism in the camps.[83] Due to the limited value of survivor testimonies and the lack of documentary sources, reconstructing the Gypsies' ordeal in the Ustaša camps proves a difficult task. Animus was typically directed against those Gypsies who had been selected for labor in the killing fields (so-called *grobari*). Some former inmates claimed that Ustaša guards made Gypsy prisoners drunk and subsequently forced them to assist in the killings, while others insisted that some Gypsy prisoners displayed sadistic tendencies and thus committed numerous atrocities. There is no doubt, however, that within a few months the Ustaša camp guards had murdered the majority of the Gypsy inmates at Jasenovac.

Gypsy Agency

Research on Gypsy persecution tends to neglect Gypsy agency. This lacuna can be attributed to the lack of documentation—collections of testimonies are rare—on the one hand and a certain romanticizing of Gypsies—the perception that Gypsies as a people organized in clans were incapable of making individual choices that could enhance survival—on the other. The tendency to exoticize Gypsies brought forward notions of illiterate Gypsies incapable of reading written orders, and thus incapable of grasping the threat to their very physical existence. Alas, the archival documentation is full of references to Gypsies pursuing their own interests, even when literally fighting for survival. Below I provide several examples that indicate various forms of Gypsy agency. I emphasize the following factors that had brought about Gypsy agency. The context of war, especially the kind of a brutal civil war that ravaged ex-Yugoslavia, made persecuted groups quickly grasp what the perpetrators were capable of. The civil war offered an option of taking up arms against the Ustaša regime, whereas the ISC's geopolitical position between Nazi Germany and Fascist Italy enabled many potential victims to escape either to Hungary or the Italian zone of occupation. Consequently, Gypsies availed themselves of different options, including writing individual petitions to the government.[84] In one particular case an entire Catholic village of seventy households filed a complaint to have been harassed by the authorities as "Gypsies" and suggested an intervention of a commission of racial experts.[85] Some Gypsies protected themselves by converting to Catholicism or Islam, or by enlisting into the ranks of the Croatian army. Most Gypsies had survived by fleeing to the Partisan or Italian-controlled areas, or in some cases even to Serbia.[86] Some of these Gypsies returned to their home villages after the war.[87] During the May 1942 deportation several Gypsies managed to escape only to be apprehended by the gendarmerie a few days later.[88] Finally, support lent by Gypsies to prisoner uprisings at Jasenovac suggests acts of active resistance.[89] Not least due to these tactics, a part of the Gypsy population of the ISC survived the war.

Conclusion

Beside Antonescu's regime in Romania, the ISC was the only country in wartime Europe that carried out mass murder of Gypsies independently of Nazi Germany.[90] Indeed, the Ustaša committed the mass murder of the so-called nomadic, non-Muslim Gypsies. The question remains open whether the regime simultaneously perpetrated the mass murder of sedentary non-Muslim Gypsies and of itinerant Muslim Gypsies. Leaving aside the figures of the 1931 census, scholars have used the rough estimates of the number of Gypsy victims in order to establish the total percentage of Gypsies killed by the Ustaša. In the end, this percentage is nearly impossible to calculate. Thus, the estimates range between 16,000 and 40,000.[91] Consequently, a comparative approach to study of different victim groups has certain limitations. Claims such as "Ustasha crimes ... against the Roma [were] even crueler and more radical than [those] against the Jews" lack a documentary basis.[92] Having said that, the death rates among the Gypsies deported to the Jasenovac camp were extremely high; the majority of Gypsy deportees had been killed within a few months after their arrival. Further research has yet to establish how an escalation of violence at Jasenovac came about and what motivated the camp guards to partake in the violence targeting specifically Gypsies.

Notes

1. Herbert Hirsch, "Genocide in Yugoslavia," in *Encyclopedia of Genocide,* ed. I. Charny, vol. 2 (Jerusalem, 1999), 634.
2. Christopher Browning, *Fateful Months: Essays on the Emergence of the Final Solution* (New York, 1991), 50f.
3. Cf. Ladislaus Hory and Martin Broszat, *Der kroatische Ustascha-Staat 1941–1945* (Stuttgart, 1964); Fikreta Jelić-Butić, *Ustaše i Nezavisna Država Hrvatska, 1941–1945* (Zagreb, 1977); John Lampe, *Yugoslavia: Twice There Was a Country* (Cambridge, 1996); Jozo Tomasevich, *War and Revolution in Yugoslavia* (Stanford, CA, 2001); Alexander Korb, "A Multipronged Attack: Ustaša Persecution of Serbs, Jews, and Roma in Wartime Croatia, 1941–45," in *Eradicating Differences: The Treatment of Minorities in Nazi-Dominated Europe,* ed. A. Weiss-Wendt (Newcastle, 2010), 145–63.
4. Lengel-Krizman has limited her research to the districts of present-day Croatia, thus leaving out those parts of the ISC that belong to Serbia and Bosnia-Hercegovina. Narcisa Lengel-Krizman, "Prilog proučavanja terora tzv. NDH: Sudbina Roma 1941–1945," *Časopis za Suvremenu Povijest* 18, no. 1 (1986): 29–42; Narcisa Lengel-Krizman, *Genocid nad Romima. Jasenovac 1942* (Zagreb, 2003); Narcisa Lengel-Krizman, "Genocide Carried Out on the Roma: Jasenovac 1942," in *Jasenovac Memorial Site: Catalogue,* ed. the Jasenovac Memorial Area Public Institution, 154–81 (Zagreb, 2006). Cf. Dragoljub Acković, "Suffering of Romas in Yugoslavia in the Second World War," *Gießener Hefte für Tsiganologie* 3, no. 1–4 (1986): 128–34; Mark Biondich, "Persecution of Roma-Sinti in Croatia, 1941–1945," in *Roma and Sinti: Under-Studied Victims of Nazism,* ed. Center for Advanced Holocaust Studies (Washington, DC, 2002); Elizabeta Jevtic, "Blank Pages of the Holocaust: Gypsies in Yugoslavia During World War II" (MA diss., Brigham Young University, 2004). For an older, less comprehensive, overviews see Dennis Reinhartz, "Aryanism in the Independent State of Croatia 1941–1945: The Historical Basis and Cultural Questions," *South Slav Journal* 9, no. 3–4 (1986): 19–25; Dennis Reinhartz, "Damnation of the Outsider: The Gypsies of Croatia and Serbia in the Balkan Holocaust, 1941–1945," in *The Gypsies of Eastern Europe,* ed. D. Crowe and J. Kolsti (Armonk, NY, 1991); Carola Fings et al., ed., *"...Einziges Land, in dem Judenfrage und Zigeunerfrage gelöst." Die Verfolgung der Roma im faschistisch besetzten Jugoslawien 1941–1945* (Cologne, 1992).
5. Tomislav Dulić, "Mass Killing in the Independent State of Croatia, 1941–1945: A Case for Comparative Research," *Journal of Genocide Research* 8, no. 3 (2006): 255–81.
6. *Deutsche Zeitung in Kroatien,* 22 February 1942.
7. Publikationsstelle Wien, ed., *Die Gliederung der Bevölkerung des ehemaligen Jugoslawien nach Muttersprache und Konfession nach den unveröffentlichten Angaben der Zählung von 1931* (Vienna, 1943), 10.

8. "Gypsy question," Commissioner of the Poglavnik in Sarajvo (Prof. Handžić) to MUP, 30 July 1941, reproduced in Lengel-Krizman, *Genocid nad Romima*, 66f.
9. Danijel Vojak, "Romi u popisima stanovništva iz 1921. i 1931. na području Hrvatske," *Migracijske i etničke teme* 20, no. 4 (2004): 447–76, 475; Bernard Gilliat-Smith, "The Dialect of the Gypsies of Serbo-Croatia," *Journal of the Gypsy Lore Society* 27, no. 3 (1948): 139.
10. Gendarmerie post Ostrožac to district administration Konjić, "Evacuation of the Gypsies," 26 May 1942, Military Archives Belgrade (hereafter: AVII), NDH/191, 3/1–1.
11. Ante Pavelić, *Die kroatische Frage* (Berlin, 1941), 28ff. Gypsies, however, were not mentioned in this pamphlet that Pavelić had written already in 1936 with the purpose of gaining Hitler's attention.
12. Poglavnik, "Možemo i tamo!," *Ustaša*, April 1934, quoted in Rory Yeomans, "Cults of Death and Fantasies of Annihilation: The Croatian Ustasha Movement in Power, 1941–45," *Central Europe* 3, no. 2 (2005): 122; see also *Hrvatska Krajina*, 30 May 1941, quoted in Tomislav Dulić, *Utopias of Nation: Local Killing in Bosnia and Herzegovina, 1941–42* (Uppsala, 2005), 219.
13. *Hrvatski Narod*, 29 August 1941, quoted in *Kroatische Presseauszüge* (Vienna), 27 September 1941.
14. Arzen Pozaić, "Srpsko Pitanje: Odakle toliki 'Srbi' u Hrvatskoj?" *Novi List*, 24 June 1941; Hermann Ginzel, *Kroatien Heute* (Zagreb, 1942), 12f.; Theodor Uzinorac, "Das Problem der Balkannomaden," in *Kroatien baut auf. Jahreslese in Wort und Bild aus der Wochenschrift "Neue Ordnung,"* ed. Neue Ordnung, vol. 2 (Zagreb, 1943), 15–20.
15. *Hrvatska Gruda*, 1 November 1941.
16. Second Croatian Army assembly to Ministry of Defense, 2 June 1942, reproduced in Antun Miletić, ed., *Koncentracioni logor Jasenovac 1941–1945, Knjiga I* (Belgrade, 1986), 294f.
17. *Donauzeitung* (Belgrade), 21 August 1942; *Grenzwacht* (Osijek), 4 September 1942. For racial-scientific literature see Gustav Küppers-Sonnenberg, "Begegnung mit Balkanzigeunern," *Volk und Rasse* 6 (1938): 183–93; Angelo Martini, "Einiges über die Seuchenlage in Südosteuropa," *Leipziger Vierteljahrsschrift für Südosteuropa* 2 (1938): 102–18; Hermann Proebst, "Die Krise des Serbentums," *Neue Ordnung*, 13 July 1941; Fritz Ruland, "Die Zigeunerfrage im Südosten," *Volkstum im Südosten*. *Volkstumspolitische Monatsschrift* 18, no. 10 (1942): 163–69; Erich Stengel, "Aus der Einsatzarbeit der Thüringer Lehrergruppe in Kroatien. Rassische und völkische Streiflichter aus Kroatien," *Mitteilungsblatt des NSLB. Gauwaltung Thüringen* 3/4 (1942); Ctibor Pokorný, "Zigeunerromantik im Verschwinden," *Slowakische Rundschau. Zeitschrift für Politik, Wirtschaft und Kultur* 3, no. 1–2 (1942), *Illustrierte Beilage*. Cf. Sevasti Trubeta, "'Gypsiness,' Racial Discourse and Persecution: Balkan Roma during the Second World War," *Nationalities Papers* 31, no. 4 (2003): 495–514.
18. *Nova Hrvatska*, June 3 1942. I am grateful to Rory Yeomans for pointing out this article to me.
19. Rory Yeomans, "Of 'Yugoslav Barbarians' and Croatian Gentlemen Scholars: Nationalist Ideology and Racial Anthropology in Interwar Yugoslavia," in *Blood and Homeland: Eugenics and Racial Nationalism in Central and Southeastern Europe, 1900–1940*, ed. M. Turda and P. Weindling (Budapest, 2006), 83–122.
20. Raul Hilberg, *The Destruction of the European Jews* (Chicago, 1961), 474.
21. David Crowe, *A History of the Gypsies of Eastern Europe and Russia* (New York, 1994), 220; Dennis Reinhartz, "Unmarked Graves: The Destruction of the Yugoslav Roma in the Balkan Holocaust, 1941–1945," *Journal of Genocide Research* 1, no. 1 (1999): 86; Jevtic, *Blank Pages of the Holocaust*, 78; Lisa M. Adeli, *From Jasenovac*

to Yugoslavism: Ethnic Persecution in Croatia during World War II (PhD diss., University of Arizona, 2004), 78; Nevenko Bartulin, *The Ideology of Nation and Race: The Croatian Ustasha Regime and Its Policies Toward Minorities in the Independent State of Croatia, 1941-45* (PhD diss., University of New South Wales, 2006), 10f; Lengel-Krizman claims that the Germans had pressured for the deportation of Gypsies to Jasenovac and their subsequent murder (Lengel-Krizman, "Prilog proučavanja terora tzv," 33). Ljubo Boban quotes contemporary accounts, according to which the deportation of Gypsies had been launched upon German requests (Boban, ed., *Hrvatska u arhivima izbjegličke vlade 1941–1943: izvještaji informatora o prilikama u Hrvatskoj* (Zagreb, 1985). For accounts that emphasize the radicalizing German influence, but do not go as far as to claim that the Germans had ordered the annihilation of the Gypsies see Irina Ognyanova, "Nationalism and National Policy in Independent State of Croatia (1941–1945)," *Topics in Feminism, History and Philosophy*, IWM Junior Visiting Fellows Conferences, vol. 6, ed. Dorothy Rogers, Joshua Wheeler, Marína Zavacká, and Shawna Casebier (Vienna, 2000), 20f; Marko Hoare, *Genocide and Resistance in Hitler's Bosnia: The Partisans and the Chetniks, 1941–1943* (Oxford, 2006); Ivo and Slavko Goldstein, *Holokaust u Zagrebu* (Zagreb, 2001); Emily Balić, "A City Apart: Sarajevo in the Second World War" (PhD diss., Stanford University, 2008).

22. Kasche to German Foreign Office, 3 May 1941, National Archives and Records Administration (hereafter: NARA), T-120/5782.
23. Lists of agents, Croatian State Archives (hereafter: HDA), Hans Helm 1/1521.
24. Michael Zimmermann, *Rassenutopie und Genozid. Die nationalsozialistische "Lösung der Zigeunerfrage"* (Hamburg, 1996), 290.
25. Alexander Korb, "La Construction nationale et Shoah: Les déportations dans l'État indépendant Croatie (1941–1945)," in *Qu'est-ce qu'un déporté? Histoire et mémoires des déportations de la Seconde Guerre Mondiale*, ed. T. Bruttmann et al. (Paris, 2009), 197–224.
26. For the so-called Madagascar plan see Christopher R. Browning, *The Origins of the Final Solution: The Evolution of Nazi Jewish Policy, September 1939–March 1942* (Lincoln, NE, 2004).
27. Some Gypsies might have been expelled to Serbia in accordance with the Croatian-German agreement on mutual expulsion of 26 June 1941. However, the evidence regarding Gypsies is unavailable (Biondich, "Persecution of Roma," 35), while the evidence exists in the case of just one Jew (Tone Ferenc, ed., *Quellen zur Nationalsozialistischen Entnationalisierungspolitik in Slowenien 1941–1945* [Maribor, 1980], 266f.). Individual Jews and Gypsies might have fled from the ISC to Serbia.
28. Yet some Jews and Gypsies had escaped to the Italian zone of occupation. See Jonathan Steinberg, *All or Nothing: The Axis and the Holocaust, 1941–1943* (London, 1990), 52ff.
29. Decree issued by the German Commissioner of the Krainburg district, 10 May 1941, printed in Ferenc, *Quellen*, 96.
30. *Neue Zürcher Zeitung*, 8 July 1941; *Neue Ordnung*, 13 July 1941.
31. Slobodan Milošević, *Izbeglice i preseljenici na teritoriji okupirane Jugoslavije 1941–1945. godine* (Belgrade, 1982), 240; Biondich, "Persecution of Roma," 43. In the case of Križevci, the resettlement would have affected 450 Gypsies.
32. Goldstein and Goldstein, *Holokaust*, 310.
33. *Novi List*, 23 June 1941; see also Uzinorac, "Das Problem der Balkannomaden," 15–20.
34. Državno Vieće, ed., *Zbornik zakona i naredaba Nezavisne Države Hrvatske*, vol. 1 (Zagreb, 1941): 1941.
35. *Novi List*, 7 June 1941.

36. Balić has emphasized this tendency in her case study of Sarajevo (*A City Apart*, 139f).
37. Ministry of the Interior to Croatian counties, 3 July 1941, Historical Museum of Bosnia and Hercegovina, NDH/1941, 1312; two weeks later, the Zagreb Police issued decree no. 13–542, according to which all Gypsies residing in the city had to register (*Deutsche Zeitung in Kroatien*, 19 July 1941); for further details see endnote 27.
38. On 10 December 1941, the postal bank accounts belonging to the Serbs, Jews, and Gypsies were confiscated. Postal Savings Bank, decree, United States Holocaust Memorial Museum (hereafter: USHMM), 1998.A.0027/1.
39. Report of the Third Military Assembly (Sarajevo) to Army Command, 13 June 1942, reproduced in Vojnoistorijski Institut, ed., *Borbe u Bosni i Hercegovini 1942. Zbornik dokumenata i podataka o narodnooslobodilačkom ratu jugoslovenskih naroda IV*, vol. 5 (Belgrade, 1953): no. 163.
40. Regardless what scholars such as Hilberg have claimed, only few instances of physical assault against Gypsies had been registered. For instance, in February 1943 a Gypsy was shot during a house search in the Syrmian village of Grk (Gendarmerie report from Vukovar, 25 February 1943, NARA, T-120/5802, fr. H313562, as quoted by Hilberg, *Destruction*, 711f).
41. An interview with the Ustaša chief of police published in the summer of 1942 makes this obvious. Long after the physical destruction had begun, he was still referring to resettlement and productive work as the core elements of Ustaša anti-Jewish policies, see Eugen Kvaternik, "Staatssekretär Kwaternik über die Entjudung Kroatiens," *Die Judenfrage* 6, no. 10 (1942): 97.
42. *Hrvatski Narod*, 14 June 1941; Jelić-Butić, *Ustaše i NDH*, 181.
43. *Hrvatski Narod*, 29 August 1941; Mladen Lorković, "Die Ustaschabewegung," *Volk im Osten. Die Zeitschrift des Südostens* 3, no. 4 (1942): 7.
44. Lengel-Krizman, "Genocide," 162f.
45. County police Nova Gradiška to county police Požega, 28 August 1942, Yad Vashem Archives (hereafter: YVA), M.70/47.
46. Biondich, "Persecution of Roma," 35f.
47. Governmental Commission for Sarajevo to MUP, 30 July 1941, printed in Lengel-Krizman, *Genocid nad Romima*, 68f.
48. Balić, *A City Apart*, 139.
49. Leopold Glück, "Zur physischen Anthropologie der Zigeuner in Bosnien und der Herzegovina. 1. Die mohammedanischen Zigeuner," *Wissenschaftliche Mitteilungen aus Bosnien und der Hercegovina* (1897): 403–33.
50. "Gypsy Question," Poglavnik's commissioner in Sarajvo, Prof. Handžić, to Ministry of the Interior, 30 July 1941, printed in Lengel-Krizman, *Genocid nad Romima*, 68f.
51. *Sarajevski Novi List*, 3 August 1941, quoted in Balić, *A City Apart*, 140.
52. "White Gypsies: Racial affiliation," Ministry of the Interior to Derventa district, 30 August 1941, HDA, 223/104, O.S. 32661/41.
53. Croatian Foreign Ministry to German Legation Zagreb, 19 June 1941, German Foreign Office Archives, Embassy Belgrade/62.
54. *Donauzeitung* (Belgrade), 21 August 1942; the same article previously appeared in *Grenzwacht* (Osijek), 4 September 1942.
55. UNS to County Police Sarajevo, 9 June 1942, AVII, NDH, 183/3/2.
56. Balić, *A City Apart*, 141.
57. Ibid., 140f.
58. UNS to County Police Sarajevo, 9 June 1942, AVII, NDH, 183/3/2.
59. *Sarajevski Novi List*, August 26 1942, quoted in Balić, *A City Apart*, 141.
60. Rajko Đurić, *Ohne Heim—Ohne Grab. Die Geschichte der Roma und Sinti* (Berlin, 1996), 284.

61. Četnik detachment Kočić to district Varcar Vakuf, 13 August 1942, USHMM, 1998. A.0028/3.
62. Franz Schönhuber, *Ich war dabei* (München, 1988), 88.
63. Nevertheless, four hundred Gypsies had apparently been deported to the Danica concentration camp in northern Croatia, where a part of them were executed (Zdravko Dizdar, "Ljudski gubici logora 'Danica' kraj Koprivnice 1941.-1942," *Časopis za Suvremenu Povijest* 34, no. 2 (2002): 64).
64. "Gypsy evacuation," UNS, decree nr. 24789, 19 May 1942, AVII, NDH/150a, 4/43; Higher Gendarmerie Command to the Gendarmerie regiments 1–6, 19 May 1942, AVII, NDH/145, 38/10–1.
65. "Evacuation of the Gypsies," gendarmerie post Ostrožac to district administration Konjić, 26 May 1942, AVII, NDH/191, 3/1–1.
66. Chief of Hum county, 2 June 1942, AVII, NDH/191, 3/1–1.
67. Dizdar gives an example from the Koprivnica district, where the local gendarme refused to collect data on the local Gypsies and thus "saved them form their certain death, since they remained in their houses and survived the war," Dizdar, "Ljudski gubici logora 'Danica'," 60.
68. *Vjesnik*, 23 April 1986.
69. Second Croatian Army Assembly to Higher Gendarmerie Command, 15 June 1942, USHMM, RG-49.003/1.
70. Korb, "La Construction nationale et Shoah," 206ff.
71. District Županja to district police, 5 June 1942, printed in Miletić, *Koncentracioni logor Jasenovac*, 299.
72. For various types of deportations see Miletić, *Koncentracioni logor Jasenovac*, 291f.; for Gypsies arriving with their animals in the Concentration Camp see Dulić, *Utopias of Nation*, 270.
73. District Županja to District Police, 5 June 1942, printed in Miletić, *Koncentracioni logor Jasenovac*, 299.
74. Report by the American Joint Distribution Committee, Belgrade, 13 March 1946, YVA, O.10/3-1-8; committee of inquiry Sremska Mitrovica, 2 April 1945, Yugoslav Archives (hereafter: AJ), 110/683.
75. "Arrest of Jews and Gypsies," County police Nova Gradiška to district police Požega, 29 August 1942, USHMM, 1999.A.0173/2; Prnjavor district to county police Nova Gradiška, 31 August 1942, Historical Museum of Bosnia and Herzegovina, UNS/1942.
76. City Police Zagreb, Criminal department to Jasenovac camp administration, 28 May 1942, reproduced in Miletić, *Koncentracioni logor Jasenovac*, 291.
77. Lengel-Krizman, *Genocid nad Romima*, 45f.
78. Poglavik's Headquarters to the Croatian Army, gendarmerie, the Ministry of the Interior, and Ustaša militias, 27 April 1942, reproduced in Miletić, *Koncentracioni logor Jasenovac*, 269f. The decree referred to communist prisoners.
79. Mirko Peršen, *Ustaški logori* (Zagreb, 1966), 159f.
80. Milko Riffer, *Grad mrtvih. Jasenovac 1943* (Zagreb, 1946): 128.
81. Lengel-Krizman, "Genocide," 168.
82. The following testimonies refer to the mass murder of Gypsies at Jasenovac: Milan Radosavljević, District Court, 10 March 1952, USHMM/1998.A.0028/4; Rade Đorđević, 26 February 1952, USHMM/1998.A.0028/1; Mahajlo Solak, county court Zagreb, 25 June 1951, USHMM/1998.A.0028/1; Miroslav Meduk, county court, 11 April 1956, USHMM/1998.A.0028/1; Dr. Josip Riboli, Croatian state commission, 28 May 1945, AJ, Fond, 110/292; interview with Miloš Despot, USHMM, Tobi Herr Collection, RG-50.468. For published memories see Riffer, *Grad mrtvih*; Nikola Nikolić,

Jasenovački logor smrti (Sarajevo, 1975). See also Rajko Đurić, "Il calvario dei Roma nel campo di concentramente di Jasenovac," *Lacio Drom* 4 (1992): 14–42.

83. Tomislav Dulić, "Mapping Out the 'Wasteland': Testimonies From the Serbian Commissariat for Refugees in the Service of Tudjman's Revisionism," *Holocaust and Genocide Studies* 23, no. 2 (2009): 263–84.
84. MUP to Ravsigur, Jewish Section, 12 June 1942, USHMM, 1998.A.0019/7.
85. Ivan Ivanović (Pitomača) to MUP, 11 August 1941, as quoted in Lengel-Krizman, *Genocid nad Romima*, 70f.
86. Some even considered joining the Četnici (Jevtic, *Blank Pages of the Holocaust*, 71–72).
87. Committee of inquiry Sremska Mitrovica, 2 April 1945, AJ, 110/683.
88. District Županja to district police, 5 June 1942, reproduced in Miletić, *Koncentracioni logor Jasenovac*, 299.
89. Legal commission in Croatia, testimony of Mihailo Petrović, 3 December 1945, AJ, 110/292.
90. For Romania see Radu Ioanid, *The Holocaust in Romania: The Destruction of Jews and Gypsies Under the Antonescu Regime, 1940–1944* (Chicago, 2000); for Hungary see László Karsai, "Zentrale Aspekte des Völkermordes an den ungarischen Roma," in *Ungarn und der Holocaust: Kollaboration, Rettung und Trauma*, ed. B. Mihok (Berlin, 2005), 103–14.
91. Vladimir Žerjavić, *Population Losses in Yugoslavia, 1941–1945* (Zagreb, 1997), 135f; Dulić, "Mass Killing," 273.
92. Goldstein and Goldstein, *Holokaust*, 595.

CHAPTER 4

ETHNIC CLEANSING OR "CRIME PREVENTION"?
DEPORTATION OF ROMANIAN ROMA

Vladimir Solonari

Deportation of Romanian Roma to Transnistria has only recently become a subject of academic research, pioneered by two Romanian historians, Dumitru Șandru and Viorel Achim.[1] The issue of deportation is sometimes included in the monographs that deal with the persecution of Jews by the Romanian authorities during World War II.[2] Among the recently published collections of primary sources, one edited by Achim is especially well executed.[3]

The authors mentioned above hold similar views on the origins of the Romanian anti-Roma policy, its aims and scope, as well as on the reactions of the Romanian population to that policy. These views can be summarized as follows. Unlike Jews, who had constantly been the object of vicious attacks of the anti-Semitic press and right-wing nationalists during the interwar period, the Roma minority occupied little space in political discourse and had not been on the receiving end of systematic, xenophobic propaganda. Thus, the decision of the Romanian dictator Ion Antonescu of May 1942 to start deporting Roma immediately came as a surprise to his underlings, as well as to the Romanian society as a whole. According to Achim, "the policy adopted with regard to the Roma was in the complete sense of the word the creation of Ion Antonescu."[4] In fulfillment of Antonescu's order, approximately twenty thousand Roma were deported to Transnistria.[5] However, the deportation turned out to have been unpopular in Romanian society: several influential Romanians, including the Queen Mother Elena, protested against it, while individual ethnic Romanians petitioned the authorities to exempt their friends and neighbors who were slated (or were believed to have been slated) for deportation. The Army protested the deportation of Roma families whose heads were concurrently deployed at the front. Due to these protests, in mid-October 1942 the deportations were terminated, and some Roma soldiers succeeded in getting their families back to Romania before the end of hostilities.

According to Achim, the deportation should be seen as an element of social policy, effectively a crime-prevention act. Although Achim admits that anti-Roma action reflected Antonescu's intentions to carry out wholesale "ethnic purification" of Romania, he insists nonetheless that the deportation should rather be viewed as part and parcel of a policy aimed at securing domestic order by authoritarian means. Along with Roma, the victims of the "ethnic purification" policy included Legionaries (i.e., members of the fascist Iron Guard party, outlawed in January 1941), Jews, religious minorities, vagabonds, beggars, prostitutes, labor duty dodgers, and others. This is why the Romanian government deported only a fraction of Roma, specifically those whom it had considered a danger to public order. At the end of the day, Antonescu's intentions to carry out wholesale "ethnic purification" remained purely declaratory, never entering the stage of practical implementation. Although nearly half of the deported Roma perished in Transnistria, this was a result of local Transnistrian authorities' incompetence rather than the original intention of the Bucharest government (unlike in the case of the deported Jews, a substantial part of whom were murdered in Transnistria).[6] Consequently, according to Achim, it is fallacious to compare Nazi and Romanian policy toward Roma, for in Germany anti-Roma policy stemmed from racial theory and was carried out consistently and relentlessly.[7]

As I demonstrate below, most of these assertions do not withstand critical scrutiny and therefore must be revisited. This chapter extensively uses primary sources, both new and previously published.[8] Most of the archival sources come from the National Historical Archives in Bucharest and National Archive of the Republic of Moldova in Chișinău. The bulk of the material is available as microfilm copies at the Holocaust Memorial Museum in Washington, DC, though some of the documents I consulted at the National Historical Archives in Bucharest. Among the published sources the most important are the collections of documents from the Romanian archives mentioned above. In addition, I used various publications on the "Roma problem" printed in Romania before and during the war, as well as individual stories of Roma survival that appeared in the anthologies by Lucian Nastasă and Andrea Varga. Finally, I extensively used the records of the sittings of the Council of Ministers from Antonescu era, along with the postwar interrogation records of Antonescu and other state and army officials.[9] This chapter examines the Romanian government's policy toward Roma, focusing on the role of government experts and mid-level officials, in particular gendarme officers, in devising and carrying out that policy. Roma's responses to the persecution are highlighted only insofar as they help to elucidate this subject.[10]

"The Roma Problem" in 1930s and early 1940s Romania

Although anti-Roma discourse in interwar Romania never reached the level of intensity of anti-Semitic propaganda, anti-Roma stereotypes were omnipresent within Romanian society. These stereotypes had deep roots in Romanian history as they fulfilled an important function in Romanian political culture. As Shannon Woodcock has persuasively argued, the conviction that Roma were second- or third-rate people, or even not human at all, had been a point of consensus in Romanian high and popular culture alike. From the time of their arrival in the territory of what is now Romania, probably in the thirteenth century, and until their emancipation in the mid-nineteenth century, all Romanian Roma were slaves owned by the state, individual noble landowners known as *boiers,* or by the monasteries. The thesis of the "second-rate quality" or "subhumanity" of Roma was meant both to justify and to naturalize their lower status. Even Romanian peasants, who themselves were in bondage to *boiers,* were convinced that, as popular proverbs would have it, "Roma is not human" and that even though "Roma [might] have money, he has no honor."[11]

The emancipation of Roma did not result in their integration into Romanian society. A great majority of Roma continued to subsist in such traditional and low-paying occupations as producing wooden wares, performing music at wedding ceremonies and other festive occasions, hawking, fortune-telling, or working for pay as temporary helpers in peasant households. Indeed, the majority of Roma were at the very bottom of Romanian society and composed its most destitute and despised stratum. It was psychologically important for Romanian peasants—who, until their emancipation simultaneously with Gyspies, and despite their bondage to *boiers,* had never been slaves—to feel different from the Roma, a condition that is sometimes referred to as "anxiety of proximity." This explains the popularity of proverbs and sayings in which such difference was articulated and objectified.[12]

Furthermore, this kind of anxiety was characteristic not only of Romanian peasants, who stood just one step above Roma on the social ladder. As Romanian historian Sorin Mitu has demonstrated, such anxiety was widely felt by the upper strata of Romanian society (Mitu has studied the formation of Romanian national consciousness in eighteenth-century Transylvania, as articulated by the local Romanian intellectuals in opposition to the anti-Romanian rhetoric of the dominant Hungarian and German upper classes). Intellectuals in particular were upset by the fact that Western observers had consistently perceived Romanians as a "backward" and "barbaric" people. Against that backdrop, Roma performed the role of a foil, since it was only with respect to them that Romanians could be secure about their superiority. The problem was, however, that Western travelers passing through the Romanian lands saw little difference between Romanian peasants and Roma, or, even worse, they sometimes referred to Romanian lands as "Roma country." The fear of being identified with Roma found its way into the classic epic of Transylvanian poet Ion Budai-Deleanu called *Gypsiad* (*Ţiganiada*) (1800–1812), which portrayed Romanian society (with all its negative features, as seen by the Enlightenment-era reformers) as a Roma caravan. This burlesque was meant to suggest that if Romanians were unable to understand how low they had fallen and to consequently change their ways, they would become veritable Roma. The humiliating comparison was intended to underscore the urgent need for reform.[13]

Falling back on Mitu's analysis, Woodcock has gone one step further, arguing that for all Romanians from the moment they acquired national self-awareness and until the present time, Roma appear as *the* significant Other, in opposition to whom they articulate their national identity. In other words, Romanians are everything that Roma are not, and therefore it is vitally important for the former to keep a symbolic distance from the latter.[14]

One does not need to agree with every one of Woodcock's claims to recognize that the low intensity of the discourse on the "Roma problem" in interwar Romania's printed media did not automatically mean that Roma were not under threat. As the most marginalized, culturally and socially isolated minority, shunned not only by those at the top but also by those at the bottom of Romanian society, Roma found themselves in the danger zone, especially due to growing nationalist and xenophobic tendencies in 1930s Romania. Besides, there were influential and vociferous groups in interwar Romania that propagated vicious anti-Roma ideas.

One such group was Romanian eugenicists, in particular members of the Iuliu Moldovan school from the Transylvanian city of Cluj. The leader of the school, Dr. Iuliu Moldovan, who had received his doctorate from the University of Vienna, and his closest associates, some of whom were also educated in German and Austrian universities and later continued their graduate studies in the United States, were proponents of Mendelism, that is, hereditary eugenics. Unlike their opponents, followers of Jean-Baptiste Lamarck, who emphasized the importance of natural environment and social conditions for the formation of character traits of individuals and social groups, Mendelian eugenicists believed that inherited qualities predetermined the biological and social worth of an individual; consequently, they tended to advocate such drastic "population policies" as forced sterilization of the hereditarily and mentally ill. Such ideas gained currency in interwar Europe and America, partially as a result of a growing concern over the rising costs of welfare at a time of economic and fiscal difficulties.[15] Although eugenicist influences in Romania were not confined to the Moldovan school, the latter was the most stable, best funded (including by the Rockefeller Foundation), and one of the most radical groups.[16]

Between 1927 and 1930, and again in 1934–1947, Moldovan edited the *Bulletin of Eugenics and Biopolitics* (*Buletin eugenic şi biopolitic*), the scholarly journal in which he and his followers advanced their ideas. Without entering into a detailed analysis of these publications, it is enough to mention that they testify to the considerable radicalization, by the late 1930s and especially in the early 1940s, of the school's views on the issues of forced sterilization, dysgenics, and racial hygiene. Racial hygiene, in particular, which was inconspicuous in the school's 1920s publications, became its priority by the late 1930s. The journal enthusiastically publicized racial hygiene practices in Nazi Germany, apparently viewing them as a model for Romania. The authors were particularly concerned about mixed marriages between ethnic Romanians and members of what they called "inferior" ethnic groups, in the first place Roma, who were seen as the most dangerous. Two prominent members of the school, Iordache Făcăoaru and Petru Râmneanţu, were evidently obsessed with the "Roma problem." To cite just one example, in the fall of 1938 Făcăoaru published an article under the telling title "Ethnic and Racial Mixing in Romania," in which he assailed the policy of assimilation of ethnic minorities in Romania, especially those deemed "biologically inferior" to ethnic Romanians. Among the latter, Făcăoaru named Turks, Tatars, Russians, Ukrainians (those two Slavic peoples, according to him, had too much "Mongol blood" in their veins), and specifically Roma. These minorities were biological "dead weight" and as such represented a "mortal threat" to the Romanian nation (called in this and similar contexts *neam*—a term that has strong biological connotations since it also means blood relationship). Further threat was attributed to "bastards" resulting from Roma interbreeding with ethnic Romanians who allegedly undermined the "average biological worth" of the Romanian nation. This is why the policy of assimilation had to be supplanted by a policy of segregation, concluded Făcăoaru. Although he never explicitly stated it, Făcăoaru implied that "biologically inferior" minorities were to be removed from Romania.[17]

In 1941, Iordache Făcăoaru's brother Gheorghe (a lawyer from the city of Craiova) published a brochure in which he exposed similar views but—unlike Iordache Făcăoaru and Petru Râmneanțu, who refrained from explaining what exactly had to be done with Roma and other "racially inferiors"—he also proposed an action plan with regard to "the Roma problem."[18] According to him, itinerant Roma had to be interned in concentration camps and subjected to forced labor, so that they "would die within the lifespan of one generation." Sedentary Roma had to be forcibly sterilized, so that their position in the national economy could be taken over by the "best representatives of the Romanian nation."[19] Finally, in 1943 Râmneanțu argued for the necessity to subject "[ethnically] foreign families and communities, especially Roma, to segregation."[20]

It is difficult to gauge the influence of the eugenicist propaganda in general, and with regard to "the Roma problem" in particular, on the Romanian society as a whole. Nevertheless, it can be argued with certainty that their views were known and shared by the Romanian wartime dictator, General (and from August 1941 Marshal) Ion Antonescu.[21] Their views were conveyed to Antonescu mainly through Dr. Sabin Manuilă, chief Romanian statistician and director of the Central Institute of Statistics.

Experts, Bureaucrats, and Roma

Like his mentor, Iuliu Moldovan, Manuilă was trained as a physician, and in 1925/26 he studied at the School of Hygiene and Public Health at Johns Hopkins University in the United States. He was one of a few recipients of the Rockefeller Foundation's scholarship for Eastern Europe, which he received in all likelihood upon suggestion of Moldovan. Among the courses that he took at Johns Hopkins University were biostatistics and biometrics. Shortly after he returned to Romania, Manuilă changed his residence from Cluj to Bucharest where he assumed a position in the government statistics department. In 1930 he was put in charge of the first (and the last) general population census carried out in Greater Romania.[22] From that date onward and until his defection to the United States from communist Romania in 1948, Manuilă served as the chief Romanian statistician. Manuilă's career reached its peak under Antonescu, who absolutely trusted his expertise. On 1 June 1941, the Conducător issued a decree forbidding all other state bodies to carry out statistical research without receiving a prior clearance from the Central Statistics Institute headed by Manuilă.[23]

Under Antonescu, Manuilă was not only the chief statistician but also the Conducător's most trusted adviser on demography and "population policies." Population policies were meant to improve the "biology" of the Romanian *neam* by means of increased birthrates, especially among the elites, prevention of sexually transmitted diseases, and sterilization of the people with disabilities. As in the case of Romanian eugenicists from the Cluj school, Manuilă's ideas became more radical in the late 1930s and early 1940s. While in the 1920s and early 1930s he had taken a relatively moderate position on "ethnic homogenization" and "biological improvement" of the Romanian nation, following the Nazi occupation of France in the summer of 1940 he became an enthusiastic supporter of negative eugenics that had been practiced in the Third Reich and that he now wanted to introduce in Romania.[24]

Antonescu wholeheartedly welcomed Manuilă's advice. On 23 May 1941, the Conducător put the following note in resolution on Manuilă's position paper on population policy: "The principal problem of the nation [*neam*] is ... race—its salvation, consolidation, development, homogenization and geographical distribution [*gruparea*]."[25] Remarkably, one of the main ideas developed in this position paper was that of the "Roma menace," and its biological aspects in particular. Manuilă identified it as "the greatest racial problem of Romania." According to him, Roma constituted "the most numerous ethnic group after Romanians, and at the same time they [were] the dysgenic and promiscuous element in our country. [Until that time] nothing [had] been done to resolve the Roma problem."[26] Like Iordache Făcăoaru, Manuilă was convinced that there were many more Roma in Romania than the 1930 census had counted, since at that time respondents had the liberty to choose their ethnicity at will. He believed that many Roma concealed their "true" identity and that the number 262,501 registered in the census had to be revised upward. However, he did not provide any guesses as to the actual number of Roma, suggesting to wait until after the data of the 1940 census had been processed (this work would never be completed).[27] Significantly, it was Manuilă's Central Statistics Institute that in 1940 published a major monograph on Roma by Romanian ethnographer Ion Chelcea, in which he advanced recommendations nearly identical to those previously formulated by Gheorghe Făcăoaru.[28]

Beside the voices of eugenicists and other specialists on "population policies" who demanded the most resolute and tough action against the "Roma menace," the Conducător listened also to other experts, who made similar recommendations, except that they advanced different arguments in favor of such a policy. For example, in early 1941 an expert in the Ministry of Labor, Health, and Social Welfare, N[icolae?] Cădere, wrote a memorandum on the causes of the spread of typhus in southern Bukovina and northern Moldova provinces. In his memorandum, Cădere referred to Roma settlements (i.e., villages entirely or partially inhabited by Roma) as hotspots of typhus due to extreme poverty and the antihygienic conditions in which Roma were accustomed to live. Many Roma only stayed in their homes during the winter time, and with the advent of spring they travelled through the nearby towns and villages looking for work, thus spreading the disease. Cădere recommended forcibly resettling those Roma in labor camps, subsequently dividing them into three categories, with different policies applied to each. The first category was those who had proclivity for farm work; they had to be settled on arable land. Those who proved capable of achieving success in other fields of economic activity constituted the second category; they had to be "guided" into those economic spheres in which they showed sufficient skills for success (Cădere failed to explain how exactly this "guidance" could be exercised). The third category was comprised of those who were incapable of performing labor. With respect to those individuals, Cădere suggested that a "daring solution [that] would liberate society from this useless and even intolerable ballast" had to be found.[29]

There is no way of knowing whether Antonescu got to read Cădere's report in the spring of 1941, yet in the fall of the same year its text did receive the dictator's attention.[30] This was due to the initiative of the secretary general of the Antonescu's office, Ovidiu Vlădescu, who in October 1941 forwarded a summary of the report to the Interior Ministry. Vlădescu requested the minister's opinion on the potential deportation of Roma across the Dniester River into Transnistria. He suggested deporting not only those categories of Roma outlined by Cădere, but "also the rest of Roma, since they constitute in their majority a permanent threat to the public health, and from the point of view of national economy [they] are a misfortune." When this summary of Cădere's memorandum together with Vlădescu reached the Conducător, he ruled that "the issue would be decided upon later."[31] Finally, on 28 May 1942, the Ministry of Justice requested the "removal" of Roma from the urban centers and their internment in forced labor camps "due to the numerous acts of thievery that they commit." Although this time Antonescu agreed with the proposal, it was never carried out in its entirety, as I will demonstrate below.[32]

The above discussion indicates that the decision to deport a part of Romanian Roma to Transnistria was not a personal whim of the Romanian dictator but reflected views and dispositions of a part—probably a considerable part—of government experts and bureaucrats. In retrospect, Antonescu proved less radical in this regard than some of his advisors and underlings.

Ion Antonescu: Toward a Fateful Decision

Nonetheless, it was Ion Antonescu who made the fateful decision, and it was he who determined the selection criteria for Roma slated for deportation as well as the timeframe within which it had to be carried out. This warrants a close look at Antonescu's political views and style of rule.

Antonescu was a right-wing politician, a radical nationalist, and a xenophobe who perceived *all* ethnic minorities as sworn enemies of the Romanian nation and who was absolutely convinced that the country's development would be inhibited unless all ethnic minorities had been, by hook or by crook, removed from Romania. From the moment he assumed power in early September 1941 and until he was deposed in a coup d'état on 23 August 1944, he was committed to complete "purification" of the country of "foreigners" (*străini*), that is, ethnic minorities. During his tenure, all ethnic minorities, save ethnic Germans who were under the protection of the Third Reich, were heavily discriminated against. However, it was the Jews who bore the brunt of his barbaric cruelty. Antonescu was personally responsible for numerous crimes against the Jews, including the campaign of mass murder of the Jews of northern Bukovina and Bessarabia in July and August 1941; the internment in ghettoes and concentration camps of those Jews in Bessarabia and northern Bukovina who had survived the initial wave of killing; the deportation of these internees, along with Jews from southern Bukovina and Dorohoi county in Moldova, to Transnistria in the fall of 1941; the mass reprisals against the Jews of Odessa in October 1941, and the expulsion of the rest of the Jewish population of this city in January 1942 to concentration camps in eastern Transnistria on the southern Buh River where most of them perished, along with deportees from Bessarabia and Bukovina, at the hands of the Romanian gendarmes, ethnic German militias, and Ukrainian policemen. According to the most recent estimates, the total number of victims of this "policy," along with those Jews who were killed in the pogroms in Bucharest in January 1941 and in Jassy in June 1941 (for which Antonescu may not be directly responsible), was anywhere between 280,000 and 380,000.[33]

The Roma were the second minority ruthlessly persecuted by Antonescu's government, even though unlike Jews, Roma were not subject to mass executions. This fact begs the question of why Antonescu, who loathed ethnic minorities in general, singled out Jews and Roma for exceptionally harsh treatment.

Apparently, the intensity of Antonescu's phobias does not contain an answer to this question. True, Antonescu's anti-Semitism and Romaphobia were vicious, but so was his animosity toward all other minorities. For example, in his address to the heads of big industrial enterprises on 14 March 1941, he argued that the problem of *newcomers*—one more derogatory term for non–ethnic Romanians—was very serious, because "they lead [the] Romanian nation to perdition as a butcher leads a beast to the slaughterhouse."[34] During the sitting of the Romanian government on 10 October 1941, Antonescu declared that "foreigners" had been exploiting the Romanian nation for centuries: "We work as slaves while they rip the benefits; we have always been slaves to the foreigners."[35]

Still, despite his xenophobia, in his practical policies Antonescu strove to take reality—geopolitical and economic—into consideration. It was his determination to account for the existing international situation, as he understood it, that explains why his approach toward the "solution" of the Jewish and Roma "problems" on the one hand and, say, German, Hungarian, Ukrainian, and Bulgarian "problems" on the other was quite different. By the summer of 1940, in light of German victory over France, Antonescu convinced himself that Germany would dominate over Europe for the decades to come. As soon as he became, with German help, a dictator, he resolved to continue the policy of an alliance with Germany, initiated by his predecessor King Carol II; in his domestic policy and his treatment of minorities he imitated Nazi policy. Antonescu was also aware that this alliance imposed serious constraints on his treatment of various minorities. For example, he granted the German minority in Romania such extensive rights that this community, which was effectively controlled by the Nazi Party, was transformed into a state within a state.³⁶ Hungarians and Bulgarians were protected by their own states, which were satellites of the Third Reich and as such could appeal to Berlin if they saw their co-nationals' interests in Romania infringed upon. Even Ukrainians had patrons in Berlin since some Nazi leaders hoped to use their national movement in the war against Bolshevism.³⁷ Thus, although all of these minorities were heavily discriminated against, none of them were subjected to the same brutalities as Jews and Roma.

The Jews were seen as the most vulnerable for it was well known that Nazis persecuted them in the most violent manner. Hitler conveyed his decision to subject Soviet Jews to the "special treatment" to Antonescu during their meeting on 12 June 1941 in Munich. On that occasion Hitler informed Antonescu of the exact date of the impending attack on the USSR and asked him whether he wanted to join Germany in this war, to which Antonescu immediately agreed.³⁸ Upon his return to Bucharest, Antonescu issued an order to start immediate preparations for cleansing Bessarabia and northern Bukovina (annexed by the Soviet Union in June 1940) of Jews.³⁹ The brutal conduct of the Romanian troops and gendarmerie vis-à-vis Jews in July and August 1941 elicited the admiration of Hitler, who in a conversation with Joseph Goebbels commended Romanians as more determined fighters against the Jews than Nazis themselves.⁴⁰

Since no country would protect Roma, they appeared to Antonescu as vulnerable a minority as were the Jews, with respect to whom one could act with impunity. Indeed, he started contemplating how to deal with the "Roma problem" almost immediately after his accession to power. The dictator shared all traditional Romanian prejudices against Roma; he was especially sensitive to the fact that foreigners had often considered Romanians "Roma-like." During his interrogation on 6 May 1946, Antonescu indignantly referred to anti-Romanian propaganda, which he believed the Hungarians had been waging so successfully that they managed to convince Europeans that "Romania was a country of Roma, [a nation which was] unable to administer itself."⁴¹ At the meeting of the Council of Ministers on 7 February 1941, and again on 4 April, Antonescu expounded on why he thought Roma were a "calamity to the country" and how they had to be combated. Roma, along with other "weak elements," he insisted, "earned their leaving without working," as well as carried and spread various diseases.⁴²

Significantly, during the 4 April meeting, when describing his observations on the way of living of Bucharest Roma, the Conducător used military lexicon. According to him, Roma "set up a big center" on the outskirts of the capital city from which they used to go every morning, together with their children, "as far as Piața Victoriei, like soldiers go in the battlefield, in loose formation. When they arrive at Piața Victoriei ... they branch off as automatons and thus they infiltrate into Bucharest and invade all marketplaces."[43] The dictator obviously saw the Roma's actions as a kind of war operation intended to destroy the Romanian nation. Hence, the state had to act resolutely and without delay. All Roma residing in Bucharest had to be identified in preparation for their deportation. Huts (*bordei*) had to be built for them in the nearby county of Ialomița where they would be put to work on big estates. Roma villages thus prepared were to be guarded by sentinels. Bucharest was to be only the beginning: In the future Roma would be removed from all Romanian cities and towns since everywhere they were a calamity, as all of them were infected by syphilis or other sicknesses.

Antonescu's order of April 1941 was not carried out for reasons which can only be surmised. Supposedly, the preparation for the war against the Soviet Union distracted his and his government's attention away from "the Roma problem." The deportation of Jews from Bessarabia and northern Bukovina in the fall of 1941 pushed this issue further into the background. The Romanian administration of Transnistria, which had to address a whole range of issues with only limited resources at its disposal, vigorously protested against the policy of "offloading" in its administrative territory hundreds of thousands of Jews.[44] Most likely, it was these protests that prompted Antonescu to postpone, on 8 October 1941, the deportation of Romanian Roma to Transnistria as had been proposed by the head of his office, Ovidiu Vlădescu.

However, on 1 May 1942, the dictator ordered the deportation of Romanian itinerant Roma.[45] During the following two to three weeks—probably as a consequence of the discussion of the "Roma problem" in the interministerial conferences, the minutes of which were either not taken or have not hitherto surfaced—the deportation plan had been expanded and rendered somewhat more specific. Before considering the content of this plan, it is important to reflect upon the question as to why violent, yet hitherto mostly "theoretical," anti-Roma rhetoric was translated into action in the spring of 1942, and not earlier.

Although no document that could have possibly prompted Antonescu's rash decision to launch deportation has surfaced to date, it is possible to infer the Conducător's logic from the general political context. The Germans' failure to capture Moscow and win the war by the fall of 1941, and the ensuing Soviet counteroffensive, had shattered Antonescu's optimism as to the war's speedy, victorious end. Once it became clear, however, that the Red Army had failed to achieve strategic breakthroughs on any but the Moscow sectors of the front, and that Germans managed to stabilize the front by the spring of 1942, Antonescu's spirits were lifted and so he regained his confidence in the victory of German arms.[46] He remained in this upbeat mood until the fall of 1942 when increasingly alarming news from the Stalingrad front—where the ill-equipped 4th Romanian Army had been experiencing mounting difficulties even prior to the Soviet counteroffensive in November—as well as the Germans' failure to deliver the promised military materiel to the Romanian troops, once again undermined his optimism, this time forever. (Antonescu, however, refused to believe in the possibility of Germany's unconditional surrender, imagining that this war, much like World War I, would end with a peace conference in which Germany and her allies, Romania included, would face the United Nations led by Britain and America.)[47]

It was during the time of renewed optimism that the deportation of Jews from the eastern provinces, which had been suspended on Antonescu's order from 13 November 1941, was resumed in May 1942.[48] It is not illogical to suppose that the decision to start deporting Roma, taken at approximately the same time, must be considered in conjunction with the decision regarding Jews, for they both fitted within the same strategy of "ethnic purification." The intensity of its pursuit ultimately depended on Antonescu's assessment of Germany's chances to win the war.

One should add that by that time Antonescu must have been aware that in the occupied Soviet territories Nazis were killing en masse not only Jews but also Roma. Particularly in the Crimea, where Einsatzgruppe D carried out mass executions of Roma, the Romanian military had participated in rounding up and convoying victims to the killing sites, according to at least one source.[49] It is uncertain whether the Romanian troops acted upon Antonescu's order or if it was the initiative of lower-level commanders. In either case, the Conducător could not remain unaware of the Nazis' "special treatment" of Roma. Since at that time Antonescu was still looking up to Hitler for guidance, it must have provided additional impetus to him to proceed from rhetoric to action with respect to Roma.

Catching and Flaying Stray Dogs: Gendarmes and Roma

Although Antonescu's order of 1 May 1942 provided exclusively for the deportation of itinerant Roma, on 17 May of the same year the state secretary in the Ministry of the Interior, Division General Constantin (Pikky) Vasiliu, ordered the police and gendarme directorates (the former oversaw urban areas and the latter rural areas) to compose by 10 June lists of Roma belonging to the following two categories: "1. Itinerant Roma. 2. Sedentary Roma (i.e., those [Roma] who, though not itinerant, [had been] sentenced by a tribunal, [were] recidivists or [had] no means of existence or occupations from which they [could] live by working in an honorable way and thus [constituted] a burden and a danger to public order)." All Roma adults belonging to these two categories had to be registered together with their spouses and children in case the latter continued living with their parents.[50] On 22 May, Antonescu issued an order to deport all those Roma "with the aim of securing order within the country and removing foreign and parasitic elements."[51] These orders set parameters for the ensuing deportation; they would remain in place until the deportation was suspended in mid-October 1942. During this whole period General Vasiliu remained in charge of the operation.

It should be noted that it was that same General Vasiliu who in early July 1941 had instructed the gendarmes dispatched to the newly "liberated" Bessarabia and Bukovina to round up and murder local Jews. Vasiliu enjoyed the unparalleled confidence of Antonescu and was renowned for his penchant for violence and brutality. Radu Lecca—an international adventurer, German spy, and Antonescu's plenipotentiary for Jewish affairs (his powers, however, did not extend to Bessarabia, Bukovina, and Transnistria)—referred in his 1960s memoirs (written in communist prison) to Vasiliu as follows: "the greatest gangster and murderer ever whelped by the Romanian gendarmerie."[52] Vasiliu fulfilled Antonescu's deportation order zealously, considering it a great opportunity to get rid of the part of Romania's population that he believed was a source of crime and disorder. Referring to the ensuing operation as *ecarisaj polițienesc* (from the French *équarissage*—flaying an animal), which can be translated as "catching and flaying stray dogs," he endeavored to deport, under any pretext, as many Roma as possible.[53]

The vague definition of categories of Roma who were subject to deportation, as well as the haste of and extralegal framework within which the whole operation was carried out, gave gendarmes and policemen practically unlimited discretionary powers over those who were regarded as Roma. In this context, it should be noted that the difference between itinerant and sedentary Roma, which existed in theory, was barely distinguishable in practice. Many Roma, especially men, used to travel long distances looking for jobs, in particular during warmer seasons, regardless of whether they had families and/or permanent domicile. Whenever gendarmes and policemen would spot such persons outside of their places of residence during that campaign, they arrested and dispatched them to Transnistria, along with the caravans of itinerant Roma who were "pushed" in guarded columns in that same direction. For example, brick-maker Chiodorean Miclescu was detained while commuting to a brick factory in Putna county (Moldova) in the company of other Roma bricklayers—all of them hired for seasonal work; the gendarmes who detained this group were convoying a column of itinerant Roma to Transnistria. According to Miclescu, who later submitted a petition requesting permission to return from Transnistria, gendarmes bluntly ordered the Roma bricklayers to join the assembled convoy and drove them to Transnistria without any proper registration or investigation. (Miclescu's petition had been denied).[54] War invalid Ion D. Păun from the village of Miloşeşti in Wallachia, requesting in a petition to the minister of the interior to allow his family to return from Transnistria, explained that they were arrested and ordered to join a group of deportees while returning home from the nearby village where they worked in the fields as hired labor.[55]

Furthermore, even to ascertain whether an individual was or was not a Roma was not always an easy matter since no official document in Romania registered its bearer's ethnic origin. In practice, gendarmes and policemen counted as Roma anyone who led a "Roma way of life" or "resided in the Roma district." Sometimes they resorted to such crude method of "ascertaining" one's ethnicity as skin color. However, given that many ethnic Romanians have a skin with a dark hue, some of them unwittingly became "suspected" of "actually" being Roma. For example, in late 1942, the mayor of the city of Târgovişte protested such police practice of ascertaining person's ethnicity, arguing that in that particular locality not only "real" Roma but also the "suspects" had been deported due to their skin color.[56] In another, no less revealing case, the police chief of the city of Galaţ had refuted the claims of an individual who protested that he was deported by mistake since he was not a Roma by saying that the latter "had Roma [skin] color, language, and [lived] among Roma." In addition, the police officer claimed that this person was a beggar, thus implying that begging was a Roma occupation.[57]

The decision regarding alleged criminality of the identified Roma slated for deportation depended on the disposition and strength of the anti-Roma prejudice of individual gendarme and police officers. Thus, the gendarme legion (county office) of Constanţa county, who had deported from the territory under its purview a record high share of Roma—24 percent of the number registered in the 1930 census, as compared to 10 percent all over the country—refused *all* petitions of those deported to Transnistria to be allowed to return to their hearths referencing military service of their husbands or siblings in the acting army. The legion's standard response to the petitioners' pleas included statements like "his main occupation is thievery" or "she has no source of income other than begging, sorcery, fortune-telling, and larceny," without providing any further proof.⁵⁸ Vasiliu considered such "expert opinions" sufficient to turn down all the petitions. At the same time, the commander of the Timiș-Toronthal gendarme legion, Major Ioan Peșchir, released from detention fourteen Roma, thus sparing them from deportation after they procured court certificates stating that they had no previous criminal records. As Peșchir related to Vasiliu, he believed those certificates were sufficient proofs to absolve the said Roma of "vague suspicions and unproved charges by which the gendarme posts' chiefs were guided [while arresting them]."⁵⁹ However, officers such as Peșchir were few and far between. The great majority of gendarme officers shared Vasiliu's enthusiasm for ridding Romania of "criminal Roma." In those rare cases when gendarmes or policemen proved more tolerant of Roma by suggesting to permit "too large" a number of them to return from Transnistria, Vasiliu did not hesitate to turn their recommendations down. As he wrote to the head of the board of police in the Ministry of the Interior, Colonel C. Tobescu, if one would follow that logic, no "capturing and flaying of stray dogs might be carried out." At least once Vasiliu ordered disciplinary punishment of a low-ranking gendarme officer for dereliction of duty, which enabled a few Roma to evade deportation (the officer's behavior could well have been intentional, as Vasiliu had suspected).⁶⁰

Deportation of Roma and the Romanian Society

There are no indications that the Romanian society as a whole was opposed to, let alone protested against, the deportation of Roma. True, Romanian archives contain a (rather limited) number of petitions by ethnic Romanians requesting to exempt individual Roma—usually the petitioner's neighbor or someone he knew—from deportation. The petitioners substantiated their requests by claiming that said persons possessed invaluable skills and had rendered vital services to the local communities, or that they were good and agreeable persons.⁶¹ However, the overwhelming majority of these petitions were submitted in late September–early October 1942 when deportation of the two categories of Roma had already been completed and a new census of Roma was conducted, following an order of Vasiliu to that effect. According to that order, the police were to register "all Roma, both those with criminal record and those who have been acquitted, so that in the spring they could be evacuated [e.g., "deported"] to Transnistria."⁶² Although this was a secret order, the ominous connection between Roma censuses and the subsequent deportation of those registered should have been crystal clear to everyone by that time. Many Roma tried to escape deportation by, among other means, persuading their neighbors and people they knew from among ethnic Romanians to write such petitions on their behalf.

Protests against the deportation of itinerant and "dangerous" sedentary Roma were conspicuous by their absence. The claim, contained in the Final Report of the International Commission on the Holocaust in Romania, that the Queen Mother and the general staff protested the deportation is based on misunderstanding, at best. The Queen Mother Elena interceded on behalf not of *all* Roma, but of one particular soldier, Zoltan Stoica, who had related to her during her visit to a hospital where he was recovering after an amputation that, while he was fighting at the front, his family was deported to Transnistria. The Queen Mother then requested the interference of Mihai Antonescu—Conducător's distant relative and his most trusted lieutenant who in 1941–1944 had served as foreign minister and deputy chairman of the Council of Ministers. In response, Mihai Antonescu ordered Stoica's family returned from Transnistria, explaining that the latter should know that "the soldier who fulfilled his duty at the front had his and his family's rights respected."[63] Despite Mihai Antonescu's lofty rhetoric, however, this decision had no bearing on the fate of other Roma soldiers' families who were ordered to remain in Transnistria, their pleas notwithstanding. Moreover, even though some Romanian army officers did intercede with the general staff on behalf of Roma men whose families had been deported to Transnistria, the general staff, after initial hesitation, discarded those pleas. To the contrary, it agreed with Vasiliu's suggestion to erase from the army's rosters the names of Roma men whose families had been deported. Consequently, those men were expelled from the ranks and ordered to join their families in Transnistrian exile. (Ironically, in spite of this decision, when in the spring and summer of 1944 Transnistria was retaken by the Red Army, the Romanian general staff recalled those Roma men who had managed, by hook or by crook, to slip back into to Romania into the army.)[64] It is true that famous composer George Enescu vehemently protested the deportation of Roma musicians; however, his noble act did not extend to the Roma community as a whole.[65]

The only public voice ever raised on behalf of the Roma belonged to Constantin Brătianu, chairman of the National Liberal Party. His strongly worded and persuasively written memorandum to Antonescu of 16 September 1942 was signed solely by him, however, and not on behalf of his party, in which his influence at the time was close to zero.[66] On the other hand, although the secret police reported on 23 October 1942 that leaders of the National Peasant Party did express support for the position taken by Brătianu, they did not seem to have presented a written protest to Antonescu, as they did in January 1942 against the persecution of the Jews.[67]

Generally, Romanian society remained notably indifferent to the suffering of the deported Roma. According to a Roma survivor who had managed to slip back into Romania from Transnistria together with a friend in the spring or summer of 1944, they had to hide their identity while begging for food, because when ethnic Romanians "heard that we were from Transnistria, and that we were Roma, they barely looked at us: 'Get out of here!'"[68] Nor can one accept Achim's suggestion that the protests of ethnic Romanians against the deportations of the Roma were instrumental in stopping them. When on 13 October 1942 Mihai Antonescu announced the suspension (effectively the end) of all deportations in the sitting of the Council of Ministers, this decision was not due to popular protests but to political calculus, in particular a revised assessment of the likely outcome of the world war. As the most recent research has showed, by that time, Antonescu had come to the conclusion that Germany would probably lose the war and that it was the right time for Romania to rebuild its relations with Western powers. Romanian leadership had ascribed to Jews enormous political influence in Great Britain and the United States, and therefore they concluded that in order to improve the relations with the two powers they needed to revisit their anti-Jewish policies, by frustrating German plans to deport Romanian Jews to the death camps in Poland and by stopping deportation of Jews to Transnistria.[69] Roma inadvertently benefitted from this policy change, even though Mihai and Ion Antonescu, while considering halting deportations, thought of Roma least of all.

Conclusion

The above analysis effectively answers the question posed in the title of this chapter, namely, whether Romanian Roma were deported as members of a particular ethnic group or as criminals. Achim regards both suppositions as plausible, yet implies that the latter rationale played a bigger role in the regime's decision making.[70] Such an interpretation is supported by some evidence, primarily the language used by Antonescu and his lieutenants on several occasions in reference to this deportation. Thus, in his order of May 1942 to start the deportation of itinerant Roma, the dictator asserted that it was a part of "general measures to remove the parasitic and disorderly elements."[71] On 10 September of the same year, the interior minister, referring to the growing crime rate, ordered the head of the police to "immediately arrest the male factors, and if their guilt has been established pending investigation, to deport them to the Roma camps in Transnistria."[72]

However, alongside these and other similar statements, one can cite from other documents indicating that for Antonescu the removal of "dangerous Roma" was part of the ethnic "purification" of Romania. That is what he said verbatim in his guidelines of 22 May 1942.[73] Nor should one forget that from Antonescu's point of view, all foreigners were "parasites" and therefore had to be removed from the body national. The fact that Roma, beside Jews, came under direct attack earlier than other minorities had to do with both his replicating Nazi policies, and the strength of his and his most trusted advisers' anti-Roma prejudices. Significantly, although the government did envisage the possibility of removing "parasitic" ethnic Romanians along with Roma, this plan had never materialized. Conversely, whenever the authorities concluded that a particular person under investigation was an ethnic Romanian and not a Roma, he/she was exempted from deportation.[74] Although not all Roma were subject to deportation, no individuals other than Roma (and Jews) were deported. It thus follows that the Romanian government's treatment of Roma in 1942–1944 was informed first and foremost by ethnic nationalism and racial anthropology. Outside of this context, the deportation could not have taken place.

Notes

1. Dumitru Şandru, "Deportatrea ţiganilor în Transnistria," *Arhivele totalitarsimului. Revista Institutului Naţional pentru Studiul Totalitarismului* 17 (1997): 23–30; Viorel Achim, "Deportarea ţiganilor în Transnistria," *Anuarulromân de istorie recentă* 1 (2002): 127–41; Viorel Achim, "Atitudinea contemporanilor faţa de deportarea ţiganilor în Transnistria," in *România şi Transnistria: problema Holocaustului: Perspective istorice şi comparative,* ed. V. Avhim and C. Iordachi (Bucharest, 2004), 201–36; Viorel Achim, *The Roma in Romanian History* (Budapest, 1998), 163–88.
2. Cf. Radu Ioanid, *The Holocaust in Romania: The Destruction of Jews and Gypsies Under the Antonescu Regime, 1940–1944* (Chicago, 2000), 225–37; International Commission on the Holocaust in Romania, *Final Report* (Iaşi, 2005), 223–42.
3. Viorel Achim, ed., *Documente privind deportarea ţiganilor în Transnistria,* 2 vols. (Bucharest, 2004). See also Lucian Nastasă and Andrea Varga, ed., *Minorităţi etnoculturale. Mărturii documentare: Ţiganii din România (1919–1944)* (Cluj-Napoca, 2001) and Vasile Ionescu, *Deportarea rromilor în Transnistria: de la Auschwitz la Bug* (Bucharest, 2000).
4. Achim, *Roma in Romanian History,* 168.
5. Transnistria was the official name of the territory between the Dniester and Southern Bug Rivers, occupied and administered by the Romanians between 1941 and 1944 following an understanding between Hitler and Antonescu.

6. According to the International Commission on the Holocaust in Romania, out of 25,000 Roma who had been deported to Transnistria, approximately 14,000 survived and 11,000 died. However, this estimate is based on the assumption that, in addition to 12,083 Roma interned in Transnistrian camps, as of March 1944 there were about 2,000 Roma "who were repatriated at different times for various reasons as well as those who had escaped from Transnistria illegally without being caught and returned" (International Commission on the Holocaust in Romania, *Final Report* [Iași, 2005], 236). I doubt the latter number was actually as high since, as I demonstrate below, Roma were rarely permitted to return, and gendarmes had been relentless in rearresting and redeporting the fugitives. The International Commission on the Holocaust in Romania was created in 2004 on the initiative of the Romanian president Ion Iliescu. It comprised academics from West Europe, the United States, Israel, and Romania—including Viorel Achim—and was chaired by the Nobel Peace Prize winner Elie Wiesel. Shannon Woodcock estimates the number of Romani deportees at more than 30,000 while M. Benjamin Thorne estimates 26,000. Both authors apparently do not provide estimates of the number of fatalities among the deportees. Cf. Woodcock, "Romanian Romani Resistance to Genocide in the Matrix of the *Țigan* Other," *The Anthropology of East Europe Review* 25, no. 2 (2007): 33; Thorne, "Assimilation, Invisibility, and the Eugenic Turn in the "Gypsy Question" in Romanian Society, 1938–1942," *Romani Studies* 21, no. 2 (December 2011): 179.
7. Achim, *Roma in Romanian History*, 168–70, 179, 182–83. The syntagma "crime prevention" in the title of this chapter is meant to encapsulate the crux of Achim's argument rather than to indicate my personal take. Thorne's article in *Romani Studies*, which advances a similar perspective to that propounded here, was published after this volume had gone to print.
8. An earlier version of this chapter appeared as an article in *Golokost i suchastnist: studii v Ukraini i sviti* (Kiev) 3, no. 1 (2008): 65–87.
9. Marcel-Dumitru Ciucă et al., eds, *Stenogramele ședințelor Consiliului de Miniștri : guvernarea Ion Antonescu*, 9 vols. (Bucharest, 1997–2006); Marcel-Dumitru Ciucă, ed., *Procesul Mareșalului Antonescu: documente,* 3 vols. (Bucharest, 1995–1998); Ioana Cracă, ed., *Procesul lui Antonescu* (Bucharest, 1995 [*Procesul marii trădări naționale* (Bucharest, 1946)]).
10. For a more comprehensive discussion of Romani victimization see Woodcock, "Romanian Romani Resistance," 28–43.
11. Shannon Woodcock, "The Țigan is Not a Man": The Țigan Other as a Catalyst for Romanian National Identity" (PhD diss., University of Sidney, 2005), 120–56; Woodcock, "Romanian Romani Resistance," 28–32.
12. Romanian sociologist Domnica I. Păun described the "anxiety of proximity" condition on the example of Bessarabian village Cornova. Cf. Păun, "Țiganii în viața satului Cornova," *Arhiva pentru știința și reforma socială* 10, no. 1–4 (1932), 525–26.
13. Sorin Mitu, *National Identity of Romanians in Transylvania* (Budapest, 2001), 75–9.
14. Woodcock. "The Țigan is Not a Man," 120–56.
15. Literature on the eugenics movement is enormous. See, for example, Mark B. Adams, *The Wellborn Science: Eugenics in Germany, France, Brazil, and Russia* (New York, 1990); Elof Axel Carlson, *The Unfit: A History of a Bad Idea* (Cold Spring Harbor, NY, 2001); Stefan Kühl, *The Nazi Connection: Eugenics, American Racism, and German National Socialism* (New York, 1994); Michael Burleigh, *The Third Reich: A New History* (New York, 2000), 345–54.
16. On Iuliu Moldovan and his school see Maria Bucur, *Eugenics and Modernization in Inter-War Romania* (Pittsburgh, 2002) and Marius Turda, "The Nation as Object: Race, Blood, and Biopolitics in Interwar Romania," *Slavic Review* 66, no. 3 (2007): 413–42; Vladimir Solonari, *Purifying the Nation: Population Exchange and Ethnic Cleansing*

in *Nazi-Allied Romania* (Washington, DC, 2010), 62–74. On other Romanian eugenicists see Marius Turda, "'To End the Degeneration of a Nation': Debates on Eugenic Sterilization in Interwar Romania," *Medical History* 53, no. 1 (2009): 77–104.

17. Iodache Făcăoaru, "Amesticul rasial și etnic în România," *Buletin eugenic și biopolitic* 9–10 (1938): 276–87. ские народа были слите удалось установить его личность, но учитывая что в сосбенности потому что ы с "мыны уровне, с

18. I am grateful to Marius Turda for sharing with me the information regarding Gheorghe Făcăoaru's identity.

19. Gheorghe Făcăoaru, *Câteva date în jurul familiei și statului biopolitic* (Bucharest, n.d.), esp. 17.

20. Petru Râmneanțu, *Sânge și glie* (Sibiu, 1943), 19.

21. On Antonescu and his regime see Dennis Deletant, *Hitler's Forgotten Ally: Ion Antonescu and His Regime, Romania 1940–44* (New York, 2006). Antonescu's official title was *Conducător*, the Romanian equivalent of *Führer*.

22. For biographical data on Manuilă see Vladimir Trebici, "Dr. Sabin Manuilă, organizatorul statisticii științifice în România," in *Sabin Manuilă: istorie și demografie: Studii privind societatea românească între secolele XVI–XX*, ed. S. Bolovan and I. Bolovan (Cluj-Napoca, 1995), 7–25 and Sorina Bolovan and Ioan Bolovan, "Introduction," in *Sabin Manuilă: Studies on the Historical Ethnography of Romania*, ed. S. Bolovan and I. Bolovan (Cluj-Napoca, 1992), 7–18.

23. Text of the decree in Central National Historical Archives in Bucharest (hereafter: DANIC), Sabin Manuilă, XII/165/1939.

24. Solonari, *Purifying the Nation*, 1–3, 88–94; Vladimir Solonari, "An Important New Document on Romanian Policy of Ethnic Cleansing During World War II," *Holocaust and Genocide Studies* 20, no. 2 (fall 2007): 268–97; Viorel Achim, "The Romanian Population Exchange Project Elaborated by Sabin Manuilă in October 1941," *Annali dell'Instituto storico italo-germanico in Trento* 27 (2001): 609–17; Viorel Achim, "Schimbul de populație in viziunea lui Sabin Manuilă," *Revista istorică* 13, no. 5–6 (2002): 133–50.

25. Manuilă's draft paper, "Population Policy" [spring 1941], DANIC, PCM-CM, 174/1940 (US Holocaust Memorial Museum [hereafter: USHMM], RG-25.013M). The fact that both Manuilă in the extant draft and Antonescu in his guidelines used a very rare form *rassă* (Romanian grammatical norms proscribe doubling consonants; the more common form is *rasă*. In this particular case, the spelling resembled that of German *Rasse* and was first used by Manuilă who, unlike Antonescu, knew German) suggests that Antonescu might have written his guidelines on that same paper.

26. Manuilă's draft paper, "Population Policy" [spring 1941], DANIC, PCM-CM, 174/1940 (USHMM, RG-25.013M).

27. See Manuilă's memorandum in Achim, *Documente privind deportarea*, vol. 1, 53–55. According to Iordache Făcăoaru's estimates, there were ca. 400,000 Gypsies in Romania in 1935, though he failed to explain how he arrived at that conclusion [Manuilă, "Inmulțirea disgenicilor și costul lor pentru societate și stat," *Buletin eugenic și biopolitic* 7, no. 4–6 (1935): 182].

28. Ion Chelcea, *Țiganii din România. Monografie etnografică* (Bucharest, 1944), 85. Chelcea suggested exempting one group of Romanian Gypsies, known as *rudari*, from deportation. He believed that, from the racial point of view, *rudari* were erroneously regarded as Gypsies while in fact they were descendants of the ancient, pre-Roman population of what is now Romania, possibly Dacians (traditionally, Romanians believe that they are the descendents of Dacians and their conquerors, Romans). Cf. Manuilă, "Inmulțirea disgenicilor și costul lor pentru societate și stat," *Buletin eugenic și biopolitic* 7, no. 4–6 (1935): 23–62, 85–101.

29. Cădere's memo, no date, National Archives of the Republic of Moldova (hereafter: ANRM), 706/1/10, vol. 2 (USHMM RG-54.002M).
30. As Thorne has recently demonstrated, Cădere's memorandum came at the heels of a whole series of initiatives emanating from Romanian public health officials and gendarme officers who, starting from 1938, identified nomadic Roma as a source of typhus epidemics and recommended various restrictions on their mobility; these recommendations, however, were only laxly enforced (Thorne, "Assimilation, Invisibility, and the Eugenic Turn," 187–89, 197–202).
31. Cădere's memo, no date, National Archives of the Republic of Moldova (hereafter: ANRM), 706/1/10, vol. 2 (USHMM RG-54.002M).
32. Achim, *Documente privind deportarea*, vol. 1, doc. no. 11, 15–16.
33. This statistic is to be found in International Commission on the Holocaust in Romania, *Final Report*, 382. I elaborated on Antonescu's worldview and his policies toward ethnic minorities in *Purifying the Nation*, esp. 136–67.
34. Lya Benjamin, ed., *Evreii din Pomânia între anii 1940–1944*, vol. 2. (Bucharest, 1996), 210.
35. Ciucă et al., *Stenogramele*, vol. 1, 184.
36. On the privileges of the German minority in Romania in 1940–1944 see Joseph B. Schechtman, *Postwar Population Transfers in Europe 1945–1955* (Philadelphia, 1962), 266.
37. On relations with Hungary see Holly Case, *Between States: The Transylvanian Question and the European Idea during World War II* (Stanford, 2009). The Reich minister of the Occupied Eastern Territories, Alfred Rosenberg, actively promoted nationalistic movements, including one in Ukraine. See Alexander Dallin, *German Rule in Russia, 1941–1945: A Study of Occupation Policies* (Boulder, CO, 1981), 107–11. In northern Bukovina and in Bessarabia Germans tried, with some success, to protect Ukrainian nationalists from Romanian impressions. See Andrej Angrick, "Im Wechspiel der Kräfte. Impressionen zur deutschen Einflussnahmene bei der Volstumspolitk in Czernowitz vor 'Barbarossa' und nach Beginn des Überfalls auf die Sowjetunion," in *NS-Gewaltherrschaft: Beiträge zur historischen Forschung und juristischen Aufarbeitung. Publikation der Gedenk- und Bildungsstätte Haus der Wannsee-Konferez*, ed. A. Gottwald et al., (Berlin, 2005), vol. 3, 318–58.
38. Paul Schmidt's transcript does not contain any mention of their discussing "the treatment of Jews in the east." However, on 16 August 1941, Antonescu complained to General Eugen Ritter von Schobert and the German ambassador in Bucharest, Manfred von Killinger, that the German army's refusal to let the Romanians deport the Jews of Bessarabia and Bukovina across the Buh River (Germans were afraid that massing hundreds of thousands of Jews in the rear of their armies would create logistical problems) was running "contrary to the guidelines which the Führer had set forth ... in Munich." Eleven days later, Karl Ritter, the German Foreign Ministry's ambassador on special duties, had informed Wehrmacht General Staff that although he was unable to find at the Foreign Ministry any mention of that discussion, Hitler and Antonescu apparently spoke on other occasions as well, and that "it was entirely possible that the question of eastern Jews was also discussed there. In any case, there was no reason to doubt the accuracy of General Antonescu's assertions." See *Documents on German Foreign Policy, 1918–1945* (Washington, DC, 1949), vol. 12, no. 614, 996–1006; vol. 13, no. 207, 318–19. Cf. Jean Ancel, "The German-Romanian Relationship and the Final Solution," *Holocaust and Genocide Studies* 19, no. 3 (Winter 2005), 255–56, and Andrej Angrick, *Besatzungspolitik und Massenmord. Die Einsatzgruppe D in der südlichen Sowjetunion 1941–1943* (Hamburg, 2003), 197–98.

39. Cf. Vladimir Solonari, "Patterns of Violence: The Local Population and the Mass Murder of Jews in Bessarabia and Northern Bukovina, July-August 1941," *Kritika: Explorations in Russian and Eurasian History* 8, no. 4 (2007): 749–87.
40. Joseph Goebbels, *Tagebücher 1924–1945*, vol. 4 (Munich, 1992), 1659–60.
41. Marcel-Dumitru Ciucă, ed., *Procesul Mareşalului Antonescu: documente*, vol. 3 (Bucharest, 1995–1998), 309.
42. Ciucă et al., *Stenogramele*, vol. 2, 181; vol. 3, 94.
43. Ibid., vol. 3, 94.
44. See report of Gheorghe Alexianu, governor of Transnistria, from November 1941 in which he recounted his (futile) efforts directed at controlling the number of deported Jews, State Archives of Chernivits Oblasti (hereafter: DACHO), 307/3/4 (USHMM, RG-31.006M).
45. Achim, *Documente privind deportarea*, vol. 1, 15–6.
46. Ioan Hudiţa, *Jurnal politic: 22 iunie 1941–28 februarie 1942* (Bucharest, 2005), 289, 305, 366. Hudiţa was deputy general secretary of the opposition National Peasant Party that had continued to exist as a network of activists (their meetings were closely monitored by the police, which did not interfere nonetheless). Hudiţa kept a detailed diary in which he had diligently entered invaluable information that reached him from various sources, including the individuals who had meetings with Antonescu and other dignitaries.
47. On the changing assessment of the prospects of war by Antonescu see Solonari, *Purifying the Nation*, 297–300.
48. By November 1941 there still remained in Bessarabia a few hundred Jews, mainly individuals who had lived for a long time in the mixed marriages with local Christians and the inmates of Costujeni mental asylum. Of the Bukovina Jews deemed indispensable for the local industry, Antonescu had allowed about 15,000 to stay; in reality close to 20,000 Jews managed to escape deportation in the fall of 1941. On Bukovina see Solonari, *Purifying the Nation*, 210–21; on Antonescu's order to suspend deportation see Ciucă et al., *Stenogramele*, vol. 5, 154. On 20 May 1942, over 200 Jews were deported from Chişinău, the capital of Bessarabia (ANRM, 67/1/6922, vol. 2). On 8 June, over 1,800 Jews were dispatched to Transnistria from the capital of Bukovina Cernăuţi and other localities (DACHO, 307/1/244 [USHMM, RG 31.006M]).
49. See deposition of an eyewitness in the files of the Soviet State Extraordinary Commission for the Investigation of the Crimes Committed by German Fascists and their Collaborators on the Territory of the USSR in the State Archives of the Russian Federation (7021/9/38). I am grateful to Mikhail Tyaglyy who provided me with this important document.
50. Achim, *Documente privind deportatrea*, vol. 1, doc. no. 3, 5–6.
51. Ibid., doc. no. 6, 9–10. Definition of these categories of Gypsies contained in Antonescu's order was somewhat different from that in Vasiliu's order, thus testifying to the haste and bureaucratic nonchalance with which this campaign had been carried out.
52. Radu Lecca, *Eu i-am salvat pe evrei din Romania* (Bucharest, 1994), 173.
53. Vasiliu's order (which contains the expression *ecarisaj poliţienesc*) reproduced in Achim, *Documente privind deportarea*, vol. 2, 104.
54. Ibid., vol. 1, docs. nos. 58, 61, 73, 107, (pp.) 89–90, 94–95, 114, 180–81.
55. Ibid., vol. 2, doc. no. 314, 116–17.
56. Ibid., vol. 1 docs. nos. 155, 188, (pp.) 238–39, 284–85.
57. Response of the police chief in Galaţ to Vasiliu's inquiry, January 1943, DANIC, 43/1943/176v (USHMM, RG 25.010M).
58. Report of the gendarme legion in Constanţa county, no date, DANIC, 43/1943/80–81v (USHMM, RG 25.010M). On ethnic composition of Greater Romania see Sabin Manuilă, *Studiu etnografic asupra populaţiei României* (Bucharest, 1940).

59. Nastasă and Varga, *Minorități etnoculturale*, doc. no. 234, 436–38.
60. Ibid., docs. nos. 223, 231, (pp.) 334–36, 345–46.
61. Petitions of ethnic Romanians on behalf of deported Gypsies reproduced in Achim, "Atitudinea contemporanilor," passim.
62. Achim, *Documente privind deprtarea*, vol. 1, 219–21, 223–24.
63. Ibid., vol. 1, doc. no. 235, 349–50.
64. For field commanders' intercessions on behalf of Roma rank-and-file see Achim, *Documente privind deprtarea*, vol. 1, docs. nos. 40, 55, 174, (pp.) 64–65, 84–85, 263; vol. 2, doc. 433, 261–63. On the position of the General Staff see ibid., vol. 1, docs. nos. 161, 215, (pp.) 244–46, 324–25; vol. 2. docs. nos. 525, 632, (pp.) 362, 486.
65. Achim, *Documente privind deportarea*, vol. 1, doc. 220, 330–31.
66. Brătianu's memo, 16 September 1942, reproduced in International Commission on the Holocaust in Romania (ICHR), *Documente*, doc. no. 202, 432. On his position in the party and the popular opinion regarding his personality see Hudița, *Jurnal politic*, [1940–1941], 110; [1941], 61; [1941–1942], 165.
67. Police report, 23 October 1942, reproduced in Achim, *Documente privind deportarea*, vol. 1, doc. no. 202, 301–12. See also National Peasant Party memo of 16 January 1941, reproduced in Ion Calafeteanu, ed., *Iuliu Maniu—Ion Antonescu, Opinii şi confruntări politice, 1940–1944* (Cluj-Napoca, 1994), 116.
68. Interview with Iona Marin in Nastasă and Varga, *Minorități etnoculturale*, 615.
69. For the best analysis of the Romanian foreign policy evolution and its effects on anti- Jewish policies see Sebastian Balta, *Rumänien und die Großmächte in der Ära Antonescu, 1940–1944* (Stuttgart, 2005), 240–98.
70. Achim, *Roma in Romanian History*, 169–70, 180–85.
71. Achim, *Documente privind deportarea*, vol. 1, doc. no. 15, 22–23.
72. Ibid., doc. no. 116, 191–92. The order was transmitted to the gendarme units on 21 September 1942 (ibid., doc. no. 141, 221–22).
73. Ibid., doc. no. 6, 9.
74. For one such case involving three women from Argeş County (Wallachia) see DANIC, 127/1942; 130/1942, vol. 2 (USHMM, RG 25.010M).

Chapter 5

Nazi Occupation Policies and the Mass Murder of the Roma in Ukraine

Mikhail Tyaglyy

After seventy years since the end of World War II the fate of the Romani population in Nazi-occupied Ukraine still remains a blank spot.[1] At the discursive level, scholars have been debating whether the Nazi mass murder of the Roma amounted to genocide. Specifically, historians have posed the question if the mass murder was premeditated and if it involved the administration at all levels.

In the case of the occupied Soviet territories, this debate is complicated by the fact that the guiding principles used by the Nazis in their treatment of the Roma differed markedly from those applied in Germany proper. Due to the input of the German administration at a lower level, the uniform policy vis-à-vis the Roma as such did not exist.[2] The existing practices to a larger degree depended on the predominance of any one occupational authority: the civil administration, the SS, or the Wehrmacht. When it came to deciding over the life and death of individual Roma, the criteria were by no means drawn directly from "racial" concepts worked out at Robert Ritter's Research Institute for Racial Hygiene and Population Biology[3] but rather were justified on the basis of their social status.

The "Gypsy policymaking" in Nazi-occupied Ukraine involved several German agencies, each one pursuing its own interests. The Einsatzgruppen C and D of the German Security Police played by far the most significant role in the process of destruction, followed by the Office of the Higher SS and Police Commander (Höhere SS- und Polizeiführer, or HSSPF), the Wehrmacht, field gendarmerie, and the civil administration of Reich Commissariat Ukraine (Reichskommissariat Ukraine, or RKU). The inconsistency of initiatives at various levels further complicated the picture, occasionally rendering the Nazi policy toward the Roma in Ukraine self-contradictory.

This chapter attempts to explicate this contradiction by addressing the following issues. First, in the absence of a comprehensive overview, I will provide a basic outline, on a province-to-province basis, of the major aspects of the Nazi campaign of extermination vis-à-vis the Roma in Ukraine. Second, I will speculate whether different branches of the Nazi occupation authorities—the military, the SS, and the civil administration—treated the Romani minority differently. Third, taking into account that some parts of the present-day Ukraine were administered by Germany's satellites, Romania and Hungary, I will look for potential differences, if any, in the persecution of the Roma in different occupation zones. Fourth, I will consider the attitudes of the local non-Romani population toward the Nazi mass murder of Roma and the effect that they might have had on the extermination policy. As an overall objective, this chapter will assess the current state of research on this particular subject and pinpoint the specific aspects that warrant further investigation.

The "Gypsy Question" as Perceived by the Wehrmacht, the SS, and the Civil Administration

During the Einsatzgruppen Trial at Nuremberg in 1947–48, the former commander of Einsatzgruppe D Otto Ohlendorf had testified that, in May or June 1941, head of the German Police and the SS Heinrich Himmler and head of the Reich Security Main Office (Reichssicherheitshauptamt, or RSHA) Reinhard Heydrich had communicated verbal orders (through intermediaries) "to protect the rear of the troops by killing the Jews, Gypsies, Communist functionaries, active communists, and all other persons who could endanger the security."[4] On the basis of this testimony some historians have concluded that the task of killing the Roma had been assigned to the *Einsatzgruppen* before Nazi Germany invaded the Soviet Union.[5] Other scholars, however, consider

Ohlendorf's statement as unreliable and question the existence of any direct order regarding Roma.[6] In his testimony Ohlendorf did not refer to any higher orders or other "rational" justifications to explain the elimination of the Romani population. While denying the distinction between Roma and Jews had ever been made, he ascertained the latter group's alleged proclivity for espionage. If a specific directive concerning the Roma had been issued, Ohlendorf would have likely mentioned it. Otherwise, Ohlendorf ascribed "asocial" characteristics to all Roma without exception and insisted that the reasons for the destruction of the two groups were identical.[7]

Heydrich's written orders did not specifically mention the Roma.[8] Among groups and individuals who were subject to "special treatment," Heydrich's deputy Heinrich Müller listed five categories: partisans, communists, Jews, the mentally ill, and "other elements dangerous to the state."[9] Nevertheless, *Einsatzgruppen* units (so-called *Einsatzkommandos* and *Sonderkommandos*) had the right "to take executive measures concerning the civilian population within the scope of their missions, upon their own responsibility."[10] In effect, the commander of a unit could, at his discretion, identify groups that "posed a threat" to the Wehrmacht. When identifying the array of "political opponents" of the regime, the *Einsatzgruppen* leaders were guided by the demands of the moment and the local situation. In addition to the shortage of food supplies and billeting space, the Soviet partisan threat was another essential factor in decision making. Under these circumstances, the decision to include the Roma—whom Nazi ideology and propaganda had declared inferior—among the groups to be exterminated seemed entirely logical to the local occupation administration. Contributing their own, negative, stereotypes of Roma, the army officers' frequent references to the potential for Romani "espionage" demonstrate just how widely the Wehrmacht's position influenced the decision to liquidate the Roma in the occupied Soviet territories and elsewhere. For example, in spring 1940 three thousand Roma were deported to the General Government of Poland from the western areas of Germany as a result of direct pressure from the Wehrmacht High Command, which wanted to rid the area of potential spies while the war with France was in progress.[11] Similarly, German army officers saw executions of Roma in Serbia in fall 1941 not as part of a general plan to wipe out Roma, but as part of a reprisal campaign and as a response to suspected espionage.[12]

Fairly often, the German occupation administration discriminated between the itinerant and sedentary Roma, between the "asocial" and "socially stable." This approach was typical of the Reich Commissioner for the Ostland (Reichskommissariat Ostland, or RKO) Hinrich Lohse.

In the fall of 1941 Lohse directed Himmler's attention to the problem created in the RKO by itinerant Roma as the group supposedly unfit for labor and responsible for spreading diseases. On 4 December 1941, he issued a decree that presented the Roma as a double threat. Arguing that Roma caused harm to the Germans by sharing information with the enemy, Lohse concluded that "they need to be treated in the same manner as the Jews."[13]

The criteria for exercising "Gypsy policy" were a subject of discussion at the Reich Ministry for the Occupied Eastern Territories (Reichministerium für die besetzten Ostgebiete, or RMO) in Berlin in June 1942. When developing a uniform policy regarding the Roma in the East, RMO official Otto Bräutigam inquired about the status of the Roma in the RKO: "I am particularly interested in whether Gypsies, in your opinion, should be subjected to the same treatment as the Jews. Also, I need information on the Gypsies' lifestyle, whether they are settled or nomadic, what their activities are, and how many mixed Roma are found in their midst." According to Guenter Lewy, the RKU received the same inquiry.[14]

There is circumstantial evidence that, following that inquiry, the RKU authorities were indeed collecting the data on the Romani population. On 10 July 1942, the rural district administration of Vysotsk in Volyn forwarded to village councils the order issued by county authorities requesting the latter to submit within five days the information about the Roma residing within their administrative borders. The inquiry contained ten questions, including the following: "How long a Gypsy lives in a village"; "Occupation/profession"; "Does he/she own land?"; and "Is he/she a real Gypsy or mixed blood?"[15] Nine village councils reported no Roma residing on their territory.[16] It is unlikely that the data collection campaign had been launched on the initiative of any particular county administration. Remarkably, the questions posed in the inquiry were essentially identical to those in Otto Bräutigam's letter. This observation indicates that, most probably, similar inquiries originating from the same source had been distributed across the RKU.

The official response from the RKO issued on 2 July 1942 cited Lohse's decree of 4 December 1941 as the basis for "Gypsy policy" and stated that the remaining Roma were a threat to the region. In July of the same year the RMO prepared a draft order, the Treatment of the Gypsies in the Occupied Eastern Territories, which prescribed: "No distinction is to be made between settled and nomadic Gypsies. Gypsies of mixed race are as a rule to be treated as Jews, particularly when they live in a Gypsy fashion or are not socially integrated." The order stipulated the following criteria to be used in determining Roma identity:

self-identification, testimonials of other group members, lifestyle, and social conditions. According to the historian Michael Zimmermann, the deliberate ambiguity of these criteria reflected the willingness of the civil administration to eventually get rid of all Roma in the area of their control.[17]

For reasons unknown, the drafting of this order continued until May 1943. The next version, however, suggested a different solution to the Gypsy Question by taking into account the difference between the itinerant and the sedentary groups, who would be placed in special camps. This time around, Roma were to be treated differently from the Jews, with no difference made between Roma of mixed origin (*Zigeunermischlinge*) and so-called purebloeded Roma. The definition of "Roma" was entrusted to Reich commissioners while the actual execution of the order was delegated to the German Security Police and the SD. The historian Guenter Lewy has attributed the change in the treatment of the Roma to the fact that the RMO and its leader Alfred Rosenberg had acted in the vein of the Roma policy in Germany proper as implemented by Himmler. In accordance with that policy, a part of Germany's Roma regarded as itinerant "and socially dangerous" was deported to Auschwitz, whereas the sedentary Roma, deemed useful, were to be dispatched to forced labor camps.[18]

On 19 October 1943, the leader of the German Security Police and SD in the RKO Friedrich Panziger let Lohse know that the Reich Criminal Police Office had notified the former of Himmler's plans concerning the Roma. Sedentary and mixed-blood Roma were subject to the same treatment as the rest of the population in the occupied territories. Itinerant Roma and half-blood persons meanwhile were assigned the same status as the Jews, to be confined to concentration camps.[19] These principles were reiterated in the RMO decree of 15 November 1943 (sent to both RKO and RKU), and the corresponding order by Lohse. According to Lewy, this decree introduced no changes in the existing situation; it effectively legalized the policy that had since long been introduced in RKO: the itinerant Roma were shot on the spot whereas the sedentary Roma still had a chance for survival. Conspicuously, no specific documents pertaining to the discussion regarding the treatment of the Roma in Reich Commissariat Ukraine have come to light until now; the policy making can only be explored at the level of civil administration in few areas.

According to the Soviet census of 1939, out of the 88,242 Roma in the whole of the country 10,443 lived in Ukraine (0.03 percent of the total population of the Ukrainian SSR).[20] Taking into account the 2,064 Roma in Crimea and a few more thousands in the former Polish and Romanian territories incorporated into the Soviet Union in 1939–40—

according to the historian Alexander Kruglov—the total Romani population in Ukraine (excluding Transcarpathia, which was part of Hungary between 1939 and 1944) hardly exceeded 20,000 persons by mid-1941.[21] However, since a part of the Roma people led an itinerant lifestyle while some Roma identified themselves as Ukrainians or Russians (and thus distorted the census data), the actual figure might be much larger.

As previously stated, due to the absence of uniform guidelines from the German Security Police and owing to local context, Nazi anti-Gypsy policies differed from one region of occupied Ukraine to another. Since the territory of what is now Ukraine was divided into several occupation zones dominated by different type of authority (military administration in left-bank Ukraine, civil administration in RKU, Romanian administration in Transnistria and West Galicia), I chose to examine the Nazi mass murder of the Roma within each of the provinces (*область*) of contemporary Ukraine separately. Unfortunately, most of the available evidence is mere statistics, and even then, incomplete. The names of the victims often remain unknown and so are the names of the perpetrators of brutalities. The objective of the following, rather sketchy, overview is to convey the scope of the Nazi Final Solution of the Gypsy Question, as it was carried out in Ukraine.

The Mass Murder of Roma Under Military Rule

The larger part of the territory of Ukraine east of the Dniester River (currently Chernihivska, Donetska, Luganska, Kharkivska, and Sumska provinces) remained for the duration of the German occupation under the jurisdiction of the Wehrmacht. Divided into several Army Rear Areas (*Rückwartiges Armeegebiet*), this part of contemporary Ukraine was administered through the local and field commandant's offices (*Ortskommandanturen* and *Feldkommandanturen*). The latter agency had not only military but also political functions, carrying out so-called pacification measures in cooperation with the SS *Einsatzgruppen*.

On 13 September 1941, on its way from Vyrva to Dederiv in Chernihiv province, Sonderkommando 4a shot dead the thirty-two members of a Romani caravan on the pretext that German ammunition had allegedly been found in a horse cart. According to a situational report (*Ereignismeldung*) of Einsatzgruppe C: "As the mob had no documents, and could not explain the origin of these items, it was executed [en masse]."[22] On 30 May 1942, in pursuance of the order by district gendarmerie, sedentary Roma working at "Stalin" collective farm were arrested and taken to the village of Baturin where eleven of them were executed. Three other Romani agricultural workers, two men and a woman from the village of Riabukhy in Dmytrivskyi district, were shot dead in the town of Bakhmach on 24 October 1942.[23]

One of the best documented executions of Romani population took place in the city of Chernihiv. On 10 July 1942, the local security police chief issued an announcement (in Ukrainian and Russian) that required the Roma to assemble "for resettlement to new places of residence." To avoid a "severe punishment" promised in the case of a failure to obey this order, the Roma flocked to Chernihiv from the surrounding towns, villages, and hamlets. The police told the Roma that they were about to be resettled in Serbia and therefore should take their money and valuables along with them. In August 1942, the Roma who had gathered in the city were taken to a local jail. According to witness testimonies, the half-naked and barefoot Roma were kept twenty-five persons per cell. On 30 September they were taken in groups to a nearby forest where they were executed.[24] According to various estimates, the number of victims ranged from few hundred to two thousand.[25]

Following the destruction of a larger part of the Romani population, the German Security Police continued hunting down individual survivors. On 20 December 1942, four Romani persons, among them three children, were brought to Chernigiv for execution from the village of Tykhoniv. Fourteen individuals were arrested in the town of Kovshyn; they, too, were executed in Chernigiv later in 1943. Seven Roma from the village of Zhuravky, Varvynskyi district, faced a firing squad in Pryluky on 25 September 1942.[26]

Along with the official documents, oral testimonies provide further details of the Nazi genocidal policies. In the summer of 1942, not far from Chernihiv a police patrol spotted a Romani caravan whose members were celebrating a wedding. The policemen ordered the Romani men to dig their own grave but took the newlyweds to the city. In Chernihiv, the newlyweds reportedly had their cheeks pierced through with a metallic rod, put the screws on both ends, and then forced to march on a leash around the city for some time. Eventually, all the eighteen families from this particular caravan were murdered.[27] The massacres continued in 1943. According to the data of the Soviet State Extraordinary Commission for the Investigation of the Crimes Committed by German Fascists and their Collaborators on the Territory of the USSR (Чрезвычайная государственная комиссия, or ChGK), 387 persons were murdered on 6 January 1943, in Novgorod-Siverskyi; 40 persons were executed on 26 February 1943, in Gorbovo; smaller groups of Roma were put to death between May 1942 and March 1943 throughout the Chernihiv province.[28]

The massacre that took place in March 1943 in the village of Gorodishche of Baturin district demonstrates most clearly the Nazis' intention to murder all the Roma irrespective of their social status and lifestyle as a security threat to the army. The Germans rounded up (on the pretext of an imminent resettlement) and subsequently executed some twenty Roma from Gorodishche and neighboring villages along with the other inhabitants regarded as Communist Party members and Soviet activists—a total of fifty-six persons. According to a Romani survivor, "Our ancestors got patches of land over here in 1861. Many of the Roma got married to the Ukrainians so that one could not really claim we were the true Gypsies, it's just that we looked like Gypsies. But the Germans disliked the Gypsies, saying the Gypsies were all untrustworthy people and that they were [Soviet] partisans."[29] The German occupation authorities used the same rationale for the mass murder of the Roma in other provinces of Ukraine.

According to ChGK records, the Romani population of Artemivsk in Donetsk province was exterminated following the destruction of the Jews in that city in late February 1942. Carried out by Sonderkommando 4b, the mass execution took place in a former alabaster mine and claimed the lives of at least twenty Roma, that is, the entire community.[30] The hunt for survivors as well as the Roma from mixed marriages continued for several months after the mass execution. Ivan Koriakin, who was married to a Ukrainian and had six children, for example, was arrested on 13 April 1942.[31] The Donetsk (until 1961 Stalino) province ChGK had concluded that the Romani population of the city of Mariupol was subjected by the Nazis to the same treatment as the Jews, who were executed en masse in October 1941.[32] Sonderkommando 10a murdered the total of forty Roma. Another *Einsatzgruppe* unit carried similar mass executions in the city of Kharkiv, in a forest park and the Drobytskyi ravine respectively. Most Roma were rounded up in the horse market in Kharkiv and in the Ordzhonikidze neighborhood. The town of Balakleia in Kharkiv province became a site of an execution of approximately fifty Roma.[33]

Up to thirty Roma were executed in the city of Sumy in mid-1942.[34] Another, larger, mass execution in Sumy province took place in the town of Leninsk on 9 and 10 January 1943. Two days earlier, local policemen arrested members of the Prokota, Moskalenko, and Pinchuk families (thirty-one of them identified by name) and fifteen other Roma. According to ChGK data, between October 1941 and February 1942 the German Security Police units carried out mass executions of Roma in at least six localities in Zaporizhia province: forty-eight persons were murdered in Mykhailivka and sixty in Pryshyb; Bereichskommando 31 of

Einsatzgruppe Halbstadt executed eighty-one persons in Molochansk; Einsatzkommando 12, seventeen in Guliaipole; Sonderkommando 10a, about one hundred in Melitopol; and Einsatzkommando 12, three hundred in Pology.[35]

The Mass Murder of Roma in Civil Administration Zone

The Reich Commissariat Ukraine with the official capital in Rivne came into existence on 1 September 1941 and remained administratively under the RMO. As of 1 September 1942, RKU comprised six general districts (*Generalbezirke*) that constitute contemporary Volyn, Rivne, Zhytomyr, Cherkasy, Dnipropetrovsk, and partially Mykolaiiv, Vinnytsa, Kherson, and Zaporizhzhia provinces, as well as Crimea and a small portion of left-bank Ukraine incorporating parts of Kiev and Poltava provinces. As the Wehrmacht advanced eastward, the military authorities transferred power in these areas to the RMO. The latter put RKU in charge of economic matters, while the security-related tasks remained within the jurisdiction of the German Security Police and SD and the Office of Higher SS and Police Commander in South Russia (Höhere SS- und Polizeiführer).

Members of Einsatzgruppe D, moving eastward in the rear of the Eleventh Army, carried out earlier mass executions of Roma in Mykolaiiv province: in September 1941 they murdered between 100 and 150 Roma, among them women and children; the number of victims of the October massacre remains unknown.[36] A further two hundred Roma were shot in the city of Mykolaiiv in January 1942.[37] A total of 120 Romani and Jewish families were killed in the former German colony of Steinberg, Varvarivskyi district, where they had been previously used as slave laborers.

The Red Army political division reported on 26 April 1942 that seven thousand Jews along with the twenty-eight Romani families were executed by the Germans in Kherson shortly after the city had been occupied.[38] Apparently, the local ChGK reported on the same event when it stated that seventy Romani women and children had been killed in Kherson in March 1942. According to one other source, in May of 1942 the Roma were ordered to assemble for deportation "to their motherland," that is, to Romania. After some three hundred Roma had gathered, they were executed en masse near the city jail, and their bodies were dumped into the ditch.[39] Fifty more Roma were put to death in the summer of 1943.[40] Another case of mass murder, which destroyed a caravan of 150, apparently was perpetrated at a local dumping ground for dead animals.[41]

The acts of mass murder also took place in Kherson suburbs. Thus, the ChGK had reported on the mass execution of twenty-six Roma (two men, twelve women, and twelve children) in Syvashi on 6 May 1942. Locked in a barn, initially the victims were told that they would be sent to Bessarabia. The names remain unknown of the fourteen persons who were murdered on 15 May in Pavlivka, not far from Syvashi. According to eyewitness accounts, the execution was carried out by the same SS commando as in Syvashi, and the Roma were similarly told of an impending resettlement. A group of eighteen Roma was arrested in the village of Bekhtera, Gola Prystan district, on 13 May 1942, taken by a truck to a nearby execution site, and shot. Just as brutally murdered were the sixteen Roma in Beryslav and, on 10 August 1942, a group of Roma in Starosoldatsk.[42]

The ethnographer Nikolai Bessonov has reconstructed the story of destruction by a German unit of a caravan near the city of Nikopol in Dnipropetrovsk province. The Germans drove a column of Romani horse carts to an antitank ditch. Once the victims realized their imminent fate, one of the Roma turned his wagon around and dashed across the field. The Germans had to abort the pursuit as their vehicles could not to run through the ploughed field. This particular individual was thus able to escape, but the remaining Roma were shot.[43] In Pokrovskyi district, in late 1942 gendarmerie and the Ukrainian auxiliary police conducted a raid, arresting and killing forty Roma.

The first documented mass execution of Roma—portrayed as "asocial elements (Gypsies)"—in Kirovograd province took place in early September 1941 and was carried out by Einsatzgruppe C.[44] According to Kruglov, the systematic destruction of the Roma began in this part of Ukraine in 1942 when seventy-three persons were shot dead at "Lenin" collective farm in Novoukraiinski district. Another twenty-seven Romani farmers were murdered in the summer of 1942 in the village of Yanychi in Chygyryn district.[45] In the city of Kirovograd, as established by the Ukrainian NKVD (Soviet Security Police) investigation commission, over six thousand Jews and one thousand Roma were "shot and tortured to death."[46]

In the fall of 1941, during an operation against "undesired elements" in the city of Poltava, the police arrested and later executed a group of Roma. Following a similar roundup in Chutovo, the arrested Roma were murdered on the outskirts of the village and their bodies dumped in the ditch. Twenty-five Romani and Jewish families, 163 persons in total, were executed on 18 May 1942, in Pyriatyn. In the town of Zinkiv an entire caravan of sixty-one men, women, and children was destroyed in 1942. With the exact date of the mass execution remaining unknown, survivors had testified that, when the executioners filled the grave up with the soil, some of the victims were still alive. Twenty-five Roma were slaughtered in February 1943 in Kobeliaky and another 250 in April 1943 in Lubny.[47] When shepherding horses sometime in 1943, a school student in Vilshanka, Lubny district, witnessed the arrival of a few truckloads of Roma: "As usual, [the trucks] were trailed by a passenger car. A horrific carnage then commenced. The people screamed, tore their hair, tried to hide under the vehicles.... Then [we] went to the grave; the place was soaked with blood, with playing cards, dresses, necklaces scattered all around."[48]

In Biloziria, Cherkasy district, not far from the town of Smila, a gravestone marks the site of a mass execution of 120 Roma who had been slain in the Tiasmyn marshes. In Zhytomir province, according to ChGK records, the mass murder of Roma took place in June 1942 in Malyn and Yanushpol, with three hundred and sixty victims respectively. A Romani survivor testified that several members of a caravan had been murdered in 1941 not far from Novohrad-Volynskyi. In the village of Golyshi, Olevskyi district, German forces killed thirty-two Roma. According to one other, unconfirmed, testimony, twenty-six Roma arrested by the Germans in Zhytomyr province had been deported to the Krakow-Płaszów concentration camp. Romani children had later been transferred from Płaszów to Litzmannstadt (Łódź)—and reportedly did return home in 1945—whereas the adults had been deported farther to Germany and France.[49]

The first act of mass murder in Volyn province was committed on 2 June 1942, when German gendarmes executed sixty-four Roma in the village of Shylovoda.[50] A similar mass execution took place the same month in Kamin-Kashyrskyi. On 17 August 1942, a German Security Police unit in Rivne reported that seventy-six Roma had been subjected to "special treatment" in Kamin-Kashyrskyi and Kovel.[51] Prior to the mass execution, Jewish and Romani prisoners were locked in the same concentration camp; over one hundred Romani victims were hastily buried in a mass grave dug out in the Jewish cemetery by a local villager. Approximately thirty Roma were put to death in 1942 in Ratno; nearly fifty were slaughtered in the spring of 1943 near Zabolottia; and, according to witness accounts, no less than sixty were shot in 1943 in the village of Vydera, Kamin-Kashyrskyi district. The 150 Romani men, women, and children who had been arrested in Kovel were executed en masse after three days spent in a local concentration camp. The twenty Roma arrested in August of 1942 in Ternopil province had been dispatched to Kremenets prison where they were later executed.[52]

In Volodymyrets district of Rivne province, not far from the village of Stepangorod, the Germans hunted down and executed fifteen Roma who had been hiding in the forest.⁵³ As reported by the Kostopol district commissar, on 21 April 1942, ninety-two Romani men, women, and children were arrested and dispatched to a forced labor camp in Ludvipol.⁵⁴ In view of the fact that these "Gypsies were a serious burden to the camp due to severe lice infestation," most likely they were eventually executed. On 15 May 1942, the commissar general of Brest-Lytovsk ordered "all nomadic Gypsies in the district to be arrested and imprisoned. For the time being, they need to be engaged in productive labor while their horses and wagons are to be confiscated." On 21 May the commissar general of Volyn-Podillia instructed district commissars "to immediately arrest all wandering tradesmen, for they spread rumors." He further prescribed to immediately arrest all itinerant Roma, to confiscate their horses and wagons, putting the latter to "rational use."⁵⁵ The ChGK has further documented the mass murder of some two hundred Roma in Sarny on 26 August 1942, and of another fifteen Roma "who had lived in the forest" in the village of Voronky in Volodymyrets district.⁵⁶

Ill-known as the site of one of the largest massacres of Jews, Babi Yar—a ravine on the outskirts of Kiev—was also an execution site for the Roma. Anatoly Kuznetsov has written in his book, *Babyn Yar:* "Fascists hunted the Roma like game. They were subject to immediate destruction like the Jews.... The Roma were taken to Babi Yar by entire caravans, and it seems that until the very last moment they could not comprehend what was about to happen to them."⁵⁷ According to unverified data, back in September 1941 three Romani caravans from Kurenivka were executed en masse behind Kyrylivska Church.⁵⁸ At least two testimonies mentioned a massacre of itinerant Roma, who arrived with their wagons, following the mass murder of Jews in late 1941–early 1942.⁵⁹ Further testimonies spoke of the destruction of thirty Romani women and children at Babi Yar in 1942. The recurrent brutalities gave birth to a popular saying in Kiev during the war: "The Germans have come—good! The Jews are kaput. The Gypsies are dead too. And so will be the Ukrainians" (*Немцы пришли—gut! Евреям kaput. Цыганам тоже. Украинцам—позже*). As of 1 April 1942, there only remained alive twenty Jews and forty Roma in Kiev. One year later, the Kiev Security Police Office had two Roma in its custody.⁶⁰

In May 1942 the German Security Police dispatched the fifty-two extended Romani families from all over the Kiev district to the nearby town of Vasylkiv and executed them.⁶¹ According to ChGK records, in August 1942 near the town of Obukhiv the Ukrainian and German policemen arrested some 250 Roma. The policemen subsequently brought the Roma to the "The Ninth of January" collective farm where they executed the prisoners next to the silage pit. The executioners received the order from Obukhiv gendarmerie chief [?] Fabisch and Obukhiv police chief Savka Zaiats.[62]

The Persecution of Roma in Transnistria

The southwestern part of prewar Ukraine, which contained a substantial number of Roma, was in 1941 occupied by Romania. Situated between the Dniester and Bug Rivers, the present Ukrainian provinces of Odessa, Mykolaiiv, and Vinnytsa constituted the so-called Transnistria Governorate. In addition, Transnistria included North Bukovina, currently the Chernivtsy province of Ukraine. As the factors contributing to the decision of the Antonescu regime to deport the Roma of Romania and Bessarabia to Transnistria have received considerable attention in scholarship,[63] the following discussion will focus on the impact of these criminal policies on the Roma, both local residents and recent deportees.

In the Odessa province the mass murder of Roma commenced as early as August 1941. In the vicinity of Koshary village in the Andre-Ivanivskyi district, a German squad ran across a Romani caravan comprising seventy people on eleven horse carts; the victims were subsequently executed at Mykolayivka.[64] Along with the Jews, beginning in June 1942, Romanian occupation authorities carried out a deportation of the Romanian and Bessarabian Roma to Transnistria (deemed an "ethnic dump"). The deportation waves sent nearly twenty-five thousand persons across the Dniester River, close to 12 percent of the total Romani population of Romania. During the initial phase, in June–August 1942, only so-called nomadic Roma were subject to deportation. In September 1942, however, the deportation order extended also to those deemed "asocial."[65]

This is how Petre Radita has described his experiences of deportation: "We were transported from Bucharest in cattle cars, having only been allowed to take with us the carry-on luggage. We rode for a few weeks with frequent stops. The nights were cold, blankets were very scarce and so was the food. As a result, many people died of hunger and freezing temperatures before we had reached the Bug River in Ukraine. Placed in huts, the survivors were forced to dig trenches."[66] The Roma were dumped in the prefectures of Golta, Ochakiv, Berezivka, and Balta, even though itinerant Roma were originally destined for Golta prefecture and sedentary Roma for Ochakiv. Many Roma travelled to Transnistria with their own horses and wagons; by order of Transnistria governor Gheorghe Alexianu from 29 July 1942, all horses and wagons would be confiscated from their owners.

On 18 December 1942, Alexianu stipulated the status of a deportee. The Roma were ordered to live in villages in groups of 150 to 350. All persons from 12 to 60 years of age were obliged to perform paid labor; each village was to appoint a Romani elder who would ensure on a daily basis that the Roma did not leave their place of residence and/or evade their labor duties. All these provisions, however, only existed on paper. In reality, the deported had no food, clothes, medicines, or any other essentials. According to one witness: "The Roma, alongside the Jews, have arrived in Golta area. All their possessions were taken away and [therefore] they were dropping like flies." A witness from the neighboring Akhmechetka village recalled that the Roma died of the same causes as the Jews, due to epidemic, starvation, and routine executions. The 3,423 surviving Roma in Kovalivka had been divided into four labor details in March 1943. The number of Roma in Golta, Kryve Ozero, Vradiievka, Liubashivka, and Domanivka who had remained alive by November was 9,567. The Roma in Kovalivka were reportedly deprived of any means of existence, forced to sell their own clothes in order to survive. The winter of 1942–43 proved deadly for the Roma in Transnistria. For example, according to an official report, due to a typhus epidemic the number of Roma in Landau district had dropped from 7,500 to anywhere between 1,800 and 2,400.[67] In an attempt to alleviate the situation, in the summer of 1943 the local authorities issued a decree disbanding labor details and prescribing to distribute the surviving Roma among the existing collective farms. This decree brought a partial relief to Roma's plight, since it provided for an opportunity to procure food and get employment. At the same time, the local administration continuously blamed Roma for their poor work ethics, proclivity to theft, vagrancy, and unwillingness to settle in one place. The local population often viewed the Roma as a superfluous element, unwilling to share the limited resources with the former. Furthermore, the itinerant Roma occasionally died at the hands of Romanian gendarmes, SS-men, or local *Volksdeutsche*. As stated by the prosecution in Ion Antonescu's court case, the prefect of the Golta district Modest Isopescu had ordered the execution of some six to eight thousand Roma. The auxiliary police units had executed an unidentified number of Roma, for instance, in the village of Schenfeld.[68] Another massacre, of some twenty Roma, took place in the village of Velyka Mechetnia in November 1943.[69]

The deportation of Roma to Ukraine caused discontent on the part of the German officialdom. Writing to his boss, Alfred Rosenberg, in August 1942, Reich Commissioner for Ukraine Erich Koch argued that the Roma arriving to the eastern bank of the Bug "as before, constitute a threat and can exercise a bad influence on the Ukrainians." Rosenberg noted that the territory in which the Roma were originally meant to be deported had been settled by ethnic Germans, and petitioned before the German Foreign Office to influence Romania on this issue. The commission for the investigation of war crimes established in postwar Romania concluded: "Tens of thousands of innocent Roma were forced into Transnistria. Half of them had suffered from typhus. Gendarmes were treating them brutally: the life of each and every Roma was in danger and the tortures were beastly. Commanding staff resorted to obscenity and established entire harems consisting of good-looking Romani women. Approximately 36,000 Roma fell victim to the Antonescu's regime." According to estimates by Donald Kenrick and Grattan Puxon, around 20,000 "pureblooded" Roma and 4,000 Roma of mixed origin were deported eastward, and nearly as many itinerant Roma travelled to Transnistria in caravans. The death toll thus might be as high as 9,000.[70] According to the Romanian historian Viorel Achim, however, out of the 25,000 Roma who had been deported to Transnistria only 14,000 survived.[71]

The Persecution of Roma in Transcarpathia and the District *Galizien*

The two other, smaller, areas that warrant separate treatment are Transcarpathia (or Carpathian Ruthenia) and the District Galizien. In March 1939 Transcarpathia declared its independence as the Republic of Carpathian Ukraine, but was immediately invaded and annexed by Hungary. In the fall of 1944 the northern and eastern parts of Transcarpathia were seized by the Soviet Army, and eventually attached to Ukraine as Zakarpats'ka province. According to the 1930 census, the number of Roma in Transcarpathia amounted to 1,442, though the actual figure may be somewhat larger. Apparently, the so-called Gypsy Question became as acute in Transcarpathia in 1940–41 as it became elsewhere. Thus, the deputy chief of Uzhan district reported on 20 September 1940 to the Hungarian Ministry of the Interior that the local authorities had taken appropriate measures to prevent Roma migration, yet could not eradicate the root of the problem. On 16 April 1941, this question came up at a separate meeting in Uzhgorod, which proposed to the minister of the Interior to lock up all Roma in special camps and use them in river dyke construction works, lumber industry, tree planting, and other types of work. At this suggestion, the participants in the meeting referred to the example of the town of Székesfehérvár where a similar solution to the Gypsy Question had been implemented for the first time in Hungary.[72]

Similar offers came from across Transcarpathia, effectively turning many caravan stopping grounds into ghettos. According to eyewitness accounts, the Roma were only able to live in the camp territory, surrounded by barbed wire and patrolled by guards, with a special permit.[73] Worn out by grueling labor, severe malnutrition, and the lack of medical care, the Roma were dying slow death while awaiting deportation to Germany's concentration camps. Following the resumption of hostilities in Transcarpathia on 15 July 1944, the German military command effectively sanctioned the previous practice by local authorities to isolate Roma in camps-cum-ghettos.[74] The actual number of Roma who perished in Transcarpathia or those who were deported to their deaths to Hungary's interior and/or German concentration camps remains unknown until today.

Very little is known today on the Nazi anti-Roma policies in District Galizien (currently Lviv, Ivano-Frankivs'k, and Ternopil provinces of Ukraine), which was a part of the General Government of Poland between 1941 and 1944. Kruglov has argued that the persecution of the Roma in the District Galizien began no earlier than February 1942. This is when the district's governor, acting pursuant to the decree issued by the General Government of Poland, prescribed to identify all Hungarian, Romanian, Slovakian, and other Roma. As a consequence, on 30 April 1942 the local welfare department reported to the General Government on the implemented "evacuation" of 536 foreign and 670 Polish Roma. Otherwise, the German treatment of the local Roma was fairly uniform. For example, in late June 1942 the gendarmerie shot twenty-five Roma in the town of Gorodok, Lviv province; a month later, the 1st company of the 133rd police battalion executed another twenty-four Roma in Rava-Ruska area. In Drogobych and Boryslav in August 1942, the Germans ordered the Roma to assemble at a local police station, subsequently deporting them to forced labor camps. During the liquidation of ghettos in 1943, the Roma were murdered along with the Jews across the towns and villages in District Galizien, for example, in Sambir in June 1943.[75]

The Case Study of Crimea

The Crimean peninsula occupies a special place in the history of the persecution of the Roma in Ukraine, and therefore warrants closer examination. What makes this region so special is its multiethnic composition (besides Russians and Ukrainians, prior to the war the Crimea was home to the Crimean Tatars). Furthermore, despite the fact that the General District of Crimea was formally a part of RKU, the real power in the German-occupied Crimea belonged to the Wehrmacht. As I will argue below, both these peculiarities influenced the Nazi treatment of the Crimean Roma.

According to the 1939 census, the Romani population of Crimea amounted to 2,064, of which 998 lived in cities and 1,066 in rural areas.[76] However, it is likely that some Roma were put down as Crimean Tatars or remained unregistered altogether. A significant number of Roma had adopted Islam and acquired the language, traditions, customs, and names of the Tatars. Simferopol, Bakhchisarai, Karasubazar (Belogorsk), and Evpatoria counted among the Crimean cities with the largest Romani communities. The destruction of the Roma and Jews in Crimea began simultaneously, in November–December 1941.

Between mid-November 1941 and March 1942, Einsatzgruppe D reported to Berlin that it had shot a total of 2,316 Roma, saboteurs, mentally ill, and so-called asocial elements.[77] These reports demonstrate that, in contrast to Jews, Roma for the most part were not singled out and put into a separate category of targeted victims. SS troops in the Crimea regarded them exclusively as asocial elements and saboteurs, regardless of their actual occupations, professional membership, or social status. Their ethnicity effectively spelled death to Crimean Roma.

According to a Romani survivor from Evpatoria, in early 1942 the German authorities compelled local Roma to report for registration. The Roma, however, went into hiding instead. In the ensuing raids the Germans apprehended more than one thousand people. The troops encircled the Romani quarters and loaded the inhabitants into trucks, with small children simply thrown into vehicles. The survivor described the execution scene at Krasnaia Gorka as follows: "I personally was in the second row of people assigned to be shot. The people in front of me were killed, and I was wounded in the shoulder. The fallen corpses covered me, so I just lay there wounded, and after the shots died down I climbed out from under the corpses and hid in the neighboring village."[78]

A Romani survivor from the village of Kamysh-Burun had told ChGK investigators that all Romani families in Kerch were imprisoned on 29 December 1941. According to him, the next day the guard detachment made up of Romanians put the Roma into twelve vehicles and took them to an antitank ditch outside of the city. The guards unloaded the people from the vehicles one by one and directed them to the ditch where German soldiers with submachine guns were waiting for them. Victims fell into the ditch after being hit by bullets from the German guns.[79] According to the findings of the Dzhankoi ChGK, about two hundred Roma had been murdered in March 1942 in gas vans in northeastern Dzhankoi along the road to Chongar; their corpses were subsequently tossed in the ditch in several layers and then buried.[80]

As of 1 November 1941, the Simferopol statistics office registered 1,700 Roma in the city. In two months' time, the numbers went down to 1,100. At the beginning of January 1943, only eight Roma remained in the city.[81] According to the recollections of eyewitnesses, the residents of Simferopol's "Gypsytown" were rounded up on 9 December 1941—the same day that the Nazis gathered the city's Krimchaks (a Turkic people practicing rabbinic Judaism). At Nuremberg, Ohlendorf's adjutant Heinz Hermann Schubert described the assembly of Roma as follows: "I went to the Gypsy quarter of Simferopol and supervised the loading of the people who were to be shot into a truck. I took care that the loading was completed as quickly as possible and that there were no disturbances or unrest on the part of the native population. Furthermore, I took care that the condemned persons were not beaten while the loading was going on."[82] Khrisanf Lashkevich described the same event differently in his diary: "The Gypsies came in crowds on carts and wagons to the Talmud-Torah [school] building. For some reason they raised a kind of green flag (the symbol of Islam) and they set a mullah at the head of their procession. The Gypsies tried to persuade the Germans that they were not Gypsies; a few identify themselves as Tatars, others as Turkmen. But their protests were ignored and they were moved into the big building."[83]

Nevertheless, according to eyewitness statements, many Roma were able to escape the massacres by fleeing the city. Some of them managed to survive by posing as Crimean Tatars. Significantly, the Crimean Tatar administration (so-called Muslim Committees were installed in each city and district center) sometimes protected the Romani minority, or at least those who practiced Islam. According to unconfirmed information, the persecution of the Roma in Simferopol stopped as a result of the intercession of the Muslim Committee with the German military command.[84] Inasmuch as the committee was formed only at the end of December 1941 or the beginning of January 1942, however, only a few Roma could have benefited from its mediation. In any case, it was a small concession on the Germans' part as they were hoping to win over the Crimean Tatars, and since much of the Romani population had already been destroyed by this time. At Nuremberg, Ohlendorf testified that the Solution of the Gypsy Question in Simferopol was indeed complicated by the fact that the Roma and the Crimean Tatars belonged to the same religion: "There were certain difficulties [in the identification of Roma], because some of the Gypsies—if not all of them—were Muslims. For this reason we considered it important not to damage relations with the Tatars, and therefore, [in seeking out and selecting Roma for extermination] we used people who understood the situation and the population."[85] Members of the Muslim Committee might have been involved in deciding which of the Roma were "essential" and which might be handed over to the Germans.

In any event, having destroyed most of the Roma in Simferopol in the first half of December 1941, the Germans apparently let the survivors be. The eyewitness Lashkevich confirmed this: "They did not manage to catch some of the Gypsies, and for reasons unknown to me, these were spared and were no longer persecuted."[86] The "Muslim factor" played an even larger role in Bakhchisarai whose Romani population remained unscathed, according to eyewitness testimonies. According to the Backchisarai Crimean Tatar oral tradition, when the Roma were assembled for "resettlement," the Muslim Greek headman of the city [?] Fenerov "went up to the weeping crowd and asked [the German] officer to pick out three [Roma] at his discretion. This was done. Fenerov brought them to the headquarters and asked them ... to take off their pants in front of the Germans. Before the amazed Germans stood ... Muslims! Fenerov then said that he could no longer be head of a city in which Muslims were being shot. The persecution was called off."[87] Whether this story is true or not, efforts to save the Roma were made not only by the municipal administration, but also by the Bakhchisarai Muslim Committee, which petitioned above all for the benefit of Roma who had gone to the same mosque as local Tatars, had spoken the same language, and had worked a trade or a retail business that benefitted the entire community.[88]

In the rural areas of the Crimean peninsula, too, the destruction of the Jewish and Romani communities was carried out simultaneously in the first half of 1942. The identification and registration of the Romani population was initiated by the field commandant offices, which issued orders to the district headmen, who in turn passed them on to the village elders. Evidently, village elders and auxiliary police actively participated in registering and rounding up Roma. The physical destruction of the Roma was the responsibility of Einsatzgruppe D and the field gendarmerie. Significantly, in rural areas and the cities alike, the killing units made no distinction between sedentary and itinerant Roma, as the following case of the Buraliev family aptly demonstrates. The parents worked on a collective farm in Karagoz village in the Staryi Krym district while their daughters went to school. According to an eyewitness, "In February 1942 a truck pulled up to the house where the Buralievs lived. Every member of the family was loaded onto the truck and taken to Staryi Krym. ... We never saw these people again, but the other villagers and I believe that they were all shot since, after the [German] troops arrived in the Crimea, the Germans killed Jews, Krimchaks, and Gypsies without mercy."[89] The seven members of the Asanov family were arrested in the Dzhuma-Eli village in the Stary Krym district and subsequently shot.[90] On 15 January 1942, Petr Fursenko and his family of six from the village of Dzhaichi in the Biiuk-Onlar district were executed "for being Gypsy."[91] In the Kolai district, thirty-two Roma were killed in the village of Terepli-Abash, six in Arlin-Barin, eight in Nem-Barin, two in Shirin, two in Mikhailovka, twenty-five in the "Bolshevik" collective farm, two in Avlach village, and three in the "Eighth of March" collective farm.[92]

As in the cities, the destruction of the Roma in the countryside was not total. Thus, the Evpatoria Field Commandant's Office related on 9 July 1942 that, according to the information provided by the local headmen in the Evpatoriia district, seventy-six Roma were still living among a total population of 91,910 people.[93] The Einsatzgruppe D reported on 8 April 1942, that "with the exception of small groups still showing up in the northern Crimea, there no longer are any Jews, Krimchaks, or Gypsies on this territory." According to a 15 June 1942 army report, however, out of a total civilian population of 573,428 in the Crimea, 405 were Roma.[94] The last references to the extermination of the Roma date to mid-1942. This does not mean, however, that there were no longer any Roma on the peninsula after that time.

The fact that in the spring and summer of 1944 the Soviet authorities had deported Roma from the Crimea, together with Crimean Tatars, Armenians, Bulgarians, and Greeks, further confirms that a small part of the Romani population did survive the Nazi occupation. When reporting on the progress of the deportation, the NKVD did not treat the Roma as a separate category, apparently assuming that the remaining Roma were Tatars. Later, however, an MVD (Ministry of the Interior) report noted that alongside the "basic contingent" (*основной контингент*) who had been deported from the Crimea in 1944 were 1,109 Roma.[95] In all likelihood, the surviving Crimean Roma belonged to the group closely related to the Crimean Tatars in their language and culture. Ironically, having been saved from Nazi persecution because of their connection to the Tatars, the Roma were subsequently persecuted by the Soviet power for the very same reason. All in all, possibly as many as one thousand Roma survived the Nazi occupation of the Crimea.

The Attitudes of the Local Population Toward the Persecution of Roma

At first glance, popular attitudes toward the persecution of the Roma appear to be of secondary importance when compared with the actual German policies. However, the actions conceived and implemented by the occupation authorities did not exist in a vacuum. The Romani quarters were situated within the existing Russian or Ukrainian neighborhoods. Under conditions of German occupation, some individuals among the local population came to play an important role in civil administration, overseeing the implementation of various German orders and decrees, including those concerning the treatment of civilians. The attitudes of non-Roma, both as individuals and figures of authority, apparently had an impact, if only limited, on the genesis of the Nazi Final Solution of the Gypsy Question. The attitudes toward victims varied depending on local and regional context, the socioeconomic profile of the Roma community in any given region, popular images of "Gypsies," and prewar interethnic relations. Without taking these factors into account, I argue, any attempt to both reconstruct and interpret the demise of the Romani minority in Ukraine during World War II would be incomplete.

So far, Nikolai Bessonov has been the first and only scholar who attempted not just to provide some examples of popular reactions toward the Nazi persecution of the Roma, but also to explicate those reactions. Thus, he has argued that the Slavic population extended support to the Romani minority, which was not at all the case with the Jews. Bessonov further stated that he "was unable to find even one case of support given by the locals to the occupiers."[96] He differentiated between political, economic, and cultural-psychological reasons as to the wide-scale aid given by the locals to the Roma: (1) Unlike Jews, Roma stayed outside politics and therefore were not responsible for the Soviet terror in the eyes of local population; (2) as horse-owners and skilled artisans, Roma maintained close contact with local farmers (for instance, in the winter season Romani families often rented a part of peasant's house); (3) traditional activities of the Roma such as fortune-telling, singing, and dancing enjoyed steady popularity among the local population. In addition, the latter generally viewed the Roma as a group poorer than themselves.[97]

However important, these observations mainly concern the relationship that had existed in rural areas, with a more complex admixture of social, professional, material, and cultural factors at play in urban centers. Indeed, the factors outlined by Bessonov apply almost exclusively to itinerant Roma, whereas sedentary, acculturated Roma were altogether well integrated into the existing social and professional structures. Furthermore, Bessonov based his analysis on popular reactions, essentially ignoring motivations and deeds of those among the local population who collaborated with the Germans. By the same token, Bessonov emphasized positive stereotypes of Roma, paying only scarce attention to plethora of negative anti-Roma stereotypes and prejudices.

As regards the social aspect of interethnic relations in wartime Ukraine, the two major forces that come under consideration are the Organization of Ukrainian Nationalists (OUN) and, later, the Ukrainian Insurgent Army (UPA), on the one hand, and the Soviet partisan movement, on the other. Although less frequently than the Jewish Question, Ukrainian nationalist propaganda also addressed the Gypsy Question. For example, the leaflets addressed by OUN to the Red Army soldiers warned the latter not to fight "along with Jews, Gypsies, and other scum."[98] On the basis of the Romani survivor's testimonies, Bessonov has summarized the current perception of the OUN by the Roma as the epitome of robbery, war crimes, and mass murder. The Roma collective memory draws a stark distinction between Ukrainian nationalists and Soviet partisans: "While the Soviet partisans were perceived as brothers, and the Roma recall 'good Germans' even among the occupiers, no kind word was reserved for Stepan Bandera's followers.... For the Roma, they were bandits that destroyed peaceful population, that is, the Poles, the Jews, the Russians, and, of course, the itinerant Roma caravans. Cases that ended up in violence, insults, and battery are remembered by the former nomads as sheer luck [in the sense of escaping death, MT]." This is how Jerzy Ficowski summarized in 1949 the experiences of the Roma at the hands of the Ukrainian nationalists in Volyn.[99] As for the OUN, presumably, it might believe that itinerant Roma were providing the enemy, be it Russians or Germans, with intelligence information. However, the shift in ideological and organizational principles of OUN and UPA in 1943 apparently changed their attitude toward the Roma for better.

The German sources have little to say as to the role of local administration and the auxiliary police in the persecution of the Roma; most information comes from the Soviet military authorities. Equally valuable prove the records of local municipalities and village councils, which were involved in registration of Roma, as well as in accounting of the property following their execution—as they did with regard to the Jews. In March 1942, the mayor of Staryi Krym, Konstantin Artsishevskii, compiled a list of the twenty Roma living in the city and its vicinity. He later testified that he had forwarded the list to the gendarmerie. The list served as a basis for subsequent arrest of the Roma by the German police, which had taken the victims to Feodosia for mass execution.[100] The Germans used auxiliary policemen for assembling, convoying, and occasionally executing the Roma, as it happened, for example, in the village of Kalanchak in Kherson province. On 8 May 1942 (possibly in June 1942) two German gendarmes, the district police chief, and his deputy arrived in Kalanchak. They ordered the local policemen (judging by names, ethnic Russians and/or Ukrainians) to assemble the Roma who it had been announced would be deported to Skadovsk. It is worth noting that all the Roma were sedentary, employed on a local collective farm. When the horse carts with the Roma and the accompanying police car reached the fruit gardens of the "Krasnyi partyzan" collective farm less than a mile from the village, the Roma were ordered to get off the carts and then led to an antitank ditch. According to the postwar interrogation of one of the policemen, some of the latter's colleagues were sent back to the district police, while the two Germans—assisted by the district police chief and the two remained policemen—killed the Roma, among them five children, six women, and two elderly.[101]

In March 1942, the German gendarmerie in the village of Abakly-Toma in Dzhankoi district ordered the headman of the rural council, his deputy, and the clerk to compile a list of the sixty Roma who lived in the village. On 28 March, when a gas van arrived in the village, these local officials helped collect the Roma and load them into a truck. The postwar Soviet investigation established that the Roma were killed and their corpses tossed out into the open in the northeastern section of Dzhankoi.[102] In the neighboring village of Burlak-Toma, the forty-five Romani residents were likewise assembled and loaded into the "gas chamber on wheels" with the assistance of the local headman and two local policemen. Once again, these Roma were sedentary and thus familiar to the local population. According to one of the witnesses: "[The Roma] were native residents of Burlak-Toma village; before the war they were members of our collective farm and they were good workers. The gassed Gypsies included old people and members of the Communist Youth League."[103]

After the war, the former policemen and village headmen mentioned above claimed that they had not known the purpose of the registration or the gas vans—or the plans of the Germans in general. There may have been some truth to these claims. The local collaborators often wanted to get rid of the Roma so that they could get hold of the victims' property. In all likelihood, they did not bother thinking of the Roma's fate. One can only speculate what would they have done if they had known what lay in store for those whose names were on the registration lists that they presented to the German authorities. One way or another, when the Roma were carried off, the headmen and the police aptly misappropriated the victims' meager possessions, including pants, a summer dress, a mattress, a record player, a suit, and slippers. One local official testified: "Of the grain that was left over from the gassed Gypsies I swapped ca. 440 pounds of wheat for sixty eggs, and in exchange for a four-month-old pig and the sixty eggs I got from the Germans one cow that had belonged to these same Gypsies."[104] Roma who lived in villages throughout the Dzhankoi district survived supposedly because the local headmen did not provide information about "their" Roma to the German administration, listing them as Tatars instead.[105] As for a possible explanation, the rural administration might indeed consider these Roma to be Tatars—owing to their religious-cultural kinship—or perhaps the village chiefs did deliberately fool the Germans knowing full well what would about to happen to these Roma.

Relatives of the dead reflected on the question of the victims' ethnic identification. In their postwar depositions to Soviet Security Police, they sometimes identified themselves and their deceased relatives as Crimean Tatars, claiming that the village headmen had handed the latter over to the Germans as "Gypsy Tatars." Thus one witness testified that "in March 1942, during the German occupation of our district, a part of the Tatar population numbering forty-five persons was assembled by local headman Krivoruchko under the designation of 'Gypsy Tatars,' even though they were all workers and poor peasants and belonged to the native, Tatar, population. I witnessed how the Germans put everyone under arrest in chief Krivoruchko's courtyard into the gas van that had just arrived."[106] Obviously, there was no consensus in society regarding the ethnic affiliation of the Roma. Some people, including the victims themselves, preferred to be considered Tatars, while others, including a portion of the Crimean Tatar population, were in no hurry to accept the Roma as "their own." This ambivalence, which did not play a substantial role in peacetime, played a crucial role under conditions of German occupation when group membership became a matter of life and death. In view of the assistance provided to the Roma in the Crimea by Muslim Committees, local communities obviously could influence, if only to a smaller extent, Nazi policy. According to existing testimonies, some Tatars in Odessa also rescued those of their Romani neighbors who practiced Islam.[107] Nonetheless, the instances of rescue remained few and far between.

Although the "Gypsy Question" never occupied a central part in the Nazi ideology, it nevertheless became a subject of a few newspaper articles published in the occupied Ukraine. For example, on 5 September 1943, the Kharkiv newspaper *Nova Ukraina* published an article under the title "The Gypsies and Europe." The article claimed: "The Gypsy problem has unveiled the site of profound degeneration.... Germans, in cooperation with the police, radically resolved the Gypsy question.... During a few thousand years of their coexistence with the civilized nations, the Gypsies have not embraced a settled way of life and remained the primordial nomadic barbarians.... The new Europe that arises from the ruins of all things obsolete, conservative, dangerous, and harmful to its nations has now decided to solve this socio-ethical problem [*Нова Європа, що постає на руїнах усього віджилого, консервативного, небезпечного й шкідливого для її народів, поставила сьогодні до розв'язання й цю проблему соціально-етичного порядку*]."[108] However, unlike the "Jewish Question," the treatment of all things Romani in the press was never consistent, and the desire to purge the references to Romani culture from popular consciousness was absent. For example, *Golos Kryma* described the performance by the Russian émigré singer Petr Leshchenko in Simferopol as follows: "On Friday, 3 December 1943, *the* émigré Petr Leshenko, who is well known for his interpretation of Gypsy songs, performed on the radio. He sang four songs in Russian, including "Farewell, My Gypsy Caravan" and his hit, "Chubchik."[109] Remarkably, similar performances of Gypsy songs were broadcast in occupied regions of Russia.[110] This fact further indicates that German occupation authorities apparently lacked a uniform, unambiguous policy toward the Roma, effectively delegating decision-making power to local agencies.

Conclusion

Some scholars who have done research on the Nazi "Final Solution of the Gypsy Question" in the occupied Soviet territories within the larger context of Nazi policies in the East refrain from evoking genocide.[111] The recent studies that deal specifically with the occupied Soviet territories, however, advance exactly this thesis. Nikolai Bessonov, for example, distinguishes three stages in the Nazi persecution of the Roma in the former Soviet territories, including Ukraine: (1) summer 1941–early 1942: the destruction of the itinerant Roma by the *Einsatzgruppen*; (2) 1942: full-fledged genocide that encompassed also the sedentary Roma; (3) 1943–44: the Roma, along with the Slavic populations, became the victims of antipartisan reprisals.[112] Alexander Kruglov essentially agrees with Bessonov when stating that "the fate of the Roma was virtually no different from that of the Jews. Like the Jews, the Roma were subjected to annihilation based solely on their ethnicity."[113] The German historian Martin Holler supports this view, though only within the context of the territories under direct military rule.[114] All three scholars acknowledge that the differentiation between the itinerant and sedentary Roma existed only on paper.

In addition to mapping the persecution of the Roma in wartime Ukraine, this chapter attempted to determine if there were any differences in the treatment of the Roma by various German occupation agencies. As far as the Germany's allies, Romania and Hungary, are concerned, their policies, however brutal, did not aim at totally destroying the Romani communities under their control. In the former case, the wish to get rid of all the elements considered alien to the ethnically pure Romanian nation led to mass deportation of a significant portion of Romanian Roma to the newly conquered areas. The local authorities in these areas, however, were incapable of providing proper living conditions for the deportees (which, obviously, did not preclude individual atrocities). As regards Hungary, the available data enforces the conclusion that Transcarpathian authorities were first and foremost interested in exploitation of Romani labor. Both cases suggest the absence of a methodical program of extermination.

The case of German perpetrators, though, appears rather different. The comparison between RKU and the military occupation zone renders few, if any, differences. Against the backdrop of the official discussions regarding the so-called Gypsy Question in RKO and RMO, one might assume that the distinction between sedentary and itinerant Roma was applied in RKU as well. This, however, does not transpire from the evidence presented in this chapter. The analysis of the documented cases of mass killing demonstrates that in the zone under German military rule nearly thirty such acts took place, peaking in 1942, while in the zone under German civil administration over fifty occurred within the same time period. Instances of the mass murder of both sedentary and itinerant Roma emerge from both zones (establishing the exact proportion is impossible since the available sources rarely contain the detailed profile of the victims, referring to them generally as the "Gypsies").

The argument that the Nazis pursued a systematic policy of genocide vis-à-vis Roma finds further corroboration in the records of the Soviet Extraordinary Commission.[115] Indeed, the ChGK records contain numerous testimonies and official reports that document the mass murder of the Roma and other civilian groups—primarily Jews—during the period of German occupation period. However, relying exclusively on this particular kind of source may pose a methodological problem: by uncovering numerous facts of destruction in any given province researchers may automatically form conclusions on the consistency of Nazi policy planning. Furthermore, as indicated above, ChGK records, as a rule, contain no specific information on the perpetrators and their motives. These methodological pitfalls have contributed to the misperception that the German occupation authorities were monolithic and that different agencies unanimously as well as methodically carried out the policy of genocide toward the Roma. Although the evidence of mass murder presented in this chapter is all-pervasive—in all probability, many atrocities committed against the Roma were undocumented—the question remains whether one can speak of a program of total extermination.

The structure of this chapter, built in accordance with administrative rather than chronological structures, imposes further limitations for analysis. The mere fact that RKU reached its maximum expanse only by September 1942 makes it difficult for the historian to know exactly which particular German agency supervised what area, who committed the acts of mass murder, when the atrocity took place, and what was the number of victims. Nevertheless, it is safe to conclude that numerous instances of mass murder in the RKU apparently were committed when any given area was still under military rule. Furthermore, even when civilian administration took over power in that particular area, they did not, as a rule, play a leading role in policymaking dealing specifically with security issues (as the case study of Crimea has demonstrated).[116]

The known cases of the civil administration using Romani slave labor (no doubt, many Roma died of exhaustion and/or due to mistreatment) further complicate the matter. The discourse advanced in this chapter pinpoints genocidal intent on the part of the Wehrmacht and the SS, but not necessarily other branches of the German occupation administration. Therefore, I would encourage scholars make a better use of the documents from different levels of civil administration—RKU, commissar general office, and district commissar office—alongside ChGK records and German security police and military reports. Not least essential for the analysis are oral testimonies of the Romani survivors who provide invaluable information not only about particular cases of mass murder but also about their experiences in forced labor camps. Despite the potential difficulties of interpretation, the 150 or so witness accounts taped in the 1990s in Ukraine (this collection is currently deposited at the University of Southern California Shoah Foundation Institute),[117] and the less voluminous but no less important archives of Ukrainian Romani organizations,[118] constitute an extremely important source.

The total number of Romani victims remains as well a subject of dispute. Statistical data, difficult to obtain anyway, is problematic due to the absence of reliable figures for each of the Ukrainian provinces under German occupation. Evidently, it has to do with the itinerant or seminomadic lifestyle of a considerable portion of the Roma population on the eve of World War II. When it comes to the death toll of Roma in Nazi-dominated Europe, the most reliable figure in my opinion was provided by Kenrick and Puxon, who estimate 200,000 victims, of which the territory of Ukraine, Belorussia, and Russia accounts for approximately 30,000.[119] According to Kruglov's estimates, close to 20,000 Roma perished within current Ukrainian borders during the war, whereas the larger percentage of victims was the Roma deported to Ukraine from

Romania.[120] Nonetheless, even this estimate is tentative, for it is based solely upon documented instances of mass murder.

As far as the Nazi mass murder of Roma in Ukraine is concerned, the available sources allow only minimum generalization, making it virtually impossible to single out the factor that would stay true for all the provinces. Obviously, the final analysis should take into account several overlapping factors rather than one. Let me begin with chronological factor. Apparently, the Nazis lacked a clearly defined anti-Roma policy at the initial stage of the war against the Soviet Union. However, as the situation on the ground evolved, this policy underwent critical transformation, and consequently had different dimensions in different places (as illustrated by the discussions in the RMO and, correspondingly, in RKO and RKU). Next come the factors of geography and the nature of the occupation regime. The specific interests of a dominant occupation structure to a certain degree determined the preferred solution of the "Gypsy Question" (the evidence overwhelmingly suggests that the Wehrmacht supported or took a direct part in the destruction of itinerant Roma, viewing them as "spies" and a potential threat to the hinterland). The third, interconnected, factor has to do with the specific circumstances that affected the process of persecution within a single geographical area or administrative unit such as the ongoing combat operations, the passing of certain military units through any given territory, or economic considerations (the first wave of mass murder was perpetrated by mobile killing squads of the German Security Police and SD, whereas the civil administration was mainly interested in exploiting Roma labor).

Notes

1. For most comprehensive publications in English and German dealing with the mass murder of Roma in Nazi-occupied Ukraine, if only in passing, see Donald Kenrick and Grattan Puxon, *Gypsies under the Swastika* (Hatfield, UK, 1995), published also in Russian translation as *Tsygane pod svastikoi* (Moscow, 2001); Michael Zimmermann, *Rassenutopie und Genozid: Die nationalsozialistische "Lösung der Zigeunerfrage"* (Hamburg, 1996); Guenter Lewy, *The Nazi Persecution of the Gypsies* (Oxford, 2000). For more recent publications see Martin Holler, *Der nationalsozialistische Völkermord an den Roma in der Besetzten Sowjetunion (1941–1944)* (Heidelberg, 2009); Martin Holler, "'Like Jews?' The Nazi Persecution and Extermination of Soviet Roma Under the German Military Administration: A New Interpretation, Based on Soviet Sources," *Dapim: Studies on the Shoah* 24 (2010): 137–76; Mikhail Tyaglyy, "Were the "Chingene" Victims of the Holocaust? The Nazi Policy toward the Crimean Roma," *Holocaust and Genocide Studies* 23, no. 1 (Spring 2009): 26–53. For Russian and Ukrainian-language publications see the special issue of *Golokost i suchastnist: studii v Ukraini i sviti* (Kiev) 6, no. 2 (2009) (also available online at: http://nbuv.gov.ua/portal/Soc_Gum/Gis/index.html).

2. For a brief overview of the fate of the Roma in the occupied Soviet territories see David Crowe, *Istoriia tsigan Skhidnoi Evropy ta Rosii* (Kiev, 2003) and Mikhail Tyaglyy, "Tsygane," in *Kholokost na territorii SSSR. Entsiklopediia* (Moscow, 2009): 1047–56; for Estonia see Anton Weiss-Wendt, "Extermination of the Gypsies in Estonia during World War II: Popular Images and Official Policies," *Holocaust and Genocide Studies* 17, no. 1 (Spring 2003): 31–61; for Lithuania see Vytautas Toleikis, "Lithuanian Roma During the Years of the Nazi persecution," in *Murders of Prisoners of War and of Civilian Population in Lithuania, 1941–1944*, ed. Christoph Dieckmann et al. (Vilnius, 2005), 267–85.
3. For Robert Ritter and the Research Institute for Racial Hygiene and Population Biology see Lewy, *Nazi Persecution of the Gypsies*, 43–49.
4. *Trials of War Criminals Before the Nuernberg Military Tribunals* (Green Series), vol. 4 (Washington, DC, [1949–1953]), 244; also see Ronald Headland, *Messages of Murder: A Study of the Reports of the Einsatzgruppen of the Security Police and the Security Service, 1941–1943* (London, 1992), 63.
5. Headland, *Messages of Murder*, 54, 63.
6. For a detailed analysis of Ohlendorf's defense strategy and the historical reliability of his testimony see Hilary Earl, *The Nuremberg SS-Einsatzgruppen Trial, 1945–1958: Atrocity, Law, and History* (Cambridge, 2009), 179–216.
7. *Trials of War Criminals*, 286–87.
8. In his 2 July 1941 directive to the heads of the SS and the police, Heydrich designated several groups of Soviet citizens as subject to execution: (1) officials of the Comintern; (2) top- and medium-level officials and radical lower-level officials of the Communist Party; (3) People's Commissars; and (4) Jews in party and state employment, and other radical elements (saboteurs, propagandists, snipers, assassins, inciters, etc.). See Yitzhak Arad et al., ed., *The Einsatzgruppen Reports: Selections From the Dispatches of the Nazi Death Squads' Campaigns Against the Jews* (New York, 1989), vii–ix.
9. Weiss-Wendt, "Extermination of the Gypsies in Estonia," 38. According to Gilad Margalit, the 20 April 1942 entry "No extermination of the Gypsies" in Himmler's diary demonstrates that the Reichsführer-SS took a more moderate stance toward the Romani population in the East than did his subordinates on the ground, and that he protested the mass murder of the Roma by the *Einsatzgruppen.* Cf. Gilad Margalit, "The Uniqueness of the Nazi Persecution of the Gypsies," *Romani Studies* 10, no. 2 (2000): 202.
10. Order of the high command of infantry forces (the so-called Brauchitsch Decree) concerning the "objectives of the security police and the SD in the infantry units," 28 April 1941, reprinted in *Trials of War Criminals,* vol. 10, 1242.
11. Michael Zimmermann, "The National Socialist 'Solution of the Gypsy Question': Central Decisions, Local Initiatives, and their Interrelation," *Holocaust and Genocide Studies* 15, no. 3 (Winter 2001): 416.
12. Guenter Lewy, "Gypsies and Jews Under the Nazis," *Holocaust and Genocide Studies* 13, no. 3 (Winter 1999): 390.
13. Crowe, *Istoriia tsigan,* 221. Reich Commissariat Ostland encompassed former Baltic States and Belorussia.
14. Lewy does not provide a reference (*Nazi Persecution of the Gypsies,* 125).
15. Rural district administration to village councils, 10 July 1942, State Archives of Rivne Oblast, R-57/1/1/2.
16. Ibid. The entire correspondence is published in Mikhail Tyaglyy, "'Nakazuiu ... pereslaty ... spysky tsiganiv': Zbir organamy vlady Raikhskomisariatu Ukraina vidomostei pro romiv u lypni 1942 r.," *Golokost i suchstnist: studii v Ukraini i sviti* 9, no. 1 (2011): 85–101.

17. Michael Zimmermann, "The Soviet Union and the Baltic States, 1941–44: The Massacre of the Gypsies," in *The Gypsies During the Second World War: In the Shadow of the Swastika,* ed. Donald Kenrick (Hatfield, 1999), 147.
18. Lewy, *Nazi Persecution of the Gypsies,* 126.
19. Crowe, *Istoriia tsigan,* 219–20; Lewy, *Nazi Persecution of the Gypsies,* 127. Zimmermann interprets this correspondence as effective guidelines to concentrate nomadic Roma and Roma of mixed race in Auschwitz-Birkenau where the SS had set up a separate "Gypsy camp" (*Zigeunerlager*) in early 1943 (Zimmermann, "The Soviet Union and the Baltic States," 148).
20. *Vsesoiuznaia perepis' naseleniia 1939 g. Osnovnye itogi* (Moscow, 1992), 58–59.
21. Alexander Kruglov, "Genotsid tsigan v Ukraine v 1941–1944 gg. Statistiko-regional'nyi aspect," *Golokost i suchastnist: studii v Ukraini i sviti* 6, no. 2 (2009): 86.
22. Alexander Kruglov, ed., *Bez zhalosti i somneniia. Dokumenty o prestupleniiakh operativnykh grupp i komand politsii bezopasnosti i SD na vremenno okkupirovannoi territorii SSSR v 1941–1944 gg.,* vol. 3 (Dnepropetrovsk, 2009), 87.
23. Nikolai Bessonov, "Genotsid tsigan Ukrainy v gody Velikoi Otechestvennoi voiny," in *Roma v Ukraini. Istorychnyi ta etnokul'turnyi rozvytok tsigan (Roma) Ukrainy (XVI–XX st.),* ed. M[?] Shvetsov (Sevastopol, 2006), 12, 15.
24. Ibid., 15.
25. Kruglov, "Genotsid tsigan v Ukraine," 93; Holler, *Der nationalsozialistische Völkermord,* 74.
26. Bessonov, "Genotsid tsigan Ukrainy," 15.
27. Ibid., 16.
28. Kruglov, "Genotsid tsigan v Ukraine," 93–94.
29. Statements, interrogations, and forensic examination by the ChGK in Chernigiv region, 17 September 1943, State Archives of the Russian Federation (hereafter: GARF), 7021/78/39.
30. Extracts from the ChGK statement in Stalino province, 30 October 1943, Yad Vashem Archives (hereafter: YVA), M.37/914.
31. Bessonov, "Genotsid tsigan Ukrainy," 10–11.
32. Extracts from the ChGK statement in Stalino province, 30 October 1943, GARF, 7021/72/2.
33. Bessonov, "Genotsid tsigan Ukrainy," 9; Kruglov, "Genotsid tsigan v Ukraine," 95.
34. Yitzhak Arad, *Katastrofa evreev na okkupirovannykh territoriiakh Sovetskogo Soiuza* (Dnepropetrovsk, 2007), 290.
35. Bessonov, "Genotsid tsigan Ukrainy," 13; Kruglov, "Genotsid tsigan v Ukraine," 96–97.
36. Andrej Angrick, *Besatzungspolitik und Massenmord. Die Einsatzgruppe D in der südlichen Sowjetunion 1941–1943* (Hamburg, 2003), 252.
37. Kruglov, "Genotsid tsigan v Ukraine," 102.
38. Head of Political Department of the 4th Army [?] Semenov to the Head of the Political Department of the Kalinin front [?] Drebednev, Central Archives of the Ministry of Defense of Russia (hereafter: TsAMO RF), 4udA/4021/177.
39. Extracts from ChGK reports in Khersonskaia oblast, 5 May 1944, Central State Archives of the Highest Authorities of Ukraine (hereafter: TsDAVOU), 4620/3/316.
40. Kruglov, "Genotsid tsigan v Ukraine," 102.
41. Bessonov, "Genotsid tsigan Ukrainy," 17.
42. Ibid., 9; Kruglov, "Genotsid tsigan v Ukraine," 102.
43. Bessonov, "Genotsid tsigan Ukrainy," 9; Kruglov, "Genotsid tsigan v Ukraine," 101.
44. Kruglov, *Bez zhalosti i somneniia,* 70.
45. Holler, *Der nationalsozialistische Völkermord,* 77.
46. Bessonov, "Genotsid Tsigan Ukrainy," 9.

47. Kruglov, "Genotsid tsigan v Ukraine," 100; Bessonov, "Genotsid tsigan Ukrainy," 9.
48. D[?] Strikha, "Dva roky nimetsko-fashists'koi okupatsii na Lubenshchini," unpublished manuscript, TsDAVOU, 4620/3/29747.
49. Bessonov, "Genotsid tsigan Ukrainy," 9, 11; Kruglov, "Genotsid tsigan v Ukraine," 99.
50. Kruglov, "Genotsid tsigan v Ukraine," 97.
51. Alexander Kruglov, ed., *Sbornik dokumentov i materialov ob unichtozhenii natsistami evreev Ukrainy* (Kiev, 2002), 397.
52. Bessonov, "Genotsid tsigan Ukrainy," 9, 11; Kruglov, "Genotsid tsigan v Ukraine," 98, 103.
53. Bessonov, "Genotsid tsigan Ukrainy," 11.
54. Kostopol district commissar [?] Löhnert to Brest-Lytovsk commissar general [?], 22 April 1942, United States Holocaust Memorial Museum (hereafter: USHMM), RG 31.017 M. I am grateful to Wendy Lower for bringing this document to my attention.
55. Commissar general of Volyn-Podillia [?] Schoene to district commissars, 21 May 1942, USHMM, RG 31.017 M.
56. Final statement of the ChGK of Rivne province, 2 June 1944, GARF, 7021/71/44.
57. Anatoly Kuznetsov, *Babii Iar. Roman-dokument* (Zaporozhie, 1991), 114.
58. Ilya Levitas, "Nerazgadannye tainy Bab'ego Iara," *Evreiskie vesti*, quoted in Alexander Kruglov, *Entsiklopediia Kholokosta. Evreiskaia entsiklopediia Ukrainy* (Kiev, 2000), 214, 222.
59. Vitalii Nakhmanovich, "Rasstrely i zakhoroneniia v raione Bab'ego Iara vo vremia nemetskoi okkupatsii Kieva 1941–1943 gg. Problemy khronologii i topografii," in *Babii Iar: Chelovek, Vlast, Istoriia. Dokumenty i materially v 5 knigakh*, vol. 1 (Kiev, 2004), 86; Kruglov, "Genotsid tsigan v Ukraine," 100.
60. Oleksii Goncharenko, "Holokost na territorii Kyivshchiny. Zagal'ni tendentsii ta regional'ni osoblyvosti (1941–1944 rr.)" (PhD diss., University of Pereiaslav-Khmelnitskii, 2005).
61. Kruglov, "Genotsid tsigan v Ukraine," 99.
62. ChGK report for the Kiev province, 7 December 1943, GARF, 7021/65/521.
63. Dumitru Şandru, "Deportatrea ţiganilor în Transnistria," *Arhivele totalitarsimului; revista Institutului Naţional pentru Studiul Totalitarismului* 17 (1997): 23–30; Viorel Achim, "Deportarea ţiganilor în Transnistria," *Anuarul roman de istorie recentă* 1 (2002): 127–41; Constantin Iordachi, ed., *România şi Transnistria: Problema Holocaustului. Persepctive istorice şi comparative* (Bucharest, 2004), 201–36; Constantin Iordachi, *The Roma in Romanian History* (Budapest, 1998), 163–88; Vladimir Solonari, "Ethnic Cleansing or Crime Prevention? Deportation of Romanian Roma," chapter in this volume.
64. Bessonov, "Genotsid Tsigan Ukrainy," 8.
65. Viorel Achim, "The Deportation of the Roma and their Treatment in Transnistria," in *Final Report*, ed. International Commission on the Holocaust in Romania (Iasi, 2005), 226–28.
66. Kenrick and Puxon, *Tsygane pod svastikoi*, 120.
67. Achim, "Deportation of the Roma," 231, 233.
68. Radu Ioanid, *The Holocaust in Romania: The Destruction of Jews and Gypsies Under the Antonescu Regime, 1940–1944* (Chicago, 2000), 234–35.
69. Statement by the ChGK on the German and Romanian atrocities in Krivoozerskii and Oktiabrskii district of Odessa province, GARF, R-7021/69/80.
70. Kenrick and Puxon, *Tsygane pod svastikoi*, 124.
71. Achim, "The Deportation of the Roma," 236.
72. May Panchuk, "Do pytannia pro stanovyshche romiv Zakarpattia v roky ugors'koi okkupatsii ta Drugoi svitovoi viyny," *Golokost i suchastnist: studii v Ukraini i sviti* 6, no. 2 (2009): 165.

73. Aladar Adam et al., ed., *Bilyi kamin' z chornoi kativni. Golokost romiv Zakarpattia* (Uzhgorod, 2006), 16, 32, 51.
74. Panchuk, "Do pytannia," 165.
75. Kruglov, "Genotsid tsigan v Ukraine," 105–6.
76. "Svedeniia o chislennosti naseleniia Kryma po perepisi 1939 g.," State Archives of the Autonomous Republic of Crimea (hereafter: DAARK), R-137/9/14.
77. Arad, et al., *Einsatzgruppen Reports*, 267, 309, 317–18, 325–26.
78. Testimony of Iakub Kurtliarov taken for the ChGK in Evpatoriia, 22 May 1944, GARF, 7021/9/35.
79. Testimony of Neisha Kemileva from Kamysh-Burun taken for the ChGK in Kerch, 8 June 1944, GARF, 7021/9/38.
80. Records of ChGK in Dzhankoi, 8 October 1944, GARF, 7021/9/193.
81. "Spravka o chislennosti naseleniia g. Simferopolia na 1 noiabria 1941g.," DAARK, R-1302/1/9/6; "Spravka 'Sostav naseleniia g. Simferopolia po natsional'nosti i rodnomu iazyku po sostoianiiu na 1 ianvaria 1942 g.,'" DAARK, R-1302/1/9/7; "Spravka o chislennosti i sostave naseleniia Simferopolia na 1 ianvaria 1943 g.," DAARK, R-1302/1/9/2.
82. *Trials of War Criminals*, vol. 4, 582.
83. From the diary of Khrisanf Lashkevich, *Peredaite detiam nashim o nashei sud'be* (Simferopol, 2002), 63.
84. Reshat Adilsha Ogly, "Kuda podevalis' krymskie tsygane?" *K'rym* 48 (1994): 2.
85. *Trials of War Criminals*, vol. 4, 290.
86. Lashkevich, *Peredaite detiam nashim*, 82.
87. Reshid Memish, "Zabytoe plemia," *Golos Kryma*, 4 September 1998.
88. The Crimea was not the only region in which Muslim religious affiliation played a role in the survival of many Gypsies. In Bosnia-Herzegovina, for example, thanks to the intervention of the Muslim clergy in 1941 and 1942, the Ustaša authorities did not include in the deportation the so-called white Gypsies—Muslims who were thoroughly assimilated and had gradually lost their language and customs. Two other local Romani groups, the Chergasi and the Karavlasi, led an itinerant lifestyle and were assimilated to a lesser degree, and were therefore subject to deportation. Cf. Yeshayahu A. Jelinek, "Bosnia-Herzegovina at War: Relations Between Moslems and Non-Moslems," *Holocaust and Genocide Studies* 5, no. 3 (Winter 1990): 289; Mark Biondich, "Persecution of Roma-Sinti in Croatia, 1941–1945," in *Roma and Sinti: Under-Studied Victims of Nazism*, symposium proceedings (Washington, DC, 2002), 36–8; Sevasti Trubeta, "'Gypsiness,' Racial Discourse and Persecution: Balkan Roma During the Second World War," *Nationalities Papers* 31, no. 4 (December 2003): 505–6.
89. Transcript of the interrogation of Vasilisa Genova, 7 June 1944, DAARK, R-1289/1/6/.
90. Testimony of the Gypsy woman Asanova to the ChGK of the Staro-Krymskii district, June 1944, DAARK, R-1289/1/6/.
91. Records of the ChGK in the Biiuk-Onlar district, 3 November 1944, GARF, 7021/9/34.
92. Records of the ChGK in the Kolai district, 15 August 1944, DAARK, 1289/1/12.
93. Field Headquarters 810 to Army Group South in Evpatoria, 9 July 1942, YVA, O-51/185/I/12.
94. Report of the Rear Area no. 553 of Eleventh Army HQ, 15 June 1942, YVA, O-51/185/II/1.
95. Nikolai Bugai, *Deportatsiia narodov Kryma. Dokumenty, fakty, kommentarii* (Moscow, 2002), 114. However, not all of those who declared Roma identity were in fact Roma. Since the deportation of Roma in 1944 was carried out apparently as a result

of an "error," some Crimean Tatars claimed to be Roma in order to be able to return to the Crimea.
96. Bessonov, "Genotsid tsigan Ukrainy," 26.
97. Nikolay Bessonov, "Tsigane SSSR v okkupatsii. Strategii vyzhivaniia," *Golokost i suchastnist: studii v Ukraini i sviti* 6, no. 2 (2009): 30–31.
98. Alexander Diukov, *Vtorostepennyi vrag. OUN, UPA i reshenie "Evreiskogo voprosa"* (Moscow, 2008), 58.
99. Jerzy Ficowski quoted in Bessonov, "Tsigane SSSR v okkupatsii," 49–50.
100. Minutes of interrogation of Konstantin Artsishevskii, 6 June 1947, Archives of the Security Service of Ukraine in the Autonomous Republic of Crimea (hereafter: ASBUARK), 10135.
101. Minutes of interrogation of Sergei Odarick, 6 December 1978, Archives of the Security Service of Ukraine in Kherson province, 8209.
102. Concluding opinion on the criminal case, 15 September 1992, ASBUARK, 7214.
103. Minutes of interrogation of Pavel Borisov, 27 April 1944, ASBUARK, 18834.
104. Minutes of interrogation of Klimentii Plots, 22 May 1944, ASBUARK, 9775.
105. Minutes of interrogation of Pavel Borisov, 27 April 1944, ASBUARK, 18834.
106. Ibid.
107. Fatima Duduchava and Evgenii Ostapovich, "Nas Riatuvali tatary," *Romani Iag* (Uzhgorod), 25 May 2005.
108. [?] Vorobiov, "Sistema ugneteniia ukrainskogo naroda nemetsko-rymynskimi okkupantami," unpublished manuscript, TsDAVOU, 4620/3/239.
109. See Vladimir Gurkovich, "Russkii pevets Petr Leshchenko, ofitser Rumynskoi armii v Krymu v 1943–1944 godakh," *Istoricheskoe nasledie Kryma* 1 (2003): 37.
110. See Boris Kovalev, *Natsistskaia okkupatsiia i kollaborationizm v Rossii, 1941–1944* (Moscow, 2003), 375.
111. According to Christopher Browning, for example, the "German policies toward the 'Gypsies' outside the Third Reich, however murderous, did not constitute genocide" (Christopher Browning, *The Origins of the Final Solution: The Evolution of Nazi Jewish Policy, September 1939–March 1942* [Lincoln, NE, 2004], 473). Guenter Lewy has argued that "the killing of the Gypsies of the Soviet Union was not part of any overall plan to exterminate all Gypsies" (Lewy, *Nazi Persecution of the Gypsies*, 128).
112. Bessonov, "Genotsid tsigan Ukrainy," 23.
113. Kruglov, "Genotsid tsigan v Ukraine," 111.
114. Holler, *Der nationalsozialistische Völkermord*, 108.
115. On the principles governing ChGK war crimes investigations see Marina Sorokina, "People and Procedures: Toward a History of the Investigation of Nazi Crimes in the USSR," *Kritika: Explorations in Russian and Eurasian History* 6, no. 4 (2005): 797–831; Kiril Feferman, "Soviet Investigation of Nazi Crimes in the USSR: Documenting the Holocaust," *Journal of Genocide Research* 5, no. 4 (2003): 587–602.
116. For the discord between civil authorities and the SS on policy issues see Wendy Lower, *Nazi Empire Building and the Holocaust in Ukraine* (Chapel Hill, NC, 2002), 126–28.
117. Anna Lenchovska, "Videosvidchennia Instytutu Fondu Shoa iak dzherelo do vyvchennia ta vykladannia istorii romiv Ukrainy u period 1941–1944 gg.," *Golokost i suchastnist: studii v Ukraini i sviti* 6, no. 2 (2009): 114–23.
118. See, for example, Evheniya Navrotska, "Antiromska politika v Zakarpatti u roky Drugoi Svitovoi viyny. Zibrannia svidchen' ta zberezhennia istorychnoi pamiati," *Golokost i suchastnist: studii v Ukraini i sviti* 6, no. 2 (2009): 124–40.
119. Kenrick and Puxon, *Tsygane pod svastikoi*, 103. Zimmermann does not provide any figures for the occupied Soviet territories, including Ukraine.
120. Kruglov, "Genotsid tsigan v Ukraine," 113.

CHAPTER 6

THE NAZI PERSECUTION OF ROMA IN NORTHWESTERN RUSSIA
THE OPERATIONAL AREA OF THE ARMY GROUP NORTH, 1941–1944

Martin Holler

The Nazi destruction of Roma in Eastern Europe remains one of the most neglected aspects of the historiography of the German occupation policies during World War II. At the same time, the Soviet case study plays a key role in establishing genocidal intent in the Nazi persecution of Roma insofar that the German attack on the Soviet Union on 22 June 1941 marked the transition toward systematic mass murder. This chapter examines the genesis and extent of the persecution of Roma in the northwestern part of Russia, which belonged to the operational area of the Army Group North (Heeresgruppe Nord) until the very end of German occupation in 1944. In addition to existing German sources, the empirical analysis draws heavily on the extensive records of the Soviet Extraordinary State Commission (Чрезвычайная государственная комиссия, or ChGK), which was established in 1942 to investigate the Nazi war crimes committed on the occupied Soviet territories.[1]

Although the Soviet sources tend to be inexact when it comes to German perpetrators, it is nevertheless possible, in most cases, to determine if a mass execution was carried out by the German Security Police and SD, the auxiliary police, and/or military units. When making a case for the systematic character of the Nazi persecution of Roma in the operational area of the Army Group North, I will draw a comparison with the Reich Commissariat Ostland (Reichskommissariat Ostland, or RKO), which remained under civil administration. Next, I will probe the question whether the (apparent) military interests prompted a radicalization of the anti-Gypsy policy up to methodical destruction. Since the amount of research done on Belorussian and Baltic Roma under Nazi rule has been greater than that on Russian Roma, I will focus mainly on the military area of northwestern Russia in my analysis.[2]

Official Policies in the Early Stages of German Occupation

Einsatzgruppe A (mobile killing unit) of the German Security Police, subdivided into smaller units—Sonderkommando 1a and 1b and Einsatzkommando 2 and 3—trailed the Army Group North into Russia in the summer of 1941. As early as the second half of July 1941, Adolf Hitler allotted the conquered areas to the newly established Reich Ministry for the Occupied Eastern Territories (Reichsministerium für die besetzten Ostgebiete, or RMO). As of fall 1941, RKO incorporated Latvia, Lithuania, and parts of Belorussia.[3] Estonia became part of the Ostland in December 1941. However, due to proximity to the front line, Estonia nominally remained under military rule, which makes it a special case.[4]

The northwestern part of Russia, conquered by the German troops in August 1941, was never handed over to the civil administration but officially remained a part of the Wehrmacht operational area. Until then the Russian regions of Pskov, Novgorod, and Leningrad composed a single administrative unit, Leningrad province (Ленинградская область). During World War II the Leningrad province was only partly occupied: while the Pskov region was firmly in German hands, one-half of Novgorod and one-quarter of the Leningrad region remained under Soviet control. The Velikie Luki region, which was originally split between the Leningrad and Kalinin provinces, fell in parts as well within the borders of the Army Group North operational area. The German occupation authorities distinguished between the front area; the areas in direct proximity to the front line—Army Area 583 (18th Army) and Army Area 584 (16th Army); and the Army Group North Rear Area (Rückwärtiges Heeresgebiet Nord).

The entire operational area of the Army Group North between the lakes Peipus and Ilmen—identified as the North section hereafter—was full of forests and swamps that provided refuge to Soviet partisans. Nevertheless, the North section did not belong to the major centers of anti-German guerilla movement until after 1943, with the partisans constituting just too weak a force to profoundly influence the course of the war, as Alexander Hill has convincingly argued.[5] As an additional, "stabilizing" factor, Jürgen Kilian has pointed out the absence of inter-ethnic tensions characteristic of other occupation zones: "The German conquerors met a homogenous [except for Finno-Ugric pockets, MH] Russian, politically rather unengaged, and predominantly rural population." Furthermore, a part of the (numerically insignificant) Jewish population had been able to escape eastward, while a majority of Soviet functionaries had been evacuated beforehand in an organized manner.[6] Another essential difference with the North section was that the occupation authorities in the areas under civil administration on the other side of Lake Peipus could count on the support of the local Baltic population, which was thought to be of relatively high "racial value." According to the Nazi racial ideology, the Russian territories were primarily inhabited by an "inferior," untrustworthy east-Slavic people. As an illustration of deep-seated distrust toward the Russian population, the German Security Police in the North section primarily recruited among Estonian and Latvian volunteers, while the local auxiliary police (*Ordnungsdienst*) remained for the most part unarmed. Furthermore, as a consequence of brutal occupation policies that followed, the military administration was soon faced with increasing unrest. The rural areas of the Leningrad province traditionally belonged to the agriculturally backward parts of Russia. Hence the strategic expulsion of the civilian population from the front areas, aggravated by the policy of deliberate starvation consistently exercised by the Wehrmacht since the beginning of the war, led to a massive refugee problem, destabilizing the security situation in the North section.[7] This constituted yet another essential difference with the former Baltic States, which were better off economically.

The extent of anti-German resistance in the North section varied from one region to another. In particular, the northern and eastern areas around Pskov remained a partisan stronghold, preventing the Germans from exercising total control. Consequently, the treatment of civilian population in and around Pskov proved the harshest, and not only by the "competent" Sonderkommando 1b but also by Wehrmacht units, first and foremost the Secret Field Police (Geheime Feldpolizei, or GFP) and Field Gendarmerie (Feldgendarmerie).[8] Thus, even outside the demarcated partisan areas, any minor incident or suspicion led to disproportionate retaliation by the Germans. Remarkably, despite the relatively low levels of guerilla activity in the North section, antipartisan operations conducted by the police and army units claimed the highest percentage of civilian deaths in this particular area.[9] Below I will examine how these and other factors affected the Nazi treatment of Roma in the Army Group North operational area.

The militarily administered territory had a relatively small, widely dispersed Romani population. According to the 1926 census, a total of 3,620 Roma lived in the area of the current Leningrad, Novgorod, and Pskov provinces. In 1939, however, 4,546 "Gypsies" were registered in the Leningrad province, not counting the city of Leningrad.[10] So-called national Gypsy collective farms, as they existed in several regions of the Soviet Union, rarely came into life in the Leningrad and Pskov regions.[11] The area with the highest proportion of Roma was in fact the city of Leningrad, which the Germans failed to capture. For this very reason, though, a great many Roma died of starvation during the 872-day siege of the city.

The German military issued several orders on the treatment of Roma in the North section. Thus, on 18 September 1941 the commander of the Army North Rear Areas (Befehlshaber im rückwärtigen Heeresgebiet Nord) General Franz von Roques ordered "itinerant and sedentary Gypsies" (*umherziehende und ortsansässigen Zigeuner*), like the Jews, to be kept under surveillance and used for labor.[12] Shortly afterward, von Roques made an explicit distinction between sedentary and itinerant Roma. According to his order from 21 November, "roaming Gypsies" were to be handed over to the Einsatzgruppe A, that is, shot, while "sedentary Gypsies, who had lived in the current place of residence for at least two years and were neither politically nor criminally suspicious," were to be left in peace until further notice.[13] The criterion of "political reliability" enabled broad interpretation by the Security Police and the military, effectively making the exemption granted to sedentary Roma obsolete. This vague notion of "political reliability" apparently remained unchanged throughout the period of German occupation. At any rate, the guidelines repeatedly issued by the Security Division 281 in 1942 and 1943 still referred to the order of November 1941.[14]

German records fail to convey whether the distinction between itinerant and sedentary Roma had actually been observed and if it had any effect on the course of persecution. In any event, the designation *itinerant* has to be treated with extreme caution in view of the ideological prejudice of the German occupation authorities and the masses of war and famine refugees, who had blurred its meaning. Fortunately, more information can be drawn from Soviet war crimes investigation.

As I will demonstrate below, the social status of Roma played no role in the practice of annihilation: the Roma were murdered because of their ethnicity.

The Wave of Killings in Spring 1942

The situational reports of Einsatzgruppe A contain references to four mass executions of Roma. In January 1942, an antipartisan combat operation in the area around Leningrad resulted in the arrest and execution of ninety-three persons, among them "a bunch of Gypsies, who made trouble [*Unwesen*] in the area around Siversky."[15] Yet another mass execution of seventy-one Roma was reported from the suburbs of Leningrad.[16] On 1 February 1942, thirty-eight Jews and a "Gypsy" were murdered in Loknia.[17] Apparently, the area of Loknia was the site of further mass executions within the same period since Einsatzkommando 1b had reported the "liquidation" of 43 Jews and 170 Roma through late February 1942.[18] Alongside the atrocities perpetrated by the SS, the biggest mass execution of Roma in the North section—a total of 128 persons according to German records—was carried out in the summer of 1942 by a military unit in Novorzhev. The available sources enable a detailed reconstruction of this particular atrocity, which I attempt in the next section.

The records of the Extraordinary State Commission offer an insight into the extent and brutality of the Nazi persecution of Roma. Evidently, the *Einsatzgruppen* reported only fragmentarily on the destruction of Soviet Roma. Although the ChGK registered no mass executions of Roma for 1941, it reported on two individual shootings. In the morning of 7 November, a thirty-member-strong German "retaliation unit"[19] executed a sixty-year-old Russian man in the village of Botanok in the Dno district (*район*). According to eyewitnesses, two Roma from the village were shot the same day, too.[20] Although the ChGK did not speculate on possible grounds for the execution of any of the three victims, the atrocity at Botanok might be a part of the mass operations against communists, "spies," and Jews in late fall 1941, during which the German Security Police "combed through" numerous villages.[21] As part of the "cleansing," the police units sometimes murdered even collective farm leaders and teachers. Without knowing either the names or occupation of the two murdered Roma, one can only speculate whether the *Einsatzkommando* had any grounds whatsoever for suspicion or if it regarded the victims as "subversive elements" solely on account of their ethnicity.

Yet, this particular execution of Roma appears to have been a singular occurrence. Overall, the ChGK records provide no answer to the question how the Germans actually treated Roma in the North section in the early stages of occupation. It seems likely, nevertheless, that the military administration increasingly subjected Soviet Roma to police surveillance and used them as slave laborers, as it was the case in Estonia.[22] At least one example supports this conjecture. In 1941 several Romani families, twenty-six persons in total, were deported to the Gdov district from Luga. Quartered with Russian peasants in the village of Filippovshchina, they were used as farm hands. Thus, the deportation apparently had an economic rationale. Nonetheless, exploitation of labor obviously was not a priority, for the Roma of Filippovshchina were eventually murdered. At the end of February 1942 a "retaliation unit" consisting of Germans, Finns, and Estonians arrived in the village. On a freezing morning, with temperatures as low as –30°C (–22°F), all Roma, most of them lightly dressed, were driven out of their houses and made to stand on a bridge at the entrance to the village. For the "repulsive entertainment" of the murderers—to quote the ChGK report—the Romani families were forced to dance in front of the assembled village community prior to their execution. Following the execution, the Russian villagers were forced to bury the dead bodies in a mass grave. A ten-year-old Romani boy, who suffered a hand injury, tried in vain to escape with the help of some farmers. According to eyewitnesses, a German officer ordered him to be buried alive.[23]

Certain details concerning this particular instance of mass murder help to explicate the motivation of the perpetrators. First, "this whole nightmare" took place in front of the entire village community. A German soldier officially declared that "the Gypsies [had been] in contact with partisans," without any prior investigation or interrogation. Initially, the "completely innocent Gypsies" calmly followed the armed SS men. Evidently, none of the eyewitnesses believed the accusation of partisan support. Instead, the villagers were deeply upset about the "savage reprisal" (*дикая расправа*) that the "German-fascist villains" (*злодеи*) carried out against the "defenseless Gypsies and their children."[24]

Second, the application of stereotypical images of Roma at the time of actual execution is revealing from a psychological point of view. The perpetrators exploited music and dance, which are the essential elements of Romani culture, to humiliate the victims. Standing out there in the freezing cold and surrounded by armed guards, the Roma of Filippovshchina were forced to perform their "last dance" on a stage formed by the bridge. The symbolic meaning of this sham performance is comparable to the Nazi humiliation of Orthodox Jewish men by cutting off their beards. Indeed this act of mass murder can be constructed as a symbolic annihilation of the entire culture.

The mass murder of the Roma in Filippovshchina marked the beginning of a whole series of massacres in the Army Group North operational areas, starting in the spring of 1942. According to the (presumably incomplete) data of the Extraordinary State Commission and the Ministry of the Interior analyzed by this author, at least 1,300 to 1,500 Roma were killed in the North section during the German occupation. Geographically, the atrocities were documented over a large territory, committed by different perpetrator groups.

In the spring of 1942, for example, twenty-one Roma were killed along with the Jews in the village of Moglino, some seven miles west of Pskov.[25] In his memoirs, former KGB official Mikhail Pushniakov has described the details of the execution as follows: "The Germans killed the Gypsy population with particular cruelty.... [Victor] Teinbas claimed during his interrogation that in order to save bullets, the members of the Sonderkommando snatched the babies from the arms of the women and smashed their heads against the cart wheels. Then they threw the dead babies into the pit. This bestiality took place before the mothers' eyes."[26] A similar scenario played out shortly thereafter in a neighboring village where some thirty Roma and Jews were shot.[27] Both mass executions took place around the time when a multifunction concentration camp came into existence near Moglino. According to Soviet postwar investigation, about three thousand civilians were murdered in the Moglino camp between 1942 and 1944. In the section of the camp meant for political prisoners, the Pskov branch office of the Estonian Security Police and SD that ran the camp incarcerated Russians, Jews, and Roma, including women and children. According to eyewitnesses, the Jewish and Romani inmates had been arrested on the ground of their ethnicity (национальность) and subsequently executed on German order by the Estonian guards. The former prisoner Pavel Anisimov stated that a group of two hundred Roma who had been dispatched to Moglino camp in the spring of 1943 were all executed en masse nearby. In the fall of the same year, the same "treatment" was accorded to a group of Roma of comparable size.[28] The analysis of ChGK and police investigation records projects 550 as the number of Roma who had been murdered at Moglino.

The ChGK had documented four mass executions of Roma that took place in April 1942, two of them in the Slantsy district. At the end of April 1942 a sixty-man "retaliation unit" that had arrived in the village of Krivitsy arrested fifteen Roma, among them children in the age between three and fourteen. The Germans lined up nine of the Roma against a fence and shot them at random (*неочерёдно*) one by one, killing the remaining six victims in the same manner. The twenty-five Roma from the nearby village of Savinovshchina were executed in similar fashion, whereas the perpetrators apparently belonged to the same SS unit.[29]

While the instances of mass murder discussed above were committed exclusively by Einsatzgruppe A units, the annihilation of the Roma in the Oredezh and Utogorsh districts of the Leningrad province was premeditated by the "SD headquarters," that is, presumably by the German Security Police Office in Oredezh. The seventy-two Roma from the town of Oredezh were executed in April 1942 at the former farmyard Vasilkovichi, which indeed served as the Security Police headquarters. Shortly thereafter, the police deported the 120 Roma from the neighboring district of Utogorsh to Oredezh, murdering them all as well at the "SD residence."[30] Remarkably, the annihilation of the Romani population in Oredezh went smoothly thanks in no small part to the Russian "traitor" Anna Ershova. The Romani survivor Anastasia Grokhovskaia testified that for an extended period of time Ershova had been working as a Field Gendarmerie informant. Reportedly, during the arrest of the Roma, Ershova showed the Germans, "who of the Gypsies was hiding where."[31] The informer Ershova is featured on the ChGK list of wanted Nazi war criminals and their local collaborators, alongside the German police chief in Oredezh, SS-Obersturmbannführer [?] Bauer.[32] The Soviet authorities failed to subsequently arrest Ershova, since she had escaped to the West with the retreating German army in 1944.

Until now, I have failed to identify even a single example when sedentary Roma, once apprehended, would be exempted from execution. Just how little the orders issued by the German military authorities had to do with the reality on the ground can be illustrated by the following example from the Novgorod province. On 21 July 1942, the village headman in the Klevitsy county (*волость*) received the following order from the administration of Soltsy: "We inform you that, should itinerant Gypsies be found in your county, you are obliged to confiscate their horses and distribute them among the needy villagers. The Gypsies should be handed over to the nearest commandant's office [*комендатура*] to perform labor."[33] However, systematic mass murder of sedentary and itinerant Roma alike can also be documented for the city of Novgorod. Thus, the argument of the Russian historian Boris Kovalev, who explained a mass execution in Novgorod through the supposed unwillingness or inability of the itinerant Roma to perform "just any work," is a crass misinterpretation due to defendants' strategies at NKVD trials.[34] In fact, military units began "cleansing" the Novgorod province of Roma two months prior to the aforementioned mass execution. As it often was the case, the German occupation authorities invoked "suspected partisan activity" as a pretext for persecution.[35]

In May 1942 thirty-eight alleged "itinerants"—among them the Massalsky family of eight—were rounded up in the Novgorod district and taken to a POW camp situated on the territory of the former Zaveriazhskie Pokosy state farm. Following the arrest of all Roma within the district, they were taken to the so-called stockyard, which served as an execution place for prisoners of war. The German executioners forced the children and teenagers to climb boards laid across an open trench before shooting them before their parents' eyes; the adults were to follow their children.[36] Those victims who only got wounded were buried alive in the trench. In order to keep it secret, the Germans forced the local civilian population who lived in the vicinity of the camp to temporarily leave their village. Nevertheless, the villagers could hear the "heart-wrenching screams" of the dying Roma even from half a mile away. With the exception of the Massalsky family, none of the victims are known by name. Curiously, most of the witnesses described the Massalskys as "itinerant Gypsies," even though the latter lived permanently in the village and knew many of them personally (Semen Massalsky, for example, worked as a conductor on the railway line between Staraia Russa and Leningrad).[37] Thus, the propensity to make Roma into "nomads" was common among not only the German perpetrators but also the local Russian population—regardless of the policy of sedentarization promoted in the Soviet Union during the interwar period. This further demonstrates just how cautiously the historian has to treat eyewitness testimonies to this effect. The fact remains that in May 1942 the German military administration in Novgorod launched a campaign of murder that targeted the Romani minority in the province, regardless of their social status or lifestyle.

The Novorzhev Massacre

The massacre of Novorzhev in the Pskov province occupies a special place in historiography. Covered extensively in both German and Soviet sources, the descriptions of the atrocity differ fundamentally, though. With regard to German records, extraordinarily detailed information is available due to an administrative investigation launched in the aftermath of the execution of 128 Roma on order of the commandant's office in Novorzhev (German: Noworshew) in the area controlled by Security Division 281 at the end of May–beginning of June 1942.[38] The massacre was committed by the Secret Field Police Group 714, presumably supported by Field Gendarmerie and the local auxiliary police.[39] In a letter to the commander of the Army Group North, the commander of the Security Division justified the execution order on suspicion of "partisan and spy activity" among the Roma due to their "itinerant lifestyle." He further argued that all the Roma, among them many men of military age, had left an unfavorable and mendacious impression and frequently contradicted themselves during their interrogation by Secret Field Police Group 714. Although the Security Division commander admitted that the guilt of the suspects had not been unequivocally proven, he nevertheless concluded that "for security and espionage reasons" their execution was warranted.[40]

After the liberation of the Pskov province in June 1944, the ChGK did as well investigate the mass crimes committed at Novorzhev. According to the results of the investigation published in the local press, the massacre unfolded as follows: In May 1942, the German occupation authorities called on Roma in the Novorzhev and Pushkinsky (Pushkinskie Gory?) districts to assemble for alleged resettlement to Southern Russia. Several families followed this call, bringing their livestock and all their belongings with them. Next the German Field Gendarmerie drove the Romani families, among them many children and the elderly, into the municipal prison of Novorzhev. In prison, the victims were severely tortured, before they were brought in trucks to the Krasnyi Lebedinets collective farm for execution. The witness Maria Chistiakova from the village of Orsha described the site of mass execution, which she had visited two days after the massacre, as follows: "A lot of dead bodies had no heads, everywhere lay chopped off [*отрубленные*] hands, feet, and hair, which the Germans had torn off the women' heads during the torture. Murdered babies lay next to their mothers."[41] Forensic expertise corroborated the witness's statement: "Several bullet shots in different parts of the body. Blows on the head inflicted by various objects resulting in the crushing [*раздробление*] of the skull. Slashing [*распарывание*] the bellies with bayonets and knives. Poisoning by toxins. Burying alive, especially children. Furthermore, the examination of the corpses revealed that a large number of dead bodies bore signs of physical torture and violence such as broken limbs, torn-off hands, feet, and heads, which were found separately from the torsos." The ChGK reported the total of over 330 bodies of the murdered Roma.[42]

The Soviet investigation contradicts the German account fundamentally, by stating a higher number of victims—a majority of whom obviously came from sedentary families and were familiar to the inhabitants of the surrounding villages and collective farms by name. Moreover, according to the Soviet interpretation, the Roma had not just been apprehended, but reported themselves voluntarily, deceived by a German call for "resettlement."

How can one then explain the discrepancy between the German and the Soviet rendition of the Novorzhev massacre? The records of the Security Division 281 indicate that in May 1942 the Novorzhev district came increasingly under partisan attacks.[43] The commandant's office and the Secret Field Police relieved the mounting pressure by destroying the local Romani population, whereby they used the methods they knew from the persecution of Jews. However, the unauthorized torture and outright murder of the Roma was regarded as a transgression of authority, since the army units had received instructions to hand over suspect Roma to the Security Police.[44] This restriction also applied to the order of the Field Headquarters 822, according to which "Gypsies were to always be treated like partisans." Used by the lower-level military authorities as a justification, this order was reversed by the Security Division commander.[45] Confronted with the unexpected criticism of the superior military authorities, the Security Division resorted to common anti-Gypsy clichés of vagabondage and espionage as to retroactively substantiate the heightened partisan activity. To this end, however, *all* Roma within the province had first to be turned into dangerous criminals who live from begging. By stating the fact that no further attacks had taken place following the mass execution of the Roma, the Security Division commander presented the murder of civilians as a successful strike against Soviet partisans.[46]

Naturally, the Soviet Extraordinary State Commission came to a different conclusion. After the recapitulation of the facts it had gathered, the commission's final report stated: "The applied methods of torture, violence, and murder had a systematic and methodical character with the intent to completely exterminate an entire ethnic group [народность]—the Gypsies."[47] The ChGK explained the German accusation of partisan activity simply as a pretext for premeditated murder.

Further atrocities committed in the area controlled by Security Division 281 confirm the conclusion drawn by the ChGK.[48] At around the same time another mass execution took place in the Pushkinskie Gory district, west of Novorzhev. As before, the commandant's office bore responsibility for the crime. In late May 1942 the German forces and the Russian auxiliary police arrested over three hundred people across the district. The prisoners were kept for a few days in the building of a secondary school, aptly transformed into a prison. According to postwar Soviet investigation, the arrest order came directly from "Commander Singer" and a certain Colonel Amel, and the prisoner population included about seventy Roma of all ages, including babies.[49] The eyewitness Konstantin Fedorov had this to say: "In May 1942 I was arrested along with other residents.... All prisoners of both sexes, including the children, were gathered in one room. Singer was in command.... I witnessed how the Germans were daily executing forty–fifty persons from this chamber for six days in a row. In the first place they shot Gypsies—men, women, and children. Thus they executed in these six days twenty-three children aged from one month to twelve years, a total of three hundred people. The executions took place east of the Rakhovo village, about 500 meters from the district capital Pushkinskie Gory."[50] Further investigation revealed that the Romani children were separated from their parents on the day of the execution and that they were murdered next to the school building in Rakhovo, whereas the corpses of the adult Roma were discovered in other mass graves.[51]

In the final analysis, the mass murder at Pushkinskie Gory targeted communists and alleged partisan supporters among the civilian population rather than specifically Roma. However, while in the case of ethnic Russians only randomly selected adults fell in the category of "suspects," the local Roma were arrested as families. The ideological depiction of Roma as incessant "partisan helpers" and/or "subversive elements" perhaps played a decisive role in the German decision to kill them en masse. The special position of the Romani victims was obvious to everyone, as best expressed in the statement of the orthodox priest Iosif Dmitriev who had been involved in the Soviet war crimes investigation. He noted that in addition to the murder of countless prisoners, the Germans had carried out "racial executions [*рассовые расстрелы*] of Gypsies and their children, from the age of six (or even babies) and up. In total, the fascists executed seventy Gypsies, including twenty-three children, whom they buried in a distance of 50 meters from the building of the secondary school."[52]

Among other victims murdered by whole families were the twenty-five "citizens of Gypsy nationality" (a standard Soviet expression) in Porkhov, located in Army Area 584. The Roma were briefly imprisoned in a camp for civilians, from where they were taken for execution.[53] The evidence gathered by the ChGK overwhelmingly suggests that the annihilation of the Roma in the operational area of Security Division 281 had a systematic character and that the military administration carried it out in its own responsibility. The commandant's offices in the southeastern part of Pskov province intended to kill every "Gypsy" they were able to lay their hands on. The collective portrayal of Roma as "partisans" and "spies" was ingrained in the anti-Gypsy racist construct of "innately subversive elements" and thus indicates genocidal intent on the part of the German perpetrators, regardless of the official pretext and specific orders that effected one or another massacre.

The 1943 Policy Shift That Was Not

The mass murder reached its peak in May and June of 1942. It is likely that most of the Roma residing in the Army Group North operational area had already been dead by the first half of 1942. Nevertheless, further executions took place at irregular intervals until the fall of 1943. In most cases the shootings were carried out by military units, in contravention of official orders, like the two instances documented for late summer 1942. Both atrocities were committed by the commandant's office 705, which exercised control over the Strugi Krasnye district and which was said to have been troubled by the ghosts of partisans (*страдала призраком партизанщины*). In August 1942 twenty-two Roma of different ages, who had been previously used as slave laborers, were executed in front of a group of civilians in the village of Khredino.[54] Once again, the systematic annihilation of Roma took priority over economic exploitation.

The following example indicates that the apprehended Roma were often refugees who had to abandon their sedentary lifestyle due to the exigencies of war. At the end of 1942 the Germans arrested a group of 122 Romani refugees (*группа цыган-беженцев*), including many women with babies, in the Loknia region in the southernmost part of the Army Group North operational area. The refugees were driven to a forest where they were executed and their corpses "simply left lying on the snow."[55] The execution was carried out by Field Gendarmerie.[56] Loknia had been the site of numerous mass executions of Roma since the beginning of 1942, as stated in the report of Sonderkommando 1b,[57] yet unconfirmed by the ChGK. The ChGK investigation confirmed, though, that at least one "Gypsy" was executed alongside Jews in the same region on 2 February 1942: on the way to the execution site, the bus that carried thirty-eight Jews stopped at the Loknia prison to pick up the Romani detainee. In summer 1942 two Romani women were shot in the Samolukovsky village. The fate of yet another five Romani families apprehended in Loknia remains unknown.[58] According to Soviet records, the orders for the arrests and executions in the Loknia region in the summer of 1942 were issued by the Field Gendarmerie chief, who supervised the mass executions carried out by ethnic Russian policemen.

The fate of the Roma depended to a larger degree on the attitudes of the local population toward the persecuted. Despite the extra manpower provided by the auxiliary police, the German Security Police and the army were in no capacity to exercise efficient control. In particular, the shortage of staff was evident in the rural areas where the Germans had to rely on the village headmen for help. Ivan Alexeiev, the headman of the Savino village in the Pozherevitsky district, obviously belonged to the ranks of "loyal" collaborators, which eventually cost him his life.⁵⁹ In March 1943 Alexeiev reported to the local Field Gendarmerie (*полевая жандармерия*) office on the twenty-three Roma (eight men, eight women, and seven children) who had just arrived to the village for business. The same day five German Field Gendarmerie officers and two Russian auxiliary policemen arrived in Savino.⁶⁰ They locked the Roma in a farmhouse (*изба*) that had been previously confiscated from Andrei Lukashev—the most important witness to the crime. Lukashev thus testified to the Soviet investigation team: "A German officer checked the documents of the Gypsies and noted everyone down [*переписал*], whereupon they were taken to another room.... I also saw the two Russian auxiliary policemen entering the warehouse. One German officer stood on a hillock while the other took two men [Roma] to the warehouse, from where he returned alone. He then took another two men to the warehouse. Afterward the policemen went to the sauna [*баня*], and that is where the German officer now took two women.... As soon as the German officers and the two policemen had distributed the belongings of the Gypsies, they left our village. In the evening of that same day I went to the warehouse and to the sauna where the German officers had taken the Gypsies. There I saw the shot men and women, among the shot Gypsies were also children."⁶¹ Geographically, the Pozherevitsy district is situated next to that of Novorzhev, but under German occupation it belonged to Army Area 584. It is likely, however, that similar cases occurred in the area of Security Division 281, and that the reminder of the Security Division to the Field Headquarters 822 to refrain from liquidating Roma and Jews but instead turn them over to the Security Police had to do with the execution of the twenty-three Roma in Savino.⁶²

At the same time, the round-up in Savino was apparently a random occurrence. One of the last (recorded) coordinated anti-Gypsy—and simultaneously anti-Jewish—operations in the North section took place in the town of Ostrov near Pskov in summer 1943. Although the ChGK identified the perpetrators simply as "Germans," this type of operation, targeting both Jews and Roma, points directly to the German Security Police.⁶³ According to the ChGK report, "In the summer of 1943 inhabitants of the town of Ostrov—the total of about two hundred Jews and Gypsies, among them old people, women, and children—were arrested and robbed of their property. The people themselves were driven out of the region to the town of Pskov and shot." The police operations against Jews and Roma were conducted separately, though shortly after one another. First, the Germans arrested about one hundred Jews at night and took them to a special camp, and from there, on trucks, in the direction of Pskov. Witnesses believed that the Jews were executed en masse somewhere near Pskov, since "not a single Jew came back into town," and all the victims' property was auctioned off or redistributed among the local population. Along the same pattern, all the local Roma—slightly over one hundred, according to witnesses—were arrested at night, detained for a while in the camp, and then deported northward; as in the case with Jews, the Romani property was offered up for sale.[64]

This description lends credence to the conclusion drawn by the ChGK, according to which the deportation of Jews and Roma from Ostrov prefigured their execution. As regards the Roma, however, the situation appears to have been more complicated. Romani survivors had told after the war that they were actually deported to Salaspils in Latvia.[65] According to O. Benarovich-Mironchuk, the male adult Roma were executed several hours after their arrival in the camp, while the Romani children were subsequently dispatched to a camp near Litzmannstadt (Łódź).[66] Another survivor, Valentin Ivanov, had insisted that some of the Romani children were later deported via Auschwitz to Mauthausen concentration camp in Austria, where they were eventually liberated by the Allies in May 1945. Altogether, about thirty Roma returned to Ostrov after the end of the war.[67]

Some statements of Benarovich-Mironchuk contradict the testimonies given by Russian eyewitnesses to ChGK in Ostrov in 1944 and 1945. Thus, Benarovich-Mironchuk told that she and the other Roma had to spend the night in the municipal prison, while the Russian witness Nadezhda Vasil'eva referred to "special camps [специальные лагеря]." Benarovich-Mironchuk stated that the deportation was carried out by train, while the ChGK spoke of German trucks.[68] Not least problematic is the assertion that the work-fit adult men had been executed at Salaspils while the unfit were spared, taking into account that in the last years of war the ability to perform physical labor offered prisoners a chance for survival. Until now, I have not been able to reconcile these contradictions.

It is certain, however, that the deportation of Roma and Jews from Ostrov took place in the summer of 1943. Apparently, the German occupation authorities let the local Roma, and probably also the Jews, stay in their houses, using them as slave laborers in the agriculture. Before the war, most of the Roma in Ostrov had worked as carters in a local cooperative (артель). After the German attack on the Soviet Union in June 1941, many of the Romani men were drafted or joined the Red Army as volunteers, leaving behind women, children, and the elderly.[69] Valentin Ivanov, who was eleven years old when the Wehrmacht entered Ostrov, insisted that he could continue with his school education alongside his Russian classmates until the deportation in 1943.[70] Evidently, the situation of Roma (and Jews) in Ostrov was unique as compared to other localities within the Army Group North operational area. Ironically, Ostrov was the exact location of Field Headquarters 822, which had issued the most radical order, according to which Roma were to *always* be treated like partisans. It was this very order that the commandant's office in Novorzhev used as pretext for the annihilation of the Romani population in this particular area.

The fact that by the summer of 1943 the Jewish population of Ostrov was still alive constitutes another exception. It is reasonable to assume, therefore, that the German authorities in Ostrov preferred the economic exploitation of Jewish and Romani labor to immediate physical destruction, as it was the case throughout the North section. The looming military defeat might have prompted the decision to "evacuate the remaining undesired elements" from northwestern Russia. This assumption is further corroborated by the fact—as stated by the ChGK—that the Germans began to kill off the remaining Soviet prisoners of war in the camps around Ostrov at roughly the same time.[71]

The available sources are insufficient to identify specific decisions and preconditions that prolonged the existence of the Jewish and Romani communities in Ostrov until the summer of 1943. It is clear, though, that the circumstances of both minority groups in Ostrov were unique within the expanse of the North section. Therefore, unlike Alexander Kruglov, I would refrain from interpreting the relatively late date of deportation as an indication of a more relaxed attitude assumed by German occupation authorities toward Soviet Roma.[72] Instead, I would encourage historians to identify the reasons that ensured the exceptional position of Ostrov throughout the entire period of German occupation. Furthermore, reports of mass executions of Soviet Roma are also available for the second half of 1943. Thus, in the fall of 1943 the Germans shot a "Gypsy named Yasha" and his entire family in the village of Lobozhi, Novgorod province.[73] As mentioned earlier, around the same time two hundred Roma were executed at the Moglino camp in Pskov province. These last recorded mass executions of Roma would certainly not have taken place if an order for deportation to camps outside the North section had indeed been issued.

The North Section and the Reich Commissariat Ostland Compared

The above discussion poses the question whether the systematic campaign of annihilation carried out in the Army Group North operational area is representative for the entire territory captured by Nazi Germany during Operation Barbarossa. In order to answer this question, next I am going to draw a comparison with Reich Commissariat Ostland (RKO) whose territory was as well secured by Army Group North, except for the southernmost part—the former Belorussian SSR—which was held by Army Group Center (Heeresgruppe Mitte). The anti-Roma policymaking in both these areas evolved rather differently, which has in part to do with the peculiarities of the administrative structures. First, in territories under civil administration, the Wehrmacht's authority was limited to military functions.[74] Second, the local elites in the former Baltic States, whom the Nazis considered to be of higher "racial value" than the Slavic peoples, were better integrated in the administration, including the police force. Despite their limited autonomy, the indigenous agencies levered certain influence on local German administration as far as the mass murder of the Roma was concerned. At the same time, the RKO was known for the intense power struggle between various branches of power.[75] This internal discord had an impact, among other things, on the anti-Roma legislation, which had remained in flux until the end of 1943. Like the military orders, most of the decrees of the civil administration and the Security Police in RKO made a distinction between sedentary and itinerant Roma, prescribing the latter group to be treated like Jews. On the other hand, the decision making with regard to the Baltic Roma had been to a larger degree shaped by the Nazi racist discourse advanced by German anthropologists and racial scientists such as Dr. Robert Ritter and endorsed by Heinrich Himmler. Hence, Roma were first and foremost regarded in RKO as "antisocial" and "work-shy elements," much less "partisan helpers" or "spies"—the absolute opposite of the Army Group North operational area.[76] Yet the correspondence and certain directives of the Ostland civil administration also contained references to "purebred" and "mixed-blood" Roma[77]—the categories less frequently invoked in the areas under military rule.

The most striking feature of the policymaking in the RKO, however, was its ambivalence, which invited local initiative. As a result, the four General Districts—Estonia, Latvia, Lithuania, and Belorussia—differed from each other remarkably as far as the Nazi persecution of Roma was concerned. In Estonia, first arrests and executions of itinerant Roma were carried out impromptu by the local auxiliary police (*Omakaitse*), with little involvement of the German Security Police during the first year of occupation. As a legal basis for persecution, the head of the German Criminal Police in Estonia, Heinrich Bergmann, cited the December 1941 RKO decree that prescribed treating "roaming Gypsies" the same way as the Jews. In May 1942, however, he had admitted that only sedentary "Gypsies" with steady employment were presently residing in Estonia. Nevertheless, thanks to the zealous local officials, a relatively large percentage of Roma ended up in prisons and camps. In October 1942, the Estonian Security Police (a subsidiary of the German Security Police) shot 243 Roma at the Harku Camp—the biggest ever mass execution of Roma in Estonia. Although the immediate cause is unclear, this mass execution signaled the beginning of a more centralized persecution policy. On 22 January 1943, Bergmann ordered the concentration of all Roma, regardless of their place of residence and work status. During the following month, more than five hundred Roma from all over the country were dispatched by the Security Police to Tallinn Central prison. Reportedly, the women and children were shortly afterward taken from Central prison for execution. In late fall 1943 Romani teenagers who had been earlier separated from their parents and lived in a children's colony near Tallinn shared the fate of the adults. According to postwar Soviet war crimes investigation, further mass executions took place in 1944. In effect, virtually none of Estonia's Roma (slightly under 800) survived the German occupation.[78]

Latvia proved the ultimate symbol of inconsistency of the anti-Roma policymaking in RKO, with the spectrum of persecution ranging from complete destruction in some provinces to relative toleration in others. The mass murders began as early as 5 December 1941, when the German Security Police shot about one hundred Roma from Liepāja, prompting the ex post facto sanction in the form of a decree issued by the Reich Commissioner for the Ostland Hinrich Lohse on 24 December.[79] According to available evidence, more than a dozen mass executions of Roma took place in Latvia in 1942.[80] In several provinces, including Rēzekne and Ventspils, the mass murder was absolute, extending to sedentary Roma in spite of official guidelines to the contrary. In Jelgava alone, 810 Roma had been executed in 1942 and 1943.[81] The German Security Police, with the help of Order Police and local auxiliary forces, thus murdered more than a half of the 3,800-strong Romani minority in Latvia. The surviving Roma received severe restrictions such as confiscation of property, police surveillance, freezing of mobility, and—in the case of Lucia Strazdiņš from Liepāja—forced sterilization (the only such case ever documented for the occupied Soviet territories in the case of Roma).[82] (Whether the RKO had anything to do with the act of sterilization is impossible to determine at this point.) Even though Romani children were generally prohibited from attending school, upon a letter of complaint from Talsi in the northwestern part of Latvia, the German civil administration in January 1943 granted permission to Romani children from sedentary families to enroll in elementary schools, pending a special request to the district commissar. To continue with the secondary education, however, was only possible with the special permission from the Reich Commissioner.[83] Inconceivably, at the exact time when sedentary Roma were granted permission to attend school, the mass executions of Roma in other parts of Latvia continued unabated, and in the neighboring Estonia the head of the German Criminal Police ordered all local Roma to be dispatched to Tallinn Central prison.

The available evidence concerning the persecution of Roma in Lithuania is not enough to reach any definitive conclusion. According to estimates, the number of Roma in Lithuania did not exceed 1,500 (the most credible figure is 1,000). The roundups and mass executions apparently began from mid-1942 onward. Romani survivors interviewed by Vytautas Toleikis single out Pravieniškės forced labor camp as a symbol of the Nazi persecution of Roma in Lithuania. Reportedly, several Roma unfit for physical work, among them children and the elderly, were shot in the camp. Survivors claimed that a majority of the work-fit Roma had been deported to Germany and France and actually returned home after the war.[84] The death toll among Lithuania's Roma is estimated anywhere between one hundred and five hundred.[85] One way or another, the majority of Roma in Lithuania miraculously survived the war.

As compared with the Baltic States, the Nazi mass murder of Roma in Belorussia was by far most extensive. The Wehrmacht commander in Belorussia, General Gustav von Bechtolsheim, ordered on 10 October 1941 the execution of Roma "on the spot." According to von Bechtolsheim, "the Jews must disappear from the countryside and the Gypsies have to be annihilated as well."[86] However, the systematic killings of Roma in the General District Belorussia began in earnest not earlier than 1942. In several cases, it was local civil administrators who issued the execution orders, usually carried out by gendarmerie and/or local auxiliary police. In Vileika, Kletsk, and Gorodishche, the Roma and Jews were executed simultaneously while in Snov the Roma were followed by Jews to the mass grave.[87] As ordered by the Higher SS and Police Commander of Central Russia and Belorussia Curt von Gottberg, SS and military units killed Roma and Jews en masse during bigger antipartisan operations.[88] According to Christian Gerlach's estimate, the Germans murdered not less than three thousand Roma in occupied Belorussia.[89]

The comparison between Reich Commissariat Ostland and the Army Group North operational area yields more differences than similarities. In terms of planning, duration, and intensity, the policy of annihilation implemented in the North section was certainly more radical. The only part of RKO that matched the North section in brutality was the General District Belorussia. Perhaps not coincidentally, the latter region became a center of partisan activity and thus evoked special "security concerns." The perceived threat to military security appears to have been the main factor that contributed to radicalization of "anti-Gypsy measures" in the areas administered by the Wehrmacht. Even though the "vagabonding Gypsy spies" remained as illusive as ever, this stereotype got a life of its own, legitimizing a systematic mass murder on racial grounds. In practice, the Romani population, regardless of its social status, was equated to Jews from spring 1942 onward. This assumption is supported by the fact that sedentary Roma were routinely murdered throughout the entire region. A close examination of the operational areas of the other two German Army Groups (Center and South), as I have done elsewhere, further corroborates the genocidal nature of the Nazi attack against the Roma.[90]

Conclusion

The Nazi genocide of Roma in the Army Group North operational area proceeded in stages. The two individual executions documented for the initial months of German occupation do not allow a definitive conclusion regarding the Nazi treatment of Roma in general. Systematic mass murder of Roma began in February and March 1942, reaching its peak in May and June of the same year. A large percentage of the Roma in the North section was murdered in the first half of 1942, with no differentiation made between itinerant and sedentary Roma.[91] This fact explains why the intensity of the persecution decreased in the second half of 1942.

Thus, the destruction of the Roma in the areas in direct proximity to the front line as well as in the North section rear area appear to be a coordinated mass operation, especially from the spring 1942 onward. As to when explicit killing order, if it ever existed, was issued still remains a subject of debate.[92] At the same time, the systematic nature of annihilation transpires from the fact that the destruction of Roma began in the rear areas of the Army Group Center, South, and North almost simultaneously.[93] Subsequent phases of destruction, carried out by different agencies, can provide a further answer to this fundamental question. Mass murder of Roma began in early 1942, and was committed mainly by Einsatzgruppe A of the German Security Police and SD. The special "Gypsy operation," with the participation of an SS *Sonderkommando* dispatched for this particular purpose to the Pskov province from neighboring Estonia, likely took place during this phase.[94]

The killing units conducted lightning raids in several Russian villages, killing the Romani inhabitants on the spot. The perpetrators explained the mass executions as a deterrent in the fight against Soviet partisans. In many cases, the remaining villagers were forced to bury the bodies of the murdered victims.

The mass executions carried out by the German Security Police in April 1942 were far better organized. In Oredezh and Utogorsh, the registration of the entire Romani population preceded the arrests. The more effective organization resulted in a significantly higher number of victims as compared to the previous, mobile operations. Furthermore, the element of deterrence was no longer important to the perpetrators; the obvious purpose was to "cleanse" the entire region of its Romani population. The same was obviously true in Ostrov, as more than one hundred Roma, who had until the summer of 1943 been used as slave laborers, were reportedly deported from that town to Salaspils.

The annihilation of Roma reached its peak in May in June 1942. The mass executions in Pushkinskie Gory, Novorzhev, and Novgorod were carried out by the Secret Field Police and the Field Gendarmerie under the commandant office's supervision. Apparently, the target was the entire Romani population since the police operations began in all three regions simultaneously, in May 1942. The deadly impact of the military became evident at that very period, namely, when the military authorities tried to reinstate their influence over the German Security Police by reclaiming responsibility for "enemy elimination" in the Army Group North operational area.[95] This interference may in part explain the extraordinary cruelty with which the murder of Roma in Novorzhev was committed. The extension of mass murder to include sedentary Roma appeared to have been a natural progression for the military, which had slight reservations only with regard to the extent of engagement of any given unit. For example, when the Field Headquarters 822 prescribed on 12 May 1942, to "*always* treat Roma like partisans," the military units that comprised the Security Division 281 had come up with the "legal" justification of their own.[96] By the time when the division commander (under the pressure of the Army Group North High Command) rebuked the commandant's office in Novorzhev and the Secret Field Police 714 for their transgression of competences and orders, the fate of the Roma in the entire province had already been sealed. This (inconsequential) reprimand further points to the existence of a tacit agreement concerning the total destruction of Roma, even if orders to the contrary had to be formally acknowledged. Ultimately, the military higher-ups were less concerned about the legal basis for the mass murder of Roma, but about the question as to who had the authority to carry it out. The fact that the order issued by the Field Headquarters 822 had to be retracted did not mean that the local military authorities actually halted the killing. One way or another, as of late summer 1942, Secret Field Police and Field Gendarmerie continued destroying any group of Roma they encountered.

Military and Security Police units alike justified the atrocities that they had committed against Roma in the Army Group North operational area by evoking the stereotypes of Roma as spies or partisans. The Russian eyewitnesses, however, pinpointed just how little those charges had to do with reality. In any event, apparently, no one among the local population believed the accusation of partisan support.[97] The Nazis' intention to extirpate the entire Romani population was just too obvious. The Soviet Extraordinary State Commission also regarded the allegation of partisan activity as a German ploy to disguise their true intention, namely, the genocide of the Romani people. According to the ChGK branch office in the Novgorod province, for example, the Massalsky family was shot "because they were Gypsies by ethnicity."[98] The Leningrad investigation team stated with regard to the mass execution at Oredezh in April 1942 that the only blemish that the German perpetrators could find with the victims was that "they were Gypsies."[99] Similar statements had been made by the ChGK branch offices in Pskov and Loknia.[100]

After months of intensive examination of Nazi mass crimes in the Pskov province, the ChGK claimed that in terms of totality and premeditation, the annihilation of Roma was comparable with that of Soviet Jews. In support of this claim, the ChGK presented the following evidence:

> The German monsters spared no one. They murdered men and women, the healthy and the ill, children and elderly people. When implementing their inhuman Nazi theory, which was based on a bestial morality, these monsters in human disguise carried out the total extermination of Soviet civilians—Gypsies and Jews—residing in the Pskov province. The only reason for their execution was their ethnic origin.... The materials gathered by the commission show that, next to the Jews, the Gypsies were subject to total extermination throughout the Pskov province.[101]

The ChGK branch office in Loknia also pointed out the exceptional status of Jewish and Romani victims, by stating that the Germans had committed "extraordinary atrocities against the Jewish population with the intent of their physical extermination," and then adding that "the German-Fascist intruders treated the Gypsies no less cruelly ... carrying out their total extermination on a massive scale under suspicion of a partisan connection."[102]

The German and Soviet records by and large corroborate the ChGK findings. The Nazi genocidal campaign carried out against the Roma in the Army Group North operational area was indeed systematic and was intended to obliterate the Romani people. Apart from the special case of Ostrov, Soviet Roma could only survive if they managed to hide their ethnic identity or escape to the forest.

Notes

1. The full name of the agency was the Soviet Extraordinary Commission for the Investigation of the Crimes Committed by German Fascists and their Collaborators on the Territory of the USSR. The ChGK records are often underestimated as a historical source. On the critical aspects of the ChGK records with reference to Soviet Roma see Martin Holler, *Der nationalsozialistische Völkermord an den Roma in der deutsch besetzten Sowjetunion (1941–1944)* (Heidelberg, 2009), 16–20.
2. It is hardly adequate to speak of "Soviet" Roma within the context of RKO, which comprised Estonia, Latvia, and Lithuania—the independent states between 1918 and 1940—and Belorussia, some regions of which had previously belonged to Poland.
3. For a general overview see Alexander Dallin, *Deutsche Herrschaft in Rußland 1941–1945. Eine Studie über Besatzungspolitik* (Düsseldorf, 1981), 95–108, 193–200.
4. Anton Weiss-Wendt, "Extermination of the Gypsies in Estonia during World War II: Popular Images and Official Policies," *Holocaust and Genocide Studies* 17, no. 1 (Spring 2003): 31–61.
5. Alexander Hill, *The War Behind the Eastern Front: Soviet Partisan Movement in North-West Russia* (London, 2005), 82–87, 120–63.
6. Jürgen Kilian, "Das Zusammenwirken deutscher Polizeiformationen im 'Osteinsatz' am Beispiel des rückwärtigen Gebietes der Heeresgruppe Nord," in *Die Polizei im NS-Staat. Beiträge eines internationalen Symposiums an der Deutschen Hochschule der Polizei in Münster*, ed. Wolfgang Schulte (Frankfurt, 2009), 305–35; Hans Heinrich Wilhelm, *Die Einsatzgruppe A der Sicherheitspolizei und des SD 1941/42* (Frankfurt, 1996), 257–58; Hill, *War Behind the Eastern Front*, 30–34.
7. On the German starvation policy see Alex Kay, *Exploitation, Resettlement, Mass Murder: Political and Economic Planning for German Occupation Policy in the Soviet Union, 1940–1941* (New York, 2006). On the deliberate starving of besieged Leningrad see Johannes Hürter, "Die Wehrmacht vor Leningrad. Krieg und Besatzungspolitik der 18. Armee im Herbst und Winter 1941/42," in *Vierteljahreshefte für Zeitgeschichte* 49, no. 3 (July 2001): 377–440.
8. See Wilhelm, *Die Einsatzgruppe A*, 277, 279–80; Hill, *War Behind the Eastern Front*, 82.
9. Kilian, "Das Zusammenwirken," 335.
10. On the number of Roma in 1926 see Tsentralnoe Statisticheskoe Upravlenie Soiuza SSR, ed., *Vsesoiuznaia perepis naseleniia 1926 goda* (Moscow, 1928–1929); A. Barannikov, *Tsygany SSSR. Kratkii istoriko-etnograficheskii ocherk* (Moscow, 1931), 36. On the number of Roma in 1939 see Russian State Archive of Economy, 1562/336/967.
11. A few Romani farmers in the Pskov province had been engaged in agriculture since the end of the nineteenth century.
12. Commander of the Army Group North Rear Areas von Roques, report, 18 September 1941, German Federal Military Archives in Freiburg, RH 22/254. I am grateful to Anton Weiss-Wendt for sharing this document with me.

13. Although the text of the order is no longer available, it was often paraphrased or referred to in subsequent orders and reports. Cf. Security Division 281 to the Commander of Army Group North, 23 June 1942, Nuremberg State Archives (hereafter: NSA), ND, NOKW 2072; Security Division 281 to Field Headquarters 822, 24 March 1943, NSA, ND, NOKW 2072.
14. Security Division 281 to Field Headquarters 822, 24 March 1943, NSA, ND, NOKW 2022.
15. See Wilhelm, *Die Einsatzgruppe A,* 260.
16. Michael Zimmermann, *Rassenutopie und Genozid. Die nationalsozialistische "Lösung der Zigeunerfrage"* (Hamburg, 1996), 260.
17. Wilhelm, *Die Einsatzgruppe A,* 259. According to Soviet postwar investigation, thirty-seven Jews were killed in this particular massacre. A twelve-year-old boy named Filanovsky survived the massacre as the German bullet narrowly missed his head. Filanovsky managed to climb out of the mass grave without being noticed, eventually making his way to the Red Army rear area and sharing his testimony with the Soviet authorities. ChGK branch office in Loknia, interrogation records of Soliu Filanovsky, 12 February 1942, State Archives of the Russian Federation (hereafter: GARF), 7021/20/13.
18. Kilian, "Das Zusammenwirken," 326.
19. The ChGK reports often used the term *retaliation unit* [карательный отряд] to describe the subdivisions of the Einsatzgruppe A. Witnesses, however, sometimes used the same term to describe military units.
20. ChGK report for the Dno district, 16 May 1945, GARF, 7021/39/316.
21. The "cleansing" of October and November 1941 extended to the entire territory under control of the Army Group North (Wilhelm, *Die Einsatzgruppe A,* 259–261). See also ChGK report for the Oredezh district, November 1944, GARF, 7021/30/245.
22. Weiss-Wendt, "Extermination of the Gypsies in Estonia," 40–44.
23. ChGK report for the Gdov district, 1945, GARF, 7021/39/457.
24. Ibid.
25. ChGK report for the Pskov province, 1945, GARF, 7021/39/455.
26. Mikhail Pushniakov, "Moglinskoe delo," unpublished manuscript. I am grateful to the Russian historian Boris Kovalev from Novgorod for sharing this manuscript with me.
27. ChGK report for the Pskov province, 1945,GARF, 7021/39/455.
28. Jury Alexeiev, "Malenkaia fabrika smerti," in *Voina na unichtozhenie. Natsistskaia politika genotsida na territorii Vostochnoi Evropy: Materialy mezhdunarodnoi nauchnoi konferentsii, Moskva, 26–28 aprelia 2010 goda,* ed. Alexander Diukov and Olesia Orlenko (Moscow, 2010), 272–86.
29. ChGK branch office in Slantsy, report no. 21, 29 November 1944, GARF, 7021/30/250.
30. Already in winter 1941–42 fifteen Roma had been murdered in Oredezh. See Wolfgang Curilla, *Die deutsche Ordnungspolizei und der Holocaust im Baltikum und in Weißrußland 1941–1944* (Paderborn, 2005), 283.
31. ChGK, interrogation records of Anastasia Grokhovskaia, 12 October 1944, GARF, 7021/30/245.
32. [Alwin?] Bauer and Ershova are explicitly listed as war criminals responsible for the murder of the Roma (ChGK report for the Leningrad province, 1945, GARF, 7021/30/1611).
33. Soltsy county administration to Klevitsy county headman, 21 July 1942, Historical State Archives Novgorod, 2113s/1/6.
34. Boris Kovalev, *Natsistskaia okkupatsiia i kollaboratsionizm v Rossii 1941–1944* (Moscow, 2004), 250.
35. According to the ChGK final report from 27 April 1945, the arrest and mass execution was ordered by a German officer named Hoffmann, the "commandant of the

German military forces" in the Novgorod province (GARF, 7021/34/368). In other witness statements, however, Hoffmann was only referred to as "officer of a street battalion" and commander of the village Borki. One way or another, the atrocity was perpetrated by a military unit.
36. ChGK branch office in Novgorod district, testimony of Danila Kuznetsov, 5 January 1945, GARF, 7021/34/368.
37. ChGK branch office in Novgorod district, report no. 34, 4 February 1945,GARF, 7021/34/368.
38. Helmut Krausnick, *Hitlers Einsatzgruppen. Die Truppe des Weltanschauungskrieges 1938-1942* (Frankfurt, 1985), 243–44; Zimmermann, *Rassenutopie und Genozid*, 265–66; Guenter Lewy, *"Rückkehr nicht erwünscht." Die Verfolgung der Zigeuner im Dritten Reich* (Munich, 2001), 204–05.
39. Kilian, "Das Zusammenwirken," 317.
40. Security Division 281 to the Commander of Army Group North, 23 June 1942, NSA, ND, NOKW 2072.
41. Valdemar Kalinin, *Zagadka baltiiskikh tsygan. Ocherki istorii, kul'tury i sotsial'nogo razvitiia baltiiskikh tsygan* (Minsk, 2005), 62–64. See also ChGK branch office in Novorzhev, interrogation records of Maria Chistiakova, 5 May 1944, GARF, 7021/39/319.
42. ChGK branch office in Novorzhev, report no. 1, 7 May 1944, GARF, 7021/39/319. Even within the ChGK records, which are full of descriptions of German atrocities, the extreme brutality with which the Germans treated the Roma in Novorzhev is striking.
43. Security Division 281 to the Commander of Army Group North concerning report on the shooting of Gypsies in Novorzhev, 23 June 1942, NSA, ND, NOKW 2072.
44. As a matter of fact, the arrested Roma had as few chances to survive when handed over to the German Security Police (Wilhelm, *Einsatzgruppe A*, 277–82).
45. Security Division 281 to the Commander of Army Group North, 23 June 1942, NSA, ND, NOKW 2072.
46. Occasionally, the *Einsatzgruppen* also manufactured success stories in their reports. Cf. Peter Klein, ed., *Die Einsatzgruppen in der besetzten Sowjetunion 1941/42. Die Tätigkeits- und Lageberichte des Chefs der Sicherheitspolizei und des SD* (Berlin, 1997), 10. Einsatzgruppe A, for example, reported in April 1942 the destruction of a dangerous group led by "communists," which in reality was a group of mental patients and their male nurses (Wilhelm, *Die Einsatzgruppe A*, 278–79)
47. ChGK branch office in Novorzhev, report no. 1, 7 May 1945, GARF, 7021/39/319. Another indication of the systematic character of persecution can be derived from Alexander Hill's mentioning that around the same time the German authorities had requested the local county administration to provide information on Roma (Hill, *War Behind the Eastern Front*, 33).
48. The ChGK branch office in Novgorod had reported two hundred Roma murdered in the Pozherevitsy district, which it evidently confused with the neighboring Novorzhev. The inaccuracy may have crept in due to the fact that the evidence stemmed from second-hand sources (ChGK to chief political commissar of the North-West Front Okorokov, 1 March 1944, GARF, 7021/34/760).
49. ChGK branch office in Pushkinskie Gory, report no. 71, 25 March 1945, GARF, 7021/39/336.
50. ChGK branch office in Pushkinskie Gory, interrogation records of Konstantin Fedorov, 12 Mai 1945, GARF, 7021/39/336. Fedorov was assigned to the prisoner group that had to bury the bodies of the executed. Having finished his assignment, he returned to the prison, to be released a few days later.
51. ChGK branch office in Pushkinskie Gory, report no. 71, 25 March 1945, GARF, 7021/39/336.

52. ChGK branch office in Pushkinskie Gory, Statement of Iosif Dmitriev, 20 April 1945, GARF, 7021/39/336. By using the phrase "racial executions" in the sense of racially motivated executions, Dmitriev apparently sought to emphasize genocidal intent in the Nazi persecution of the Roma.
53. ChGK report for the Porkhov district, 30 April 1945, GARF, 7021/39/328. This particular mass execution presumably took place in the period between March and June 1942.
54. ChGK branch office in Strugi Krasnye, report, 17 May 1945, GARF, 7021/39/339.
55. ChGK branch office in Loknia, report, 15 December 1944, GARF, 7021/20/13.
56. Ministry of the Interior office in Pskov, interrogation records of Nikolai Gavrilov, 16 August 1947, United States Holocaust Memorial Museum (hereafter: USHMM), RG-06.025.
57. Kilian, "Das Zusammenwirken," 326.
58. ChGK branch office in Loknia, report, 15 December 1944, GARF, 7021/20/13.
59. Ivan Alexeiev was assassinated by partisans in 1943.
60. Soviet Security Police administration in the Leningrad province, interrogation records of Andrei Lukashev, 29 March 1945, GARF, 7021/39/325.
61. Ibid.
62. Security Division 281 to Field Headquarters 822, March 24, 1943, NSA, ND, NOKW 2022.
63. This assessment is corroborated by the statement of the former commander of the Field Headquarters 822 Karl Georg Sasse, who stood trial in Pskov in 1947–48. Sasse testified that the order to deport the Roma came from the SD (read: German Security Police), interrogation records of Karl Georg Sasse, 29 October 1947, USHMM, RG-06.025.
64. ChGK branch office in Ostrov, report, 28 August 1944, GARF, 7021/30/1736.
65. Donald Kenrick and Grattan Puxon, *Sinti und Roma—die Vernichtung eines Volkes im NS-Staat* (Göttingen, 1981), 104; Vladimir Litvinov, *Operatsiia "Chernyi diatel." Dokumentalnaia povest'* (Kiev, 1981), 134–36, 144. I am grateful to the Ukrainian historian Alexander Kruglov from Kharkov for pointing out to me the testimony of O[?] Benarovich-Mironchuk quoted in Litvinov's book; I also thank the Russian ethnographer Nikolai Bessonov from Moscow for sending me a scanned copy of the relevant pages.
66. Litvinov, *Operatsia,* 135–36.
67. Kenrick and Puxon, *Sinti und Roma,* 104.
68. Litvinov, *Operatsia,* 135; ChGK branch office in Ostrov, report, 28 August 1944, GARF, 7021/30/1736.
69. Litvinov, *Operatsia,* 133–34.
70. Kenrick and Puxon, *Sinti und Roma,* 104.
71. ChGK branch office in Ostrov, report, 28 August 1944, GARF, 7021/30/1736.
72. Cf. Alexander Kruglov's review on my recent book in *Golokost i suchasnist: studii v Ukraini i sviti* (Kiev) 6, no. 2 (2009): 216. As a further proof of presumed shift in the Nazi treatment of Roma in the occupied Soviet territories Kruglov gives the following example: A group of twenty-six Roma captured in the Zhitomir region in February 1943 was not shot on the spot, as it would have happened before, but was deported to Krakow-Plaszów concentration camp in the General Government of Poland. While the children were transferred to Litzmannstadt (from where they returned to Ukraine in 1945), the adult Roma were dispatched as slave laborers to Germany and France. Cf. Alexander Kruglov, "Genotsid tsygan v Ukraine v 1941–1944 gg. Statistiko-regional'nyi aspect," *Golokost i suchasnist: studii v Ukraini i sviti* 6, no. 2 (2009), 99. However, one has to take into account that, as part of the Reich Commissariat Ukraine, the General District of Zhitomir was under civil administration, which

makes it difficult to compare with the "Gypsy policies" in the Army Group North operational area.
73. Ministry of the Interior office in Novgorod, interrogation records of Mikhail Obodkov, 1 November 1947, USHMM, RG-06.025.
74. Kilian, "Das Zusammenwirken," 311. This also concerns Estonia, even though this constituent part of RKO featured an admixture of military and civil rule.
75. For the power struggle within the RKO see, for example, Dallin, *Deutsche Herrschaft*; Andreas Zellhuber, *"Unsere Verwaltung treibt einer Katastrophe zu ...": Das Reichsministerium für die besetzten Ostgebiete und die deutsche Besatzungsherrschaft in der Sowjetunion 1941-1945* (Munich, 2006).
76. RKO, decree, 24 December 1941, German Federal Archives in Berlin (hereafter: BAB), R 90/147. Identical copies of the RKO decree deposited at Yad Vashem in Jerusalem and German Federal Archives in Ludwigsburg are dated 4 December 1941. This inconsistency led Michael Zimmermann to believe that the decree was meant as an ex post facto justification of a mass execution of Roma at Liepāja on 5 December 1941 (Cf. Zimmermann, *Rassenutopie und Genozid*, 269, 471).
77. See, for example, Reich Ministry for the Occupied Eastern territories in Berlin to RKO, 11 June 1942, BAB, R 90/147.
78. Weiss-Wendt, "Extermination of the Gypsies in Estonia," 31–61; Anton Weiss-Wendt, *Murder without Hatred: Estonians and the Holocaust* (Syracuse, NY, 2009), 144–46; Anton Weiss-Wendt, "Vinishchennia tsiganskogo narodu u krainakh Baltii (1941–1944): tsentral'ni rishennia i mistsevi initsiativi," *Golokost i suchasnist: studii v Ukraini i sviti* 6, no. 2 (2009): 53–61; Ruth Bettina Birn, *Die Sicherheitspolizei in Estland 1941-1944. Eine Studie zur Kollaboration im Osten* (Paderborn, 2006), 185–89.
79. It should be emphasized that the RKO decree was directed against "Gypsies wandering about in the countryside," while the Roma murdered in Liepāja were apparently sedentary city dwellers.
80. Andrew Ezergailis, *The Holocaust in Latvia, 1941-1944: The Missing Centre* (Riga, 1996), 188, 288; Zimmermann, *Rassenutopie und Genozid*, 271.
81. Zimmermann, *Rassenutopie und Genozid*, 271.
82. Liepāja police chief to the city prefect, 10 December 1941, reprinted in *Der Prozess gegen die Hauptkriegsverbrecher vor dem Internationalen Militärgerichtshof in Nürnberg, 14. November 1945 bis 1. Oktober 1946*, vol. 8 (Nuremberg, 1947), 345. According to the prefect, the unfortunate woman was sterilized on 9 January 1942.
83. School department of the General Commissioner for Latvia to the director of education and culture in Riga, 27 January 1943, BAB, R 92/92 (By mistake, Zimmermann has identified this file as R 90/90).
84. Vytautas Toleikis, "Lithuanian Roma During the Years of the Nazi Occupation," in *Murders of Prisoners of War and of Civilian Population in Lithuania, 1941-1944*, ed. Christoph Dieckmann et al. (Vilnius, 2005), 269–78. Until now, no French or German documents regarding Romani slave laborers from Lithuania have come to light.
85. According to Arūnas Bubnys (as quoted by Toleikis), the Nazis murdered anywhere between 100 and 150 Roma in Lithuania. Toleikis himself gives the figure 500, though he does not back it up with any empirical data. In Christoph Dieckmann's analysis, the death toll among Lithuania's Roma was about 200—out of the estimated 1,000 living in Lithuania in 1941 See Dieckmann, *Deutsche Besatzungspolitik in Litauen 1941-1944* (Göttingen, 2011), 1397.
86. Orders of the General Gustav von Bechtolsheim from 10 October and 24 November 1941, reprinted in *Einsatz im "Reichskommissariat Ostland." Dokumente zum Völkermord im Baltikum und Weißrußland 1941-1944*, ed. Wolfgang Benz et al. (Berlin, 1998), 77–78.

87. On the Nazi destruction of Roma in Belorussia see Christian Gerlach, *Kalkulierte Morde. Die deutsche Wirtschafts- und Vernichtungspolitik in Weißrußland 1941 bis 1944* (Hamburg, 1999), 1063–67; Martin Dean, *Collaboration in the Holocaust: Crimes of the Local Police in Belorussia and Ukraine, 1941–44* (New York, 2000), 44, 59, 83, 100–102. On the Snov massacre see Eric Haberer, "The German Police and the Genocide in Belorussia, 1941–1944. The 'Second Sweep': Gendarmerie Killings of Jews and Gypsies on January 29, 1942," *Journal of Genocide Research* 3, no. 2 (2001): 207–18.
88. Peter Klein, "Curt von Gottberg—Siedlungsfunktionär und Massenmörder," in *Karrieren der Gewalt. Nationalsozialistische Täterbiographien*, ed. Klaus-Michael Mallmann and Gerhard Paul (Darmstadt, 2004), 95–103.
89. Gerlach, *Kalkulierte Morde*, 1066.
90. Cf. Holler, *Der nationalsozialistische Völkermord*, 53–100.
91. This conclusion further confirms the assumption of Wolfgang Wippermann, who doubted whether any sedentary Roma had still been alive in the German-occupied Soviet territories by 1943. Cf. Wolfgang Wippermann, "Nur eine Fußnote? Die Verfolgung der sowjetischen Roma. Historiographie, Motive, Verlauf," in *Gegen das Vergessen. Der Vernichtungskrieg gegen die Sowjetunion*, ed. Klaus Meyer and Wolfgang Wippermann (Frankfurt, 1992), 75–90.
92. The commander of German Security Police in Estonia Martin Sandberger asserted during his postwar trial the existence of a so-called Führer order to exterminate Roma, Jews, and Soviet functionaries. At the same time, Sandberger swore that he had not been aware of the order issued by the Commander of the Army Group North Rear Areas on 21 November 1941. Cf. Weiss-Wendt, "Extermination of the Gypsies in Estonia," 55f.
93. Holler, *Der nationalsozialistische Völkermord*, 53–100. The only exception to the rule was the Nikolaev region and the Crimea in southern Ukraine, where Einsatzgruppe D headed by Otto Ohlendorf began to indiscriminately destroy Romani communities as early as late fall 1941.
94. Cf. Pavel Kurovsky's testimony at the *Mere-Gerrets-Viik* war crimes trial in Tallinn in 1961, quoted in Weiss-Wendt, "Extermination of the Gypsies in Estonia," 54.
95. Wilhelm, *Die Einsatzgruppe A*, 282–83.
96. Nevertheless, the military units appeared to have been conscious of exceeding their own authority, exemplified by the consistent efforts to ensure that no civilians witnessed atrocities.
97. The civilian population could clearly distinguish between the cases in which the "retaliation units" were hunting partisans and those in which the charge of illicit activity served as a pretext for premeditated mass murder. In some cases, witnesses differentiated between "communists" and "partisans" on the one hand and "completely innocent civilians" on the other. None of the cases that I have examined indicate that the Romani victims had anything to do with Soviet partisans.
98. ChGK branch office in the Novgorod district, report no. 30, 4 February 1945, GARF, 7021/34/368.
99. ChGK report for the Leningrad province, 1945, GARF, 7021/30/1611.
100. ChGK branch office in Novorzhev (of the Pskov province), report no. 1, 7 May 1945. GARF, 7021/39/319 ChGK branch office in Loknia, report, 15 December 1944, GARF, 7021/20/13.
101. ChGK report for the Pskov province, 1945, GARF, 7021/39/455.
102. ChGK branch office in Loknia, report, 15 December 1944, GARF, 7021/20/13. For comparison of Jewish and Romani victimization by the Nazis see my recent article, "'Like Jews?' The Nazi Persecution and Extermination of Soviet Roma Under the German Military Administration: A New Interpretation, Based on Soviet Sources," *Dapim: Studies on the Shoah* 24 (2010): 137–76.

CHAPTER 7

THE JUSTICE SYSTEM OF THE FEDERAL REPUBLIC OF GERMANY AND THE NAZI PERSECUTION OF THE GYPSIES

Gilad Margalit

One of the long unresolved issues of the Holocaust has been the recognition of Gypsies as victims of Nazi racial persecution, a step necessary to make them eligible for compensation. This chapter analyzes the judicial inquiries into this matter held in the Federal Republic of Germany from the late 1940s through the mid-1960s.[1] I argue that a perpetuation of prewar racial biases compromised the findings in the Gypsy case and led to the exoneration of "racial scientists" such as Robert Ritter, whose activities were instrumental in the persecution of Gypsies. I conclude, moreover, that the attitude of the judicial system with regard to the Gypsies has been reflected in its dealings with other persecuted groups, including Jews.

From the late 1940s to the mid-1960s, the justice system of the Federal Republic of Germany (FRG) conducted an investigation into issues related to the Nazi persecution of the Gypsies, in particular appeals for compensation by Gypsy survivors of the Holocaust. The compensation authorities refused to recognize the plaintiffs as victims of the Nazis. In dealing with this question, the justice system often ruled in favor of the state, relying on a Nazi document as a legal underpinning for its decisions. Known as the Auschwitz-Decree (*Erlass*), this document, which was promulgated by Chief of the German SS and the Police Heinrich Himmler on 29 January 1943, ordered the deportation of the majority of German Gypsies to the Auschwitz-Birkenau death camp.[2] The postwar justice system cited this decree in overruling the appeals of Gypsies persecuted before January 1943. The document was referred to also in dismissing investigation procedures conducted by the prosecution authorities against Robert Ritter, the Reich's chief expert on the Gypsy question, and against his assistant, Eva Justin. This chapter explores the failure of the legal system to come to terms with the racial biases against the Gypsies manifested in German law and culture both before and after the Nazi period. In so doing, the chapter points out the system's larger failure to come to terms with much of the persecution perpetrated during the Nazi period.

The "Auschwitz-Decree" and the Compensation of Gypsy Victims

The compensation laws enacted in Germany after 1945 recognized eligibility only for victims whose persecution derived from political, racial, or religious motives.[3] Gypsies persecuted before the publication of the Auschwitz-Decree allegedly were not persecuted for these motives, so compensation authorities did not recognize them as actual victims of Nazism. In trials conducted between 1950 and 1953, the judicial system concurred with the opinion of the compensation authorities. While the racial nature of the 1943 Himmler decree has never been contested,[4] some of the first commentaries on the Federal Compensation Law (BEG) supported a restrictive (nonracial) interpretation of earlier persecution of Gypsies. Two of the authors of these commentaries, Hans Wilden and Otto Küster, both senior officials in the compensation authorities of the Federal Republic of Germany, had prior experience in this area. The section they authored concerning Gypsies in the 1955 commentary on the Compensation Law began thus:

> Since the beginning of time, the Gypsies have been regarded by Western civilized nations (*Kulturvölker*) as a state plague (*Landplage*). No one can claim that actions taken against them before 1933 constituted racial persecution. The Gypsies' character (antisocial behavior, crime, the wandering drive) were occasion for combating them.[5]

This declaration accepted at face value the Nazi regime's formal excuse for persecuting the Gypsies. Basing their argument on the precedent of maltreatment of German Gypsies before 1933, Hans Wilden and Otto Küster argued that the decision to send those people to concentration and death camps before 1943 was not racially inspired. Turning back Gypsy appeals in the 1950s against the authorities' refusal to recognize them as victims of the Nazis, the courts repeatedly concluded that their *racial* persecution began only with the issuance of the Auschwitz-Decree.[6]

The facts show otherwise. Antecedents in German maltreatment of Gypsies notwithstanding, racial motives were interwoven with official Nazi policy toward the Gypsies as early as 1936 with the publication of the commentary to the Nuremberg Laws, and they were explicitly expressed by various decrees of the criminal police beginning that year.[7] The position adopted by the judicial system of the FRG in the 1950s expressed a rather moderate claim: it acknowledged that the massive deportation of Gypsy families from Germany to Auschwitz *was* the result of racial motives. Yet a contradictory belief was widespread among postwar police experts and compensation authorities: few experts maintained the persecution of Gypsies (either before or after 1943) did not derive from racial motives.[8]

The claim that Nazi *racial* persecution of the Gypsies actually began in 1943 was neither asserted nor mentioned in the 1950 discussions with the compensation authorities on the eligibility of the Gypsies for compensation. The available evidence suggests that this argument had been raised for the first time between 1948 and 1950, during the prosecutorial investigation of Ritter. The claim subsequently appeared in a 1951 police newspaper article written by Rudolf Uschold, a Bavarian police expert on the Gypsies.[9] Uschold had specialized in this field during the Third Reich, and he remained active in the area from 1946 to 1951, as a member of the Information Agency Concerning Gypsies (Nachrichtenstelle über Zigeuner) in the Munich police headquarters, known within the bureaucracy as the "Gypsy Police" (Zigeunerpolizei).[10] He appeared as an expert witness both during the Ritter investigation and in the numerous 1950–1953 eligibility appeals of Gypsies against the compensation authorities.[11]

Uschold's view was not accepted by all of the police experts on Gypsy matters. As I have indicated above, some of them even suggested that the whole persecution of Gypsies during the Third Reich was not racial at all.[12] The "post-1943" formula, then, occupied a middle ground between those who denied that Gypsies were persecuted on racial grounds and those who regarded Nazi treatment of Gypsies as analogous in motive to Nazi persecution of Jews. Senior German-Jewish officials within the compensation authorities of the FRG took the latter position.[13] Constituting a compromise view, the Auschwitz-Decree thus served as a watershed criterion to determine the eligibility of Gypsies for recognition as victims of Nazism, depriving such status for the survivors of the first deportation of German Gypsies to the General Government of Poland in May 1940 (there were 2,330 Gypsies, only half of whom survived). By 1956, this approach had been adopted by the Federal Supreme Court (Bundesgerichtshof, or BGU) of the FRG.

The court did not hesitate to apply this stricture, rejecting the appeal of a Gypsy deported to Poland in May 1940: the latter had challenged the compensation authority for its refusal to recognize his confinement in Polish ghettoes and camps as racial persecution. In their verdict, the judges gave a formalistic interpretation of the Nazi terms (such as *resettlement*), thereby echoing the common position of the compensation authorities. Further, no attempt was made by the court to verify the squalid circumstances in which the Gypsies deported to Poland had lived during this period (e.g., by summoning witnesses who could describe the reality of life there).[14]

The part of the verdict that might have given rise to any perception of prejudice by the judges against the Gypsies seemed carefully formulated to shield them from accusations of racism. This part was presented as an objective review of the historical and social background of the persecution of Gypsies in Germany. It began with a description of the circumstances in which the image of the Gypsies was consolidated within German culture, determining that the Gypsies' vagrancy was perceived by the settled society as unstable (*unstetes Leben*). This way of life, the verdict indicated, was associated with occupations such as commerce, entertainment, art, and the like, which "did not always enjoy much appreciation in the surrounding society." The judges emphasized that their assertions did not constitute moral criticism of the Gypsies, but rather mere reflection of public perception of them. At a certain stage the verdict shifted from summarizing public opinion to citing pseudoscientific explanations from the racial-criminological literature blemishing the Gypsies:

> As most Gypsies opposed quitting their nomadic life and being integrated into the settled population, they were perceived as *Asoziale*. They tended, as experience shows, toward crime, especially theft and fraud. They totally lack the moral instinct to respect the property of others, because as primitive people they are governed by unrestrained, dominating instinct.[15]

The verdict denied any possibility of granting compensation to Gypsies persecuted before 1943.

In the face of this reality, Kurt May, a Jew heading the central office of the United Restitution Organization (URO) in Frankfurt, was one of the few people in the FRG who worked intensively to revise the court's ruling. May regarded the verdict as a gross mistake, and acted on several levels to correct it. He encouraged Hans Buchheim, a historian at the Institute for Contemporary History (IfZ) in Munich, to investigate the May 1940 deportation of Gypsies to Poland, and even assisted him in doing so.[16] May sent letters to and had discussions with representatives of the compensation authorities and with members of the political and judicial systems. Furthermore, he asked his friend, Franz Calvelli-Adorno, the president of the senate of the Regional Court of Appeal (Oberlandesgericht, or OLG) in Frankfurt, to publish an article on the issue, a move that turned out to be of paramount importance.[17] May understood that, in order to generate a revision in the ruling of the Supreme Court, he needed to recruit a member of the judicial system whose pro-Gypsy stance would not appear to be based upon self-interest.

This was not the first time in post-1945 Germany that German Jews had defended the rights of Gypsies to be compensated as victims of Nazi persecution. In 1950 Marcel Frenkel and Philip Auerbach, both senior officials in the compensation authorities in the FRG, protested against the position of their German colleagues in the Coordination Committee of Compensation Offices for denying the Gypsies eligibility. The Germans maintained that the Gypsies had been persecuted not for racial motives, but rather for asocial behavior (*Asozialität*) and crime.[18] It was not incidental that German-Jewish, rather than non-Jewish German officials who dealt with these questions, demonstrated more sensitivity for the injustice done to the Gypsies.

Without gainsaying moral concern, Jewish involvement with, and concern for, the discrimination against the Gypsies seems to have derived, at least in the early 1950s, largely from deep concern regarding the future of the Federal Republic. Auerbach worried that the denial of compensation for Gypsies, on the pretext that their persecution by the Nazis was not a result of racial factors, but rather a legitimate action to eradicate crime, might serve the West German compensation authorities as a precedent to deny Jews compensation for the persecution they had suffered.[19] By the late 1950s this fear had dissipated, and Kurt May apparently acted primarily out of identification with the Gypsies, and in outrage against the injustice inflicted upon them by the justice system of the FRG.

In 1961 and under the advice of May, Calvelli-Adorno published a sharp critique of the BGH verdict; he invalidated the acceptability of the commonly advanced argument predicated on the perceived antisocial behavior of the Gypsies. Calvelli-Adorno criticized the "anticipated collective identification" of the Gypsies, based on fixed and unchangeable racial properties, [that] Gypsies are identical to *Asozial*.... The injustice done to Gypsies must be defined as racial persecution. The individual Gypsy was treated as asocial only because he belonged to the Gypsy race. This membership was enough to differentiate him from the rest of the population and to subject him without investigation to illegal and cruel treatment.[20]

The publication of the article was an important contribution to the German discourse on Gypsy victims of Nazism, a discourse that had been gaining momentum in the FRG press since the late 1950s.[21] Moreover, it influenced the FRG judges to revise the BGH's ruling.[22] On 23 May 1963, reversing verdicts of the Cologne district court, the BGH ruled on the appeals of Gypsies who had fled Germany in 1939, after having been examined by members of Robert Ritter's Health Office. The plaintiffs argued that the research conducted by Ritter and his subordinates should be regarded as racial persecution, and that Gypsies were entitled to compensation. The high court accepted their arguments, and for the first time ever the German judicial system recognized Ritter's pseudoscientific activity as Nazi persecution. The court, two members of which had been judges in 1956, revised its previous decision that racial persecution of the Gypsies began only in 1943, and ruled that its actual origins were in 1938.[23] Unfortunately, some of those who should have benefited from the revised ruling were no longer alive.

The "Auschwitz-Decree" and the Persecutors

The offices of the public prosecutor (Staatsanwaltschaft) in the FRG initiated criminal investigation procedures against dozens of policemen, officials, and scientists who had participated in the Nazi persecution of Gypsies, but did not find it proper to bring most of them to trial.[24] Accordingly, let me examine now the investigation procedures employed in connection with two individuals who held key positions within the Nazi system dealing with the Gypsies.

The individuals in question were scientists from the field of racial hygiene, known in the Anglo-Saxon world as *eugenics*. This pseudoscientific discipline was internationally recognized as a legitimate field of inquiry before the Nazis came to power.[25] Although none of these scientists was a member of the Nazi Party, the inevitable racial consciousness was confirmed by the roles they fulfilled.[26] Furthermore, they were integrated into the bureaucratic machinery of the Nazi state through their efforts to translate these radical racial ideas into the social policies of the Third Reich. Like the technocrats who consolidated the final solution to the "Jewish problem," the thinkers and designers of the final solution to the "Gypsy problem" (*endgültige Lösung der Zigeunerfrage*) were "desk criminals" (*Schreibtischtäter*), who themselves took no part in murdering or sterilizing Gypsies. All of these racial researchers worked in the framework of the Racial Hygiene and Demographic Biology Research Unit (*Rassenhygienische und Bevölkerungsbiologische Forschungsstelle*), which operated from 1937 to 1944 under the direction of Robert Ritter in the Reich Health Office.[27] This unit worked closely with the Reich Criminal Police (RKPA) under the command of Arthur Nebe, and with the criminal police stations throughout the Nazi state.[28] Ritter and his assistants collected data from police files about Gypsies, as well as anthropological and genealogical information from the Gypsies themselves.[29] The Gypsies did not respond willingly to these examinations of racial researcher Ritter and his colleagues, who tried to overcome their resistance with incentives, and also reportedly with threats and the exercise of brute force, under the protection of policemen who accompanied them.[30]

The data collected by Ritter's team enabled the purported experts to prepare racial-hygienic opinions about each of the approximately 24,000 Gypsies examined by mobile team units. The opinions, which classified the extent of the Gypsies' "racial purity," were then submitted to the criminal police.[31] Ritter had already argued in 1935 that experience showed Gypsy "mongrels" (*Mischlinge*) to be clearly inclined toward crime and *Asozialität*, in contrast to "racially pure (*reinrassige*) Gypsies.[32] At the time, the only solution Ritter had foreseen for the "mongrel" population was mass sterilization and incarceration.[33] It was not long, however, before such a sentence for thousands of "mongrel" men, women, and children led directly to confinement in concentration camps and consequently to death by starvation, disease, or gas.

The decisions of the public prosecutor's office in Frankfurt to terminate the investigation procedures against Ritter in 1950, and against his assistant, Eva Justin, in 1960, and not to bring them to trial, were part of a broader pattern. The two educated defendants were regarded as people whom circumstances had thrown into an extreme situation, and in which they involuntarily had carried out their duties.[34] Put differently, some German courts did not adjudge such crimes perpetrated during the Nazi period as having been committed out of free will, but rather as actions forced upon the actors by a dictatorship. Therefore, no personal responsibility for their deeds was adduced, and no accountability imposed.[35] Their Gypsy victims, however, faced quite a different attitude from the FRG justice system. Gypsies who had agreed to be sterilized (a term some testified that they had not fully understood), under threat of deportation to the concentration camps, were regarded as responsible for the sterilization performed on them.[36]

In addition to his work at the Reich Health Office, Ritter also headed, beginning in 1942, the Institute for Criminal Biology of the Security Police (Sicherheitspolizei).[37] There he helped design—and I believe that the evidence shows that he did so enthusiastically—the "Gypsy policy" of the Third Reich, and thus played a central role in the Gypsies' fate.[38] His future assistant, Eva Justin, was a nurse in the children's ward of the psychiatric clinic of Tübingen University, where Ritter served as a psychiatrist and where he met her in 1934. When Ritter was appointed in 1936 to head the racial-hygienic research unit of the Reich Health Office, he brought Justin and some other Tübingen colleagues along with him to Berlin. In 1943, Ritter helped Justin earn a PhD from Humboldt University in Berlin. In the framework of her activity in the Racial Hygiene Unit, Justin made anthropological measurements and took blood samples from Gypsies.[39] She also signed hundreds of racial opinions, in which she determined that many Gypsies were "mongrels," and thus condemned them to sterilization or deportation to concentration camps. In her doctoral thesis she recommended the sterilization of all Gypsy children who had been removed from their parents' homes and had received a German education, since she thought that they were hopeless and could not be improved.[40] In so doing, Justin had a hand in the fate of many Gypsies.

In October 1948, the public prosecutor in Frankfurt initiated an investigation of Ritter who, having undergone the denazification process in 1947, had served as the principal youth physician in the city's Municipal Health Service.[41] The investigation was opened following a complaint filed by the Bavarian State Commissioner on behalf of victims persecuted by Nazism for political, racial, and religious reasons. The basis of this complaint was the evidence of German Gypsies who had come to know Ritter in the course of his activity in the Third Reich.[42] The principal claim against him was that his research and other actions had been instrumental in the compulsory sterilization of large numbers of Gypsies, and had been similarly instrumental in the deportation of thousands to concentration camps during the war, making him partially responsible for their deaths.

Other sections charged Ritter with physically injuring the Gypsies he examined for research purposes, and with showing cruelty toward them. He also was accused of concealing during his denazification information regarding his alleged membership in the SS.[43] The investigation lasted for almost two years, during which time dozens of witnesses were interviewed throughout Germany. In August 1950 the chief prosecutor in Frankfurt, Dr. Hans K. Kosterlitz, decided to terminate investigation procedures, and closed the file; in his opinion the results did not warrant an indictment of Ritter.[44] A few years after Ritter's death, the investigation file was officially destroyed.[45] Of the entire file, only the summary of the investigation and the decision of the chief attorney to close it remained, so that it absolutely was no longer possible to examine either the evidence or Ritter's statement in full. However, it is possible that a copy of the file survived, for in the summary of the investigation of Eva Justin, conducted in 1959, it is implied that the prosecutors were familiar with the evidence in the Ritter file.[46]

In February 1959 then, less than nine years after the investigation procedures against Ritter had been terminated, the pattern repeated itself when the chief prosecutor in Frankfurt opened a criminal investigation against Eva Justin on charges of abetting mass murder. Justin had worked as a child psychologist in the health service of Frankfurt municipality since her completion of the denazification process in 1948.[47] In late 1958 Sigmund S. Wolf, a linguist and the compiler of a Gypsy-language dictionary, attacked Justin for her work during the Third Reich. The most severe accusation was that she had conducted research and catalogued for the Reich Security Main Office (RSHA) the personal data of about 20,000 Gypsies, with the aim of physically eliminating them. She was also charged with spreading the notion of the advisability of sterilizing Gypsies, pressuring Gypsies to accept voluntary sterilization, and perjuring herself in Ritter's denazification procedure.[48]

The resolution that the racial persecution of the Gypsies began in 1943, the year when Himmler promulgated the Auschwitz-Decree, heavily influenced the decision of the public prosecutor in Frankfurt to terminate investigation procedures against Ritter and Justin. In each case, prosecutors accepted the defendant's claim of innocence on the basis that Ritter and his team completed their research on the Gypsy issue before 1943, thereby making it possible to argue that their activity should not be regarded as racial persecution.[49]

Ritter argued that he did not know to what extent, if any, the research material he collected was used in the framework of the mass deportation of German Gypsies to Auschwitz-Birkenau that had begun in March 1943, and thus strongly denied having anything to do with that deportation. The prosecution also accepted the formalistic claim that since the criminal police had not published the Auschwitz-Decree, Ritter could not have known about its existence. He further asserted that he became aware of the deportations to Auschwitz only after the war.[50]

It is worth stressing too that ten years later the same argument was instrumental in the termination of the investigation against Justin. The prosecutor acknowledged that the racial-biological opinions about the Gypsies that Ritter and his team prepared through 1942 had served as grounds for the Law Concerning the Gypsies (*Zigeunergesetz*), which was to be enacted together with the Law Concerning *Asoziale*.[51] The prosecutor's assertion that the law's intent was to regulate the lives of Gypsies in the Reich in order to prevent additional mixing of blood, distinctly proved the researchers' awareness of the racial nature of this law, which was no different from the 1935 Law for the Protection of German Blood and Honor, one of the Nuremberg Laws.[52]

But with this legal formalism the prosecution ignored the illegal nature of the Law Concerning the Gypsies. It also determined that Justin could not have known, when preparing the opinions, that they would serve as a basis for illegal actions in the framework of Himmler's subsequent 1943 Auschwitz-Decree, inflicting death and sterilization on many Gypsies.[53] In accord with this formalistic approach, the prosecution excluded Ritter and his institute from the list of criminal organizations that shaped the "Gypsy policy" of the Third Reich.

In the course of the investigation of Justin, more than twenty thousand personal files of Gypsies were collected from the various branches of the criminal police throughout the FRG.[54] Had these files been examined during the investigation of Ritter, his opinions written after the publication of the Auschwitz-Decree would have surfaced. However, according to the prosecution, not even one file containing racial opinions signed by Justin was located. Today we know that Justin signed hundreds of racial opinions (*gutachtliche Ausserungen*) on Gypsies.[55]

The Perpetrator as Anti-Nazi Fighter

An apologetic composition Ritter wrote in 1947, when he applied for a post in the municipal health service of Frankfurt, can help us to reconstruct his lost statement of defense. In this essay, Ritter presented his own version of the Nazi persecution of the Gypsies, and his part in designing the Reich's "Gypsy policy."[56]

The above document also helps clarify the context and meaning of various assertions in the investigation summary. For example, in the later document, in addition to a reference to the head of the Criminal Police, Arthur Nebe, the prosecutor mentioned that Nebe was executed for complicity in the 20 July 1944 attempt on Hitler's life.[57] Prima facie, this information is irrelevant to the issue in the summary of Ritter's investigation. The emphasis on Nebe's opposition to Hitler, while ignoring his murderous role as the commander of Einsatzgruppe B, suggests that not only Nebe but also Ritter's treatment of the "Gypsy problem" should be regarded as an integral part of their opposition to Hitler and Nazism. The prosecutor accepted Ritter's main rejoinder that he should not be held responsible for the fate of the Gypsies in the Third Reich and that the fields in which he engaged, racial hygiene and criminal biology, were legitimate scientific areas having no connection to the racial ideology of Nazism.[58] In short, Ritter's defense presented him as a persistent opponent of Nazism, even before Hitler came to power. By 1947, when Ritter was declared denazified, he presented two genuine notes he had written for a local newspaper in Cologne, which had published them in 1931. In these notes, he criticized Nazism from a conservative rightist viewpoint, accusing it of mobilizing youth by means of hatred, terror, and murder.[59] Ritter claimed as well that in early 1932 he had sent Paul von Hindenburg a letter warning him against Hitler. Ritter insisted that, out of a sense of political responsibility as a psychiatrist, he had tried to bring to the attention of the Reich president Hitler's "doubtful nature, his resistance to orderly work, his susceptibility to mood swings, his ruthlessness, and the unfair conspiracies deriving from this restlessness."[60] No copy of this alleged letter to Hindenburg survives.

Ritter tied his recommendations on the Gypsy issue in the Third Reich to his alleged opposition to Nazism. An important layer in his defense was his own evidence that in the first International Congress for Population Science, which had convened in Berlin in 1935, he had already heard that the SS planned "to solve the Gypsy problem in one blow."[61] Ritter added that the speakers, whose names he did not mention, belonged to the offices dealing with racial policy, and that they referred to a plan to put Gypsies on a ship and sink it in the Mediterranean Sea.[62] Ritter recounted this story in a letter written during the process of the investigation.[63] This argument that as early as 1935 the intention of the SS was to murder all the Gypsies enabled Ritter to present as humane his own recommendations to sterilize and to incarcerate in family camps both the *Asoziale* and the Gypsy "mongrels," which earlier research had led him to conclude constituted more than 90 percent of German Gypsies.[64]

Ritter argued that when he learned of these murderous intentions he decided to do everything he could to prevent any unfair and inhumane treatment of the Gypsies.[65] The prosecutor's office accepted this argument, as well as Ritter's implied claim that Nebe's and his action concerning the Gypsy issue in the Third Reich were important aspects of their opposition to Hitler's regime. Ritter utilized Nebe's fabricated, false image as an anti-Nazi resistance fighter. He used a few books that had been published after the war by Nebe's partners in the resistance, some of them former Gestapo members stung by being presented as bloodthirsty, brutal barbarians. In their 1946 memoirs, Hans Bernd Gisevius and Fabian von Schlabrendorff attempted to whitewash Nebe's crimes.[66] In their search for legitimization, they highlighted Nebe's involvement in the resistance against the Nazi regime, and portrayed him as an antithesis to this negative image of the Gestapo and other "law and order" organs of the Nazi state. He was presented as a professional policeman who contributed to the modernization of criminal investigation techniques in Germany, and as an opponent of Nazism.[67]

Schlabrendorff depicted Nebe as "a determined anti-Nazi under a mask of an SS leader," and even claimed that in some thousands of cases Nebe sabotaged Hitler's murderous commands.[68] He bluntly denied Nebe's involvement in the mass executions of Einsatzgruppe B, claiming that the latter had been carried out without his, Nebe's, knowledge or consent. Today, of course, we know much more about the scope of his dreadful crimes, for example, his idea to use gas in the framework of the Euthanasia project, his direct responsibility for mass killings in the occupied Soviet Union, and his involvement in the persecution and subsequent mass murder of Gypsies.[69]

Ritter was attentive to the need prevailing among the majority of the German public, and apparently also any members of the prosecutor's office, to believe that the Nazi system included some decent people too. According to his version of the story, after meeting Nebe, Ritter felt that that man was open to accommodation of humane concerns; the police official could be of assistance in preventing brutal actions against the Gypsies. According to Ritter, he laid before Nebe his fears of the "fanatics," and the latter responded approvingly, apparently proposing that Ritter conspire with him against those who wanted to exterminate all Gypsies.[70] The prosecution accepted Ritter's argument that Nebe was the one who initiated the recording, registration, and collection of data on all the Gypsies and vagrants inside the Reich. Ritter's own correspondence with the German Research Community (Deutsche Forschungsgemeinschaft, or DFG) from 1935 onward implied that he supported this limited action and, from 1939 if not earlier, expressed that support openly.[71]

Victims and Perpetrators at the German Courts

The way in which the Frankfurt chief prosecutors handled the investigation files against Ritter and Justin, despite the decade that lay between them, was virtually identical. First, they rejected the respondent's responsibility for the direct implications of their deeds. Instead, the accountability for persecution of the Gypsies was fully attributed to Himmler, who promulgated the Auschwitz-Decree in early 1943, as well as to anonymous figures defined as "fanatic SS people" who wanted to exterminate all German Gypsies. The charges leveled against Ritter and Justin attributed blame to their colleagues and to individuals high in the Nazi hierarchy who already were dead at the time of the investigation. Some of the Gypsy accusations about Ritter's brutality were thought more properly to be actions attributable to his former colleague, Karl Moravek, who was killed in the war. Later, Justin's alleged role in the dissemination of the notion of sterilization was attributed to Ritter, who had died several years earlier.[72]

The defendants themselves were presented as scientists who tried to solve legitimately a difficult social problem. After the prosecution examined Ritter's writings about the Gypsies, it accepted his nonverifiable and surprising assertion that his scientific publications constituted proof of his revulsion with any radical racial doctrine of the Nazi regime.[73] The prosecution's position, however, ignored Ritter's explicit writings, as well as the basic racial assumptions interwoven in his theories about Gypsies. It reveals, moreover, an uncritical attitude toward the whole notion of "racial hygiene" and the "solutions" its experts recommended concerning the Gypsies and other fringe groups in German society. In both investigations, the prosecution preferred the evidence of Ritter and Justin, their colleagues in the institute, and the criminal police, over that of the Gypsy victims.

In the investigation of Ritter, the prosecution even questioned the possibility of reaching a verdict on the basis of Gypsy-supported evidence, a position grounded in the learned opinion of the accused himself. As evidence that Gypsies were unreasonable, the prosecutor presented one Gypsy man's claim that Ritter had beaten up his brother-in-law, as well as the testimony of a Gypsy woman that he had addressed her in a vulgar and humiliating manner: "It is hard to believe that an educated man like the defendant was able to resort to such ill-treatment."[74] Ritter built his case around "scientific" literature published before the Nazis came to power, and which was thus considered to be free of racism. His position, furthermore, was supported by Rudolf Uschold, the policeman who not only shared Ritter's perceptions, but expressed them publicly in police magazines.[75] The summary of the public prosecutor's argument implied too that he accepted Ritter's contention that the Gypsies, most of whom were illiterate, could not distinguish between reality and imagination,[76] and that the *Asoziale* amongst them believed wrongly that Ritter was responsible for the death of their family members in the concentration camps, and therefore were prepared to accuse him falsely.[77] Ritter submitted to the prosecutor racial-hereditary opinions about the families of some of the witnesses—opinions prepared by people from his own institute under the Nazi regime.[78] In the end, the evidence of several Gypsy witnesses, including family members who initiated the investigation, was disqualified by the prosecution on the grounds of their criminal past.[79]

The policy of the justice system toward the Nazi persecution of the Gypsies was strongly influenced by the negative image of this minority, an image rooted in German culture. A collection of citations from literature on Gypsies (possibly compiled by an assistant on orders from the compensation board, or *Entschädigungskammer*, in Munich) revealed the hostile attitude toward the Gypsies that prevailed in the judicial system. This collection, which to all appearances was oriented and prepared in accordance with a jurist's instruction, looked to contemporary as well as classic literature and, not surprisingly, found "scientific" support for the argument that Gypsies were *Asoziale* and deeply involved in crime. Most of the citations, in fact, came from criminological literature influenced by the racial ideas of the Third Reich. Amazingly, one of them was an article by Robert Ritter. Citing Heinrich M. G. Grellmann's classic 1787 work on the Gypsies, the anonymous collector chose the parts reflecting negative attitudes toward the Gypsies. In the spirit of the Enlightenment, however, Grellmann had called for integrating the Gypsies into the state and making them useful citizens. In contrast, only a few lines from Martin Block's less biased book were cited.[80] Thus it was not only the Nazis who preferred racial explanations for the Gypsy phenomenon; these ideas preceded Nazism and were widely popular in German *Kultur*.[81]

Sterilizing Gypsies as an Unpunishable Act

Apparently, during the investigation procedures dealing with Ritter and with Justin, the prosecution intentionally obscured the significant difference between the illegal sterilization of Gypsies during the Third Reich and the sterilization performed according to the 1933 Law for the Prevention of Genetically Diseased Offspring (*Gesetz für Verhütung erbranken Nachwuchses*).[82] The related judicial decisions that were consolidated in postwar Germany determined that the act dealing with Gypsies was not a typical Nazi law, but should be understood in light of the perceptions that guided German legislators before 1933, as well as of parallel legislation in other countries. Collectively, these decisions ignored the fact that since 1924 Hitler had adopted the principles of racial hygienic theory and made them an integral part of Nazi ideology. They also denied that the only Weimar legislators who tried to initiate legislation in the spirit of 1933 were primarily members of the Nazi Party or other radical rightist parties.[83] The decisions further dismissed any possibility of indicting physicians involved in carrying out this law. The British Martial Law and the Allies Control Council did not abrogate them, but the courts for hereditary health, which were the relevant ruling bodies, were not reestablished after 1945, and so decrees of sterilization were no longer issued in Germany.[84]

The legal situation regarding compulsory sterilization of Gypsies and Jews for racial motives, however, was entirely different. Doctors who participated in compulsory sterilization on racial grounds were severely punished by the Allies for crimes against humanity, and for causing injury to their victims.[85] The prosecutors accepted Ritter's claim that he supported sterilization only in accordance with the law; in so doing, they obscured the inherently illegal nature of the sterilization of Gypsies. The legal authorities of the Third Reich themselves knew that applying the law for the prevention of hereditary diseases to the sterilization of Gypsies was technically illegal.[86] In cases when sterilization of Gypsies was performed under the authority of that law and in some measure of accord with the procedure defined therein, there was still substantial deviation from the provisions of the law, because the Gypsies did not voluntarily agree to the sterilization but succumbed to coercion, threats, and sometimes direct force.[87] Likewise the sterilizations were not performed in order to prevent hereditary illnesses, but were undertaken from racial considerations. The very classification of a person as a "mongrel" labeled him as inclining toward criminal behavior, and brought with it a sentence to sterilization.

The prosecution's approach, then, was idiosyncratic. The prosecution argued that as long as Ritter sought to implement this law for the sake of preventing crime by *Asoziale* and "asocial mongrels," his perceptions should be regarded as legally binding and should not be juridically denounced.[88] By doing so, the prosecution transformed what should have been an indictment of crimes against humanity, committed under the inspiration of a racial ideology, into legal actions that even amounted to a demonstration of humane responsibility toward future generations.

To repeat then, the prosecution accepted Ritter's claim that resorting to sterilization during the Third Reich was a legitimate method of combating crime, and that these methods allegedly were limited only to a group of Gypsy "mongrels" inclined toward crime because of asocial characteristics these "defectives" had inherited from their non-Gypsy ancestors.[89] In their semantics, Ritter and the prosecution conveyed the impression that the target population for sterilization and confinement was only a minority of the Gypsies, while according to Ritter's own classification, the "mongrel *Asoziale* constituted more than 90 percent of Gypsies in the Reich." In 1947, Ritter wrote that the number of pure Gypsies in the territory of the Reich had not exceeded four thousand.[90] All the remaining Gypsies in the Reich, more than twenty thousand people, were intended for sterilization or incarceration in concentration camps. There is no need to quibble here over the mathematics of a few percentage points; the principle is clear enough.

During its investigation of Justin, the prosecution expressed a similar attitude toward the sterilization of Gypsies. In late 1943, she had submitted a report about a Gypsy who claimed that his 1941 classification by Ritter's institute was incorrect; he was not, he insisted, a "Gypsy mongrel," and he objected to undergoing sterilization. Justin determined that there was no reason to change the designation. The prosecutor stated his opinion that Justin had indeed assisted in an attempt to cause severe physical injury, but he felt that no legal action should be taken against her inasmuch as the expected punishment would be imprisonment for not more than six months.[91] Moreover, because seventeen years had elapsed since the commission of the offense, it was entirely possible that even that punishment might be halved.

The prosecutor also found grounds for reducing the punishment on the basis of Justin's youth and inexperience (she was thirty-five years old in 1943), and the supposition that she was subject to the full influence of her teacher, Robert Ritter. Furthermore, during the investigation she had dissociated herself from her previous conceptions.[92] The prosecution accepted without reservation Justin's version of one other of her recommendations to sterilize a Gypsy "mongrel" woman who had wanted to marry a German. Justin had argued that there were three reasons to sterilize the woman. First, the sterilization was supposed to overcome the prohibition set by the Nuremberg Laws on marriages between Germans and non-Aryans. Second, she claimed that since the girl had grown up amongst Germans, she could not go back to her original Gypsy family. And finally, Justin asserted that since the girl's relatives were *Asoziale*, it was possible that her descendants would also be *Asoziale*, and thus her sterilization should be regarded as a preventive measure. The prosecutor accepted Justin's arguments and concluded that without sterilization, the life and fate of this girl would have been threatened. In this statement he sanctioned the argument, which was also implied in Ritter's investigation, that in recommending the sterilization of the Gypsies, Ritter and Justin in fact protected the *Asoziale* among them from a much more brutal fate than that planned for them by the Nazis.[93]

Conclusion

The demonstrated attitude of the judicial system of the Federal Republic in the prosecution of those responsible for persecuting and murdering the Gypsies in the Third Reich reflected its general attitude with regard to all acts of genocide committed during the Nazi regime, including the extermination of European Jews.[94] In the 1950s and 1960s, the justice system of the FRG was an integral part of the civil service that remained from the Nazi regime, and continued to function in the post-Nazi period without many significant changes in personnel.[95] During the Third Reich, this system had played a central role in legitimizing the regime's criminal policy and, in effect, acted as an accomplice to its crimes. According to Jörg Friedrich, the attitude of the postwar justice system toward its defendants reflected the attitude toward its own deeds in the Nazi regime, such that many of the bureaucrats identified with the defendants and the "problematic" situation in which they found themselves.

The decision to terminate the investigation of these two racial researchers reveals a conflict. On the one hand, there was the prosecutors' understanding and perhaps even identification with the defendants and their situation. On the other, there was the need to dissociate themselves from the Nazi crimes—brought upon them by the political culture in the FRG and their status as officials in the new democratic German state. The limited publication of prosecution decisions and the legal protection accorded their writers afforded almost an "intimate" character to the rulings of the system. This in turn enabled bureaucrats, in their references to the Nazi crimes, to deviate from the rules of public expression on Nazism prescribed in the political culture of the FRG. The language of the verdicts and the prosecutions decisions included many characteristics of the semipublic postwar German discourse on Nazi crimes, the public voicing of which was taboo, and was usually conducted at home or in the pub.[96]

Yet Friedrich's explanation is only partial. There was no substantial change in the attitude of the prosecution in the FRG toward racial researchers of the Third Reich even in the 1980s, when key positions in the system were largely transferred to a generation that had no personal responsibility for its activities during the Nazi era. In 1985 the prosecution in Stuttgart terminated investigation procedures against two of Ritter's colleagues, Sophie Ehrhardt and Adolf Würth, following a complaint submitted by the Association of German Sinti (Verband Deutscher Sinti). The two were accused of offenses similar in severity to those attributed to Justin.[97] Although legally it would have been difficult for the prosecution to prove the Gypsies' claim that the opinion Erhardt and Würth prepared might prove their responsibility for assisting in murdering the Gypsies, the way in which the investigation was terminated was reminiscent of the prosecutor's approach in Justin's case: the defendants were exempted from any further consideration of their possible guilt.

In the decision to terminate the investigation, the prosecutor argued that the defendants' participation in Ritter's research was a legitimate scientific activity.[98] The prosecutor further relied, without any reservation, on the allegedly objective opinions of two anthropologists whose work easily can be read as racially biased. One, Hans Jürgens, had even published a book in 1961 in which one may perceive the spirit of racial hygiene; it dealt with *Asozialität* as a biological and socio-biological problem. (The term *Sozialbiologie* replaced, under the influence of the denazification policy established by the Allies in occupied Germany, the illegitimate term *Rassenbiologie*.)[99] Obscuring that author's approach, the prosecutor emphasized that Jürgens's family had been persecuted by the Third Reich.[100] In the decision to terminate the investigation, it would have been possible to relate in an entirely different way to the deeds of the accused, even if the prosecutor were unable, as he claimed, to bring them to trial. The prosecutor's opinion explicitly stated that there was serious intention in the 1930s to prevent the biological reproduction of the Gypsies, and to do so by sterilization (leading inevitably to their extinction),[101] a clearly illegal intention. In Ritter's file summary in the DFG, published no later than 1984, as well as in some of his articles, evidence indicated that the aim of the research on the Gypsies, in which Würth and Ehrhardt took part, was to give scientific legitimization to the idea of using sterilization for solving the *Asoziale* problem.[102]

All of Ritter's partners in the Gypsy research project were familiar with his scientific work and knew that Ritter believed *Asozialität* to be a direct consequence of intermingling of races. They must also have been aware that Gypsies classified as "mongrels" through information extracted from those individuals were intended for sterilization. In light of the above, it is hard to see how anyone could doubt that Würth and Ehrhardt knowingly participated in acts designed to carry out a criminal plan for mass sterilization of the German Gypsies.

One possible conclusion is that the prosecution in effect lent itself to the acquittal of accomplices to what others would call crime. It also expressed a myth that in time became a collective German memory. According to this myth, the Nazi upper ranks alone initiated the crimes, and the SS hangmen alone performed them. In this way, the army, the public administration, the scientific community and, of course, the wider public had little or nothing to do with the Nazi crimes.

This myth was generated in the political culture of postwar Germany under the inspiration of the Allies' reeducation policy and in the face of the psychological difficulty of coping with the scope of the crimes and the extent of civil involvement in them. The attitude of the system's bureaucrats revealed some of the denial mechanisms through which postwar German society came to grips with the wide dimensions of public collaboration in the crimes of the Nazi regime. This myth also made it easier for Germans to endure the guilt that the Allies' propaganda mechanisms imposed on them during the short period of denazification. While it could be argued that all Germans were collectively responsible for the horrors, the myth created a partition between the Nazi regime and civil society. The politicians and bureaucrats of the Federal Republic of Germany believed, in contrast to the Allies' denazification policy, that the normal functioning of the new state's apparatus depended not on the purging without compromise of all officials who had taken part in Nazi crimes, but rather on obscuring the deep involvement of officials and German civil servants in planning and organizing the crimes.[103] Transforming this myth into a collective memory of the German consciousness ensured that it became entrenched in the next generation.

Notes

1. This chapter previously appeared as an article in *Holocaust and Genocide Studies* 11, no. 3 (Winter 1997): 330–50. Reprinted by permission of Oxford University Press.
2. RSHA letter from January 29, 1943 (so-called Auschwitz-Decree). Michael Zimmermann, *Rassenutopie und Genozid. Die nationalsozialistische "Lösung der Zigeunerfrage"* (Hamburg, 1996), 303ff. Although Himmler's order on deportation of certain groups of Gypsies to the concentration camps was issued on 16 December 1942, the German criminal police began assembling deportee lists on the basis of the abovementioned RSHA letter (Schnellbrief). Hence I date Auschwitz-Decree by January 1943 rather than December 1942.
3. Ingeborg Becker, Harald Huber, and Otto Küster, *Bundesentschadigungsgesetze (BEG). Kommentar* (Berlin, 1955), 50; Franz Calvelli-Adorno, "Die rassische Verfolgung der Zigeuner vor den 1 Marz 1943," *Rechtsprechung zum Wiedergutmachungsrecht (RzW)*, 12 December 1961, 529ff; Arnold Spitta, "Entschadigung fur Zigeuner? Geschichte eines Vorurteils," in *Wiedergutmachung in der Bundesrepublik Deutschland,* ed. L. Herbst and C. Goschler (Munich, 1989), 385ff.
4. A list of sentences of German courts in which the appeals of German Gypsies against the compensation authorities were rejected: Becker et al., *BEG* (1955), 50. See also

the following sentences: District Court (OLG) Munich, 8 September 1952, W-EG 30/52 in City Archives Bremen (hereafter: StA Bremen), IV 54–08–13; OLG Munich, 15 September 1952, W-EG 51/52, StA Bremen, IV 54–08–13; OLG Stuttgart, *RzW* 1953; OLG Munich, *RzW* 1953; OLG Oldenburg, December 17, 1955, quoted in Marcel Frenkel: *Entschädigungsrecht—Entscheidungen,* Nr. 327; Federal Supreme Court (BGH), 7 January 1956, IV ZR 211/55, *RzW* 1956.
5. Becker et al., *BEG,* 48.
6. Ibid., 50.
7. Michael Zimmermann, *Verfolgt, vertrieben, vernichtet. Die nationalsozialistische Vernichtungspolitik gegen Sinti und Roma* (Essen, 1989), 20, 24.
8. "A racial persecution against the Gypsies, contrary to the persecution of the Jews, simply should be denied." Quoted in Hans Eller, "Die Zigeuner—Ein Problem," *Kriminalistik* 8 (1954): 126.
9. Rudolf Uschold, "Das Zigeunerproblem," *Die Neue Polizei* 5, no. 4 (1951): 60.
10. Main State Archives Düsseldorf (hereafter: HStA Düsseldorf), trial against Dr. Hans Maly et al., rep. 231, no. 1535. This department was integrated as a section of the Bavarian central office for criminal identification (Zentralamt für Kriminal-Identifizierung), very likely because it held a rich collection of fingerprints and other articles useful in the identification of Gypsies.
11. A letter of Rudolf Uschold to Eva Justin, 6 June 1953, StA Bremen, IV 54–11–30/6; OLG Munich, EK 34/51, 21 September 1951.
12. Eller, "Die Zigeuner—Ein Problem," 126.
13. Gilad Margalit, *Germany and Its Gypsies: A Post-Auschwitz Ordeal* (Madison, WI, 2002), 102–16.
14. For living conditions of the deported German Gypsies in Poland, see Zimmermann, *Rassenutopie und Genozid,* 176–84.
15. Verdict of the BGH, IV ZR 211/55, 7 January 1956.
16. Hans Buchheim, "Die Zigeunerdeportation vom Mai 1940," in Frenkel, *Entschädigungsrecht, Abhandlungen,* 136ff; Hans Günter Hockerts, "Anwalte der Verfolgten. Die United Restitution Organisation," in Herbst and Goschler, *Wiedergutmachung,* 269ff.
17. Hockerts, "Anwalte der Verfolgten," 269ff.
18. Bayerisches Ministerium der Justiz 109–1SA. Beiakte zu den Generalakten Wiedergutmachung nationalsoz. Unrecht auf vermögensrechtl. Ged. Protokol über die Sitzung des Koordinierungsausschusses der 11 Länder, 17 March 1950, 46–50. See also Margalit, *Germany and Its Gypsies,* 102–16.
19. Bayerisches Ministerium der Justiz 109–1SA. Beiakte zu den Generalakten Wiedergutmachung nationalsoz. Unrecht auf vermögensrechtl. Ged. Protokol über die Sitzung des Koordinierungsausschusses der 11 Länder, 17 March 1950, 46.
20. Calvelli-Adorno, "Die rassische Verfolgung," 532.
21. The first article of the newspaper *Frankfurter Allgemeine Zeitung* on the Nazi persecution: Zigeuner—die Nomaden unter uns," 16 January 1954.
22. Christian Pross, *Wiedergutmachung. Der Kleinkrieg gegen die Opfer* (Frankfurt, 1988), 105ff.
23. Verdict of the BGH, 23 May 1962, IV ZR 221/61 (OLG Cologne); sentence of the BGH, 23 May 1962, IV ZR 198/61 (OLG Cologne), Institut für Zeitgeschichte Munchen (hereafter: IfZ), 3058/62. This verdict only solved partly the problem of compensation for Gypsies persecuted by the Nazi regime. See also Henning Stanicki, "Zur Problematik der Anspriiche von Zigeuner nach dem BEG-Schlussgesetz," *RzW* 9 (12 December 1968), 529ff.
24. A survey of the investigation procedures and the trials conducted in the FRG against perpetrators who participated in the persecution of the Gypsies during the Third

Reich. Decision in the preliminary proceedings against Prof. S. Ehrhardt and Dr. A. Würth, 21 November 1985, public prosecutor's office Stuttgart-3 (19) Js 921/81.
25. Robert Proctor, *Racial Hygiene: Medicine Under the Nazis* (Cambridge, MA, 1988); Paul Weindling, *Health, Race and German Politics Between National Unification and Nazism, 1870–1945* (Cambridge, 1993).
26. Ritter denied after 1945 that he ever had been a member of the Nazi Party or any other Nazi organization. After he was presented in a document of the American Military Government in Germany (OMGUS) as a member of the Nazi party and the SS, OMGUS initiated in 1949 an investigation against Ritter accusing him of supplying false information in his denazification process. Inquiry at the Berlin Document Center reveals that the charges against Ritter ultimately were dismissed (Ritter investigation files in Hessian Main State Archives Wiesbaden [hereafter: Hess. HStA Wiesbaden], 501/1547 Riek-Ritt; Hess. HStA Wiesbaden, 520/F7019). Benno Müller-Hill, *Tödliche Wissenschaft. Die Aussonderung von Juden, Zigeunern und Geisteskranken 1933–1945* (Hamburg, 1984), 153, 156. In a June 1937 letter of recommendation for Ritter addressed to the DFG, written by the president of the Reich Health Office, Hans Reiter, the former was described as "one of the few young scholars who follows his research drive in an almost fanatic devotion, and is totally free of selfish consideration." German Federal Archives Koblenz (hereafter: BAK), R73/14005.
27. Hans Reiter, *Das Reichsgesundheitsamt 1933–1939. Sechs Jahre nationalsozialistischen Führung* (Berlin, 1939), 356.
28. Dr. Ritter's personal file (PA), Ritter "Erläuterungen zu unseren Asozialen und Zigeunerforschungen," 20 May 1947, City Archives Frankfurt (hereafter: StA Frankfurt), 18.576; report of Ritter to the DFG from 20 January 1940, BA Koblenz R 73/14005-A.
29. *Das falsche Wort. Wiedergutmachung an Zigeunern (Sinte) in Deutschland?* A film of Melanie Spitta and Katrin Seibold (1987).
30. HStA Düsseldorf, Rep. 231, no. 1535.
31. PA Robert Ritter, "Erläuterungen zu unseren Asozialen, und Zigeunerforschungen," 20 May 1947, StA Frankfurt 18.576.
32. Ritter's letter to the president of the DFG from 12 February 1935, BAK, R 73/14005. In his reports and publications of later years this position is much clearer (Cf. a report to the DFG from 20 January 1940).
33. Robert Ritter, "Erbbiologische Untersuchungen innerhalb eines Züchtungskreis Zigeunermischlingen und 'asozialen Psychopathen,'" in *Bevölkerungsfragen*, ed. H. Harmsen and F. Lohse (Munchen, 1936), 713–18.
34. Jörg Friedrich, "Confronting the Past: The Attitude Towards Nazi War Criminals in the Federal Republic," in *"Normal Relations": Israeli-German Relations* (in Hebrew), ed. M. Zimmermann and O. Heilbronner (Jerusalem, 1993), 62.
35. Ibid., 60; Ingo Müller, *Hitler's Justice: The Courts of the Third Reich* (Cambridge, MA, 1991), 249–50.
36. In his decision to suspend the judicial proceeding against Ritter, the public prosecutor argued: "The attestations of the witnesses imply that they voluntarily agreed to undergo a sterilization. ... Their statements make it clear that they agreed to undergo sterilization in order to prevent their deportation to the concentration camps." HStA Düsseldorf, Rep. 231/1535. The resolution of the public prosecutor to suspend the judicial proceeding against Justin read as follows: "The girl herself applied for the sterilization." HStA Düsseldorf, Rep. 231/1540.
37. Joachim S. Hohmann, *Robert Ritter und die Erben der Kriminalbiologie. Zigeunerforschung im Nationalsozialismus und in Westdeutschland im Zeichen des Rassismus,* Studien zur Tsiganologie und Folkloristik 4 (Frankfurt, 1991), 136ff, 146ff.
38. Ibid., 130; Zimmermann, *Verfolgt, vertrieben, vernichtet,* 33ff.

39. Reimar Gilsenbach, *Oh Django, sing deinen Zorn: Sinti und Roma unter den Deutschen* (Berlin, 1993), 97–133.
40. Eva Justin, "Lebensschicksale artfremd erzogener Zigeunerkinder und ihrer Nachkommen," *Veröffentlichungen aus dem Gebiete des Volksgesundheitsdienstes* 57, no. 4 (1944): 121.
41. PA Dr. Ritter, StA Frankfurt, 18.576.
42. StA Stuttgart, Js 5582/48; HStA Düsseldorf, rep. 231, Nr. 1535.
43. HStA Düsseldorf, rep. 231, no. 1535.
44. Ibid.
45. The registration of the destruction of the file on the Ritter investigation, Hess. HStA Wiesbaden, 461/29090.
46. HStA Düsseldorf, rep. 231, no. 1536.
47. PA Dr. Eva Justin, StA Frankfurt, 92.546.
48. HStA Düsseldorf, rep. 231, no. 1535.
49. The resolution of the public prosecutor to suspend the judicial process against Ritter, HStA Düsseldorf, rep. 231, no. 1535; the resolution of the public prosecutor to suspend the judicial process against Justin, HStA Düsseldorf, rep. 231, no. 1540.
50. HStA Düsseldorf, rep. 231, no. 1535.
51. HStA Düsseldorf, rep. 231, no. 1540.
52. Also known as one of the Nuremberg Race Laws.
53. "From the subjective respect the burden of proof does not fall on the defendant. He had not known or could not have assessed when he gave his opinion, that an unlawful decree would be issued on 29 January 1943." HStA Düsseldorf, rep. 231, no. 1540.
54. List of files, HStA Düsseldorf, rep. 231, no. 1540.
55. HStA Düsseldorf, rep. 231, no. 1540; Zimmermann, *Rassenutopie und Genozid,* 150.
56. PA Robert Ritter, "Erläuterungen zu unseren Asozialen, und Zigeunerforschungen," 20 May 1947, StA Frankfurt, 18.576.
57. HStA Düsseldorf, rep. 231, no. 1535.
58. Ibid.
59. Robert Ritter, "NS und Jugend," *Kölnische Zeitung,* 11 January 1931; Robert Ritter, "Mehr gegenseitige Achtung," *Kölnische Zeitung,* 25 January 1931.
60. PA Robert Ritter, "Erläuterungen zu unseren Asozialen, und Zigeunerforschungen," 20 May 1947, StA Frankfurt 18.576.
61. Ibid.
62. Ritter's letter from 28 April 1949, quoted in Hermann Arnold, *Die NS-Zigeunerverfolgung: Ihre Ausdeutung und Ausbeutung. Fakten,Mythos, Agitation, Kommerz* (Aschaffenburg, 1989), 9.
63. HStA Düsseldorf, rep. 231, no. 1535.
64. Ritter, "Erbbiologische Untersuchungen," 713ff.
65. PA Robert Ritter, "Erläuterungen zu unseren Asozialen, und Zigeunerforschungen," 20 May 1947, StA Frankfurt 18.576.
66. Hans Bernd Gisevius, *Bis zum bittern Ende,* vol. 1 (Zurich, 1946), 217; Fabian v. Schlabrendorff, *Offtziere gegen Hitler. Nach einem Erlebnisbericht* (Zurich, 1946), 49.
67. Schlabrendorff, *Offtziere gegen Hitler,* 49.
68. Ibid., 62.
69. Niels Weise, "Reichskriminaldirektor Arthur Nebe—Dissident und Opportunist," in *Portraits zur Geschichte des deutschen Widerstands,* ed. Matthias Stickler (Rahden, 2005), 245–60.
70. PA Robert Ritter, "Erläuterungen zu unseren Asozialen, und Zigeunerforschungen," 20 May 1947, StA Frankfurt 18.576.
71. In his letter to the Deutsche Notgemeinschaft of 12 February 1935, Ritter emphasized that the results of his research on the Gypsies had great significance to the

policy of the criminal police and to the state's activity in the field of racial hygiene. BAK, R73/14005.
72. For a survey of Moravek's research activities, see Hohmann, *Robert Ritter,* 271–75; HStA Düsseldorf, rep. 231, no. 1535; HStA Düsseldorf, rep. 231, no. 1540.
73. HStA Düsseldorf, rep. 231, no. 1535.
74. Ibid.
75. Rudolf Uschold, "Das Zigeunerproblem," *Die Neue Polizei* 5, no. 3 (1951): 38–40; ibid., no. 4: 60–62.
76. HStA Düsseldorf, rep. 231, no. 1535.
77. Ibid.
78. Ibid.
79. Ibid.
80. District Court Munich I, October 13, 1951, IfZ, MA-21. Heinrich Moritz Gottlieb Grellmann, *Historische Versuch über die Zigeuner, betreffend die Lebensart und Verfassung, Sitten und Schicksale dieses Volkes seit seiner Erscheinung in Europa und dessen Ursprung* (Göttingen, 1787); Martin Block, *Zigeuner. Ihr Leben und ihre Seele* (Leipzig, 1936).
81. The entries on Gypsies in the post Weimar-era German encyclopedias supply an irrefutable proof for this claim.
82. Zimmermann, *Verfolgt, vertrieben, vernichtet,* 57–60.
83. Gisela Bock, *Zwangssterilization im Nationalsozialismus. Studien zur Rassenpolitik und Frauenpolitik* (Opladen, 1986), 24ff, 79.
84. Franz Neukamp, "Ist die Unfruchtbarmachung von Menschen immer strafbar?" *Neue Juristische Wochenschrift* 3, no. 20 (1950): 773ff.
85. Ibid.
86. Zimmermann, *Verfolgt, vertrieben, vernichtet,* 57ff.
87. Martha Adler's testimony on the pressure put on her husband by the racial researcher and the police to undergo a sterilization, HStA Düsseldorf, rep. 231, no. 1536.
88. HStA Düsseldorf, rep. 231, no. 1535.
89. Ibid.
90. Ritter's report on his research, 20 January 1940, BAK, R 73/14005; PA Robert Ritter, "Erläuterungen zu unseren Asozialen, und Zigeunerforschungen," 20 May 1947, StA Frankfurt 18.576.
91. HStA Düsseldorf, rep. 231, no. 1540.
92. Ibid.
93. Ibid.
94. Friedrich, "Confronting the Past," 57–77; Müller, *Hitler's Justice,* 249ff.
95. Friedrich, "Confronting the Past," 66.
96. Ibid.; Ruth Wodak, et al., *"Wir sind alle unschuldige Täter!" Diskurshistorische Studien zum Nachkriegsantisemitismus* (Frankfurt, 1990), 210ff.
97. Decision in the preliminary proceedings against Prof. S. Ehrhardt und Dr. A Würth, 21 November 1985, public prosecutor's office Stuttgart-3 (19) Js 921/81.
98. Ibid.
99. Ibid.; Hans W. Jürgens, *Asozialität als biologisches und sozialbiologisches Problem* (Stuttgart, 1961); Lau Mazirel, "Die Verfolgung der 'Zigeuner' im Dritten Reich. Vorgeschichte ab 1870 und Fortsetzung bis Heute," in *Essays über Naziverbrechen,* 149ff.
100. Decision in the preliminary proceedings against Prof. S. Ehrhardt und Dr. A Würth, 21 November 1985, public prosecutor's office Stuttgart-3 (19) Js 921/81.
101. Ibid.
102. Karl Heinz Roth, "'Erbbiologische Bestandsaufhahme.' Ein Aspekt 'auszumerzender' Erfassung vor der Entfesslung des Zweites Weltkrieges," in *Erfassung zur*

Vernichtung. Von der Sozialhygiene zum "Gesetz über Sterbehilfe," ed. K. H. Roth (Berlin, 1984), 94. As far as I know, this was the earliest publication of documents from Ritter's personal file in the DFG.
103. Norbert Frei, *Vergangenheitspolitik. Die Anfänge der Bundesrepublik und die NS-Vergangenheit* (Munich, 1996).

CHAPTER 8

DISENTANGLING THE HIERARCHY OF VICTIMHOOD
COMMEMORATING SINTI AND ROMA AND JEWS IN GERMANY'S NATIONAL NARRATIVE

Nadine Blumer

Introduction

In Germany, a country that has experienced "commemoration saturation" or "an inflation of memory," the Roma genocide can be more accurately described in terms of a *Lücke der Erinnerung*—a gap of remembrance in the national historical narrative of persecution.[1] Official recognition of the Nazi genocide of Sinti and Roma—the standard term used in Germany—in 1982 did not quell public and political debates regarding the legitimacy of comparing the Nazi persecution of Roma with that of Jews. These debates were rooted in a long-standing controversy regarding the so-called singularity thesis, according to which the Jewish Holocaust occupied a special place in the history of genocide, thus making it impossible for other victim groups to claim a similar experience of persecution and suffering.[2]

The debates about representation of the past and acknowledgment of victimization resurfaced in the early planning phase of a Central Holocaust Memorial in Berlin (hereafter: Holocaust Memorial), proposed in 1988 by a German citizen's initiative to be dedicated to the Jewish victims. The catalyst was a full-page petition published in the German daily *Der Tagesspiegel* by Romani Rose, chairperson of the Zentralrat deutscher Sinti und Roma (Central Council of German Sinti and Roma, or Sinti/Roma Central Council). Rose argued, "The Holocaust also means the annihilation of 500,000 Sinti and Roma." Thus began a new phase of contestation over the Nazi genocide's uniquely Jewish character, and the moral and political responsibility of the German state toward acknowledging past injustice committed against other victim groups.

Rose put a new spin on old debates by drawing on this long-established (albeit contentious) vocabulary of uniqueness, and expanded the concept to include the Sinti and Roma victims of genocide. He emphasized equality in suffering, that is, the shared fate of Jews and Sinti and Roma under the Nazis. According to him, this historical link would help both groups to establish collective forms of commemoration and achieve equal standing in the German Holocaust narrative. Thus, Rose wrote that the term "'uniqueness,' commonly used to describe the Jewish genocide, refers in equal measure to the genocide of the Sinti and Roma across National Socialist occupied Europe.... The Federal Government, the Berlin Senate and the individual state governments must honor their obligation vis-à-vis the Sinti and Roma by supporting a shared site of remembrance in Berlin for the victims of genocide."[3] This petition, along with several others published by Rose in the wake of the proposal to build reunified Germany's first national Holocaust Memorial, marked the genesis of the "Memorial to the Sinti and Roma Persecuted under the National Socialist Regime" (hereafter: Sinti/Roma Memorial), a project yet to be completed, twenty years later, and the subject of this chapter.[4]

This chapter examines how the very idea of the Sinti/Roma Memorial arose as a direct response to the proposal to build a central commemoration site for the Jewish victims of the Nazis. From the outset, the evolution of the memorials and the memory narratives of both victim groups became intertwined. In the phase of memorial planning that followed, the competing interests of various memory actors collided as each sought to stake a claim in the German national narrative—itself in a phase of redefinition following reunification in 1990. What started as a non-Jewish German citizen's initiative soon embroiled Sinti and Roma leadership, the Jewish political establishment in Germany, and various state actors (e.g., members of the Bundestag and Berlin municipal officials). Equally contentious was the geopolitics of the "New Berlin," reinstated in 1990 as the capital city of a reunified Germany, which was expected to accommodate an ever-increasing number of national memorials. Many of these new memorials thus came to symbolize the merger of East and West German histories as well as their divergent ideologies of commemoration.[5]

In order to show how memory narratives are shaped and reshaped in competition and exchange between multiple actors at different times according to changing ideological positions, I will deal primarily with the initial stage of memorial debates. These debates can be traced back to 1988 when the Holocaust Memorial was originally proposed, soon followed by initiatives to include mention of the Sinti and Roma victims within the same memorial structure. Rejection of a shared site by Chancellor Helmut Kohl in 1993, and the 1999 German government resolution to build the "Central Memorial to the Murdered Jews of Europe," along with separate memorials to each of the other victim groups, marked the end of that stage of the debates. I conclude by examining the relevance of parliamentary decisions that have led to the formation of a "memorial network"—a configuration in which the memories of individual victim-group experiences are scattered across a memorial landscape in the form of detached memorial structures, yet brought together through various administrative, pedagogical, research, and commemorative activities. Today, this memorial network reflects how Germany's three national Holocaust memorials (Central Memorial to the Murdered Jews of Europe, Memorial to the Homosexuals Persecuted under the Nationalist Socialist Regime, and Memorial to the Sinti and Roma Persecuted under the National Socialist Regime) are legally conjoined, with the Jewish Holocaust Memorial maintaining a commanding presence in both the city's and country's memorial landscape.[6] I argue that this framework has the potential to increase recognition and memory of the Nazi genocide of the Sinti and Roma.

Drawing on a relational understanding of memory production, I use Sebastian Conrad's concept of "entangled memories" to describe how plans for the Holocaust Memorial were, from the start, circumscribed by longstanding debates about the uniqueness of Jewish suffering, fears of relativizing the history of Nazi mass murder, and postunification concerns over conflating Germany's histories of the Nazi and the Communist past. Conrad maintains that collective memories of the past do not originate within one country but rather take shape through processes of connection and exchange between different actors, discourses, practices, and time periods.[7] It is this "entangled" perspective, I argue, that enables us to *disentangle* the "contest over ownership, appropriation, and meaning" or "pathology of ownership," which marks much of the historiography of the Nazi genocide, and which came to a head in response to the Holocaust Memorial initiative of the late 1980s.[8] Furthermore, this framework helps us to identify the specific individuals and institutions within and outside Germany involved in the complex process of memory production (e.g., state actors, members of civil society, and victim group representatives). Finally, the evolution of the memorial debates indicates that memory does matter in Sinti and Roma communal politics, challenging the blanket generalization of Roma as a "people without history."

Memory and Emergent Discourses of Victimhood

Postwar German historiography has been laden with debates over the "uniqueness" or "singularity" of suffering, going back to the immediate postwar period when the dominant national discourse framed the German nation as the sole victim of the Nazi regime, Soviet terror, but also Allied occupation.[9] According to Hannah Arendt, this time period was characterized by a "conspiracy of silence" regarding Jewish victimization.[10] While the West-German government officially acknowledged the Nazi persecution of the Jews (the program of reparations to the State of Israel [*Shilumim* in Hebrew] launched by Konrad Adenauer in 1952 was among the most notable initiatives), it had less to do with the victims but with Adenauer's political will to refashion West Germany into a "reliable nation, one no longer to be associated with its predecessor regime."[11] It was not until the 1960s, however, that the "myth of German victimization" was renegotiated and for the most part abandoned (although it has resurfaced periodically).[12] For the first time in postwar history, talk of Jewish persecution entered the civil and political spheres of society. The new narrative that framed the Nazi genocide—and specifically the mass murder of Jews—as an incomparable and unprecedented event in the history of persecution and mass death came about largely as the result of the campaign of Jewish lobby groups (located primarily in Israel and the United States) to pressure the West-German government for restitution.[13]

The uniqueness discourse continued to gather momentum in the late 1970s and 1980s, especially in the United States.[14] On the one side of the debate were those scholars who asserted the Jewish character of the Nazi genocide and its fundamental singularity based on criteria such as scale, intent, technology, and bureaucracy.[15] On the other side were those who argued that the Holocaust not only entailed the murder of millions of non-Jews but also was comparable to other genocides throughout history.[16] In Germany, the so-called *Historikerstreit* (Historians' Dispute), which erupted in 1985, responded to these external discourses and ultimately became the most publicized episode related to the ongoing debate about the singularity of the Holocaust.[17]

The gradual entry of the Sinti and Roma genocide into Germany's national narrative, starting in the late 1970s, can only be understood in the context of this preexisting environment of commemoration, that is, an environment already sensitive to relativization and competing claims of victimization and suffering. In the following section I give a brief overview of the postwar political mobilization of the German Sinti and Roma, showing in particular how these activities have stemmed from community-organized efforts to gain acknowledgement of and compensation for genocide.[18] In many ways these mobilization efforts mirrored the earlier work of Jewish lobby groups in respect to the Nazi persecution.

Postwar Exclusion and Mobilization of Sinti and Roma in Germany

A 1956 ruling of the West German Supreme Court concluded that the Nazi mass deportations and executions of the Sinti and Roma (German: *Zigeuner*) were carried out as a part of a "legitimate struggle against criminals." Specifically, the court ruled that persecution was racially motivated only since December 1942 when Himmler issued the so-called Auschwitz-Decree leading to the deportation of 23,000 Sinti and Roma from eleven European countries. All other edicts promulgated between 1936 and 1942 were interpreted by the court as "preventive security measures of the police," even though there is ample evidence pointing to racial motives in official Nazi policy from as early as 1936.[19] The German State thus not only failed to recognize the full extent of racial persecution of Sinti and Roma, but also framed Nazi anti-Gypsy policies as "punishment" and "retribution" for their imputed criminality. In practical terms, this meant that Sinti and Roma survivors, especially those persecuted prior to the enactment of the "Auschwitz-Decree," were excluded from state policies of restitution (*Wiedergutmachung*) for most of the postwar period. It was not just in the realm of the courts, however, that Nazi persecution of Sinti and Roma went unrecognized, but also across all levels of German society. Activists and scholars alike have documented numerous examples of persistent Nazi-like policies directed against the Sinti and Roma in the postwar years such as the so-called *Zigeunergesetze* (Gypsy Laws) enacted by the Allied administration, which restricted movement and employment.[20] The title of an earlier German-language publication on the Nazi persecution of Sinti and Roma, *Gassed at Auschwitz, Persecuted Until Today*, aptly captures the sentiment.[21]

Influenced by the rise of the international Roma civil rights movement and its emergent project of Romani nationalism in the early 1970s, Sinti and Roma activists in Germany increasingly joined NGOs in order to promote their moral and financial claims. The year 1979 was a turning point as the discourse on persecution moved from the courtrooms to street protests, sit-ins, press statements, and eventually into the sphere of public memory. Activism in these early years was mainly due to the support of a German human rights organization, Gesellschaft für bedrohte Völker (Society for Endangered Peoples, or the Society). Building upon the precedent established by Jewish lobby groups in previous decades, president of the Society Tillman Zülch worked with Sinti activists to organize protests, hunger strikes, and commemoration ceremonies in former sites of persecution.[22] The commemoration ceremony at the former Bergen-Belsen concentration camp in 1979, which drew an impressive number of international dignitaries, was the first public event of its kind that honored the plight of Sinti and Roma victims and survivors and simultaneously advocated for the recognition of Sinti and Roma as an integral part of contemporary German and European society. Among the 2,500 guests were Sinti and Roma activists and community leaders from Germany and thirteen other European countries, survivors and their descendants, German parliamentarians, president of the European Parliament (and Holocaust survivor) Simone Veil, and Jewish community leaders.[23]

The Bergen-Belsen commemoration was followed in April 1980 by another large-scale and highly publicized event, this time a fourteen-day hunger strike, held by twelve Sinti men on the grounds of the former Dachau concentration camp. The protesters demanded recognition of Nazi persecution, reparation payments, and an end to ongoing institutionalized discrimination. As a direct response, the center-left SPD party committed itself to combating discriminatory policies on the federal level. The hunger strike also led to the establishment of a culture center for the Sinti and Roma in the city of Dachau.[24]

The abovementioned efforts culminated in the establishment of the Central Council of German Sinti and Roma in February 1982. When visiting the newly opened offices of the Central Council in Heidelberg the following month, West German chancellor Helmut Schmidt was the first German head of state to officially recognize the racially motivated genocide of 500,000 European Sinti and Roma by the Nazi regime. In so doing, Chancellor Schmidt indirectly endorsed a distinction that is integral to the political work of many Sinti and Roma leaders to the present day, namely, that the Sinti and Roma people were *victims* of Nazi mass murder, not *criminals* who allegedly posed a threat to the Third Reich. It is not a coincidence, I would argue, that the Sinti/Roma Central Council was established around the same time as the state acknowledgement of genocide. Modeled after the Israeli *Shilumim,* the Sinti/Roma Central Council was effectively founded in order to channel federal and states funds as compensation to (the few remaining) Sinti and Roma survivors of Nazi persecution.[25] Thus, we can trace the origins of the Sinti/Roma Central Council to a mobilization campaign around the discourse on victimization that drew predominantly on preexisting forms of institutionalized memory of Jewish persecution.[26] In the remainder of this chapter, I show how the Central Council's effort to include Sinti and Roma victims into Germany's Holocaust Memorial epitomizes the entangled processes of memory production, involving interrelated social and political actors, historical precedents, and ideological rifts.[27]

Debating a Hierarchy of Victims

In the summer of 1988, German media personality Lea Rosh and historian Eberhard Jäckel proposed construction of a central Holocaust memorial in Berlin—"to set a visible sign in the country of the perpetrators."[28] According to Jäckel, it was unacceptable that "in the 'land of the perpetrators' there was no central memorial dedicated to *all* of the European *Jewish* victims of the Holocaust, to this unparalleled act of genocide [emphasis added]."[29] By January 1989, Rosh founded the citizens' initiative, Perspektive Berlin, and published a series of newspaper petitions outlining its objective, "[t]o finally build a visible memorial in Berlin to the millions of murdered Jews."[30] The petition carried signatures of support from many of Germany's foremost intellectuals and politicians such as Günter Grass, Christa Wolf, Willy Brandt, and Otto Schilly. Rosh made clear from the start that "the construction of this memorial should in no way be a matter of the Jews, that is, the victims. Rather this is a matter for the descendants of the perpetrators."[31]

Opposition was quick to come from individuals and groups concerned about the exclusion of non-Jewish victims from the proposed Holocaust memorial. Among the dissenting voices, head of the Sinti/Roma Central Council Romani Rose proved most vocal. Rose responded to the founding of Perspektive Berlin, and its successor, the Förderkreis zur Errichtung eines Denkmals für die ermordeten Juden Europas (Association for the Memorial to the Murdered Jews of Europe, or the Association), with a series of articles, open letters, and petitions in major German newspapers and magazines. In a 1989 article titled "A Memorial for All Victims," he demanded the construction of a *shared* memorial to the Jewish and Sinti and Roma victims of genocide. "[A memorial] that refers exclusively to the Jewish people," argued Rose, "implies a hierarchy of victims. This is hurtful and insulting to the victims of genocide and the survivors from the Sinti and Roma minority." In the years to come, accusations of creating a "hierarchy of victims"—the ranking of victim groups on a continuum of suffering—turned the German press into a battleground over questions of "appropriate forms" of historical representation. Moreover, it influenced the political decision-making process regarding the first federally sanctioned Holocaust memorial to be built in the new old capital of the reunified German state.

If Not a Shared Memorial Then at Least a Shared Memorial Site: Negotiations Between State Actors and Ethnic Leaders

In February 1994, five years after Rose's initial petition, the parties involved reached a compromise that favored dedicating the central Holocaust Memorial exclusively to Jewish victims. Almost simultaneously, the federal government committed 2 million toward the construction of a *separate* memorial to the Sinti and Roma victims on a parcel of land between the Brandenburg Gate and the Reichstag. Donated by the city of Berlin, the site was situated some 650 meters (2,000 feet) from the Holocaust Memorial. Construction Senator Wolfgang Nagel (SPD) described the location as a "dignified and appropriate site that is also associated with the grounds for the Jewish memorial." Rose ultimately expressed satisfaction with the site, as did Ignatz Bubis, head of the Jewish Central Council, and then Bundestag president Rita Süssmuth.[32]

This decision was preceded by complex, sometimes hostile, negotiations between a constellation of social and political actors. The Sinti and Roma political establishment communicated directly with Jewish community leaders in an effort to establish a common front. Jewish leaders responded while simultaneously engaging in negotiations with German state and Berlin officials regarding the Central Holocaust Memorial, which they had previously claimed to have no interest in.[33] Decisions taken by the government deferred primarily to the wishes of the Jewish establishment; the non-Jewish Citizens' Association, which had initially proposed the Holocaust Memorial, remained involved in all stages of negotiation. Earlier historiographical debates over Nazi crimes and German reunification rendered these exchanges especially contentious, situating them squarely in the realm of German national identity.

In March 1991 the Sinti/Roma Central Council submitted an official request to the Berlin Senate to build a memorial dedicated to the murdered Sinti and Roma, ideally as part of the structure commemorating the Jewish victims. In September of the same year, Berlin mayor Walter Momper (SPD) assured representatives of the Central Council that they would receive equal consideration with the Jews when it came to the decision concerning a Holocaust memorial.[34] In March 1992, Berlin cultural senator Ulrich Roloff-Momin (independent) and federal minister Rudolf Seiters (CDU) allocated a plot of land close to Hitler's Reich Chancellery and the so-called Death Strip that ran alongside the Eastern side of the Berlin Wall as the future site of the Central Holocaust Memorial. No mention was made of the Sinti and Roma at this time.

This decision turned the ongoing political debate into a vicious public conflict between Romani Rose and Heinz Galinski, then head of the Jewish Central Council, and later his successor, Ignatz Bubis. The heated exchange between the Jewish and the Sinti and Roma Central Councils exposed the entanglement of memory work. Despite pervasive claims from the Citizens' Association, as well as from Jewish intellectuals and community leaders, that it was a "non-Jewish project," Germany's Jewish establishment had nonetheless become deeply involved with the plans for the Holocaust Memorial. Notably, the Jewish Central Council made its first public statement regarding the memorial in response to a newspaper article written by Rose. In that article, Rose accused the Jewish Central Council of "distorting historical fact" by refusing to include the Sinti and Roma in the memorial project. Galinski addressed Rose in an open letter that emphasized the former's longstanding commitment to non-Jews' commemorative initiatives, specifically those of the Sinti and Roma. He went on, however, to describe "particular reasons," that is, the Nazi treatment accorded to "Jewish but not other groups," which portended to legitimize the construction of a "site of remembrance for the six million murdered Jews of Europe."[35]

Several months later the Ministry of the Interior reached a compromise with the Senate Department for Cultural Affairs to erect two separate memorials: one for the Jewish victims and another for the Sinti and Roma victims. This decision, however, did not compel the Sinti/Roma Central Council to abandon its campaign. Rather, the Central Council simply changed its demands, shifting attention from a shared *memorial* to a shared memorial *site*. Specifically, Rose lobbied for a Sinti and Roma Memorial that would stand in "geographic proximity" to and "share the artistic design" of the Holocaust Memorial for the Jews. In a full-page ad published simultaneously in *Der Tagesspiegel* and *Der Frankfurter Rundschau*, Rose emphasized that Nazi policies of annihilation had been directed against Jews and Sinti and Roma, and asserted the historical uniqueness of the Nazi persecution of *both groups*. To strengthen his argument, Rose cited a speech given by Galinski a decade earlier at the newly opened Sinti/Roma Central Council in which the latter not only spoke with compassion about the persecution of the Sinti and Roma, but also acknowledged the "existential similarity" between the two groups and their shared experience of "systematic annihilation" by the Nazis. In that very speech he had also criticized the German government for failing to recognize the genocide of the Sinti and Roma people for over thirty years.[36]

Bubis, in his capacity as the new head of the Jewish Central Council (appointed in the wake of Galinski's death), rejected Rose's demand, arguing that geographic proximity and shared artistic design between the two memorials would be impossible. Since the Holocaust Memorial would symbolize, among other things, a graveyard for the victims, Bubis referred to Jewish religious law, which prohibits the sharing of cemetery space with non-Jews.[37] At most, he was willing to accept that the two memorials could share an "analogous horticultural design" with "possibly the same variety of trees," but only insofar as they were separated by at least 200 meters (650 feet) and thus were obviously disconnected.[38] Bubis's reasoning was deemed legitimate by the Berlin Senate which, in October 1992, once again indicated its preference for the construction of two separate memorials: "As stated, the Senate has committed itself to building a memorial of equal worth for the murdered Sinti and Roma of Europe. Although this memorial will stand on a separate site, the murder of the European Sinti and Roma will be commemorated in an appropriate manner."[39]

The decisive moment in this struggle over political, symbolic, and physical space came in the lead-up to Chancellor Kohl's plan to rededicate the Neue Wache (Käthe Kollwitz's bronze pieta of a mother mourning her dead son) as "the Federal Republic of Germany's central site of commemoration for all victims of war and tyranny."[40] Aside from the problem of Christian iconography embodied by the sculpture, the re-rededication of the Neue Wache reawakened unease not just about the notion of comparability and relativization, which had underpinned the *Historikerstreit* and the earlier singularity debates, but also more recent fears developed in the wake of reunification about conflating memory of the Nazi and Communist dictatorships in Germany. In an attempt to rebut these accusations, and "as a gesture of reconciliation," Chancellor Kohl promised Bubis—who had threatened to skip the inauguration ceremony of the Neue Wache—that the Holocaust Memorial would be dedicated exclusively to the Jewish victims.[41] In late 1993, Chancellor

Kohl indeed spoke out officially against the idea of a shared memorial, insisting instead on "distinct sites of remembrance." By so doing, Kohl not only sanctioned an earlier decision by Berlin politicians to situate the Holocaust Memorial on 20,000 square meters in the designated location south of the Brandenburg Gate, but also (re)affirmed the dominance of Jewish victimhood in Germany's politics of commemoration.

Rose immediately protested this decision, publishing two consecutively dated full-page advertisements in the press and using strategic language meant to appeal to German memory culture: "The uniqueness of the Holocaust [that] pertains to Jews and Sinti and Roma in Europe is not a form of relativization!"[42] In both ads, Rose emphasized the shared and unique experience of Jewish and Sinti and Roma victimhood and suffering as to invalidate the notion that comparison of the two groups would in any way relativize the history of the Holocaust:

> Fifty years after the end of [the Nazi crimes] there is still no centrally located national Holocaust memorial in the capital city of Berlin that commemorates the historically singular genocide of 500,000 Sinti and Roma and six million Jews. The Berlin Senate's resolution to erect a national Holocaust Memorial in memory of the murdered Jews of Europe ... south of the Brandenburg Gate on government property near the future American embassy is for this reason unacceptable.... *The singularity of the Holocaust means that both memorials must be built concurrently on this site.* ... [T]he design of both memorials must guarantee that state gestures [*staatliche Gesten*] of national or international mourning and remembrance, and ceremonies and wreath-laying for the murdered Sinti and Roma are conducted in the same way as they are for the murdered Jews. [emphasis added][43]

Throughout the memorial debates, the strategy used by Rose and the Central Council to incorporate the memory of Sinti and Roma persecution into Germany's spaces of commemoration was meant to achieve parity with the more established memory discourses of Jewish victimhood. Central to this endeavor was an expanded version of the thesis of singularity, that is, an attempt at redefining the hierarchy so as to include Sinti and Roma alongside Jewish victims. As evident from the abovementioned examples, Rose and the Central Council were not so much trying to forge a memory niche of their own (which could potentially make them susceptible to accusations of relativizing history) as they were trying to find a way of sharing the central position of Jewish memory in the German national narrative. As suggested by journalist Igal Avidan: "Rose, who on the one hand speaks out against the classification of victims into first and second class, claims on the other hand that persecution against the 'Gypsies' was more methodically enacted than against the Jehovah's Witnesses."[44]

Earlier in this chapter I discussed the reasons why the Nazi persecution of the Jews was not automatically integrated into mainstream public and political discourse immediately following the war; it was only after years of lobbying that the experience of Jewish victimization became widely known, discussed, and ultimately incorporated in the realm of restitution and identity politics (in Germany and elsewhere). It is thus the particularity of the *process* of making Jews into victims that Rose adopted as a model for his own group. This attempt at gaining recognition on par with Jewish victims is pronounced in the frequent references made by the Sinti/Roma Central Council to Bundestag president Roman Herzog's 1997 statement equating the Nazi persecution of the Jews and the Sinti and Roma:[45]

> The genocide against the Roma and Sinti was carried out with the same motive of racial madness, the same intention and the same will of deliberate and final destruction, as that against the Jews. Throughout the entire area under National Socialist influence they were systematically murdered, family-by-family, from small children to the elderly.[46]

The Central Council had originally intended to inscribe this quotation onto the Sinti and Roma memorial structure and continues to make frequent reference to it at commemoration ceremonies and in media publications.[47]

"Who Does the Holocaust Belong to?" Media Debates

Parallel to government decision making and political jockeying between the heads of the Jewish and Sinti and Roma Central Councils, a heated media debate took place among intellectuals, politicians, and the general public, as well as the key players directly involved in the memorial's planning. Letters to the editor frequently described this first phase of debates as a "religious war" (*Glaubenskrieg*) over the "right way to remember Nazi victims."[48] Rhetoric was often couched in an ontological discussion of the fundamental premise of Nazi ideology, and consequently prescribed what form Germany's first national Holocaust Memorial should take and whom it should commemorate.

Historian Jäckel of the Association instantly ruled out the possibility of a shared memorial based on a familiar premise: anti-Semitism was the core of Nazi ideology and therefore persecution of the Jews overshadowed all other Nazi crimes. Jäckel argued that any attempt to compare the persecution of the Jews with that of any other group would amount to relativizing history.[49] Another member of the Association, philosopher Margherita von Brentano, echoed Jäckel when she wrote that anti-Semitism was "not only an element of National-Socialism, but its center."[50] For this reason, she concluded, Germany's Holocaust Memorial must be dedicated exclusively to the Jewish victims.

The Association and its supporters were especially opposed to the idea of a joint memorial, and defended their position in newspaper articles by drawing on a rhetoric of historical precision rooted in the thesis of singularity: "Because every victim group has a distinct history, it would be disastrous to blend them together."[51] Such "generalizations of memory" (*Pauschalisierung der Erinnerung*), they argued, risked belittling both the specificity of the victim experience and the criminal intent of the perpetrators. Jäckel explained, "If we are to include Sinti and Roma in this memorial, then we will have to also mention the Slavs and the mentally handicapped who were murdered in accordance with the same racial theories. We will then end up with a general memorial that is no longer specific enough to really help us remember anything."[52] Lea Rosh has been quoted as rather cynically saying that, "we would then also be expected to commemorate the soldiers or the German housewife who was killed by bombs."[53] The first director of the Association Jakob Schulze-Rohr made a similar statement that his intentions were to "simply prevent an oversimplification of past events by throwing all victims into the same pot. If you were to commemorate just everyone, you may as well include in the memorial the SS soldier who threw away his weapons and surrendered."[54]

As an addendum, newspaper articles written by Association members and its supporters made sure to emphasize that a Jewish-only dedication would in no way devalue the suffering of other groups; to counter claims that the Holocaust Memorial would unwittingly introduce or reinforce a hierarchy of victims, organizers maintained that each of the victim groups should indeed have a memorial space of its own.[55]

What this line of reasoning obscures, however, is that the real point of contention was not so much the particularity of the *actual* history of Jewish persecution (i.e., whether it was in fact the center of Nazi racist ideology), as it was about the ways in which this history has been and should be represented. This is evident in the fact that opponents of a shared memorial were not only concerned about accurately documenting the past, but also about symbolically representing the future of a newly reunified Germany. Director of the "Topography of Terror" museum Reinhard Rürup, for example, championed plans to dedicate the Holocaust Memorial exclusively to Jewish victims based on the premise that, "fundamentally, it is about showing that the new Germany, still in a process of formation, is ready to seriously grapple with the National

Socialist past."[56] The memorial debates engendered a public discourse that typically defined the Jewish-only dedication as "moral redemption for the [German] nation."[57] By placing memory of Jewish victimization at the center of Germany's self-perception as a nation, supporters of an exclusive Holocaust Memorial were ultimately reinforcing the dominant position of Jewish victims over "other" victim groups in Germany's narrative of commemoration, and by extension, in the broader context of German national identity.

Newspapers also printed numerous articles advocating for a shared memorial to both Jewish and Sinti and Roma victims (and occasionally other victim groups as well). Not dissimilar to the motivation of those arguing in favor of an exclusive Jewish memorial, the individuals promoting a shared memorial were primarily interested in the symbolic implications of commemoration; these concerns dovetailed with the restructuring of Berlin's topography and political identity.

Romani Rose's allegation of a victim hierarchy was frequently quoted in the press along with phrases claiming that an exclusive Jewish memorial would result in "a classification of the dead into first and second class [citizens]," "a reenactment of the Nazi selection process," and "a subsequent triumph of the National Socialists, for today victim groups are being divided and counted up against one another [as they once were in the past]."[58] Accordingly, philosopher Günter Freudenberg referred to the Holocaust Memorial as an "outrage" and asked, "With what right can we determine that only one segment of the greater victim population is worthy of remembrance?"[59] Gerhard Schoenberner, founding director of the memorial site "House of the Wannsee Conference," criticized the idea of an exclusive Jewish memorial, arguing that it would not only be a sign of utter disrespect vis-à-vis the dead but would also have the effect of narrowing the very dimensions of the Holocaust. He then added, "It is horrible to think that that the dead have been posthumously ranked."[60] With the pithy question, "Whom does the Holocaust belong to?" journalist Avidan captured the essential point of contention in the debate.[61]

In response to the suggestion put forth by the Association that each victim group was entitled to its own memorial space, opponents inundated the press with expressions suggestive of a "deluge of new memorials." In their view, if each victim group would indeed get its own memorial, the New Berlin would be transformed into a "memorial mile," "ensemble of memorials," "buffoonery of remembrance," "federal memorial park for the victims of National-Socialism," "Berlin memory avenue," and a "macabre Disneyland."[62] These phrases were intended to point out the absurdity entailed in the construction of separate memorials for each of the victim groups as well as to suggest that the most appropriate form of honoring all victims of genocide would be to build one memorial dedicated to them all. Opponents of the Association thus regarded the idea of building separate memorials as affirmation, in visual and concrete form no less, of a victim hierarchy. Condemningly, and with marked symbolic import, Reinhart Koselleck wrote, "The variously colored triangles worn by concentration camp inmates are returning after fifty years, re-created in memorials."[63]

The extent to which Berlin's topography mattered to both sides of the memorial debates must be understood in the context of German reunification, see by many as a key moment in which to write German identity anew. For Rose and the Sinti/Roma Central Council, reunification suggested a discursive opening in the country's commemoration space, a space that had for a long time been reserved for Jewish victims. This is why physical proximity—be it in a shared memorial or on a shared memorial site—was so important in the evolution of the Central Council's campaign.

The issue of the memorial's location was also one of essence to city planners seeking to redesign and promote Berlin as a world-class, cosmopolitan city of the new millennium, politicians, and those members of civil society fearing that the row of memorials would leave the city overrun by memories of past atrocities and national guilt.[64] Mayor of Berlin Eberhard Diepgen used polemic terms such as *Denkmaleritis* (loosely translated as "Memorialitis," or infection-like spread of memorials) in order to condemn plans for building a series of memorials in and around Berlin.[65] For him, the "new" Berlin was not only the home of the German government, but also the "workshop of Germany unity." Diepgen presented Berlin as a key element in the process of creating a united Germany, of rediscovering a wider German nationhood."[66]

It is thus clear that all sides of the memorial debates were effectively fighting not only for an "appropriate" form of representing history, but also for a suitable representation of the *new* Germany and the chance to be inscribed in it. The debates highlight the very inextricability of these two processes—(re-)shaping memory and (re-)defining identity.

Resolving the Hierarchy of Victims?

On 25 June 1999, debates regarding shared versus individual memorials were carried over into a plenary session of parliament.[67] The language of "victim hierarchy" was at the center of the session as parliamentarians sought a way of sifting through a decade's worth of disputes over the form, content, and meaning of the Holocaust Memorial. Bundestag president Wolfgang Thierse (SPD), who opened the session, immediately broached the issue by reminding his colleagues that whatever decision they reached would inevitably reflect Germany's moral commitment to all victim groups of Nazism:

> [T]oday we must decide: do we want to dedicate this memorial to the murdered Jews of Europe or to all of victims persecuted and murdered by the National Socialists? This decision is not easy for me. Significant is Reinhard Kosellek's [sic] urgent plea that we, as perpetrators, have no right to arrogate a hierarchy of victims. More virulently, he adds: doing so would serve to reinforce those categories defined by the SS and then used to annihilate their victims.... Against this backdrop we must ensure that our decision today does not in any way represent disrespect to the other victim groups—the Sinti and Roma, the politically persecuted, the homosexuals, and the mentally handicapped. We remain committed to providing an honorable remembrance of their respective fates.[68]

This declaration of support for all victim groups set the tone for the rest of the plenary session as members of parliament from all sides of the political spectrum deliberated on how to most honorably commemorate all Nazi victims. The parliamentary session ended with a vote that put forth the motion to expand the dedication of the Holocaust Memorial so that it would include, in addition to Jewish victims, mention of "all of the other victims of the National Socialist crimes against humanity." The motion did *not* pass, with 325 members of parliament voting against and 218 in favor of a shared memorial to "all victims."[69] Subsequently, the Bundestag committed itself to funding construction of separate memorials in the capital city to "the other victims of National Socialism." Although articulated in vague terms, this pledge set in motion more concrete measures for commemorating other victim groups, to be taken at a later date.

Toward a Memorial Network

Design of the Holocaust Memorial was another key issue on the plenary session's agenda, with a majority vote going to the "Peter Eisenmann II design." This particular proposal consisted of an aboveground field of 2,711 concrete stelae—commonly referred to as the *Stelenfeld* (field of stelae)—along with an underground Place of Information (*Ort der Information,* or PI). The primary function of the PI was to supplement the abstract aboveground memorial structure with detailed historical information. It was also meant to link together other memorials and memorial sites (e.g., former concentration camps) in Germany and across Europe, including those dedicated to or encompassing the history of non-Jewish victims. The PI would be run by a Foundation for the Memorial to the Murdered Jews of Europe (hereafter: Foundation), an independent entity under public law committed to "ensuring that all victims of National Socialism are remembered and honored appropriately."[70]

By voting to institutionalize the memory of "other victim groups" in the PI and directing responsibility to the Foundation, the Bundestag partially resolved the conflict over establishing a "memorial mile" (consisting of the Holocaust Memorial flanked on all sides by smaller memorials to the other victim groups) versus building one memorial dedicated to all victim groups equally. From its establishment in April 2000 and until the inauguration of the Holocaust Memorial in 2005, the Foundation's advisory board concentrated primarily on the planning and realization of the PI's exhibit. While the exhibition would cover mainly the Nazi persecution of Jews in 1933–1945, members of the advisory board—representatives of historical research institutes, survivor associations, museums, and various youth groups—deliberated how to integrate the experience of non-Jewish victim groups into the exhibit's historical narrative. Today, visitors to the PI will notice scattered mention of non-Jewish victims, Sinti and Roma in particular, in the historical chronology 1933–1945 on display in the foyer, in the Room of Places that documents the Nazi sites of terror across Europe, and in the computer databases available for individual use at the end of the exhibit. The PI also features a collection of video testimonies from Jewish and non-Jewish survivors.[71]

As a significant development, in July 2009 the Bundestag granted the Foundation full administrative control over the Homosexual Memorial and the unfinished Sinti/Roma Memorial, with funds coming from the Federal Government Commission for Culture and the Media and earmarked specifically for these two memorials. Uwe Neumärker, current director of the Foundation, commented that the 1999 parliamentary resolution, which pledged to "contribute to the honorable memory of all victims," was only made clear in the 2009 legal amendment. Neumärker further explained that while the Foundation now has administrative control over the other two memorials, decisions are reached in conjunction with respective victim group associations (in the case of the Sinti/Roma Memorial, the Sinti/Roma Central Council, the Sinti Alliance, and since recently also the Jenischer Bund).[72]

The fact that the Foundation is now in charge of the other two national memorials has generated several pedagogical and research initiatives. Specifically, the Foundation helps to bring the visitors to the

Jewish Holocaust Memorial in direct contact with the histories of the other victim groups, as well as provides the newer memorials with access to the Foundation's extensive infrastructure (e.g., personnel, research tools, library and archival materials, office space, political and social networks). Since 2011, the PI has been running an educational workshop on the Nazi persecution of the Sinti and Roma for high-school students, inclusive of a guided tour of the memorial site, albeit still unfinished.[73] The homepage of the Holocaust Memorial currently features Germany's three national Holocaust memorials positioned alongside one another.[74] Beneath the photograph of each memorial is an Internet link that takes visitors to the respective website; the Foundation is in charge of administering the websites and updating information, which in the case of the Sinti/Roma Memorial includes a detailed map indicating the site's location, a chronology of the Nazi persecution of the Sinti and Roma, and information about the Memorial's design and architect (by Israeli Dani Karavan).[75]

Other ways in which the Foundation may support the Sinti and Roma Memorial depend on its eventual completion. For example, there are plans to prepare a printed leaflet about the Memorial and to make it available at the PI.[76] The Foundation is entrusted with applying to the Berlin district office for "blue sign markers" indicating the direction and distance to the Sinti and Roma Memorial (these signs are typical in Berlin for all tourist and memorial sites). While most guided tours organized by the Foundation take visitors to the aboveground field of stelae at the Holocaust Memorial, at least one tour covers a range of Berlin memorials dedicated to other victim groups. Following its completion, the Sinti/Roma Memorial will be incorporated into this particular tour.

Decisions taken at the Bundestag plenary session on 25 June 1999, as well as more recent government legislation, point to the formation of a "memorial network." The Jewish Holocaust Memorial maintains a dominant position in this network, however, not least due to the fact that the Jewish Holocaust Memorial Foundation is now in charge of the other victim group memorials; there are currently no reciprocal relations evident in this network. Although other victim groups' narratives are now incorporated into the PI's exhibit and are cursorily mentioned in the organized tours of the field of stelae, the Jews maintain their status as archetypical victims and the Jewish Holocaust remains the focal point of the Foundation's activities.[77] Thus, while the state has clearly increased efforts at integrating the narratives of other victim groups, suggesting a widening of German space for genocide commemoration, the memorial *network*, in the fullest sense of the word, is unbalanced.

Conclusion

On 12 January 2010, the Sinti/Roma Central Council issued a press release deploring the commemorative activities of the Saxony Memorial Foundation, charged with equating the Nazi genocide with injustices committed by Communist regimes. Specifically, the Sinti/Roma Central Council demanded that the Saxony Memorial Foundation "elevate the memory of National Socialist crimes" by establishing "an independent advisory council composed of representatives of Nazi victim groups that can work separately from and independently of other organizations involved with post-1945 issues."[78]

About one year later, on 16 December 2010, the Documentation and Cultural Centre of German Sinti and Roma issued a press release announcing that Simone Veil, former president of the European Parliament, was the winner of the "European Civil Rights Prize of the Sinti and Roma" (a 15,000 prize administered by the Sinti/Roma Central Council and the Manfred-Lautenschläger Foundation, awarded biannually to an individual, group, or institution that has shown commitment to improving the human rights of the Sinti and Roma minority). Veil received the prize as "a personality who was one of the first to fight for the recognition of the victims of the National-Socialist genocide of Sinti and Roma." As both a Jew and a Holocaust survivor, Veil's show of solidarity with the Sinti and Roma community since 1979 has made her into an important symbol for many of the Sinti and Roma leaders engaged in memory politics.[79]

The two press releases suggest that issues raised and debated over a period of twenty years in the context of building a Central Holocaust Memorial in a reunified Germany still resonate today. Those issues include the entangled relationship between memory of Jewish and Romani persecution in Germany's culture of commemoration; "appropriate" definitions of victims and their implications; the role played by the German state in the process of interpreting and institutionalizing national memory; and the integration of separate remembrance narratives as they have developed in postwar East and West Germany. The issues debated and decisions taken cut through differing political interests, interpretations of the past, and visions of the future. In this chapter I have analyzed the evolution of Germany's national memorials as a way of disentangling these processes and showing how memory narratives are shaped and imbued with symbolic meaning. I argue that by tracing the evolution, or biography, of a memorial we can better recognize the social relations and identities mobilized in the process.

Recent developments reveal yet another level of entanglement. By linking up the three national memorials and creating a memorial network, the German state has made it clear that while issues of uniqueness, relativization, and victim rivalry continue to dominate German public and political discourse, efforts are indeed underway to create space in mainstream channels of commemoration for "other" discourses of victimhood. Predictably, it has generated friction between the ever-increasing number of memory projects underway in post-Holocaust, post-Wall Germany.[80] From a purely visual standpoint, the Holocaust Memorial's 2,711 concrete stelae literally hover above the single stele comprising the Homosexual Memorial and the still unfinished (and also much smaller) Sinti/Roma Memorial. However, if we are to understand memory and its representation as a dynamic process involving multiple actors and interrelated historical events, then the entangled constellation of identities and legacies of persecution outlined in this chapter indicates that the politics of Sinti and Roma commemoration, like the unfinished memorial itself, is still a work in progress.

Postscript

Shortly before this chapter went to print, the Memorial to the Sinti and Roma of Europe Murdered Under National Socialism opened in Berlin on 24 October 2012. Over 1,200 guests were present at the inauguration ceremony, including Chancellor Angela Merkel, Federal President Joachim Gauck and Bundestag President Norbert Lammert, as well as numerous international media outlets.[81]

Notes

1. *Der Spiegel*, 11 May 2007.
2. Dan Stone, "The Historiography of Genocide: Beyond 'Uniqueness' and Ethnic Competition," *Rethinking History* 8, no. 1 (2004): 128; Gavriel Rosenfeld, "The Politics of Uniqueness: Reflections on the Recent Polemical Turn in Holocaust and Genocide Scholarship," *Holocaust and Genocide Studies* 13, no. 1 (1999): 29–30; Alan Rosenbaum, ed., *Is the Holocaust Unique? Perspectives on Comparative Genocide* (Boulder, CO, 1996), 3.
3. *Tagesspiegel*, 11 April 1989.
4. This is the official name of the memorial, as approved by the Bundestag on 20 December 2007.
5. On the respective ideologies of commemoration in West versus East Germany see Jeffrey Herf, *Divided Memory: The Nazi Past in the Two Germanys* (Cambridge, MA, 1997).

6. Since the inauguration of the memorial for the Jewish victims in 2005, in popular discourse it has been referred to as the "Holocaust Memorial"; since its inauguration in 2008, the memorial for the Homosexual victims has been commonly referred to as the Homosexual Memorial.
7. Sebastian Conrad, "Entangled Memories: Versions of the Past in Germany and Japan, 1945–2001," *Journal of Contemporary History* 38, no. 1 (2003): 86–87. See also Michael Rothberg, *Multidirectional Memories: Remembering the Holocaust in the Age of Decolonization* (Stanford, CA, 2009); Daniel Levy and Natan Sznaider, "Memory Unbound The Holocaust and the Formation of Cosmopolitan Memory," *European Journal of Social Theory* 5, no. 1 (2002): 89.
8. Daphne Berdahl, "Dis-Membering the Past: The Politics of Memory in the German Borderland," in *A User's Guide to German Cultural Studies*, ed., S. Denham et al. (Ann Arbor, MI, 1997), 325–26.
9. Levy and Sznaider, "Memory Unbound," 94. See also Bill Niven, ed., *Germans as Victims: Remembering the Past in Contemporary Germany* (London, 2006).
10. Hannah Arendt, "The Aftermath of Nazi Rule: Report From Germany," *Commentary* 10, no. 4 (1950): 342–53.
11. Jeffrey K. Olick, "What Does It Mean to Normalize the Past? Official Memory in German Politics Since 1989," *Social Science History* 22, no. 4 (1998): 551.
12. Cf. Helmut Dubiel, *Niemand ist frei von der Geschichte. Die nationalsozialistische Herrschaft in den Debatten des Deutschen Bundestages* (Munich, 1999).
13. Jean-Michel Chaumont, *La concurrence des victimes. génocide, identité, reconnaissance* (Paris, 1997). For a description of these developments in the US context see Jeffrey C. Alexander, "On the Social Construction of Moral Universals: The 'Holocaust' From War Crime to Trauma Drama," *European Journal of Social Theory* 5, no. 1 (2002); Peter Novick, *The Holocaust in American Life* (New York, 1999); For the Israeli context, see Tom Segev, *The Seventh Million: The Israelis and the Holocaust* (New York, 1991).
14. Rosenfeld, "Politics of Uniqueness," 30.
15. Cf. Steven Katz, "The 'Unique' Intentionality of the Holocaust," *Modern Judaism* 1, no. 2 (September 1981): 161–83; Eberhard Jäckel, *Hitlers Herrschaft* (Stuttgart, 1986); Deborah Lipstadt, *Denying the Holocaust: The Growing Assault on Truth and Memory* (New York, 1993); Yehuda Bauer, *The Holocaust in Historical Perspective* (Seattle, 1978).
16. Cf. David E. Stannard, "Uniqueness as Denial: The Politics of Genocide Scholarship," in *Is the Holocaust Unique?* ed. A. Rosenbaum, 163–208; Ward Churchill, *A Little Matter of Genocide: Holocaust and Denial in the Americas 1492 to the Present* (San Francisco, 1997).
17. Wolfgang Wippermann, *Auserwählte Opfer? Shoah und Porrajmos im Vergleich. Eine Kontroverse* (Berlin, 2005), 92–93. The *Historikerstreit* focused on the (West) German state's accountability for the Nazi crimes. Rather than comparing experiences of victimization, as in earlier debates, conservative Right-leaning historians broached the topic of perpetration, seeking to establish historical precedent to Nazi crimes. The intellectual left regarded such arguments as an attempt to "free Germany from its particular stain, thus facilitating the resurgence of a sense of national pride" (Levy and Sznaider, "Memory Unbound," 99). See Rudolf Augstein et al., eds, "*Historikerstreit.*" *Die Dokumentation der Kontroverse um die Einzigartigkeit der nationalsozialistischen Judenvernichtung* (Munich, 1987).
18. The German Sinti and Roma's lobbying for recognition and restitution can also be interpreted as a collective form of self-identification, which at the same time corresponds to and diverges from the identity politics of the European Roma civil rights movement (Grattan Puxon cited in Wippermann, *Auserwählte Opfer?*, 75).

19. Gilad Margalit, "The Representation of the Nazi Persecution of the Gypsies in German Discourse after 1945," *German History* 17, no. 2 (1999): 222.
20. Even though German citizenship was restored to Sinti and Roma survivors following the war, many individuals then had their citizenship once again revoked in the 1950s by the interior ministries of the German states on the premise that they had obtained citizenship illegally. See Gilad Margalit, "German Citizenship Policy and Sinti Identity Politics," in *Challenging Ethnic Citizenship: German and Israeli Perspectives on Immigration*, ed., D. Levy and Y. Weiss (New York and London, 2002), 110.
21. Tilman Zülch, ed., *In Auschwitz vergast, bis heute verfolgt. Zur Situation der Roma (Zigeuner) in Deutschland und Europa* (Reinbek, 1979).
22. Andrew Woolford and Stefan Wolejszo, "Collecting on Moral Debts: Reparations for the Holocaust and Porajmos," *Law & Society Review* 40, no. 4 (2006): 871–901; Yaron Matras, "Phases in the Development of Romani Political Movement," seminar taught at the Summer School in Romany Studies at the Central European University in Budapest, 1 July 2009.
23. Gesellschaft für Bedrohte Völker, ed., *Sinti und Roma im ehemaligen KZ Bergen-Belsen am 27. Oktober 1979* (Göttingen and Vienna, 1981).
24. Margalit, "The Representation," 223; Gesellschaft für Bedrohte Völker, *Sinti und Roma*, 18.
25. Matras, "Phases in the Development."
26. See also Roni Stauber and Raphael Vago, ed., *The Roma: A Minority in Europe. Historical, Political and Social Perspectives* (Budapest, 2007); Gilad Margalit, *Germany and its Gypsies: A Post-Auschwitz Ordeal* (Madison, WI, 2002); Sławomir Kapralski, "Identity Building and the Holocaust: Roma Political Nationalism," *Nationalities Papers* 25, no. 2 (1997): 269–83.
27. The Central Council (and Romani Rose in particular) has played a dominant role in the development of the Sinti/Roma Memorial and most other issues related to Sinti and Roma memory politics in Germany. The analysis presented in this chapter is thus limited to the interaction between German authorities and the Central Council, the organization that they have clearly chosen as the representative voice of all Sinti and Roma in Germany (even though the Central Council is in fact comprised entirely of Sinti members, and is not necessarily representative of all German Sinti). For a detailed overview of the Sinti and Roma minority in Germany, and the internal divisions within the minority, see Gilad Margalit and Yaron Matras, "Gypsies in Germany—German Gypsies? Identity and Politics of Sinti and Roma in Germany," in *The Roma: A Minority in Europe*, eds., Stauber and Vago, 203–16.
28. Bürgerinitiative Perspektive Berlin e.V., ed., *Ein Denkmal für die ermordeten Juden Europas. Dokumentation 1988–1995* (Berlin, 1995), 14. For background information on the Central Memorial for the Murdered Jews of Europe, see Peter Carrier, *Holocaust Monuments and National Memory Cultures in France and Germany Since 1989: The Origins and Political Function of the Vél' d'Hiv' in Paris and the Holocaust Monument in Berlin* (New York, 2005); Claus Leggewie and Erik Meyer, *"Ein Ort, an den man gerne geht." Das Holocaust-Mahnmal und die deutsche Geschichtspolitik nach 1989* (Berlin, 2005); Irit Dekel, "Public Passages: Political Action in and Around the Holocaust Memorial, Berlin" (PhD dissertation, New York University, 2008).
29. Interview with Eberhard Jäckel, 30 January 2009.
30. *Frankfurter Rundschau*, 30 January 1989.
31. Press release, 17 March 1995, in *Der Denkmalstreit—das Denkmal? Die Debatte um das „Denkmal für die ermordeten Juden Europas." Eine Dokumentation*, ed., U. Heimrod et al. (Berlin, 1999), 271.
32. *Tageszeitung*, 11 November 1994.

33. See, for example, Rafael Seligmann, "Genug bemitleidet. Gegen ein deutsches Holocaust-Memorial," *Der Spiegel,* 16 January 1995; Michael Wolffsohn, "Am Tatort sollt ihr eingedenken. Gegen die Wattierung der Erinnerung durch zentrale Gedenkstätten," *Frankfurter Allgemeine Zeitung,* 24 July 1994.
34. Heimrod et al., *Denkmalstreit,* 28.
35. Ibid., 93.
36. *Der Tagespiegel* and *Frankfurter Rundschau,* 14 September 1992.
37. Wippermann, *Auserwählte Opfer?* 110. Otherwise, there were few, if any, Jewish leaders who accepted the interpretation of the memorial site as a symbolic cemetery. See Paul Spiegel, president of the Jewish Central Council from 2000–2006 (*Der Spiegel-Online,* 11 May 2005).
38. *Tageszeitung,* 18 November 1993.
39. Heimrod et al., *Denkmalstreit,* 109.
40. For the history of Neue Wache's multiple dedications see Karen Till, "Staging the Past: Landscape Designs, Cultural Identity and *Erinnerungspolitik* at Berlin's Neue Wache," *Ecumene* 6, no. 3 (1999): 251–83.
41. Gerd Knischewski and Ula Spittler, "Remembering in the Berlin Republic: The Debate About the Central Holocaust Memorial in Berlin," *Debatte: Journal of Contemporary Central and E. Europe* 13, no. 1 (2005): 28.
42. *Tagesspiegel,* 16 December 1993.
43. *Die Zeit,* 17 December 1993.
44. Similarly, Rudolph Kraft wrote that Central Council representatives refused to share a memorial with the homosexual and Communist victims of Nazis based on the fact that neither of these groups were persecuted on racial grounds (*Die Zeit,* 24 July 1992).
45. Michael Zimmermann, "The Berlin Memorial for the Murdered Sinti and Roma: Problems and Points for Discussion," *Romani Studies* 17, no. 1 (2007): 18.
46. Roman Herzog, *Rede zur Eröffnung des Dokumentations- und Kulturzentrums Deutscher Sinti und Roma, 16 March 1997.*
47. Natasha Winter of the Cologne-based Sinti Allianz, however, opposed historical comparison of the Gypsy genocide (the Allianz's preferred terminology) and the Jewish genocide. This particular dispute was extensively covered in the media and went on for years, ultimately to be resolved by the Commission for Culture and the Media in 2007. Historian Jäckel was the most vocal supporter of Winter's (successful) campaign to remove this particular quote from the center of the memorial. The quote will, however, be integrated into the chronology of the Nazi persecution of the Sinti and Roma, to be displayed at the memorial site.
48. *Der Spiegel,* 18 June 1991.
49. *Die Zeit,* 7 April 1989. See also Jäckel cited in Avidan, *Tageszeitung,* 31 July 1991.
50. Heimrod et al., *Denkmalstreit,* 58.
51. *Der Freitag,* 20 March 1992.
52. *Tagesspiegel,* 8 March 1991.
53. *Der Freitag,* 20 March 1992.
54. *Tageszeitung,* 13 April 1989.
55. See, for example, Brentano cited in Heimrod et al., *Denkmalstreit,* 58; Bernhard Schulz, *Tagesspiegel,* 3 July 1990.
56. *Tagesspiegel,* 3 July 1990.
57. Carrier, *Holocaust Monuments,* 201. See also *Frankfurter Allgemeine Zeitung,* 22 September 1995.
58. *Der Spiegel,* 18 June 1991; *Focus,* 15 August 1994.
59. Heimrod et al., *Denkmalstreit,* 73.
60. *Die Tageszeitung,* 30 September 1992.

61. *Die Tageszeitung*, 31 July 1991.
62. *Focus*, 15 August 1994; *Tagesspiegel*, 26 March 1998; *Die Zeit*, 24 July 1992.
63. *Der Spiegel*, 3 February 1997.
64. Karen Till, *The New Berlin: Memory, Politics, Place* (Minneapolis, 2005), 193.
65. Heimrod et al., *Denkmalstreit*, 122.
66. Allan Cochrane, "Making up Meanings in a Capital City: Power, Memory and Monuments in Berlin," *European Urban and Regional Studies* 13, no. 1 (2006): 6.
67. German Bundestag, plenary session proceedings 14/48, 25 June 1999, http://dip21.bundestag.de/dip21/btp/14/14048.pdf (accessed 25 May 2010).
68. Ibid., 4086.
69. Ibid., 4128. Note that Thierse voted against the motion.
70. Quoted on the Foundation's website, http://www.holocaust-mahnmal.de/en/thememorial/foundation.
71. *Bericht 2003, 2004, 2005. Stiftung Denkmal für die Ermordeten Juden Europas* (Berlin, 2005), http://stiftung-denkmal.de/ (accessed 25 May 2010).
72. Interview with Uwe Neumärker, 1 March 2010.
73. Information (in German) about the workshop is available at: http://www.stiftung-denkmal.de/besuch/angebote-fuer-schulen/workshops.html (accessed 23 February 2012).
74. http://www.holocaust-mahnmal.de/ or http://stiftung-denkmal.de/ (accessed 23 February 2012).
75. The website of the Sinti/Roma Memorial is available at: http://www.stiftung-denkmal.de/en/memorials/sinti-and-roma-memorial.html#c952 (accessed 23 February 2012).
76. The PI is now one of Berlin's most visited tourist sites (*Tageszeitung*, 5 May 2010). Since opening in 2005, more than 3.1 million people have visited the underground PI. Visitor statistics available at: http://www.stiftung-denkmal.de/en/memorials/the-memorial-to-the-murdered-jews-of-europe.html (accessed 23 February 2012).
77. Irit Dekel, "Ways of Looking: Observation and Transformation at the Holocaust Memorial, Berlin," *Memory Studies* 2, no. 1 (2009): 80.
78. Romani Rose, press release, 12 January 2010, http://zentralrat.sintiundroma.de/ (accessed 25 May 2010).
79. Press release, 8 December 2010, http://www.sintiundroma.de/index/ (accessed 25 May 2010).
80. The most contentious of the current memorial projects is the memorial for German expellees, administered by the state-funded Foundation for Flight, Expulsion, and Conciliation. For more information see http://www.dhm.de/sfvv.
81. See, for example, articles in *die Tageszeitung*, 24 October 2012; *BBC News*, 24 October 2012; *New York Times*, 24 October 2012; *Le Monde*, 25 October 2012; *Haaretz*, 25 October 2012.

CHAPTER 9

THE AFTERMATH OF THE ROMA GENOCIDE
FROM IMPLICIT MEMORIES TO COMMEMORATION

Sławomir Kapralski

This chapter assesses the impact of the Nazi persecution of the Roma on Romani identities in postwar Europe. My argument builds on a critical assessment of Lech Mróz's conception of Romani "non-memory that does not mean forgetting" and Michael Stewart's idea that the Roma remember through implicit memories "embedded in dealings with others" but do not commemorate the past. I argue that the issue of memory largely depends (1) on the diversified nature of persecution that particular groups suffered from; (2) on the changing dynamics of perceptions influenced by the development of the Holocaust discourse and transformation of the past into a "symbolic asset"; and (3) on the changing dynamics of identity-construction processes that characterize particular Romani groups. The main question that I am asking in this chapter is how Roma remember the atrocities of World War II and how that remembrance becomes an element in various constructions of Romani identities.

Memory and Identity

The persecution of the Roma under Nazi rule has emerged as a topic of scholarly research and public discourse relatively recently. The long period of silence regarding the murder of approximately half a million people[1] calls for an explanation. Among various interpretations we may find a conception, according to which the historical dimension of identity is of no relevance to Roma. According to this conception, the Roma allegedly are a "people without history," who neither store and share memories of the past nor conceptualize themselves in terms of a desired future.[2]

The corresponding perception of the Romani identity is ingrained in a model of the essentialized "substance" of "Romness" that is identical with or fully represented in the everyday life of Romani people. Hence, Romani identity does not have a historical dimension. Instead, it perpetuates a suprahistorical cultural idiom, *Romanipen*—a normative system and worldview that constitute the essence of "being Rom." The interpretation of the memory void in terms of the alleged irrelevance of history to Roma coexists with a more recent conception, according to which Roma do remember the past, but it is a different form of remembrance from the one we may find in a modern society. Nonreflective and nondiscursive, this "implicit memory" is supposedly embedded in the Roma relations with the non-Romani world, and in the way they organize their social life. The concept of implicit memory fits with a "relational" vision of Romani identity, according to which it is mainly the nature of the relations with the non-Romani world, as well as the relations between particular structural units within Romani communities, that determine the identity of a group. In this interpretation, echoing Fredrik Barth's theory of identity, it is the nature of the social border separating groups that determines group identity, not the cultural contents that it circumscribes.[3]

What both interpretations have in common is the belief that the Roma do not engage in conscious acts of commemoration referring to past events important to the community. The former, "substantive" approach assumes that remembrance has no bearing on Romani identity and, as a matter of fact, does not even exist among Roma. The latter, "relational" approach presupposes that Romani memories are incognizant. Therefore, remembrance does not exist as a means of communication among Roma people, though it may still be present, encoded in the social landscape of Romani life.

I argue that both approaches neglect the instances when memory has actually been voiced and reflected upon within Romani communities, and that these acts of remembrance are often associated with and facilitated by commemorative practices. Furthermore, I suggest that those instances of remembrance and commemoration may call for yet another, "temporal," or historical, theory of identity in which the present self-definition of a group depends on its members' idea of who they were in the past.[4] As a result, the members of a group develop a sense of its "constancy over time," that is, an ability of those living in the present to bring the "past into conjunction with an anticipated future."[5] By "temporal" or historical construction of identity I understand a synthesis of the aspects of identity that have been inherited (based on past events regarded as important by the community), the potential aspects (based on the group's projection into the future), and those aspects experienced as the most important in the present.[6] Naturally, this synthesis (or "constancy" as Anthony Giddens calls it) may take very different forms. In fact, modern identities can be built on the principle of difference; a group defines itself in the present as distinct from that it was in the past and assumes that in the future it will be once again different from what it is now.[7]

Here I should add that the term *Roma* applies to an array of highly differentiated groups which may have little in common in spite of the otherwise very important political projects of constructing some commonalities for the purpose of uniting these heterogeneous populations.[8] This is a mixed blessing for those of us writing on Roma. On the one hand, whatever we may want to say about "Roma" in general has a great chance of being false in the presence of a group that may constitute an exception. On the other hand, much of what we may want to say about "Roma" has a chance of being true because of a probability that there exists a community that would validate our statement. It is not my intention, therefore, to claim that "Roma" do remember and do commemorate. What I want to say is that some Romani groups preserve memories of wartime atrocities, accompanied by commemorative practices. I further claim that those memories and practices are important for our understanding of the contemporary processes of identity building among Roma.

With regard to the problem of identity, there may well be groups whose identities could best be captured as an effort to keep *Romanipen* alive and intact. There may also be groups that create their identities as symbolic walls separating the Romani social universe from the non-Romani world. And finally, there may be groups that, with the help of commemorative ceremonies, reflect on what happened to them in the past and try to imagine their future according to that reflection. There may also be a group characterized by all three processes occurring simultaneously.[9] The issue is not exactly whether "Romani identity" is substantial, relational, or developmental, but rather what is the proportion of those aspects of identity in a particular group at any given moment.

Having said that, the temporal aspects of Romani identity are of particular importance for my research, as they may point toward the processes that could contribute to forming the future Romani identities. In the spirit of poststructuralist criticism, I want to avoid an essentializing approach to identity that sees it as a petrified substance, relation, or process. Instead, I view identity as a cultural text, which is a result of numerous interactions and social practices within the group and across group boundaries, and which evokes a multitude of meanings, historical codes, memories, and images.[10]

Roma: Mute or Muted?

I distinguish between three main interpretations of the long-lasting silence surrounding the Roma suffering during World War II. One interpretation refers to the particular nature of the suffering inflicted; another refers to the way Roma suffering has (not) been documented and perceived (in relation to the development of the Holocaust discourse); and yet another refers to the particularities of Romani culture or the Roma social status. The last mentioned construal gained some currency in Romani studies, usually in the form of a claim that it was "traditional Romani culture" that prevented the Roma from remembering their tragedy. For example, Jan Yoors—fascinated by the ability of Roma to survive in harsh conditions—has pointed out that traditional Romani culture is oriented toward life and that the Roma collective memory does not store traumatic experiences. "I often wondered," he commented, "at their strange, inexplicable lack of traumatic reactions to their often violent personal persecutions. I observed, and eventually learned to understand, their rejection of hate or personal bitterness as a response to outside pressures."[11]

In his follow-up book, which focused on the time of the war, Yoors adopted further elements of the Holocaust discourse and presented the basic facts of the Nazi genocide of Roma. Nevertheless, his story remained a narrative of survival against all odds, a tale of the victory of life over death. According to Yoors, the extermination of the Roma has not been documented and remembered, even by the Roma themselves, "due to the Gypsies' own lack of a sense of history." "Even though over half a million of them were massacred," he continued, "they are content to remain forgotten and unnoticed."[12] This opinion may be tainted by the European (somewhat romanticized) stereotype of "people without history,"[13] or may perhaps be attributed to the fact that Yoors lived with rather traditional Romani groups (who had escaped the brunt of Nazi genocide). Coincidentally, the same year that Yoors's second book was published, representatives of various Roma groups gathered near London at a meeting (known since then as the First World Romani Congress), which, among other things, adopted the Romani anthem and the national flag. The next Congress, held in Geneva, addressed a petition to the United Nations member states to recognize the Roma as a "distinct nation;" the third Congress, held in 1981 in Göttingen, was entirely devoted to the Nazi persecution of Roma.

Apparently, "traditional culture" with its "focus on life," "living in the present," or "tabooed death," cannot be solely responsible for the silence surrounding Romani tragedy.[14] In my view, the following three factors offer a much better explanation: the particularity of the persecution of Roma, the general perceptions of Nazi atrocities in the postwar period, and the development of the Holocaust discourse. Only then, elements of "traditional culture" and some aspects of the social standing of Roma could feature as factors mediating the influence of these three processes.

As far as the nature of the persecution of Roma is concerned, the pattern of destruction of Roma was different from that of Jews. The vast majority of Roma victims lost their lives not in the death camps but in the summary executions carried out throughout the Nazi-occupied Eastern Europe by *Einsatzgruppen* and auxiliary police units. A significant number of Roma died from the inhumane conditions in the numerous concentration and forced labor camps to which they had been deported. The crimes against Roma were much more "decentralized": decision making occurred at various levels of the Nazi terror apparatus and was implemented by different units of the SS, the army, and the police. The allies of Nazi Germany performed a much more important role in murdering Roma than in the annihilation of Jews. The degree and nature of persecution varied depending on a number of factors such as place, the kind and level of the involved institutions, the particular constellation of interests, relations between different agencies, and ideological framework.

Although the Nazis' conception of "Roma" was built upon racist ideology, on the level of concrete decisions and legal acts the racial thought was concealed behind labels such as "asocial," "work-shy," or "socially unadjusted people." The difference drawn by racial scientists and some Nazi officials between "racially pure Gypsies" and "Gypsies of mixed origin" (*Mischlinge*), along with shifting policies toward those groups, further contributed to the postwar misconceptions and silence regarding the nature of the crimes committed against Roma. Finally, it is not always easy to reconstruct the chain of decisions that led to the mass murder of Roma.[15]

In Germany, Austria, and the Protectorate of Bohemia and Moravia the persecution of Roma was premeditated, based on traditional practices of registration and surveillance of Romani groups by the police. Step by step, under the growing impact of racial ideology, Roma people were segregated from the rest of the society by means of discriminatory legal acts, internment in the special "Gypsy camps," and imprisonment in concentration camps. From Germany, the road led to the Jewish ghettos in occupied Poland and then into the gas chambers of death camps. In the occupied territories of the Soviet Union, Roma were executed en masse by the SS, Wehrmacht, and the police. In Poland both methods were in use. In the satellite countries, the plight of Roma differed significantly. Whereas in Bulgaria Roma essentially escaped persecution, the Antonescu regime in Romania implemented the Nazi concept of destruction through labor (*Vernichtung durch Arbeit*) by dispatching thousands of Roma to labor camps and settlement areas in Transnistria where many of them died of hunger, diseases, and inhumane living conditions. In Croatia, local fascists executed thousands of Roma in the Jasenovac camp, without resorting to the method of industrialized mass murder perfected by the Nazis.[16]

It should also be noted that the silence surrounding the fate of the Roma during World War II is by no means unique. As Peter Novick has argued, in the years immediately following the war, the Holocaust was not a highly debated issue. In the United States, the Holocaust became a subject of public discourse only in the 1970s.[17] Owing to the subsequent prominence of the Holocaust discourse, we may have a wrong impression it has always been the case. Rather, the postwar debates focused on the "crimes against humankind" at large, without paying much attention to the crimes perpetrated against specific population groups.[18] The word *holocaust* (not yet capitalized at that time) was occasionally used during and immediately after World War II to describe the "totality of the destruction wrought by the Axis."[19] Once the discourse was established, however, it turned into a narrative that focused on the Jewish suffering, its unprecedented character and incommensurability with the suffering of other victim groups. This narrative has strengthened the view that the extermination of the Jews "finds ... no parallel with the persecutions of the other groups by the Nazis, [it] does not matter whether it happened to Russians, Serbs, Czechs, Sinti, Roma, homosexuals or political opponents."[20]

Within this context, the situation of the Roma has not changed significantly. While previously they could not frame their memories in a discourse for the lack of discourse as such, since it has been developed, Roma have not been granted the right to use it as their own. Whenever interpreted as the unique event, any association of the term *Holocaust* with non-Jewish victims of Nazi terror has been treated as an attempt to dilute its meaning and to offend the memory of its actual victims. Nonetheless, the Holocaust discourse created a context in which Roma interested in their past have searched for concepts and ideas to give meaning to their plight under the Nazis. As a result, some of the Romani activists decided to fight for the acceptance of Roma as victims of the Holocaust along with Jews, while others have been looking for a different language altogether to describe the fate of Roma. The latter has been advanced either for political reasons (e.g., to avoid a conflict with certain Jewish organizations), or upon the insistence of some of the activists that Romani history should be debated with the help of Romani concepts, independently of other visions of history.

Ian Hancock's passionate defense of the right of the Roma to be included in the Holocaust discourse could be an illustration of the first strategy.[21] The linguistic convention of the International Romani Union to portray Roma as the victims of a "holocaust" (lowercase) illustrates the attempt to present Roma as victims of a genocide that is of a similar character and yet different from the Holocaust.[22] Finally, Ian Hancock's attempt to create a new periodization of Romani history with *O baro Porrajmos* (translated by Hancock as "The Great Devouring") as its crucial element can illustrate the third strategy, as can other attempts, critical of Hancock's concept for linguistic and cultural reasons, and advocating instead, for example, the term *Samudaripen* ("genocide" or "mass murder").[23]

In my opinion, the alleged lack of historical memory among Roma cannot be attributed to specific features of Romani culture. More crucial is the way in which Roma were persecuted, the way their suffering has been documented, the rather slow development of the narrative of the Holocaust, and the problem of incorporating Roma within that narrative. In general, the perception of Roma as "people without memory" has come about as a consequence of the following factors: the dominant stereotype of Roma in modern culture; the process of "differential deprivation of history" of those marginalized;[24] the process of "othering" certain categories by denying them the right to participate in "our" temporal order;[25] and eventually the process of the "erasing of interconnections" between the dominant majority and marginalized and exploited minorities.[26]

My main argument is that Roma are not "mute" in regard to their past. If they do not bring it to the attention of others, if they do not actively commemorate collective trauma (as has been the case until recently), it is rather because they have been a "muted group" in the sense given to this term by Edwin Ardener—a group that for various reasons was unable to express itself through the socially dominant structures (linguistic, symbolic, and those related to action).[27] Among other factors that have contributed to making Roma into a "muted group" is the low level of education or political organization within many Romani communities. This situation, however, started changing recently, making the claim that "Roma do not remember" hard to sustain. However, the old paradigm is still informing academic discourse, making some authors overlook or disregard the growing interest in the past among Roma, as well as the increasing role that interest plays in Romani politics, including the politics of identity. In the next section I will outline recent approaches to the problem of Romani memory. Although these analyses are to a certain degree influenced by the traditional way of thinking, they explore new possibilities for interpreting Romani memory.

Michael Stewart: Memory Embedded in Social Relations

Michael Stewart dissociates his approach from more traditional ethnology, by consciously focusing on the "ways in which ... the past is 'remembered' among Gypsy populations" rather than on the way in which Roma obliterate or forget their past.[28] Stewart has argued that Roma do remember the past (or rather the past "is remembered" for them), but this is a special kind of memory, unsupported by any kind of active commemoration, "implicit" or "embedded" in the relations between Roma and the non-Roma world. However, he is ambiguous regarding the status of the Roma memory. Although he claims it does exist—individual memories of the wartime atrocities "have been handed on through time and ... turned into shared memories"—one wonders how this process would have been possible owing to a "general lack of interest in matters past among the Roma," unless memory has been re-created, for example during commemorative ceremonies.[29]

A part of the problem is that Stewart's generalization shares the fate of any other general statements about "Roma." It is false, since there are instances of interest in the past among Roma and there take place Romani commemorations (in fact, Stewart himself gives a few examples in his text). It seems that Stewart has adopted sort of a Durkheimian approach to identity; as in Durkheim's concept of "social fact," in Stewart's approach there are more or less fixed and objectified cultural patterns ("things Roma do") and there is the level of everyday life with its activities that may be the manifestation of the pattern but may as well be subversive or neutral regarding that pattern. It all depends on whether we take the pattern (as Stewart seems to be doing) or the life itself as the area in which we search for the elements that make up the identity of the group in question. If we go for the first option, we end up claiming that "Roma do not commemorate." If we go for the second, performative concept of identity, we may conclude that (some) Roma (sometimes) do engage in acts of commemoration.

Stewart's main argument is based on yet a different concept of Romani identity—one we know from his earlier work—that falls within the "relational" approach. A good example of the way memory works, according to this approach, is Stewart's observation that when in 1988 the "skinheads panic" broke out in Hungary, the Hungarian Roma instantly turned to the vocabulary related to the time of World War II to describe their fears. Since that kind of vocabulary was not used in public discourse concerning skinheads, Stewart has rightly claimed that Roma had employed that language on their own, as a frame of reference that gave meaning to the situation they currently experienced. Conversely, we may say that the contemporaneous events helped to evoke the Roma wartime memories.[30] What Stewart says means basically two things. First, the way Roma think of their past is not completely isolated from the cultural frames with which they interact. Second, it is the content and the form of the interactions with non-Roma that encode and store the memories of the past for the Roma (and perhaps that sometimes serve as the prompt itself, as in the case of the skinheads).

It seems that Stewart has a preference for the second option, namely that interactions with non-Roma are Romani "mnemonic devices," since they "store" the Romani history and serve as a reminder of the past and of Romani identity. "What I wish to suggest," Stewart writes, "is that the Roma of Harangos [a village in Hungary where Stewart has conducted his fieldwork] are able to live without much of what we think of as 'history' because they have their relations with us, the *gaźe*, the non-Gypsies, to remind themselves 'who they are' and who they have been, and thus to help them recognize the nature of the durational world in which, despite their best efforts, they are condemned to live."[31] When writing about the Roma of Harangos, in whose case this observation may as well be true, Stewart avoids generalizations. The problem is, however, that there is a tendency in Stewart's approach to apply the conclusions from his fieldwork in Harangos to the situation of Roma in general. According to Stewart, the majority of Roma remember in an indirect way, with their memories embedded in the oppressive relations with non-Roma. These relations remind Roma first and foremost of threat and danger, of living in a "state of siege" and daily humiliation. They sustain the memory of forced assimilation, discrimination, oppression, and exclusion.[32] This is the kind of Romani past that the outside world "remembers for" Roma.

Needless to say, this is a largely simplified picture based on a vision of Roma as a passive group. Even though oppression is an essential feature of Romani history, it is not the full history of Roma and their relations with non-Romani society. This view does not take into account Romani proactive strategies of survival, treating the Romani people as if they have been molded exclusively through policies and attitudes of non-Roma. If the whole complex of Romani memory is embedded in Roma non-Roma relations, and if those relations are as described by Stewart, then one should wonder how Roma remember their survival, so much stressed by Yoors, and how they construct their identity as the "superior party" vis-à-vis non-Roma—as noticed by Stewart himself.[33]

The static picture of Roma as passive and oppressed recipients of external intimidation informs Stewart's misplaced criticism of Isabel Fonseca[34] and her claim that for Roma "recovery of 'memory' will be an act of cultural empowerment, and hence the route to cultural self-discovery."[35] Despite Stewart's claim to the contrary, Fonseca does not imply that Roma have no memory, no self, and no culture. What Fonseca actually says is that in the world in which the remembered past has the function of legitimizing power, those excluded from the realm of memory have no power. Thus, the struggle for Romani memory (different from that "embedded in the relations with the non-Roma world") signifies the fight for empowerment. In a world defined by the modern European sense of history, one can live in the "continuous present," having memories stored in social relations. That, however, would amount to a marginal existence. Many Romani activists understand that very well and thus engage in commemorative ceremonies or in the production of narratives, largely ignored by Stewart as incongruent with his "Harangos-based" picture of Roma.

This brings me to the second problem with Stewart's approach, namely, his notion of the solid "border" between the Roma and non-Roma worlds, as well as the perception of the Roma world as homogeneous. The nature of the interactions between Roma and non-Roma is rather complex, partly due to the fact that the non-Roma world is not monolithic in its attitudes towards Roma. It consists of many different layers and institutional settings, some of them openly hostile to Roma, others neutral, and still others embracing and supporting Romani efforts to improve their situation. Hence, there is no single "frame of memory" embedded in the social relations, precisely because there is no single pattern defining these relations.

Nor is there a single "Romani memory," for the Roma are heterogeneous as a people. There are groups who prefer to stay away from the limelight, undisturbed by the non-Roma world, and there are Romani activists and intellectuals who strive to bring the Roma case to the attention of the general public. Stewart has effectively excluded the latter segment of Romani society from consideration as not really belonging to "Romness." One can see it in the way Stewart interpreted the story of Ilsa Schmidt, who has worked through her traumatic experience by means of sharing her personal recollections with the staff of the Documentation and Cultural Center of German Sinti and Roma in Heidelberg (the Center is known, among other things, for its commemorative activities that include regular visits to Auschwitz-Birkenau).[36] According to Stewart, Schmidt belongs to a minority whose memory is shaped by narratives and activities, and whose identity is connected with a remembered and emotionally appropriated history. This type of memory, according to Stewart, is fostered by institutions like the Heidelberg Center and is conditioned by circumstances such as the changing policies within the German State.

If this is the case, then the memory pattern we observe here is precisely based on social relations and/or interactions, in line with Stewart's approach. These relations, however, are determined by a much more differentiated nature of both Roma and non-Roma worlds and a more permeable border separating them than Stewart is willing to admit. Besides, I do not see why memory can be attributed to Roma only when embedded in oppressive relations. There are other forms of Romani memory that are discursive, owing to the positive transformations within the non-Roma world. Finally, there are Romani memories that emerge out of Romani commemorative practices.

Naturally, one may still argue that these forms of remembrance are available only to a tiny fraction of Roma. However, the intellectuals and activists—people genuinely interested in the history of their own group—are always a minority in any given society. Their activities may not be widely known within the larger society, and their ideas may be dismissed as unconventional. Yet, we need to study nonrepresentative ideas and commemorative practices if we want to learn about the frames of memory that characterize any given society. I do not see any reason why we should not do the same in the case of Roma.

Lech Mróz's "Non-Memory That Is Not Forgetfulness"

Lech Mróz, a Polish ethnologist working in the field of Romani studies, has adopted a perspective similar to Stewart's.[37] His perspective on memory and identity is social, or relational, though the elements of the substantial approach and the focus on "traditional Romani culture" are also present in his interpretation. He claims that it is the peculiar nature of contemporary relations with non-Roma that prompts a particular Romani way of remembrance. Mróz labeled this way of remembrance "non-memory that is not forgetfulness." This concept comprises two ideas. Mróz tends to agree with Stewart that traditional Romani culture cannot provide a frame in which Roma could remember their past, the war time in particular. Contrary to Stewart, however, Mróz argues that Roma do remember (or do not forget, to be precise) their past, and that this memory is an outcome of conscious acts of remembrance that include commemoration. The main difference between these two approaches is the status of the relations between Roma and non-Roma. For Stewart, those relations are static, conforming to the pattern of Romani history replete with persecution and discrimination, while Mróz sees them as more complex and dynamic, transforming the ways Roma look at their own past.

According to Mróz, the experience of the Nazi persecution caused a cultural trauma—a situation in which the categories of traditional culture could no longer perform their role as the regulators of social life and frames of interpretation that could give meaning to the world. For Mróz, the *Zigeunerlager* (Gypsy camp) at Auschwitz-Birkenau could serve as a metaphor for what happened to Romani culture and social life. In the *Zigeunerlager*, people of different sexes and ages, belonging to different Romani groups—including those individuals who would otherwise never sit together because of ritual rules concerning purity that separated them—were herded in the limited space of the camp, which meant the violation of the essential principles of Romani culture.[38] In such conditions, it was impossible to follow rules concerning hygiene and proper conduct, which caused frustration and shame (in the ritual sense associated with pollution as well as psychologically), even if the rituals were occasionally suspended by the leaders of some groups.

The survivors associated the experience of the camp, and the war in general for that matter, not only with oppression and the threat of physical elimination but also with the destruction of a whole symbolic universe supported by cultural patterns (which was tantamount to cultural death). They learned first-hand that there are situations in which the elaborated protective mechanisms of traditional culture can offer no defense against an external threat.

This analysis may help us to better understand the nature of the Romani silence regarding their victimization. After Mróz, I argue that this silence was caused less by the horror of death, but rather by the fact that the only means Roma had at their disposal to counter that horror—the rules of their culture—was corrupted and could no longer offer any meaningful interpretation, ritual protection, or even hope. That is why the Romani memory was traumatic, according to Mróz. It was traumatic less in the sense of a psychological wound but in the sense of cultural inadequacy—the discomfort caused by the impossibility of finding an expression for individual experiences within cultural categories.

Hence, Mróz regards Romani memory of the war as "mute" or implicit. The traces left by the experience of terror can be only detected through "silences," that is, cultural voids. This is not a case of the repression of trauma, however, as Mróz seems to suggest. In more general terms, this means that the classic approach to trauma as a psychological mechanism of repression of a disturbing and horrifying experience cannot adequately render the Romani experience and perhaps the experience of the Holocaust survivors at large. Saul Friedländer has observed that the period of latency "that followed the war in regard to talking or writing about the Shoah ... should not be equated with massive repression exclusively.... The silence did not exist *within* the survivor community. It was maintained in relation to the outside world, and was often imposed by ... the shame of telling a story that must appear unbelievable, and was, in any case, entirely out of tune with surrounding society."[39]

Among Roma, too, the memory persisted and, whenever voiced, it became an expressed recollection. Emmanuel Filhol's research on the Romani inmates of the internment camps in Vichy France shows that this might have been the case. Filhol concluded that, contrary to widespread views, Roma do remember:

> When questioning ex-internees, I realized to what degree the internment drama was engraved into the collective and individual memories of the witnesses. The memories linked to the trauma of the camps had not changed. What struck me was the extraordinary precision with which the witnesses were able to remember and relate the many ordeals they had lived through. ... Surprisingly, the Gypsy narrators had not spoken a great deal to those close to them, perhaps since the memory of those lost and the past in general is not part of their culture, as it is the case with other peoples.... [T]hey were relating this dramatic event for the first time to a non-Gypsy.[40]

Filhol's respondents did not repress their experiences: they did not communicate them within the Romani community because of the lack of a code by means of which their experience could be conveyed. They could be silent vis-à-vis the non-Romani world for similar reasons: the lack of a code (prior to the development of the Holocaust discourse); the lack of access to the code; the lack of education; or the reluctance of the surrounding world to let Roma use that code.

The Jewish survivors described by Friedländer shared their memories within the survivors community, but they remained by and large voiceless vis-à-vis the external world, for the latter did not want to listen. Only later, having benefited from the already developed Holocaust discourse and an expanded interest in the fate of the victims, Roma could share their memories with researchers (as outsiders), while remaining silent about their suffering within their own communities. This implies that the factor determining whether a particular form of memory is "voiced" or "mute" is not necessarily a mechanism for repressing trauma, and only to a certain degree it is the "culture" of a particular "community of memory" (in a sense that it provides [or does not provide] the current frame of expression). What really matters is the existence (or nonexistence) of a network of interactions via which we can and do communicate about our past.

The situation regarding this network started to change, particularly in Eastern Europe, along with the changes affecting the relations with the non-Roma. New configurations have emerged, owing to (more or less forced) assimilation and the shrinking of the distance between Roma and non-Roma—a consequence of settling the formerly itinerant groups and relocating those already settled into towns and industrial regions. In the process, Roma have been exposed to mass media, education, and popular culture—including the culture of remembrance and commemoration—which have gradually created new forms of memory conducive to Roma conceptualizing their experiences.

Mróz concluded his argument as follows: Roma do and will remember due to greater exposure to non-Romani frames of memory. In other words, Roma will remember, but at the price of being "less Roma" from the viewpoint of traditional culture. They will remember within and thanks to the non-Romani frames, which gradually become open for the Roma and used by them, becoming therefore "less non-Romani," as we might say. Despite the sense of nostalgia in Mróz's thesis, he grasps the most important point, namely, that Roma no longer constitute an isolated island in contemporary society. They do interact with non-Roma, and these interactions involve a great deal of sharing of accessible cultural elements. This means that the Roma way of remembering will cease to be traditional, but it does not mean it will cease to be Romani. Thus, we may interpret the title of Mróz's paper—non-memory that is not forgetfulness—as an affirmation that the lack of expression does not yet mean the lack of memory, and that memory can be voiced and essentialized only as a part of the modernization process. Often expressed within "non-Romani" cultural frameworks, memory will become an element of the new identity-constructs developed by people who nevertheless define themselves as Roma.

Romani Commemoration

The conjecture that Roma do not commemorate their past is a consequence of the older approach to Roma as "people without history and memory" that overlooks the existing forms of commemoration as not "essential" to Romani life. This section describes the Caravan Memorial—a commemorative practice of Roma in Southern Poland—to show certain important features of the relationship between memory and identity among Roma today.

The Caravan Memorial (*Tabor Pamięci*) is organized jointly by the Regional Museum in Tarnów, a town in southern Poland, and the Social-Cultural Association of Roma in Tarnów, an organization representing a segment of Tarnów's Roma community. The Roma who live in Tarnów belong mostly to the Carpathian group, the members of which used to live (and still do live) a sedentary life in the mountains, working mostly as blacksmiths and seasonal construction workers. It is one of the poorest and highly differentiated Romani groups in Poland that lacks the elaborated and institutionalized system of specific values (*Romanipen*) that characterizes other groups of Roma in Poland. Other Roma in Poland tend to look down on this group for having forgone the traditional ways of Romani life. In the 1950s, many of the members of this group moved to urban centers, attracted by the opportunities offered by new industrial projects. For the extremely poor mountain Roma, the possibility of obtaining a permanent job and an apartment in a block of flats meant a radical improvement of their living conditions. The Social-Cultural Association of Roma in Tarnów—perhaps the first of its kind in Poland—performed an important role in integrating newcomers into the local community and securing their status and well-being. More traditional Roma, however, have criticized the organization for collaborating with the Communists, and therefore betraying the Romani way of life.

The Roma who have settled in Tarnów received help from the curator of the Regional Museum, Adam Bartosz. Bartosz is an ethnographer and an expert on Romani culture who set up the first permanent exhibition in Poland on the Romani history and culture. This exhibit is on display at the ethnographic branch of the local museum, serving as a "place of encounter" where Romani culture is presented to non-Romani audiences.

The two institutions—the Social-Cultural Association of Roma and the local museum—are behind the idea of "reconstructing" a Romani "tabor" (caravan). The element of "reconstruction" (or rather "invention") is obvious not only because the idea came from a non-Romani ethnographer, but also because the caravan—an integral element of a nomadic lifestyle—does not belong to the tradition of those who participate in the event, namely, sedentary Roma who settled in the Carpathians four hundred years ago. Nevertheless, for the participants, the caravan may signify the universal Romani values to which they would like to adhere. Some of the Carpathian Roma have developed a growing interest in *Romanipen* and in various institutions of other Romani groups (like *Shero Rom*, the judiciary authority of the Polska Roma group), which they believe may help to strengthen the identity of their own group. Paradoxically, because of their lack of contact with other Roma in Poland, it is the non-Romani ethnographer who has been mediating between the Carpathian Roma and institutions of "traditional Romani culture."

The first Caravan Memorial took place in 1996, and by now it has become a regular occurrence. The Caravan departs from the Ethnographic Museum that houses the Romani exhibition. Prior to the departure, the participants receive a blessing from the Roman-Catholic Chaplain of the Roma in Poland, the non-Romani priest Reverend Stanisław Opocki. Elements of Roman Catholicism, the dominant religion in Poland, are evident on many other occasions during the Caravan ceremony. Apart from the central role that Reverend Opocki plays, local parish priests usually welcome the travelling group wherever it arrives; these clergymen also attend commemorative ceremonies at the sites of mass execution and pray there together with the participants of the Caravan. They also perform the wedding or christening ceremonies that sometimes take place during the Caravan.

The Caravan's first stop is at the Monument of the Victims of Auschwitz in Tarnów, the site from which on 14 June 1940, the first transport of Polish (non-Romani and non-Jewish) prisoners departed for Auschwitz. The Caravan participants light candles, and musicians play a sorrowful tune. Occasionally, there are speeches given by influential Romani participants of the Caravan. The participants then proceed to a memorial plaque commemorating the mass murder of Tarnów's Jewish community. Afterward, the Caravan moves to a cemetery in the Krzyż district of Tarnów where the city's Roma bury their dead. The participants of the Caravan commemorate their deceased just as they would during All Souls and All Saints Days, that is, through prayer, music, and pouring vodka on the graves.

The next stop is Żabno, the site of a mass grave of Roma who were murdered in the summer of 1943. The participants pray at the grave, light candles, lay flowers, and sing mourning songs and the Romani anthem. The Romani flag is displayed at this and other commemorative ceremonies during the Caravan. The local priest, together with Reverend Opocki, leads prayers while the mayor of the town, along with some of the more recognizable participants of the Caravan, make speeches. From Żabno, the Caravan proceeds to its final destination, Szczurowa. In this village, on 3 August 1943, ninety-three Roma (including women, children, and the elderly) were killed by the German police. Szczurowa is thus the largest known site of summary executions of the Roma in the vicinity of Tarnów. Relatives of the murdered have always visited Szczurowa; their visits have unintentionally acquired the form of a ritual, and involve a walk from the site of the former settlement of the Szczurowa Roma to the local cemetery where they were executed and subsequently buried. I contend that, even if the Caravan Memorial does belong to the category of invented tradition, it is nevertheless ingrained in spontaneous family and group rituals.

In Szczurowa, the participants of the Caravan are welcomed by the local parish priest. He takes visitors to the grave of the murdered Roma where, after the prayer, the names of the murdered Roma are read out loud. The atmosphere is solemn and sorrowful. In the presence of local authorities and the inhabitants of Szczurowa, the most important speeches are reserved for this part of the ceremony. When the ceremony is finished, the participants of the Caravan prepare an encampment at the camping site in Dołęga near Szczurowa, where the Caravan stays for the next few days. In the evening, Romani musicians give a concert for the local audience, which usually includes the regional authorities. By means of the concert, the Tarnów Romani community expresses its gratitude to the people of Szczurowa for taking care of the mass grave of the murdered Roma. The next day, the activities shift to the local church where the participants of the Caravan attend a religious service (sometimes accompanied by wedding ceremonies or christenings). These ceremonies are followed by private celebrations held in the encampment. Afterward, the Caravan returns to Tarnów, sometimes visiting other cemeteries where Roma have been buried along the way.

This is a synthetic picture of the Caravan, as it has been functioning in the first two years of its existence.[41] Among the Caravan's participants are usually the Roma of Tarnów and other Carpathian Roma from southern Poland. The organizers are keen on inviting influential members of the Polish Roma community as well as prominent activists from international Romani organizations. The organizers can thereby gain recognition of the Caravan within the two most important frameworks in which contemporary Romani authority operates, "traditional" and "modern." Those persons not only add prestige and legitimacy to the Caravan within various Romani circles, but also perform an important educational role as well as an integrative function. The traditional leaders educate young participants of the Caravan about the Romani tradition and, in a way, integrate them into the bigger, stronger, and more respected groups of Roma living in Poland. This is particularly important in the case of the small, poor, and relatively isolated groups of Carpathian Roma. The modern leaders educate participants about the current Romani politics and thus integrate them into the discourses on modern Romani identity. The presence of these two categories of leaders, discourses, and identities aired during a single event shows that it is possible to synthesize tradition and modernity—the elements of traditional Romani identity and the need for a modern, politicized identity of the Roma as a nation.

Among the non-Romani participants of the Caravan, one can find staff members of Tarnów's Museum, scholars with academic interests in the Romani community, and above all journalists. A number of non-Roma, including local authorities, priests, and occasional spectators, have also taken part in some of the events of the Caravan. The Caravan is actually quite popular among the local population; the concerts in particular are well attended. Alongside the Roma from southern Poland, three other groups of participants in the ritual help to create communication channels for the external frames of reference in which the Caravan of Memory can be placed. Thus, the presence of the influential members of other groups of Polish Roma helps to situate the Caravan within the Romani tradition and to legitimize it within the framework of traditional authority. The members of the international Romani organizations constitute the group of Caravan participants who provide a link to modernity by defining the place of Roma in the contemporary world. Finally, participation of non-Roma in the ceremonies testifies to the legitimate place of Roma within larger Polish society.

There are three major sites laden with symbolism that the participants visit as part of the Caravan Memorial. The most important of these are, of course, the sites of mass executions of the Roma, which have become focal points of the group's memory and by extension, group identity. The visit to Tarnów's cemetery evokes private memories of the participants while the stop at the Auschwitz monument and the memorial plaque to Jewish victims refers to both the Holocaust discourse and the discourse of Polish national suffering. Thus the collective memory of the wartime physical destruction draws upon the resources of individual memories on the one hand, and on the symbolism of the Holocaust on the other. In a way, the presence of these three different sites in one ritualized event, their spatial proximity and symbolic similarity, helps to synthesize the different meanings into a coherent message by means of the external discourses.

The three symbolic frameworks of the Caravan perform a similar, synthesizing function. The symbolism of traditional Romani life has been contained in such elements of the Caravan as camping, meetings with the "elders," getting together inside the extended family, and jointly playing music. Another form of symbolism has been brought to the ritual through the display of the Romani national flag and performance of the Romani anthem during commemorative ceremonies. Lastly, religious symbolism has been introduced at various stages of the ritual with the purpose of presenting Roma as an integral part of a predominantly Catholic society.

Thus, one can speak of three interwoven processes that take place in the course of the Caravan. First, one can speak of an agent of the ritual—a group of Roma from southern Poland that combines the traditional way of Romani life with modern Romani identities and with an openness toward the non-Romani world. Second, the ritual symbolically invests this group with a collective memory that refers to the fate of the Roma during World War II and simultaneously integrates both individual and family memories into the generalized memory and symbolism of the Holocaust. Finally, the ritual provides three different symbolic frameworks for the memory of the group: traditional, national, and religious. These three processes—connected through ritual and transformed into a symbolic message—provide an opportunity to comprehensively integrate the "invented tradition" of the Holocaust victims into collective memory and popular discourses of the Roma, thus making them a cornerstone of their contemporary identity.

Conclusion

The silence surrounding the fate of Roma under Nazi rule is a matter of the past by now, even though it still has not entered social consciousness, as it should. The contributing factors to that silence, however, seem to be on the wane. Thus, I have criticized the conjecture that a peculiar nature of Romani culture prevents Roma from remembering their traumatic experience. Among the factors that accounted for the silence, I argued, has been the particularity of Romani genocide, the way it has been (not) documented, and the way Roma have been perceived by majority population. I have further questioned the "trauma repression" approach, pointing out that it is rather the existence (or nonexistence) of the social structure of interactions in which Roma may (or may not) communicate their suffering. In my interpretation, Roma are not "mute," but they may be "muted" by the societies within which they exist.

Traditional Romani culture has undergone a process of transformation: Roma are better educated and organized today than ever before; there is a growing awareness among Roma that the struggle to improve their lives will take place mainly on non-Romani territory and by using methods particular to the non-Romani world. As a consequence, we are witnessing the process of political organization of Roma. An important part of that process is the construction of a new collective identity that would transcend the existing divisions between Romani groups and incorporate the concept of a "community of fate" characterized by a distinctive vision of Romani history. Roma are increasingly more interested in their past, and acts of commemoration help to "evoke a future imaginable throughout the past."[42] Ian Hancock's efforts to include Roma in the Holocaust commemoration, ceremonies by German Sinti commemorating deportations to concentration camps, annual commemorations by groups of Polish Sinti and Roma marking the dissolution of the *Zigeunerlager* at Birkenau, the new tradition of commemorating the "resistance action" at Birkenau, visits to Auschwitz-Birkenau organized by Romani activists from Eastern Europe, and also the Caravan Memorial described above—these and similar symbolic acts show that commemoration is not at all alien to Roma.

Jointly organized by Romani and non-Romani organizations, these acts of commemoration refer to many different discourses, symbols, and forms of expression. This strengthens the notion of "implicit memory," namely, that the relations between Roma and non-Roma are crucial factors for construction of Romani collective memory and identity. I have argued that: (1) Romani memories are not always "implicit" and "embedded," but rather explicit and reflexive, reenacted through commemorative ceremonies; (2) Romani memory and identity are constructed in the course of a complex relationship between different Romani groups on the one hand, and between Roma and non-Roma on the other; (3) it is the status of the relationship between Roma and non-Roma that forms Romani attitudes toward the past (rather than having past events derived from this relationship); (4) in order to comprehend Romani identities one must combine the traditional substantive and relational perspectives and temporal or historical perspective, which views the Romani past as reconstructed in accordance with the contemporary needs of Romani politics, and creates a framework within which particular Romani groups can conceptualize their existence.

If I am right with my conclusions, then the Roma are not significantly different from other groups when it comes to identity. Contemporary identities, as James Clifford has observed, no longer presuppose the continuity of culture and traditions.[43] Groups inevitably construct their identities out of fragments—the reassembled images of the past circulated in the media, in symbols and languages that are originally not "theirs." I argue that, in the light of the presented criticism, this description aptly presents the way contemporary Roma conceptualize the relation between memory and identity today.

Notes

1. This figure is a rough estimate.
2. This approach can be illustrated by Stewart's remark concerning the identity of Roma, which is neither the "myth of shared ancestry" nor the "dream of future reunion," but "a place of their own ... in which they could feel at home ... a social space composed according to their own ethic of relatedness." [Michael Stewart, *The Time of the Gypsies* (Boulder, CO, 1997), 28.] Stewart's conception of Romani identity is, however, different from that of the "people without history."
3. Fredrik Barth, "Introduction," in *Ethnic Groups and Boundaries: The Social Organization of Cultural Difference*, ed. F. Barth (Boston, 1969).
4. David Lowenthal, *The Past is a Foreign Country* (Cambridge, 1985).
5. Anthony Giddens, "Living in a Post-Traditional Society," in *Reflexive Modernization: Politics, Tradition and Aesthetics in the Modern Social Order*, ed. U. Beck et al. (Stanford, CA, 1994), 80.
6. Michel Bassand, *Identité et développment régional* (Bern, 1991), 13.
7. Niklas Luhmann, *Observations on Modernity* (Stanford, CA, 1998), 3.
8. Wim Willems, *In Search of the True Gypsy: From Enlightenment to Final Solution* (London, 1997), 6–7.
9. This typology may be correlated with internal stratification of a group in terms of gender, age, education, income, etc. The image of homogeneous, cohesive entities cultivated in research might have been true in the past but does not necessarily correspond to the current situation of many Roma groups.
10. Heidrun Friese, "Introduction," in *Identities: Time, Difference, and Boundaries*, ed. H. Friese (New York and Oxford, 2002), 5.
11. Jan Yoors, *The Gypsies* (New York, 1967), 7–8.
12. Jan Yoors, *Crossing* (Prospect Heights, IL, 1988 [1971]), 38.
13. Katie Trumpener, "The Time of the Gypsies: A 'People Without History' in the Narratives of the West," *Critical Inquiry* 18, no. 4 (Summer 1992): 843–84; Eric R. Wolf, *Europe and the People Without History* (Berkeley, CA, 1982).
14. Here I am falling back on the criticism of my earlier work by Alaina Lemon [Alaina Lemon, *Between Two Fires: Gypsy Performance and Romani Memory from Pushkin to Postsocialism* (Durham, NC, 2000), 167.] See also Slawomir Kapralski, "Identity Building and the Holocaust: The Roma Political Nationalism," *Nationalities Papers* 25, no. 2 (1997): 269–83.

15. Michael Stewart, "How Does Genocide Happen?" in *Questions of Anthropology*, ed. R. Astuti et al. (Oxford, 2007).
16. Michael Zimmermann, "Die nationalsozialistische Zigeurnerverfolgung in Ost- und Südosteuropa. Ein Überblick," in *Der nationalsozialistische Genozid an den Roma Osteuropas. Geschichte und künstlerische Verarbeitung*, ed. F. Fischer von Weikersthal et al. (Cologne, 2008).
17. Peter Novick, *The Holocaust and Collective Memory: The American Experience* (London, 2001), 1–2.
18. Alan S. Rosenbaum, "Introduction to the First Edition," in *Is the Holocaust Unique? Perspectives on Contemporary Genocide*, ed. A. S. Rosenbaum (Boulder, CO, 2001), 3.
19. Novick, *The Holocaust and Collective Memory*, 20.
20. Robert S. Wistrich, "Antisemitismus in 20. Jahrhundert. Ein Überblick," in *Antisemitismus in Osteuropa. Aspekte einer historischen Kontinuität*, ed. P. Bettelheim et al. (Vienna, 1992), 21.
21. Ian Hancock, "Uniqueness, Gypsies and Jews," in *Remembering for the Future. Working Papers and Addenda*, vol. 2, *The Impact of the Holocaust on the Contemporary World*, ed. Y. Bauer et al. (Oxford, 1989); Ian Hancock, "Gypsy History in Germany and Neighboring Lands: A Chronology Leading to the Holocaust and Beyond," in *The Gypsies of Eastern Europe*, ed. D. Crowe and J. Kolsti (Armonk, NY, 1991); Ian Hancock, "Responses to Porrajmos: The Romani Holocaust," in Rosenbaum, ed., *Is the Holocaust Unique?*
22. Andrzej Mirga and Nicolae Gheorghe, *The Roma in the Twenty-First Century: A Policy Paper* (Princeton, 1997).
23. Ian Hancock, *We Are the Romani People. Ame sam e Rromane dzene* (Hatfield, 2002); Lev Tcherenkov and Stéphane Laederich, *The Roma*, vol. 1, *History, Language, and Groups* (Basel, 2004).
24. Zygmunt Bauman, *Mortality, Immortality and Other Life Strategies* (Cambridge, 1992).
25. Johannes Fabian, *Time and the Other: How Anthropology Makes its Object* (New York, 2002).
26. Wolf, *Europe and the People Without History*.
27. Edwin Ardener, "Belief and the Problem of Women," in *Perceiving Women*, ed. Shirley Ardener (London, 1975).
28. Michael Stewart, "Remembering Without Commemoration: The Mnemonics and Politics of Holocaust Memories Among European Roma," *Journal of Royal Anthropological Institute* 10, no. 3 (2004): 561.
29. Ibid., 563.
30. Ibid., 565.
31. Ibid., 575.
32. Ibid., 575–76.
33. Ibid., 572.
34. Isabel Fonseca, *Bury Me Standing: The Gypsies and Their Journey* (London, 1995).
35. Stewart, "Remembering Without Commemoration," 573.
36. Ibid., 568.
37. Mróz's article that I review here appeared earlier than Stewart's text.
38. Lech Mróz, "Niepamięć nie jest zapominaniem. Cyganie-Romowie a Holokaust," *Przegląd Socjologiczny* 49, no. 2 (2000): 108.
39. Saul Friedländer, "Trauma, Memory and Transference," in *Holocaust Remembrance: The Shapes of Memory*, ed. G. H. Hartman (Oxford, 1994), 259.
40. Emmanuel Filhol, "The Internment of Gypsies in France (1940–1946): A Hidden Memory," in *Ethnic Identities in Dynamic Perspective. Proceedings of the 2002 An-*

nual Meeting of the Gypsy Lore Society, ed. S. Salo and C. Prónai (Budapest, 2003), 13.
41. In the last few years, the Caravan's main camping site was at Bielcza, a village in the vicinity of which Germans carried out mass executions of Roma. Noteworthy is the growing participation of Romani children, brought by buses from their settlements in the Carpathians, for whom the Caravan is meant as a lesson in the history of their people.
42. David McCrone, *The Sociology of Nationalism: Tomorrow's Ancestor.* (London, 1998), 52.
43. James Clifford, *The Predicament of Culture: Twentieth-Century Ethnography, Literature, and Art* (Cambridge, MA, 1996).

SELECTED BIBLIOGRAPHY

Achim, Viorel. *The Roma in Romanian History.* Budapest, 1998.
———. "The Romanian Population Exchange Project Elaborated by Sabin Manuilă in October 1941." *Annali dell'Instituto storico italo-germanico in Trento* 27 (2001): 609–17.
———. "Deportarea țiganilor în Transnistria." *Anuarulromân de istorie recentă* 1 (2002): 127–41.
———. "Atitudinea contemporanilor fața de deportarea țiganilor în Transnistria," in *România și Transnistria: problema Holocaustului: Perspective istorice și comparative,* ed. V. Avhim and C. Iordachi, 201–36. Bucharest, 2004.
———. ed. *Documente privind deportarea țiganilor în Transnistria,* 2 vols. Bucharest, 2004.
Acković, Dragoljub. "Suffering of Romas in Yugoslavia in the Second World War." *Gießener Hefte für Tsiganologie* 3, no. 1–4 (1986): 128–34.
Ancel, Jean. "The German-Romanian Relationship and the Final Solution." *Holocaust and Genocide Studies* 19, no. 2 (Fall 2005): 252–75.
Angrick, Andrej. *Besatzungspolitik und Massenmord. Die Einsatzgruppe D in der südlichen Sowjetunion 1941–1943.* Hamburg, 2003.
Arad, Yitzhak, et al., eds. *The Einsatzgruppen Reports: Selections from the Dispatches of the Nazi Death Squads' Campaigns Against the Jews.* New York, 1989.
Arnold, Hermann. *Die NS-Zigeunerverfolgung: Ihre Ausdeutung und Ausbeutung. Fakten, Mythos, Agitation, Kommerz.* Aschaffenburg, 1989.
Balić, Emily. "A City Apart: Sarajevo in the Second World War." PhD diss., Stanford University, 2008.
Balta, Sebastian. *Rumänien und die Großmächte in der Ära Antonescu, 1940–1944.* Stuttgart, 2005.
Baranowski, Julian. *Zigeunerlager in Litzmannstadt 1941–1942/The Gypsy Camp in Łódź/ Obóz cyganski w Łodzi.* Łódź, 2003.
Benz, Wolfgang et al., eds. *Einsatz im "Reichskommissariat Ostland". Dokumente zum Völkermord im Baltikum und Weissrussland 1941–1944.* Berlin, 1998.
Bessonov, Nikolai. "Genotsid tsigan Ukrainy v gody Velikoi Otechestvennoi voiny," in *Roma v Ukraini. Istorychnyi ta etnokul'turnyi rozvytok tsigan (Roma) Ukrainy (XVI–XX st.),* ed. M[?] Shvetsov, 4–28. Sevastopol, 2006.

———. "Ob ispol'zovanii terminov 'Porajmos' and 'Holocaust' v znachenii 'genotsid tsygan'." *Golokost i suchasnist: studii v Ukraini i sviti* 2, no.1 (2007): 71–82.
———. "Tsigane SSSR v okkupatsii. Strategii vyzhivaniia." *Golokost i suchastnist: studii v Ukraini i sviti* 6, no. 2 (2009): 17–52.
Birn, Ruth Bettina. *Die Sicherheitspolizei in Estland 1941–1944. Eine Studie zur Kollaboration im Osten.* Paderborn, 2006.
Blumer, Nadine, "From Victim Hierarchies to Memorial Networks: Berlin's Holocaust Memorial to Sinti and Roma Victims of National Socialism." PhD diss., University of Toronto, 2011.
Bock, Gisela. *Zwangssterilization im Nationalsozialismus. Studien zur Rassenpolitik und Frauenpolitik.* Opladen, 1986.
Browning, Christopher. *The Origins of the Final Solution: The Evolution of Nazi Jewish Policy, September 1939–March 1942.* Lincoln, NE, 2004.
Bucur, Maria. *Eugenics and Modernization in Inter-War Romania.* Pittsburgh, 2002.
Burleigh, Michael, and Wolfgang Wippermann. *The Racial State: Germany, 1933–1945.* New York, 1991.
Carrier, Peter. *Holocaust Monuments and National Memory Cultures in France and Germany Since 1989: The Origins and Political Function of the Vél' d'Hiv' in Paris and the Holocaust Monument in Berlin.* New York, 2005.
Center for Advanced Holocaust Studies, ed. *Roma and Sinti: Under-Studied Victims of Nazism.* Washington, DC, 2002.
Cracă, Marcel Dumitru, ed. *Procesul lui Antonescu.* Bucharest, 1995.
Crowe, David, and John Kolsti, ed. *Gypsies in Eastern Europe.* Armonk, NY, 1991.
Curilla, Wolfgang. *Die deutsche Ordnungspolizei und der Holocaust im Baltikum und in Weissrussland ss1941–1944.* Paderborn, 2006.
Czech, Danuta. *Kalendarium der Ereignisse im Konzentrationslager Auschwitz-Birkenau 1939–1945.* Reinbek bei Hamburg, 1989.
Dallin, Alexander. *Deutsche Herrschaft in Rußland 1941–1945. Eine Studie über Besatzungspolitik.* Düsseldorf, 1981.
Dean, Martin. *Collaboration in the Holocaust: Crimes of the Local Police in Belorussia and Ukraine, 1941–44.* New York, 2000.
Dekel, Irit. "Ways of Looking: Observation and Transformation at the Holocaust Memorial, Berlin." *Memory Studies* 2, no. 1 (2009): 71–86.
Delclitte, Christophe. "La catégorie juridique 'nomade' dans la loi de 1912." *Hommes & Migrations* 1188–89 (June–July 1995): 23–30.
Deletant, Dennis. *Hitler's Forgotten Ally: Ion Antonescu and His Regime, Romania 1940–44.* New York, 2006.
Diukov, Alexander. *Vtorostepennyi vrag. OUN, UPA i reshenie "Evreiskogo voprosa."* Moscow, 2008.
———, ed. *Voina na unichtozhenie. Natsistskaia politika genotsida na territorii Vostochnoi Evropy: Materialy mezhdunarodnoi nauchnoi konferentsii, Moskva, 26–28 aprelia 2010 goda.* Moscow, 2010.
Dulić, Tomislav. *Utopias of Nation: Local Killing in Bosnia and Herzegovina, 1941–42.* Uppsala, 2005.
———. "Mass Killing in the Independent State of Croatia, 1941–1945: A Case for Comparative Research." *Journal of Genocide Research* 8, no. 3 (September 2006): 255–81.
Đurić, Rajko. "Il calvario dei Roma nel campo di concentramente di Jasenovac." *Lacio Drom* 4 (1992): 14–42.
———. *Ohne Heim—Ohne Grab. Die Geschichte der Roma und Sinti.* Berlin, 1996.
Earl, Hilary. *The Nuremberg SS-Einsatzgruppen Trial, 1945–1958: Atrocity, Law, and History.* Cambridge, 2009.
Ezergailis, Andrew. *The Holocaust in Latvia, 1941–1944: The Missing Centre.* Riga, 1996.

Feferman, Kiril. "Soviet Investigation of Nazi Crimes in the USSR: Documenting the Holocaust." *Journal of Genocide Research* 5, no. 4 (2003): 587–602.
Ficowski, Jerzy et al. *Wieviel Trauer und Wege. Zigeuner in Polen.* Frankfurt, 1992.
Filhol, Emmanuel. "The Internment of Gypsies in France (1940–1946): A Hidden Memory." *Ethnic Identities in Dynamic Perspective. Proceedings of the 2002 Annual Meeting of the Gypsy Lore Society,* ed. S. Salo and C. Prónai, 11–17. Budapest, 2003.
———. "Le sort des Tsiganes dans le Limousin pendant la Second Guerre mondiale." *Revue des sciences, des lettres et des arts de la Corrèze* 108 (2006): 67–90.
———. *Un camp de concentration français: Les Tsiganes alsaciens-lorrains à Crest 1915-1919.* Grenoble, 2004.
Filhol, Emmanuel, and Marie-Christine Hubert. *Les Tsiganes en France: un sort à part (1939–1946).* Paris, 2009.
Fings, Carola et al., eds. *"...Einziges Land, in dem Judenfrage und Zigeunerfrage gelöst." Die Verfolgung der Roma im faschistisch besetzten Jugoslawien 1941–1945.* Cologne, 1992.
Fischer von Weikerstahl, Felicitas et al., eds. *Der nationalsozialistische Genozid an den Roma Osteuropas. Geschichte und künstlerische Verarbeitung.* Cologne, 2008.
Fogg, L. Shannon. "'They Are Undesirables': Local and National Responses to Gypsies during World War II." *French Historical Studies* 31, no. 2 (Spring 2008): 327–58.
———. *The Politics of Everyday Life in Vichy France: Foreigners, Undesirables, and Strangers.* Cambridge, 2009.
Fonseca, Isabel. *Bury Me Standing: The Gypsies and Their Journey.* New York, 1996. London, 1995.
Freund, Florian. "Der polizeilich—administrative Zigeunerbegriff. Ein Beitrag zur Klärung des Begriffes 'Zigeuner'." *Zeitgeschichte* 30, no. 2 (March–April 2003): 76–90.
———. *Oberösterreich und die Zigeuner. Politik gegen eine Minderheit im 19. und 20. Jahrhundert.* Linz, 2010.
Freund, Florian et al. *Vermögensentzug, Restitution und Entschädigung der Roma und Sinti, Veröffentlichungen der Österreichischen Historikerkommission.* Vienna, 2004.
Gerlach, Christian. *Kalkulierte Morde. Die deutsche Wirtschafts- und Vernichtungspolitik in Weissrussland 1941 bis 1944.* Hamburg, 1999.
Gesellschaft für Bedrohte Völker, ed. *Sinti und Roma im ehemaligen KZ Bergen-Belsen am 27. Oktober 1979.* Göttingen and Vienna, 1981.
Gilsenbach, Reimar. *Oh Django, sing deinen Zorn: Sinti und Roma unter den Deutschen.* Berlin, 1993.
Goldstein, Ivo, and Slavko Goldstein. *Holokaust u Zagrebu.* Zagreb, 2001.
Haberer, Eric. "The German Police and the Genocide in Belorussia, 1941–1944. The 'Second Sweep': Gendarmerie Killings of Jews and Gypsies on January 29, 1942." *Journal of Genocide Research* 3, no. 2 (2001): 207–18.
Hancock, Ian. *The Pariah Syndrome: An Account of Gypsy Slavery and Persecution.* Ann Arbor, MI, 1987.
———. "Uniqueness of the Victims: Gypsies, Jews, and the Holocaust." *Without Prejudice: International Review of Racial Discrimination* 1, no. 2 (1988): 42–67.
———. "Responses to Porrajmos: The Romani Holocaust," in *Is the Holocaust Unique? Perspectives on Comparative Genocide,* ed. A. S. Rosenbaum, 39–64. Boulder, CO, 1998.
Hanschkow, Juliane. "Etikettierung, Kriminalisierung und Verfolgung von 'Zigeunern' in der südlichen Rheinprovinz zur Zeit des Kaiserreiches und der Weimarer Republik 1906 bis 1933," in *Zigeuner und Nation. Repräsentation—Inklusion—Exklusion,* ed. Herbert Uerlings and Julia-Karin Patrut, 249–71. Frankfurt, 2008.
Hantarrède, Guy. "Les Tsiganes au camp des Alliers (novembre 1940–mars 1946)." *Etudes Tsiganes* 13, no. 1 (1999): 120–31.

Headland, Ronald. *Messages of Murder: A Study of the Reports of the Einsatzgruppen of the Security Police and the Security Service, 1941–1943.* London, 1992.
Heinschink, Mozes, and Ursula Hemetek, eds. *Roma. Das unbekannte Volk. Schicksal und Kultur.* Vienna, 1994.
Hill, Alexander. *The War Behind the Eastern Front: Soviet Partisan Movement in North-West Russia.* London, 2005.
Hoare, Marko. *Genocide and Resistance in Hitler's Bosnia: The Partisans and the Chetniks, 1941–1943.* Oxford, 2006.
Hohmann, Joachim. *Zigeuner und Zigeunerwissenschaft. Ein Beitrag zur Grundlagenforschung und Dokumentation des Völkermords im "Dritten Reich."* Marburg, 1980.
———. *Geschichte der Zigeunerverfolgung in Deutschland.* Frankfurt, 1988.
———. *Robert Ritter und die Erben der Kriminologie. "Zigeunerforschung" im Nationalsozialismus und in Westdeutschland im Zeichen des Rassismus,* Studien zur Tsiganologie und Folkloristik 4. Frankfurt, 1991.
Holler, Martin. *Der nationalsozialistische Völkermord an den Roma in der besetzten Sowjetunion (1941–1944).* Heidelberg, 2009.
———. "'Like Jews?' The Nazi Persecution and Extermination of Soviet Roma Under the German Military Administration: A New Interpretation, Based on Soviet Sources." *Dapim: Studies on the Shoah* 24 (2010): 137–76.
Hürter, Johannes. "Die Wehrmacht vor Leningrad. Krieg und Besatzungspolitik der 18. Armee im Herbst und Winter 1941/42." *Vierteljahreshefte für Zeitgeschichte* 49, no. 3 (July 2001): 377–440.
International Commission on the Holocaust in Romania. *Final Report.* Iași, 2005.
Ioanid, Radu, *The Holocaust in Romania: The Destruction of Jews and Gypsies Under the Antonescu Regime, 1940–1944.* Chicago, 2000.
Ionescu, Vasile. *Deportarea rromilor în Transnistria: de la Auschwitz la Bug.* Bucharest, 2000.
Jelinek, A. Yeshayanu. "Bosnia-Herzegovina at War: Relations Between Moslems and Non-Moslems." *Holocaust and Genocide Studies* 5, no. 3 (Winter 1990): 275–92.
Jevtic, Elizabeta. "Blank Pages of the Holocaust: Gypsies in Yugoslavia during World War II." MA diss., Brigham Young University, 2004.
Kalinin, Valdemar. *Zagadka baltiiskikh tsygan. Ocherki istorii, kul'tury i sotsial'nogo razvitiia baltiiskikh tsygan.* Minsk, 2005.
Kapralski, Sławomir. "Identity Building and the Holocaust: Roma Political Nationalism." *Nationalities Papers* 25, no. 2 (1997): 269–83.
Karsai, László. "Zentrale Aspekte des Völkermordes an den ungarischen Roma." *Ungarn und der Holocaust: Kollaboration, Rettung und Trauma,* ed. B. Mihok, 103–14. Berlin, 2005.
Kay, Alex. *Exploitation, Resettlement, Mass Murder: Political and Economic Planning for German Occupation Policy in the Soviet Union, 1940–1941.* New York, 2006.
Kenrick, Donald, and Grattan Puxon. *The Destiny of Europe's Gypsies.* New York, 1972.
———. *Gypsies Under the Swastika.* Hatfield, UK, 1995 / *Tsygane pod svastikoi.* Moscow, 2001.
———, eds. *The Gypsies During the Second World War: The Final Chapter.* Hertfordshire, 2007.
Kilian, Jürgen. "Das Zusammenwirken deutscher Polizeiformationen im 'Osteinsatz' am Beispiel des rückwärtigen Gebietes der Heeresgruppe Nord," in *Die Polizei im NS-Staat. Beiträge eines internationalen Symposiums an der Deutschen Hochschule der Polizei in Münster,* ed. Wolfgang Schulte, 305–35. Frankfurt, 2009.
Klein, Peter, ed. *Die Einsatzgruppen in der besetzten Sowjetunion 1941/42. Die Tätigkeits- und Lageberichte des Chefs der Sicherheitspolizei und des SD.* Berlin, 1997.

Knesebeck, Julia von dem, *The Roma Struggle for Compensation in Post-War Germany.* Hatfield, 2011.

Knischewski, Gerd, and Ula Spittler. "Remembering in the Berlin Republic: The Debate About the Central Holocaust Memorial in Berlin," *Debatte: Journal of Contemporary Central and E. Europe* 13, no. 1 (2005): 25–42.

Korb, Alexander. "La Construction nationale et Shoah: Les déportations dans l'État indépendant Croatie (1941–1945)." *Qu'est-ce qu'un déporté? Histoire et mémoires des déportations de la Seconde Guerre Mondiale,* ed. T. Bruttmann et al., 197–224. Paris, 2009.

———. "A Multipronged Attack: Ustaša Persecution of Serbs, Jews, and Roma in Wartime Croatia, 1941–45." *Eradicating Differences: The Treatment of Minorities in Nazi-Dominated Europe,* ed. A. Weiss-Wendt, 145–63. Newcastle, 2010.

———. *Im Schatten des Weltkriegs. Massengewalt der Ustaša gegen Serben, Juden und Roma in Kroatien, 1941–45.* Hamburg, 2012.

Kovalev, Boris. *Natsistskaia okkupatsiia i kollaboratsionizm v Rossii 1941–1944.* Moscow, 2004.

Krausnick, Helmut. *Hitlers Einsatzgruppen. Die Truppe des Weltanschauungskrieges 1938–1942.* Frankfurt, 1985.

Kruglov, Alexander. "Genotsid tsigan v Ukraine v 1941–1944 gg. Statistiko-regional'nyi aspect." *Golokost i suchastnist: studii v Ukraini i sviti* 6, no. 2 (2009): 83–113.

———, ed. *Bez zhalosti i somneniia. Dokumenty o prestupleniiakh operativnykh grupp i komand politsii bezopasnosti i SD na vremenno okkupirovannoi territorii SSSR v 1941–1944 gg.* Dnepropetrovsk, 2009.

Leggewie, Claus, and Erik Meyer, *"Ein Ort, an den man gerne geht." Das Holocaust-Mahnmal und die deutsche Geschichtspolitik nach 1989.* Berlin, 2005.

Lemon, Alaina. *Between Two Fires: Gypsy Performance and Romani Memory from Pushkin to Postsocialism.* Durham, NC, 2000.

Lengel-Krizman, Narcisa. "Prilog proučavanja terora tzv. NDH: Sudbina Roma 1941–1945." *Časopis za Suvremenu Povijest* 18, no. 1 (1986): 29–42.

———. *Genocid nad Romima. Jasenovac 1942.* Zagreb, 2003.

———. "Genocide Carried Out on the Roma: Jasenovac 1942." *Jasenovac Memorial Site: Catalogue,* ed. Jasenovac Memorial Area Public Institution, 154–81. Zagreb, 2006.

Lewy, Guenter. "Gypsies and Jews Under the Nazis." *Holocaust and Genocide Studies* 13, no. 3 (Winter 1999): 383–404.

———. *The Nazi Persecution of the Gypsies.* Oxford, 2000.

Lípa, Jiri. "The Fate of the Gypsies in Czechoslovakia under Nazi Domination." In *A Mosaic of Victims: Non-Jews Persecuted and Murdered by the Nazis,* ed., M. Berenbaum, 207–15. New York, 1990.

Lucassen, Leo. *Zigeuner. Die Geschichte eines polizeilichen Ordnungsbegriffes in Deutschland 1700–1945.* Cologne, 1996.

Luchterhandt, Martin. *Der Weg nach Birkenau. Entstehung und Verlauf der nationalsozialistischen Verfolgung der 'Zigeuner.'* Lübeck, 2000.

Margalit, Gilad. "Die deutsche Zigeunerpolitik nach 1945." *Vierteljahrshefte für Zeitgeschichte* 45, no. 4 (1997): 557–88.

———. "The Representation of the Nazi Persecution of the Gypsies in German Discourse after 1945." *German History* 17, no. 2 (1999): 221–40.

———. "The Uniqueness of the Nazi Persecution of the Gypsies." *Romani Studies* 10, no. 2 (2000): 185–210.

———. *Germany and Its Gypsies: A Post-Auschwitz Ordeal.* Madison, WI, 2002.

Marushiakova, Elena, and Veselin Popov. "Kholokost i tsygane. Konstruirovanie novoi natsional'noi mifologii." *Golokost i suchstnist: studii v Ukraini i sviti* 4, no. 2 (2008): 29–42.

Milton, Sybil. "The Context of the Holocaust." *German Studies Review* 13, no. 2 (1990): 269–83.

———. "Gypsies and the Holocaust." *The History Teacher* 24, no. 4 (1991): 375–87.

———. "Nazi Policies Toward Roma and Sinti." *Journal of the Gypsy Lore Society* 2, no. 1 (1992): 1–18.

Mirga, Andrzej, and Nicolae Gheorghe. *The Roma in the Twenty-First Century: A Policy Paper.* Princeton, NJ, 1997.

Mróz, Lech. "Niepamięć nie jest zapominaniem. Cyganie-Romowie a Holokaust." *Przegląd Socjologiczny* 49, no. 2 (2000): 89–114.

Müller-Hill, Benno. *Tödliche Wissenschaft. Die Aussonderung von Juden, Zigeunern und Geisteskranken 1933–1945.* Hamburg, 1984.

Museum of Auschwitz-Birkenau, ed. *Memorial Book: The Gypsies of Auschwitz-Birkenau*, 4 vols. Munich, 1993.

Nastasă, Lucian, and Andrea Varga, eds. *Minorități etnoculturale. Mărturii documentare: Țiganii din România (1919–1944).* Cluj-Napoca, 2001.

Navrotska, Evheniya. "Antiromska politika v Zakarpatti u roky Drugoi Svitovoi viyny. Zibrannia svidchen' ta zberezhennia istorychnoi pamiati." *Golokost i suchastnist: studii v Ukraini i sviti* 6, no. 2 (2009): 124–40.

Pernot, Mathieu, ed. *Un Camp pour les Bohémiens: Mémoires du camp d'internement pour nomades de Saliers.* Arles, 2001.

Peschanski, Denis. *Les Tsiganes en France 1939–1946.* Paris, 1994.

Pohl, Dieter. *Die Herrschaft der Wehrmacht. Deutsche Militärbesatzung und einheimische Bevölkerung in der Sowjetunion 1941–1944.* Munich, 2008.

Reinhartz, Dennis. "Unmarked Graves: The Destruction of the Yugoslav Roma in the Balkan Holocaust, 1941–1945." *Journal of Genocide Research* 1, no. 1 (1999): 81–89.

Rose, Roman, ed. *Der nationalsozialistische Völkermord an den Sinti und Roma.* Heidelberg, 1995.

———, ed. *"Den Rauch hatten wir täglich vor Augen." Der nationalsozialistische Völkermord an den Sinti und Roma.* Heidelberg, 1999.

Şandru, Dumitru. "Deportatrea țiganilor în Transnistria." *Arhivele totalitarsimului. Revista Institutului Național pentru Studiul Totalitarismului* 17 (1997): 23–30.

Sigot, Jacques. "La longue marche vers l'internment des Tsiganes en France pendant la seconde guerre mondiale." *Etudes tsiganes* 13, no. 1 (1999): 19–28.

Solonari, Vladimir. "An Important New Document on Romanian Policy of Ethnic Cleansing During World War II." *Holocaust and Genocide Studies* 20, no. 2 (fall 2007): 268–97.

———. "Patterns of Violence: The Local Population and the Mass Murder of Jews in Bessarabia and Northern Bukovina, July–August 1941." *Kritika: Explorations in Russian and Eurasian History* 8, no. 4 (2007): 749–87.

———. *Purifying the Nation: Population Exchange and Ethnic Cleansing in Nazi-Allied Romania.* Washington, DC, 2010.

Sorokina, Marina. "People and Procedures: Toward a History of the Investigation of Nazi Crimes in the USSR." *Kritika: Explorations in Russian and Eurasian History* 6, no. 4 (2005): 797–831.

Stauber, Roni, and Raphael Vago, ed. *The Roma: A Minority in Europe. Historical, Political and Social Perspectives.* Budapest, 2007.

Steinberg, Jonathan. *All or Nothing: The Axis and the Holocaust, 1941–1943.* London, 1990.

Stewart, Michael. *The Time of the Gypsies.* Boulder, CO, 1997.

———. "Remembering Without Commemoration: The Mnemonics and Politics of Holocaust Memories Among European Roma." *Journal of the Royal Anthropological Institute* 10, no. 3 (2004): 561–82.

Thorne, B. Benjamin. "Assimilation, Invisibility, and the Eugenic Turn in the 'Gypsy Question' in Romanian Society, 1938–1942." *Romani Studies* 21, no. 2 (December 2011): 177–205.
Thurner, Erika. *Nationalsozialismus und Zigeuner in Österreich.* Vienna, 1983.
Toleikis, Vytautas. "Lithuanian Roma During the Years of the Nazi Persecution," in *Murders of Prisoners of War and of Civilian Population in Lithuania, 1941–1944,* ed. Christoph Dieckmann et al., 267–85. Vilnius, 2005.
Trials of War Criminals Before the Nuernberg Military Tribunals, vols. 1–42. Washington, DC, 1949–1953.
Trubeta, Sevasti. "'Gypsiness,' Racial Discourse and Persecution: Balkan Roma during the Second World War." *Nationalities Papers* 31, no. 4 (2003): 495–514.
Trumpener, Katie. "The Time of the Gypsies: A 'People Without History' in the Narratives of the West." *Critical Inquiry* 18 (Summer 1992) : 843–84.
Turda, Marius. "The Nation as Object: Race, Blood, and Biopolitics in Interwar Romania." *Slavic Review* 66, no. 3 (2007): 413–42.
———. "'To End the Degeneration of a Nation': Debates on Eugenic Sterilization in Interwar Romania." *Medical History* 53, no. 1 (2009): 77–104.
Tyaglyy, Mikhail. "Tsygane," in *Kholokost na territorii SSSR. Entsiklopediia,* 1047–56. Moscow, 2009.
———. "Were the "Chingene" Victims of the Holocaust? The Nazi Policy toward the Crimean Roma." *Holocaust and Genocide Studies* 23, no. 1 (Spring 2009): 26–53.
———. "'Nakazuiu … pereslaty … spysky tsiganiv': Zbir organamy vlady Raikhskomisariatu Ukraina vidomostei pro romiv u lypni 1942 r." *Golokost i suchstnist: studii v Ukraini i sviti* 9, no. 1 (2011): 85–101.
Vojak, Danijel. "Romi u popisima stanovništva iz 1921. i 1931. na području Hrvatske." *Migracijske i etničke teme* 20, no. 4 (2004): 447–76.
Wagner, Patrick. *Hitlers Kriminalisten. Die Deutsche Kriminalpolizei und der Nationalsozialismus.* Munich, 2002.
Weiss-Wendt, Anton. "Extermination of the Gypsies in Estonia During World War II: Popular Images and Official Policies." *Holocaust and Genocide Studies* 17, no. 1 (Spring 2003): 31–61.
———. *Murder without Hatred: Estonians and the Holocaust.* Syracuse, NY, 2009.
———. "Vinishchennia tsiganskogo narodu u krainakh Baltii (1941–1944): tsentral'ni rishennia i mistsevi initsiativi." *Golokost i suchasnist: studii v Ukraini i sviti* 6, no. 2 (2009): 53–61.
Wilhelm, Hans Heinrich. *Die Einsatzgruppe A der Sicherheitspolizei und des SD 1941/42.* Frankfurt, 1996.
Willems, Wim. *In Search of the True Gypsy: From Enlightenment to Final Solution.* London, 1997.
Wippermann, Wolfgang. "Nur eine Fussnote? Die Verfolgung der sowjetischen Roma. Historiographie, Motive, Verlauf," in *Gegen das Vergessen. Der Vernichtungskrieg gegen die Sowjetunion,* ed. Klaus Meyer and Wolfgang Wippermann, 75–90. Frankfurt, 1992.
———. *Wie die Zigeuner. Antisemitismus und Antitsiganismus im Vergleich.* Berlin, 1997.
———. *Geschichte der Sinti und Roma in Deutschland. Darstellung und Dokumente.* Berlin, 2000.
———. *"Auserwählte Opfer?" Shoah und Porrajmos im Vergleich. Eine Kontroverse.* Berlin, 2005.
Wolf, R. Eric. *Europe and the People Without History.* Berkeley, CA, 1982.
Woodcock, Shannon. "The Țigan Is Not a Man": The Țigan Other as a Catalyst for Romanian National Identity." PhD diss., University of Sidney, 2005.

———. "Romanian Romani Resistance to Genocide in the Matrix of the Țigan Other." *Anthropology of East Europe Review* 25, no. 2 (2007): 28–43.

Woolford, Andrew, and Stefan Wolejszo. "Collecting on Moral Debts: Reparations for the Holocaust and Porajmos." *Law & Society Review* 40, no. 4 (2006): 871–901.

Yoors, Jan. *The Gypsies*. New York, 1967.

Žerjavić, Vladimir. *Population Losses in Yugoslavia, 1941–1945*. Zagreb, 1997.

Zimmermann, Michael. *Verfolgt, vertrieben, vernichtet. Die nationalsozialistische Vernichtungspolitik gegen Sinti und Roma*. Essen, 1989.

———. "Der nationalsozialistische Genozid an den Zigeunern und der Streit zwischen 'Intentionalisten' und 'Funktionalisten'." In *Von der Aufgabe der Freiheit. Festschrift für Hans Mommsen zum 5. November 1995*, ed. C. Jansen et al., 413–26. Berlin, 1995.

———. *Rassenutopie und Genozid. Die nationalsozialistische "Lösung der Zigeunerfrage."* Hamburg, 1996.

———. "Zigeunerpolitik im Stalinismus, im 'realen Sozialismus' und unter dem Nationalsozialismus. Ein Vergleich." In *Lager, Zwangsarbeit, Vertreibung und Deportation. Dimensionen der Massenverbrechen in der Sowjetunion und in Deutschland 1933 bis 1945*, ed. D. Dahlmann and G. Hirschfeld, 111–32. Fulda, 1999.

———. "Zigeunerbilder und Zigeunerpolitik in Deutschland. Eine Übersicht über neuere historische Studien." *Werkstatt Geschichte* 9, no. 25 (May 2000): 35–58.

———. "The National Socialist 'Solution of the Gypsy Question': Central Decisions, Local Initiatives, and Their Interrelation." *Holocaust and Genocide Studies* 15, no. 3 (Winter 2001): 412–27.

———. "The Berlin Memorial for the Murdered Sinti and Roma: Problems and Points for Discussion." *Romani Studies* 17, no. 1 (2007): 1–30.

———, ed. *Zwischen Erziehung und Vernichtung. Zigeunerpolitik und Zigeunerforschung im Europa des 20. Jahrhunderts*. Stuttgart, 2007.

Zülch, Tilman, ed. *In Auschwitz vergast, bis heute verfolgt. Zur Situation der Roma (Zigeuner) in Deutschland und Europa*. Reinbek, 1979.

Contributors

Nadine Blumer completed her doctoral dissertation in the department of sociology at the University of Toronto on the memorial politics of the Sinti and Roma in Germany. Her recent article in the *Journal of Ethnic and Migration Studies* looks at issues of homeland, ethno-diasporic identity, and Holocaust education programs for Jewish youth. She is currently teaching international migration at the University of Toronto.

Shannon L. Fogg is associate professor of history at Missouri University of Science and Technology. Dr. Fogg is the author of *The Politics of Everyday Life in Vichy France: Foreigners, Undesirables, and Strangers* (2009). She is currently working on a project that explores the spoliation of Jewish apartments in Paris during World War II and postwar restitution.

Florian Freund is an independent historian affiliated with the University of Vienna, Austria. He is a member of the editorial board of the scholarly journal *Zeitgeschichte;* between 1999 and 2002 he served on the Austrian Historical Commission. Dr. Freund is the author of numerous books on the persecution of Jews and Roma in Austria, Nazi concentration camps, and postwar restitution. His major study, *Die Vernichtung der österreichischen "Zigeuner" 1938–45,* will be published shortly.

Martin Holler is a PhD candidate at Humboldt University in Berlin, majoring in German and East European history and Slavic literature. He is the author of *Der nationalsozialistische Völkermord an den Roma* *in der besetzten Sowjetunion (1941–1944)* (2009) and is currently completing his dissertation on Soviet Roma during World War II.

Sławomir Kapralski is lecturer in sociology at the Warsaw School of Social Sciences and Humanities in Poland. He is the author of *Values and Sociological Knowledge* (1995) and *A Nation From the Ashes? The Holocaust and Romani Identities* (forthcoming), and the editor of *The Jews in Poland* (1999) and *Memory, Space, Identity* (2010). Dr. Kapralski is a member of the editorial board of *Studia Romologica*.

Alexander Korb is lecturer in modern European history at the University of Leicester, England. He is currently working on a research project on Ustasha mass violence against Serbs, Jews, and Roma during World War II. He is the author of *Reaktionen der deutschen Bevölkerung auf die Novemberpogrome* (2008) and the co-editor of *Nationalsozialistische Lager. Neue Beiträge zur Verfolgungs- und Vernichtungspolitik und zur Pädagogik in Gedenkstätten* (2006). His newest book, *Im Schatten des Weltkriegs. Massengewalt der Ustaša gegen Serben, Juden und Roma in Kroatien 1941–1945*, was published in January 2013.

Gilad Margalit is associate professor of history at the University of Haifa in Israel, and deputy director of the Haifa Center for German European Studies. He is the author of *Germany and Its Gypsies: A Post-Auschwitz Ordeal* (2002) and *Guilt, Suffering, and Memory: Germany Remembers Its Dead of World War II* (2010).

Vladimir Solonari is associate professor of history at the University of Central Florida. His book, *Purifying the Nation: Population Exchange and Ethnic Cleansing in Nazi-Allied Romania,* was published by Woodrow Wilson Center Press in cooperation with Johns Hopkins University Press in 2010. Dr. Solonari is the author of a number of articles on Romanian, Moldovan, and Soviet history. His current research focuses on the social history of southwestern Ukraine under the Romanian occupation during World War II.

Mikhail Tyaglyy is research associate at the Ukrainian Center for Holocaust Studies in Kiev and the executive editor of the scholarly journal *Голокост і сучасність: studii v Ukraini i sviti* (Holocaust and Modernity: Studies in Ukraine and the World). He is the author of the book on the Holocaust in the Crimean peninsula, *Места массового уничтожения евреев Крыма в период нацистской оккупации полуострова, 1941–1945*

(2005). His articles on Nazi anti-Semitic propaganda in Ukraine and on Nazi persecution of the Gypsies appeared in *Holocaust and Genocide Studies*.

Anton Weiss-Wendt heads the research department at the Center for the Study of the Holocaust and Religious Minorities in Oslo, Norway. He is the author of *Murder Without Hatred: Estonians and the Holocaust* (2009) and *Small-Town Russia: Childhood Memories of the Final Soviet Decade* (2010), and the editor of *Eradicating Differences: The Treatment of Minorities in Nazi-Dominated Europe* (2010) and *Racial Science in Hitler's New Europe, 1939–1945* (with Rory Yeomans, 2013). He is currently writing a book on the Soviet Union and the Genocide Convention.

Index

A
Achim, Viorel, 96–97, 113, 134
Adenauer, Chancellor Konrad, 208
Adriatic Sea, 11, 78–79
Aghet, 23
Ahnenerbe, 62
Alexeiev, Ivan, 165–66
Alexianu, Gheorghe, 132–33
Alliers camp, 38
Allies, 14, 39, 167, 195, 198–99, 208–209
Allies Control Council, 195
America. *See* United States of America
Anfal, 23
Anisimov, Pavel, 159
Anschluss, 54–55
anti-Roma legislation, 2, 14–15, 18–19, 27–30, 39, 44–52, 54–56, 65–66, 78–79, 183
anti-Roma stereotypes 3, 19, 45–46, 48, 67, 98–99, 140, 174, 194
anti-Semitism, 8, 75, 80, 88, 96, 98, 105, 216–17
Antonescu, Ion, 13–14, 89, 96–98, 101–109, 112–14, 132–34, 234
Antonescu, Mihai, 112–13
Ardener, Edwin, 236
Arendt, Hannah, 208
Arles, 38
Armenians, 4, 23, 139
Army Group Center, 169, 172
Army Group North, 153–75

Army Group North Rear Areas, 154, 156
Army Group South, 172
Artemivsk, 127
Artsishevsky, Konstantin, 141
"Aryans," 12, 17, 62, 79, 81–82, 84, 196
asocial behavior, Roma accused of, 52, 54–55, 65, 122, 129, 132, 169, 182, 184–87, 191, 193–94–98, 233
Association for the Memorial to the Murdered Jews of Europe, 211, 216–19
Association of German Sinti. *See* Central Council of German Sinti and Roma
Association of Roma in Poland, 22. *See also* Poland
Auerbach, Philip, 185
Auschwitz-Birkenau camp, 2–3, 5, 9, 11, 16, 19, 37–38, 62–64, 73–74, 77, 87, 124, 167, 182–83, 189, 240, 244, 248. *See also Zigeunerlager*
Auschwitz-Birkenau State Museum, 3, 22, 239
Auschwitz decree, 5, 19, 38, 62, 182–84, 189–90, 193, 209
Austria, 1–2, 5–6, 11, 15–16, 18–19, 44–67, 82, 167, 234
Austrian Lands. *See* Austria
auxiliary police, 18, 129, 133, 138, 141, 154–55, 162–63, 166, 169, 171, 233
Avidan, Igal, 215, 218
Axis, 14, 234

B

Babi Yar, 12, 131
Bakhchisarai, 17, 136, 138
Bakhmach, 126
Balakleia, 127
Baldinger, Josef, 50
Balić, Emily. See Greble-Balić, Emily
Balkans, 63, 75–76, 80
Balta, 132
Baltic States, 8, 10, 57, 154–55, 169, 171.
   See also Estonia; Latvia; Lithuania
Bandera, Stepan, 141
Banija region, 85
Barbarossa, Operation, 6, 11, 169
Barth, Fredrik, 230
Bartosz, Adam, 243
Bauer, Yehuda, 4
Bavaria, 48, 183, 188
Bechtolsheim, General Gustav von, 171
Belgium, 37
Belgrade, 75–76, 82
Belogorsk, 136
Belorussia, 10, 146, 154, 169, 171–72
Benarovich-Mironchuk, O[?], 167
Berenbaum, Michael,
Bergen-Belsen camp, 210
Bergmann, Heinrich, 169–70
Berlin, 15, 20, 54–56, 62, 66, 77, 106,
   123, 136, 188, 191, 206, 211–12, 215,
   218–19, 222, 224
Berlin Senate, 206, 213–15
Berlin Wall, 213
Beryslav, 129
Bessarabia, 104–107, 109, 129, 132
Bessonov, Nikolai, 8, 24, 129, 140–41, 144
Biondich, Mark, 80
Block, Martin, 194
Bloxham, Donald, 9
Blumer, Nadine, 20
Bohemia, 50, 64. See also Czechoslovakia
Böhmer, Anton, 58
Bolshevism, 106
Boryslav, 135
Bosnia-Herzegovina, 17, 49, 74–75, 81–83
Brandenburg Gate, 212, 215
Brandt, Chancellor Willy, 211
Brătianu, Constantin, 112–13
Bräutigam, Otto, 123
Brentano, von Margherita, 217
Brest-Lytovsk, 131
Britain. See Great Britain
British Gypsy Council, 21

Browning, Christopher, 5
Bruck on Leitha, 58
Bubis, Ignatz, 212–14
Bucharest, 97–98, 102, 105–107, 132
Buchenwald camp, 3, 22
Buchheim, Hans, 185
Budai-Deleanu, Ion, 99
Bug River, 105, 132
Bukovina, 103–107, 109, 132
Bulgaria, 3, 11, 234
Bulgarians, 105–106, 139
Bundestag, 206, 212, 216, 220–22, 224
Burgenland, 11, 15–16, 48, 52–55, 57–60, 65

C

Cădere, N[icolae?], 103–104
Calvelli-Adorno, Franz, 185
Camargue region, 33–34, 38
Caravan Memorial, 243–48
caravans, 12, 99, 109, 125–26, 129,
   131–32, 135, 141, 244
Carinthia, 47
Carol, King II, 105
Carpathian Roma, 243–45
Carpathian Ruthenia. See Transcarpathia
Catholicism. See Roman Catholicism
CDU. See Christian Democratic Union of Germany
Central Council of German Sinti and
   Roma, 5, 20–22, 198, 206, 210–11,
   213–16, 219, 221, 223
Central Holocaust Memorial in Berlin,
   20, 205–207, 211–18, 220–24
Central Information Office for Gypsies, 52
Central Memorial to the Murdered Jews
   of Europe. See Central Holocaust
   Memorial in Berlin
Chelcea, Ion, 103
Chełmno. See Kulmhof death camp
Cherkasy province, 128, 130
Chernihiv, 125–26
Chernivtsy province, 132
children, 2, 10, 12, 15, 32, 35–36, 50,
   53–54, 56, 109, 128, 142, 158–59,
   161–67, 170, 188
Chișinău, 97
Chistiakova, Maria, 162
Christian Democratic Union of Germany
   (CDU), 213
Christianity, 53, 214

Christian Socialist Party of Austria, 53
civil right movement. *See* Romani civil rights movement
Clifford, James, 249
Cluj, 100, 102
Cologne, 186, 191
Communist Party, 127
communists, 31, 121–22, 127
Communist Youth League, 7, 142
Conducător. *See* Antonescu, Ion
Conrad, Sebastian, 207
Constanța county, 110
Craiova, 101
Crimea, 11, 16–17, 108, 124, 128, 135–39, 146
criminality, alleged of Roma, 50–52, 54–55, 61, 66, 83, 111, 113–14, 133, 163, 182, 184, 194–95
Croatia. *See* Independent State of Croatia
Czechoslovakia, 48, 52. *See also* Bohemia
Czechs, 234
Czerniaków, Adam, 11

D

Dachau camp, 3, 210
deportations, 2–3, 5–6, 8–12, 14, 16–17, 38, 46, 48–49, 53, 56–65, 73, 76–78, 80–81, 83–87, 96–97, 103–105, 107–14, 124, 128, 130, 132–33, 135, 139, 142, 145, 147, 167–68, 171, 184–85, 187–89, 234, 244, 248
Diepgen, Eberhard, 219
Dmitriev, Iosif, 164
Dniester River, 103, 125, 132
Dnipropetrovsk province, 128–29
Dno region, 157
Documentation and Cultural Center of German Sinti and Roma, 22, 223, 239
Donetsk province, 125, 127
Dorohoi county, 104
Drogobych, 135
Dulić, Tomislav, 4, 74
Durkheim, Émile, 236
Dzhankoi, 11, 136, 142

E

Eastern Europe, 6, 16, 101–102, 153, 233, 242, 248. *See also* Europe; Western Europe
East Germany, 207, 223. *See also* Germany; West Germany

Edict for the Preventive Combating of Crime, 55
Ehrhardt, Sophie, 198
Einsatzgruppen, 1, 5, 7, 9, 12, 60, 108, 121, 125, 127–29, 136, 138–39, 144, 154, 156–57, 160, 172, 190, 192, 233
Einsatzgruppen Trial, 121. *See also* Nuremberg Trials
Einsatzkommandos, 122, 128, 154, 157. *See also* Einsatzgruppen; Sonderkommandos
Eisenmann, Peter, 220
Eisenstadt, 58
18th German Army, 154
Elena, Queen Mother, 97, 112
Enescu, George, 112
Ershova, Anna, 160
Esterházy estate, 59
Estonia, 154, 158, 169–72. *See also* Baltic States
Estonians, 155, 158–59
Estonian Security Police, 159, 170
ethnic Germans. *See* Volksdeutsche
eugenics, 100, 186. *See also* racial hygiene
"European Civil Rights Prize of the Sinti and Roma," 223
European Parliament, 22, 210, 223
Europe, 1, 6, 13, 18–20, 22–23, 28, 39, 51, 62, 76, 89, 100, 105, 143, 146, 206, 214, 221, 229. *See also* Eastern Europe; Western Europe
euthanasia, 192
Evpatoria, 136
executions. *See* mass executions
expropriation of property, 60, 78, 85–86, 132, 141–42, 166–67

F

Făcăoaru, Gheorghe, 101, 103
Făcăoaru, Iordache, 100–102
Federal Compensation Law, 182
Federal Republic of Germany. *See* West Germany
Federal Supreme Court, 184–86, 209
Fedorov, Konstantin, 164
Feldbach, 63
Feodosia, 141
Ficowski, Jerzy, 141
Field Headquarters 822, 163, 166, 168, 173–74
Field gendarmerie. *See* gendarmerie

Fighting Against the Gypsy Nuisance
    edict, 47
Fighting the Gypsy Plague order, 55
Filhol, Emmanuel, 37, 241
Filippovshchina village, 158–59
Final Solution of the Gypsy Question, 3,
    6–7, 11–12, 53, 60, 77–78, 85, 105,
    124–25, 134, 137, 140–41, 143–44,
    147, 187
Final Solution of the Jewish Question,
    4–6, 11–12, 14, 60, 73, 77–78, 105,
    141, 144, 187. See also Holocaust
Finno-Ugric minorities, 155
Finns, 158
First World War. See World War I
Flossenbürg camp, 3
Fogg, L. Shannon, 6, 13, 15, 17, 19
Fonseca, Isabel, 238
forced labor, 12, 16, 49, 54–56, 58–61, 76,
    78–79, 87–88, 101, 103–104, 133–35,
    145–47, 158, 165, 167–68, 171, 233
Foundation for the Memorial to the
    Murdered Jews of Europe, 221–22
France, 2, 5–6, 13–15, 17–19, 27–40, 102,
    105, 122, 130, 171, 241. See also
    Vichy regime
Franco-Prussian war, 28
Frank, Hans, 57
Frankfurt on Main, 184–85, 187–90, 192
Frenkel, Marcel, 185
Freudenberg, Günter, 218
Freund, Florian, 6, 11, 15–16, 18
Friedlander, Henry, 3, 9
Friedländer, Saul, 241–42
Friedman, Philip, 3
Friedrich, Jörg, 197
Fursenko, Petr, 139
Fürstenfeld, 61, 63

G
Galaţ, 110
Galicia, 11, 125, 134–35
Galinski, Heinz, 213–14
gas vans, 11, 142–43
Gauck, Joachim, 224
Gdov region, 158
gendarmerie, 12, 84–85, 98, 105–106,
    108–11, 121, 133–34, 138, 141–42,
    155, 160, 162, 165–66, 171, 173–74
General Government of Poland, 11,
    57–58, 61, 122, 135, 184
Geneva, 233

Genocide Convention, 1
Gerlach, Christian, 171
German Criminal Police, 15, 55, 58, 62,
    64, 124, 169, 187, 190, 193
German Empire. See Germany
German Foreign Office, 134
Germans, 6, 11, 17–18, 32, 34, 37, 40, 45,
    76–77, 83, 105, 107, 123, 127–30,
    135, 137–38, 140–43, 156, 158–65,
    168, 196, 199. See also Nazis;
    Volksdeutsche
German Security Police, 8, 10, 12, 61,
    121, 124–28, 130–31, 146–47, 154–
    57, 160, 163, 165–66, 169–74. See
    also Einsatzgruppen; Reich Security
    Main Office
Germany, 1–5, 18, 20–21, 31, 46, 53–54,
    60–61, 64–66, 72–73, 81, 87, 97, 100,
    102, 104–108, 113, 120–21, 124,
    130, 152, 169, 171, 183–84, 186–99,
    205–24, 233–34, 239. See also East
    Germany; West Germany
ghettos, 1, 11, 15–16, 49, 60–62, 65, 135,
    184, 234
Giddens, Anthony, 231
Gieger, Anton, 56
Gisevius, Hans Bernd, 192
Glan canal, 59
Goebbels, Joseph, 106
Golta, 132–33
Göring, Hermann, 57
Gorodishche village, 127, 171
Gorodok, 135
Gottberg, Curt von, 171
Göttingen, 21, 233
Gradina killing site, 87–88
Grass, Günter, 211
Graz, 50
Great Britain, 5, 108, 113
Greble-Balić, Emily, 74, 81–83
Greece, 3, 78
Greeks, 78, 138–39
Greiser, Arthur, 60
Grellmann, M. G. Heinrich, 51, 194
Grokhovskaia, Anastasia, 160
Gross, Hans, 50–51
Guliaipole, 128
Gypsiad (Ţiganiada), 99
Gypsy Edict, 46–47, 65–66

H
Hamburg, 21

Hancock, Ian, 23, 235, 248
Hantarrède, Guy, 38
Harangos village, 237–38
Harku camp, 170
Hartberg, 61
Heidelberg, 22, 210, 239
Herzog, Roman, 216
Heydrich, Reinhard, 56–61, 121–22
Hill, Alexander, 155
Himmler, Heinrich, 2, 5, 19, 38, 54–56, 60–63, 121, 123–24, 169, 182, 189–90, 193, 209
Hindenburg, von Paul, 191
Hitler, Adolf, 6, 19, 60, 106, 108, 190–92, 195, 213
Historikerstreit, 208–209, 214
Holler, Martin, 4, 6–8, 10, 12, 16, 18, 144
Holocaust, 4, 10, 20–21, 24, 72, 181, 205–206, 208–209, 211, 215, 218, 223–24, 229, 232–35, 241–42, 246–48. See also Final Solution of the Jewish Question
"Holocaust" TV miniseries, 21
Holodomor, 23
homosexuals, 234
"House of the Wannsee Conference" memorial site, 218
Hubert, Marie-Christine, 37
Humboldt University, 188
Hungarians, 99, 105–106
Hungarian Statistics Bureau, 47
Hungary, 3, 11, 15, 45–48, 73, 77, 82, 89, 121, 125, 134–35, 145, 237
Hussein, Saddam, 23
Hutus, 4

I
Ilmen Lake, 155
indemnification, 3
Independent State of Croatia, 2, 8, 11–13, 17, 72–90, 234. See also Ustaša
Innsbruck, 58
Institute for Contemporary History, 185
Institute for Criminal Biology of the German Security Police. See Research Institute for Racial Hygiene and Population Biology
International Congress for Population Science, 191
International Military Tribunal at Nuremberg, 7
International Romani Union, 21, 235

Iro, Karl, 50
Iron Guard, 97. See also Legionaries
Islam, 16–17, 82–83, 89, 136–37, 143. See also Muslims
Isopescu, Modest, 133
Israel, 208, 211
Italy, 3, 73, 89
itinerant Roma. See sedentary vs. itinerant Roma
Ivano-Frankivs'k province, 135
Ivanov, Valentin, 167

J
Jäckel, Eberhard, 211, 216–17
Jasenovac camp, 8–9, 14, 18, 72, 74, 76, 79–80, 84–90, 234
Jassy, 105
Jehovah's Witnesses, 215
Jelgava, 170
Jenischer Bund, 221
Jewish Central Council (Germany), 212–14, 216
Jews, 4, 5–6, 8–12, 14, 16–20, 24, 28, 31–32, 35, 55–57, 60–61, 72–73, 75, 78–82, 88, 90, 96–97, 104–109, 113–14, 121–24, 127–31, 133, 135–36, 138–41, 144–45, 155–59, 163, 165–69, 171–72, 174, 181, 183, 185, 195, 197, 205–24, 233–34, 244
Johns Hopkins University, 101
Joseph, Keiser Franz I, 45
Judaism, 137
Judenrat, 11
Jürgens, Hans, 198
Justin, Eva, 19, 182, 187–90, 192–94, 196–99

K
Kalinin province, 154
Kamin-Kashyrskyi, 130
Kapralski, Sławomir, 20
Karavan, Dani, 222
Kasche, Siegfried, 77
Kattowitz, 63
Kenrick, Donald, 21, 134, 146
Kerch, 136
Kharkiv, 125, 127, 143
Kherson, 124, 128–29, 141
Kiev, 12, 128, 131
Kilian, Jürgen, 155
Kirovograd, 129
Klagenfurt, 58

Kletsk, 171
Koch, Erich, 133
Kohl, Chancellor Helmut, 207, 214–15
Kollwitz, Käthe, 214
Korb, Alexander, 8, 12, 14, 16–17
Koriakin, Ivan, 127
Koselleck, Reinhart, 219–20
Kosterlitz, K. Hans, 189
Kovalev, Boris, 160
Kovalivka, 133
Kovel, 130
Kovshyn, 126
Krakow-Płaszów camp, 130
Križevci, 78
Kruglov, Alexander, 125, 129, 135, 144, 146, 168
Krymchaks, 137–39
Kulmhof camp, 1–2, 11, 16, 49, 62
Kurds, 23
Küster, Otto, 182–83
Kuznetsov, Anatoly, 131

L

Lackenbach camp, 59, 64–66
Lalleri, 5, 62
Lamarck, Jean-Baptiste, 100
Lammert, Norbert, 224
Landau district, 133
Lashkevich, Khrisanf, 137–38
Latvia, 154, 167, 169–70. See also Baltic States
Latvians, 155
Lausanne, Treaty of, 78
Law Concerning *Asoziale,* 190
Law Concerning the Gypsies, 190
Law for the Prevention of Genetically Diseased Offspring, 54, 194
Law for the Protection of German Blood and Honor, 190
League of Nations, 53
Lebrun, President Paul, 30
Lecca, Radu, 109
Lechner, Josef, 45–46, 49
Legionaries, 97. See also Iron Guard
Lemkin, Raphael, 8
Lengel-Krizman, Narcisa, 74, 81, 85
Leningrad, 12, 156–57, 161
Leningrad province, 154–56, 160
Leninsk, 127
Leshchenko, Petr, 144
Lewy, Guenter, 3–4, 8, 123–24
Liepāja, 170

Lilienfeld, 58
Linas-Montlhéry camp, 32
Linz, 58, 66
Lithuania, 154, 169, 171. See also Baltic States
Litzmannstadt ghetto, 1, 11, 15–16, 49, 60–62, 64, 130, 167
Łódź ghetto. See Litzmannstadt ghetto
Lobozhi village, 168
Lohse, Hinrich, 122–24, 170
Loknia, 157, 165, 174
London, 21, 233
Lower Austria, 47, 61, 65. See also Austria; Upper Austria
Ludvipol camp, 131
Luga, 158
Lugansk province, 125
Lukashev, Andrei, 166
Lviv province, 135

M

Madagascar, 11
Malines, 37
Manuilă, Sabin, 101–103
Margalit, Gilad, 3–5, 19
Mariupol, 127
Marseille, 37
Massalsky, Semen, 161, 174
mass executions, 5, 12, 87–88, 104–105, 108–109, 125–35, 142–43, 154, 157–68, 170–75, 245
Mattersburg, 61
Mauthausen camp, 3, 167
Maxglan camp, 56–57, 59
May, Kurt, 184–85
Mediterranean Sea, 191
Melitopol, 128
Memorial to the Homosexuals Persecuted under the Nationalist Socialist Regime, 207, 221–22, 224
Memorial to the Sinti and Roma Persecuted under the National Socialist Regime, 20, 206–207, 212–13, 221–22, 224
Mendelism, 100
mentally disabled, 100, 217. See also people with disabilities
Merkel, Chancellor Angela, 224
Miclescu, Chiodorean, 110
Milton, Sybil, 3
Mischlinge, 5, 55, 195, 198. See also *Zigeunermischlinge*

Mitu, Sorin, 99
mixed marriages, 127, 196
Moglino, 159, 168
Moldavia. *See* Moldova
Moldova, 46, 97, 103
Moldovan, Iuliu, 100–102
Molochansk, 128
Momper, Walter, 213
Mongols, 101
Moravek, Karl, 193
Moravia, 64. *See also* Czechoslovakia
Moscow, 107
Mróz, Lech, 229, 239–43
Müller, Heinrich, 122
Müller-Haccius, Otto, 57
Munich, 106, 183, 185, 194
Muslim Committees, 17, 137–38, 143
Muslims, 13, 74, 81–84, 89, 137–38. *See also* Islam
Mykolaiiv province, 128, 132

N
Nagel, Wolfgang, 212
Nastasă, Lucian, 98
National Liberal Party (Romania), 112
National Peasant Party (Romania), 112–13
Natzweiler camp, 3
Nazi Germany. *See* Germany
Nazi Party, 105, 186, 195
Nazis, 2, 5, 11, 13–14, 17–23, 55, 57, 60, 64–65, 89, 106, 108, 120, 127, 137, 145, 147, 168, 174, 181–82, 186, 193, 206, 214, 218, 220, 233–35. *See also* Germans; *Volksdeutsche*
Nebe, Arthur, 58, 187, 190–92
Neue Wache, 214
Neumärker, Uwe, 221
Neureiter, Bernhard Wilhelm, 54
Neusiedl am See, 52
Niederdonau district, 54, 58, 60, 63
New York City, 22
Nikopol, 129
NKVD. *See* Soviet Security Police
"nomadism," 15, 19, 28–33, 37
Normandy, 39
Novick, Peter, 234
Novgorod, 154, 160, 161, 173
Novgorod province, 156, 160, 168, 174
Novhorod-Siverskyi, 126
Novohrad-Volynskyi, 130
Novorzhev massacre, 12, 157, 161–64, 166, 168, 173

Nuremberg Laws, 12, 79, 183, 190, 196
Nuremberg Trials, 137. *See also* Einsatzgruppen Trial

O
Oberpullendorf district, 58, 66
Oberwart, 53, 61–63
Obukhiv, 131–32
Ochakiv, 132
Odessa, 104, 132, 143
Ohlendorf, Otto, 121–22, 137
Opocki, Reverend Stanisław, 244–45
Oredezh region, 160, 173–74
Organization of Ukrainian Nationalists (OUN), 18, 141
Orthodox Church, 13, 16, 74
Osijek, 82
Ostmark. *See* Austria
Ostland. *See* Reich Commissariat Ostland (RKO)
Ostrov, 166–68, 173, 175
Ottoman Empire, 4

P
Pacific Ocean, 11, 53
Panziger, Friedrich, 124
Paris, 39
partisans. *See* Soviet partisans; Tito Partisans
Păun, D. Ion, 110
Pavelić, Ante, 13–14, 73, 82, 84, 86
Pavlivka, 129
Peipus Lake, 155
people with disabilities, 102. *See also* mentally disabled
Perspective Berlin, 211
Peșchir, Ioan, 111
Pétain, Marshal Philippe, 15, 28, 32, 36
Piața Victoriei, 107
Poglavnik. *See* Pavelić, Ante
Pohl, Dieter, 6
Poland, 1, 3, 5, 11, 16, 21, 37, 56–57, 64, 113, 124, 135, 184–85, 234, 243–48
Poles, 57, 141
Pology, 128
Poltava, 128–29
Porkhov, 164
Porrajmos, 23–24, 235
Portschy, Tobias, 54–55
POWs. *See* prisoners of war
Pozherevitsky region, 165–66
Pravieniškės camp, 171

prisoners of war, 3, 161, 168
Protectorate of Bohemia and Moravia, 5, 60, 234
Pryluky, 126
Pskov, 159, 162, 166–67, 174
Pskov province, 154–56, 161, 164, 168, 172
Pushkinskie Gory, 162–64, 173
Pushniakov, Mikhail, 159
Putna county, 110
Puxon, Grattan, 21, 134, 146

R

racial hygiene, 54, 76, 100, 191, 193, 195. *See also* eugenics
Racial Hygiene and Demographic Biology Research Unit, 187
racial theory, 48, 51, 97, 169, 181, 186–87, 193, 217, 233
Radita, Petre, 132
Rainer, Friedrich, 56
Râmneanţu, Petru, 100–101
Rava-Ruska, 135
Ravensbrück camp, 3, 22
Red Army. *See* Soviet Army
Reich Commissariat Ostland (RKO), 122–24, 147, 154, 169–72
Reich Commissariat Ukraine (RKU), 121, 123–25, 128, 135, 145–47
Reich Commissioner for the Strengthening of Germandom, 56. *See also* Himmler, Heinrich
Reich Criminal Police Office (RKPA), 55–56, 58–59, 62, 66
Reich Ministry for the Occupied Eastern Territories (RMO), 123–24, 128, 145, 147
Reich Security Main Office (RSHA), 6, 56–58, 63, 66, 121, 189. *See also* Heydrich, Reinhard
Reichstag, 212
Renard, Berthe, 34,
rescue efforts, 81–82, 137–38, 140
Research Institute for Racial Hygiene and Population Biology, 3, 120, 188, 194, 196
Rēzekne, 170
Riefenstahl Film, 59
Ritter, Robert, 3, 19, 62, 120, 169, 181–83, 186–99
Rivesaltes camp, 35
Rivne province, 128, 130
RKPA. *See* Reich Criminal Police Office
Rockefeller Foundation, 100–101

Roloff-Momin, Ulrich, 213
Romani civil rights movement, 21–22, 210, 235
Roman Catholicism, 74, 89, 244, 247
Romanes language, 23
Romania, 2, 9, 11–12, 14, 17, 77, 89, 96–114, 121, 124, 128, 132–35, 145–47, 234
Romanians, 14, 17, 97–102, 106, 110–13, 136
Romanipen, normative system of, 230–31, 243–44
Romani World Congresses, 21, 23, 233
Roques, General Franz von, 156
Rose, Romani, 5, 20, 22, 206, 211–16, 218–19
Rosenberg, Alfred, 124, 133–34
Roser, Franz, 49
Rosh, Lea, 211, 217
Rotenthurm, 61
RSHA. *See* Reich Security Main Office
Rürup, Reinhard, 217
Russia, 2, 4, 8, 16, 146, 153–75
Russians, 7, 17, 101, 125, 135, 141, 155, 157–61, 163–67, 234. *See also* Slavs
Rwanda, 4

S

Sachsenhausen camp, 3
Salaspils camp, 167
Saliers camp, 15, 33–38
Salzburg, 47, 56, 58, 59, 64, 66
Sambir, 135
Samudaripen, 235
Şandru, Dumitru, 96
Sarajevo, 74, 82–83
Sarny, 131
Sava River, 76, 87
Savino, 165–66
Saxony, 223
Schabas, William, 4
Schilly, Otto, 211
Schlabrendorff, von Fabian, 192
Schmidt, Chancellor Helmut, 210–11
Schmidt, Ilsa, 239
Schoenberner, Gerhard, 218
Schubert, Heinz Hermann, 137
Schulze-Rohr, Jakob, 217
Schutzstaffel (SS), 11–12, 14, 54, 64, 120–21, 133, 136, 146, 157, 171, 189, 191, 193, 199, 220, 233–34
Schwarzach in Pongau, 56
Second World War. *See* World War II

Security Division 281, 156, 161–64, 166, 173
sedentary vs. itinerant Roma, 1, 9–10, 15, 17, 46–47, 74, 82–83, 109, 122, 124, 140, 144–45, 156, 160–61, 169–70, 172
Seiters, Rudolf, 213
Sémelin, Jacques, 44
Serbia, 6, 17, 59, 73, 75–77, 82, 89, 122, 126
Serbs, 12–14, 72–73, 75, 77–80, 85, 87, 234
Shaw, Martin, 4
Shoah Foundation, 8, 146
Simferopol, 17, 136–38, 144
Sinti, 2, 5, 19, 23, 62, 234, 248
Sinti Alliance, 221
16th German Army, 154
Slantsy district, 159
Slavonia, 85
Slavs, 8, 12, 16, 101, 140, 144, 155, 169, 217. See also Russians
Slovakia, 3, 77, 135
Smila, 130
Snov, 171
Social-Cultural Association of Roma in Tarnów, 243–44. See also Tarnów
Social Democratic Party of Austria, 53
Social Democratic Party of Germany (SPD), 210, 212–13, 220
Society for Endangered Peoples, 21, 210
Soltsy, 160
Solonari, Vladimir, 9–10, 13–14, 17
Sonderkommandos, 122, 125, 127–28, 154, 155, 159, 165, 172. See also Einsatzgruppen; Einsatzkommandos
Soviet Army, 107, 112, 128, 134, 141, 167
Soviet Extraordinary Commission for the Investigation of the Crimes Committed by German Fascists and their Collaborators on the Territory of the USSR (ChGK), 7–8, 126–31, 136, 145–46, 153, 157–60, 162–68, 174–75
Soviet partisans, 7, 18, 122, 127, 141, 155–56, 161–63, 168–69, 172–74. See also Tito Partisans
Soviet Security Police (NKVD), 18, 129, 139, 143
Soviet Union, 1–7, 10–12, 14, 16, 60, 66, 106–108, 120–22, 124, 144, 147, 152–75, 192, 234. See also Russia

SPD. See Social Democratic Party of Germany
SS. See Schutzstaffel
Stalingrad, 108
Staraia Russa, 161
Starosoldatsk, 129
Staryi Krym, 138, 141
Steinberg, 128
sterilization, forced, 2, 5, 14, 53, 76, 100–102, 170, 187–89, 191, 193–97
Stewart, Michael, 24, 229, 236–40
St. Germain, Treaty of, 48, 53
Stoica, Zoltan, 112
St. Pantaleon-Weyer, 59, 61
St. Pölten, 58
Strasbourg, 22
Strazdiņš, Lucia, 170
Strugi Krasnye, 165
Stuttgart, 198
Styria, 47, 52, 54, 56–61, 64
Sumsk province, 125, 127
Süssmuth, Rita, 212
Syvashi, 129
Szczurowa village, 245
Székesfehérvár, 134

T
Tallinn Central prison, 170–71
Talsi, 170–71
Târgovişte, 110
Tarnów, 21, 243–48. See also Social-Cultural Association of Roma in Tarnów
Tatars, 17–18, 101, 135–39, 143. See also Crimea
Teinbas, Victor, 159
Ternopil province, 135
Thierse, Wolfgang, 220
Third Reich. See Germany
Tito Partisans, 18, 76, 83, 85–86, 89. See also Soviet partisans
Tobescu, Colonel C., 111
Toleikis, Vytautas, 171
"Topography of Terror" museum, 217
Transcarpathia, 125, 134–35, 145
Transnistria, 14, 96–97, 103–105, 107, 109–14, 125, 132–34, 234
Transylvania, 51, 99–100
Treblinka camp, 11
Tübingen University, 188
Turkmens, 137
Turks, 4, 78, 100

Turner, Dr. Harald, 6, 77
Tutsi, 4
Tyaglyy, Mikhail, 6–8, 10–12, 14, 16–18
typhus, 14, 16, 62, 103, 133–34
Tyrol, 47

U
Uiberreither, Siegfried, 54, 56
Ukraine, 2, 4, 10, 12, 16, 120–47
Ukrainian Insurgent Army (UPA), 141
Ukrainians, 12, 23, 101, 105–106, 125, 127, 129, 133, 135
United Nations, 22, 108, 233
United Restitution Organization, 184
United States Holocaust Memorial Museum, 8, 97
United States of America, 3, 5, 100–102, 108, 113, 208, 234
University of Southern California Shoah Foundation Institute. *See* Shoah Foundation
University of Vienna, 100
Upper Austria, 45, 47, 50, 52, 59, 66. *See also* Austria; Lower Austria
Uschold, Rudolf, 183, 193
USSR. *See* Soviet Union
Ustaša, 4, 8, 11–13, 17–18, 72–90
Uštice camp, 87
Utogorsh district, 160, 173
Uzhgorod, 134

V
Vagabond Law, 44–47
Varga, Andrea, 98
Vasil'eva, Nadezhda, 167
Vasiliu, General Constantin, 108–109, 111–12
Vasylkiv, 131
Veil, Simone, 210, 223
Velikie Luki, 154
Ventspils, 170
Ventzki, Werner, 61
Vichy regime, 6, 13, 15, 17, 27–28, 31–35, 38–40, 241. *See also* France
Vienna, 44, 50, 58, 64, 66
Vileika, 171
Vinnytsa province, 128, 132
Vlădescu, Ovidiu, 103–104, 107
Volksdeutsche, 14, 99, 104–105, 133–34. *See also* Germans; Nazis
Volyn, 12, 57, 123, 128, 130–31, 141
Vorarlberg, 47

W
Wagner, Hans, 53
Waidhofen on Thaya, 63
Wallachia, 46, 110
Warsaw, 11
Warthegau, 60–61
Washington, DC, 97
Wehrmacht, 8, 57, 60, 73, 120–22, 125, 128, 135, 146, 154–55, 160, 167, 169, 171–72, 234
Weimar Republic, 195
Western Europe, 15–16, 18, 61. *See also* Eastern Europe; Europe
West Germany, 7, 17, 19, 21, 181–99, 207–10, 214, 223. *See also* East Germany; Germany
Wilden, Hans, 182–83
Wolf, Christa, 211
Wolf, S. Siegmund, 189
Woodcock, Shannon, 98–99
World War I, 48, 79, 108
World War II, 4, 6–8, 12–13, 18, 21, 22, 27–28, 30, 45, 72, 96, 120, 140, 146, 153–54, 229, 232, 234, 237, 247
Würth, Adolf, 198

X
xenophobia, 28, 31, 96, 100, 104–105

Y
Yeomans, Rory, 76
Yoors, Jan, 232–33, 238
Young Turks, 4
Yugoslavia, 3, 6, 18, 59, 72–74, 77, 89

Z
Żabno, 245
Zagreb, 13, 77, 85–86
Zaiats, Savka, 132
Zakarpats'ka province, 134
Zaporizhzhia province, 127
Zemun, 75–76, 84–85
Zigeunerlager, 63–64, 234, 240, 248. *See also* Auschwitz-Birkenau camp
Zhytomyr province, 128, 130
Zigeunermischlinge, 9, 56, 60, 62–63, 132, 134, 187–88, 191, 196, 233. *See also Mischlinge*
Zimmermann, Michael, 3–4, 9, 124
Zinkiv, 129
Zülch, Tillman, 210
Županja district, 85

War and Genocide

General Editors: Omer Bartov, Brown University; A. Dirk Moses, European University Institute, Florence, Italy/University of Sydney

There has been a growing interest in the study of war and genocide, not from a traditional military history perspective, but within the framework of social and cultural history. This series offers a forum for scholarly works that reflect these new approaches.

"The Berghahn series Studies on War and Genocide *has immeasurably enriched the English-language scholarship available to scholars and students of genocide and, in particular, the Holocaust."*—**Totalitarian Movements and Political Religions**

Volume 1
The Massacre in History
Edited by Mark Levene and Penny Roberts

Volume 2
National Socialist Extermination Policies: Contemporary German Perspectives and Controversies
Edited by Ulrich Herbert

Volume 3
War of Extermination: The German Military in World War II, 1941/44
Edited by Hannes Heer and Klaus Naumann

Volume 4
In God's Name: Genocide and Religion in the Twentieth Century
Edited by Omer Bartov and Phyllis Mack

Volume 5
Hitler's War in the East, 1941–1945
Rolf-Dieter Müller and Gerd R. Ueberschär

Volume 6
Genocide and Settler Society: Frontier Violence and Stolen Indigenous Children in Australian History
Edited by A. Dirk Moses

Volume 7
Networks of Nazi Persecution: Bureaucracy, Business, and the Organization of the Holocaust
Edited by Gerald D. Feldman and Wolfgang Seibel

Volume 8
Gray Zones: Ambiguity and Compromise in the Holocaust and Its Aftermath
Edited by Jonathan Petropoulos and John K. Roth

Volume 9
Robbery and Restitution: The Conflict over Jewish Property in Europe
Edited by Martin Dean, Constantin Goschler and Philipp Ther

Volume 10
Exploitation, Resettlement, Mass Murder: Political and Economic Planning for German Occupation Policy in the Soviet Union, 1940–1941
Alex J. Kay

Volume 11
Theatres of Violence: The Massacre, Mass Killing and Atrocity in History
Edited by Philip G. Dwyer and Lyndall Ryan

Volume 12
Empire, Colony, Genocide: Conquest, Occupation, and Subaltern Resistance in World History
Edited by A. Dirk Moses

Volume 13
The Train Journey: Transit, Captivity, and Witnessing in the Holocaust
Simone Gigliotti

Volume 14
The "Final Solution" in Riga: Exploitation and Annihilation, 1941–1944
Andrej Angrick and Peter Klein

Volume 15
The Kings and the Pawns: Collaboration in Byelorussia during World War II
Leonid Rein

Volume 16
Reassessing the Nuremberg Military Tribunals: Transitional Justice, Trial Narratives, and Historiography
Edited by Kim C. Priemel and Alexa Stiller

Volume 17
The Nazi Genocide of the Roma: Reassessment and Commemoration
Edited by Anton Weiss-Wendt

Volume 18
Judging "Privileged" Jews: Holocaust Ethics, Representation, and the "Grey Zone"
Adam Brown

Volume 19
The Dark Side of Nation States: Ethnic Cleansing in Modern Europe
Philipp Ther

Volume 20
The Greater German Reich and the Jews: Nazi Persecution Policies in the Annexed Territories 1935-1945
Edited by Wolf Gruner and Jörg Osterloh

Volume 21
The Spirit of the Laws: The Plunder of Wealth in the Armenian Genocide
Taner Akçam and Umit Kurt

Volume 22
Genocide on Settler Frontiers: When Hunter-Gatherers and Commercial Stock Farmers Clash
Edited by Mohamed Adhikari

www.ingramcontent.com/pod-product-compliance
Lightning Source LLC
Chambersburg PA
CBHW072147100526
44589CB00015B/2126